The Logics of
Party Formation

The Logics of Party Formation

ECOLOGICAL POLITICS IN
BELGIUM AND WEST GERMANY

Herbert Kitschelt

Cornell University Press

Ithaca and London

First published 1989 by Cornell University Press.

International Standard Book Number 0-8014-2252-3
Library of Congress Catalog Card Number 88-31871

Printed in the United States of America

*Librarians: Library of Congress cataloging information
appears on the last page of the book.*

*The paper in this book is acid-free and meets the guidelines for
permanence and durability of the Committee on Production
Guidelines for Book Longevity of the Council on Library Resources.*

Contents

Preface

When I began lecturing on West German politics at American universities in the early 1980s, my hosts favored no theme as much as the rise and future of the German Greens, then a tiny ecology party that had not managed to gain even one seat in the German parliament. Similarly, among American political science graduate students with some interest in West German politics, nothing appeared to stimulate their imagination more than the emergence of the "new social movements" and the Green party. While political science students in the late 1960s and early 1970s had been inspired by the French May 1968 and the Italian Hot Autumn of 1969, in the 1980s many began to look at West Germany. For the first time, West German politics was shedding its reputation as a "boring" subject of comparative political study. It began to offer a hope and a new avenue for democratizing modern societies and orienting them toward more enlightened values that aspired to something beyond material wealth and military power.

I originally expected that although the West German ecology party had some attractiveness for the American political Left, it would offer little promise of scholarly investigations yielding broad new empirical and theoretical insight into the transformation of politics in modern democracies. I anticipated that the Greens were riding a brief issue-oriented cycle, both with West German voters and with academic researchers, which was unlikely to leave a lasting imprint on existing democratic institutions. The themes of the new party would soon be adopted by its competitors, and the exigencies of electoral competition would force it to abide by the same rules of vote getting and to develop the same organizational structures as its competitors in the West German party system. For this reason I was confident that political science had already developed the tools and theoretical instruments for analyzing and predicting the future of the new party.

Examining the Greens more closely, however, I began to revise my initial impression. First of all, I found that they are not an isolated phenomenon but only one of a far-flung cohort of new parties in Western Europe. Among American scholars and in the U.S. mass media, focus on the Greens appeared to be locked into the narrow confines of an explanation that characterizes the Greens as an outgrowth of "German exceptionalism." I was determined, however, to understand the conditions surrounding the emergence of ecology and related parties in several countries. Thus I decided to take an in-depth look at the Belgian ecology parties Agalev and Ecolo in addition to the Greens.

I soon discovered that studying ecology parties in Belgium and West Germany would be more fruitful for the theoretical analysis of party politics than I had expected. Most students of political parties in the past twenty years have focused on the *individual* level of political action, on the *sociological* and rational bases of voting decisions, or on the *systems* level in studying competition and cooperation among parties and the impact of parties on public policy. What remained relatively neglected, however, were the *organizational* level of party politics—internal decision making and strategy formation—and the interorganizational networks of interest intermediation between state and civil society.

In the literature on parties at least four propositions, some held implicitly, others made explicitly, appear to lie behind this lack of scholarly interest in the intra- and interorganizational dynamics of political parties: (1) a more or less unqualified acceptance of Michels' law of oligarchy; (2) a belief in the irrelevance of party organization and activism in the age of mass media campaigning; (3) a general disenchantment with the ability of parties to reform society and recast procedures of democratic decision making; and (4) a normative belief that elections alone are the standard of democratic politics and have absolute priority over the influence of small groups of party activists in regard to party strategy and policy choice. My study of ecological politics leads me to conclude that all of these propositions need to be qualified, rejected, or reformulated. In particular, I have found that parties are not nearly as constrained by electoral competition as many scholars have argued. To modify Stein Rokkan's well-known phrase: Votes count, but in party politics ideas and activists matter. In other words, parties can contribute to political innovation in contemporary democracies. Furthermore, they can institutionalize reforms through new patterns of internal organization and decision making and external linkages to civil society and the state.

I thank the German Marshall Fund for a fellowship that enabled me to conduct research on the German and Belgian ecology parties over the course of 1985. I also express my gratitude to the many party activists in both countries who were generous with their time, answering my questions and correcting my perceptions of their political work. Although they will not always agree with my interpretations and conclusions, I hope they will find them worthy of reflection and discussion. I am especially indebted to two activist-scholars and friends who helped me get started. Staf Hellemans of the sociology department at the University of Leuven provided me with entrée to the Flemish ecology party Agalev and helped me gather countless documents and a wealth of materials on it. Helmut Wiesenthal of the sociology department at the University of Bielefeld allowed me to use his extensive archive on the West German Greens and made important suggestions for the conduct of my research. Both Staf and Helmut deepened my understanding of European ecology parties not only through many discussions but also by commenting on a first draft of this book. I am also indebted to Russell J. Dalton, Peter Katzenstein, Peter Lange, Peter Merkl, Claus Offe, and George Tsebelis, who read the first draft and made many valuable comments. Needless to say, they have not always concurred with my approach. For ignoring some of their fine suggestions, I take full responsibility. Finally, I thank Elaine Madison, whose interest in European ecology parties and steadfast insistence that they deserve serious investigation prompted me to undertake this research.

I have previously presented some materials appearing in Chapters 1, 4, 6, and 7 in my articles "Left-Libertarian Parties: Explaining Innovation in Competitive Party Systems," *World Politics* 40, no. 2 (January 1988), copyright © by Princeton University Press; adapted with permission of Princeton University Press; and "Organization and Strategy of Belgian and West German Ecology Parties: A New Dynamic of Party Politics in Western Europe?" *Comparative Politics* 20, no. 2 (January 1988). I am grateful to the publishers of both journals for their consent to borrow from these articles here.

HERBERT KITSCHELT

Durham, North Carolina

The Logics of
Party Formation

Introduction

When the newly elected Green members of the German parliament carried a tree withered by acid rain into the opening session of the tenth Bundestag in the spring of 1983, they were convinced that their arrival marked a watershed in the development of West German democracy. The dead tree in parliament, as well as the Green deputies' unconventional clothing, symbolized both a point of arrival and a point of departure for a political and cultural movement that had already spanned a period of close to twenty years.

It was an arrival because most Green parliamentarians saw themselves as representatives of German protest movements and social experiments dating back to the 1960s. Many had personally participated in important early episodes such as the student movement and anti–Vietnam War protests. Later activities involved struggles for women's rights and reproductive freedom, uncurtailed civil liberties, environmental protection, the shutdown of nuclear power plants, and an end to urban real-estate speculation. Moreover, efforts to effect cultural and institutional change through self-help groups of women, foreign residents, and medical patients, and experiments with cooperative enterprises, theater groups, and unconventional news media, figured prominently among these new movements. In the 1980s many of these activities were integrated into a broad movement against the stationing of new medium-range nuclear missiles in Western Europe.

Green parliamentary politics also constituted a departure because, for the first time, a political party had been elected to parliament that promised to represent the political and cultural protest movements of the postwar generations. Previous efforts to push the German Social Democrats closer to the demands of the protest groups had failed. And the considerable number of New Left Maoist, Trotskyist, and independent groups and sects of the 1970s espoused doctrinaire Marxist programs that found little if any popular support.

Only the Greens succeeded in uniting enough of these diverse voices of protest to become a serious contender in the competition among parties.

In Belgium a Walloon and a Flemish ecology party, Ecolo and Agalev, jointly entered the national parliament in November 1981. This electoral success surprised even the small core of party activists. Here, too, the newly elected deputies emphasized their political agenda with a symbolic gesture: they arrived on bicycles to the opening session of parliament. The Belgian ecology parties also looked back on a history of New Left, feminist, ecology, peace, and neighborhood movements and forward to a new combination of extraparliamentary mobilization and intraparliamentary party competition. As in West Germany, the Belgian parties emerged only when efforts to articulate the demands of protest movements in the 1960s and 1970s were thwarted by the existing socialist, liberal, and Christian democratic parties.

The Belgian and West German ecology parties belong to a cohort of left-libertarian West European parties that are committed to similar objectives, are supported by similar electoral constituencies, grow out of similar institutional environments, and face almost identical strategic problems. In this sense Agalev, Ecolo, and the Greens are not unique to peculiar national political cultures but constitute examples of a widespread phenomenon significant for our understanding of political change in contemporary Europe. Left-libertarian parties appeal to young, highly educated voters who work predominantly in the service sector, particularly in public personal services (education, health care, welfare). Their programs are left-wing because, in the socialist tradition, they affirm solidarity and equality and reject the primacy of markets and allocation efficiency as the final arbiters of social development and justice. They follow libertarian thinking, however, in rejecting the socialist vision of centralist planning and party organization and calling for a society in which individual autonomy and citizen participation in public affairs have priority.

Left-libertarians thus criticize the policies as well as the procedures and institutions that underlie the post–World War II social compact between capital and labor revolving around the Keynesian welfare state. Substantively, left-libertarians argue that advanced industrial democracies have put too much emphasis on income growth and economic security and lack sufficient concern with the production, preservation, and distribution of collective and intangible goods, such as an intact physical environment and a communal social infrastructure protected from both market competition and bureaucratic regulation. Procedurally, they trace the centrality of material economic growth and bureaucracy back to the dominance of economic producer groups that prevail in the political process through the organizational efficiency and resources of centralized mass parties and interest groups.

Conventional socialist, liberal, and conservative parties in particular have become the target of left-libertarian attacks because they are viewed as vehicles of interest intermediation that remove citizens at least three steps from the locus of policy formation. First, citizens must choose from broad packages of policies put together by competing parties and cannot influence individual policies by voting. Second, hierarchical party organizations stand between citizen preferences and party policies. Third, in order to partake in government, parties often compromise with each other and with interest groups, a process over which voters have no control. Critics of West European parliamentary party democracies recognize that parties are not simply transmitters of well-defined interests from civil society into politics. More realistically, they constantly reformulate and transform voters' demands through the deliberations of their own activists, internal decision making, and the leadership's choice of alliance strategies. It is this "politics of institutional form" that left-libertarians are particularly concerned about.

While the Keynesian welfare state has muted class conflict, its institutions have given rise to new political and cultural tensions that feed into a crisis of political participation. Existing representative organs and political organizations are not able to represent new left-libertarian demands. As a consequence new left-libertarian movements and parties challenge both the *form* and the *substance* of policy making in the Keynesian welfare state. Because they see political form and substance as interdependent, left-libertarians have tried to organize according to a new model of citizens' mobilization which, they hope, will eventually enable them to enact policies creating a more decentralized, libertarian, and participatory society with less emphasis on economic competition and growth. Left-libertarians have engaged in protest movements with loose alliances of federated, egalitarian organizations with little hierarchy or formalization of decision-making procedures. They have attempted to build their parties in the same mode.

To understand the rise and the persistence of left-libertarian politics, it is crucial to examine the ways and the extent to which this new political force is able to change patterns of political participation in European democracies. Left-libertarian challenges are still too recent to determine whether they have a far-reaching substantive impact on the policies of modern welfare states. But because of the interdependence of form and content in policy making, development of innovative practices for organizing new interests today may be a necessary, though not sufficient, condition for left-libertarian politics' having a considerable impact on contemporary democracies.

Most conventional thinking on party organization and competition would tell us that parties face severe difficulties in developing dramatically new organizational forms and strategies. Party theorists from Weber (1919) to Downs (1957), Duverger (1954), and Kirchheimer (1966) have been mesmerized by the role of electoral competition and view it as the final and decisive determinant of party structures and strategies. According to this perspective, it is functionally almost inevitable that innovative parties will eventually adopt a common logic of electoral competition and accommodate to the prevailing organizational and strategic patterns their competitors employ. Because parties compete according to a common set of institutional rules and must consider maximizing electoral support and parliamentary representation as their overriding concern, they will sooner or later gravitate toward an "efficient" model of organization and strategic choice that is essentially similar for all competitors. Innovative forms of party politics represent nothing but short-term aberrations from the norm.

If new and innovative forms of party organization and strategy do persist, we need intellectual tools to understand this phenomenon different from the one provided by the conventional "functionalist" view of party organization, which interprets the role of parties in terms of systemic imperatives, be they called stability, adaptation, equilibrium, or political capacity. We must reconsider behavioral and rational actor-oriented studies of parties and "structural" approaches to party organization and political decision making.[1] These strands of investigations have focused on three factors that affect the organization and strategy of political parties, often in ways contradicting the imperatives of electoral competition. First, parties rely on political activists with ideas, personal commitments to party involvement, and the rational intellectual capacity to pursue their political objectives. These activists may leave an imprint on parties regardless of systemic imperatives. Second, the organizational rules and decision-making procedures that parties initially develop take on an independent life and are difficult to adjust to the competitive electoral marketplace. Third, parties in most modern democracies are immersed in more complex institutions of interest intermediation between state and civil society than simple competition theories suggest. They are linked to interest groups, they recruit political leadership personnel, and they develop public policy in conjunction with interest groups and the state executive.[2] These institutional ties and networks of communication among voluntary associations, parties, and state executives may alter whatever organizational form and strategy a logic of electoral competition would expect parties to adopt.

Thus, the starting point of my investigation of Belgian and West German

---

1. Eldersveld's (1964) work is still the theoretically and empirically most outstanding contribution to the behavioral tradition. For the rational actor perspective, Robertson (1976) and Schlesinger (1984) have made valuable contributions. For the structuralist perspective, see Harmel and Janda (1982), Janda (1980), Riggs (1968; 1975), and Schonfield (1983).

2. Because of the multiplicity of tasks modern parties engage in, a simple and comprehensive definition of political parties remains elusive. The term "party" is enmeshed in a Wittgensteinian language game wherein it assumes different, though related, meanings depending on the theoretical and empirical context in which it is used. For a definition of "party" see Crotty (1970), King (1969), Steininger (1984).

ecology parties is a theoretical framework and set of propositions that identify forces and conditions affecting the choice of organizational form and strategy in political parties. From this perspective, the pursuit of a logic of party competition is only one possible outcome of organization and strategy, an outcome that depends on the internal composition and alliance of party activists and on external institutional and conjunctural factors I specify in Chapter 2. My theoretical framework should be applicable to a wide range of political parties. But left-libertarian ecology parties represent especially useful test cases because they envision new patterns of party organization and strategy that diverge from what conventional theory mandates in a European parliamentary democracy. In fact, I argue, a deterministic interpretation of the logic of party competition is unfounded. Ecology parties, and left-libertarian parties more broadly, are indeed developing new organizational and strategic features that clearly set them apart from their competitors. Party activists translate a new vision of interest intermediation between citizens and state into party organization and strategy. In this process they build on patterns of mobilization similar to those employed by the parties' left-libertarian movement constituencies. In other words, left-libertarian parties engage in a *logic of constituency representation* rather than a pure *logic of party competition*. In this sense, the crisis of participation in many modern democracies is leading to a significant innovation opposed to conventional patterns of interest intermediation.

This proposition, however, must be qualified in three vital respects. First, the pursuit of a new form of organization in ecology parties produces results that are in agreement neither with a logic of party competition nor with the intended logic of constituency representation. These "perverse effects" (Boudon 1977) are a continuous source of conflict and change within left-libertarian parties. Second, organization and strategy vary with the social and institutional context in which the parties are located. In settings where left-libertarian movements are highly mobilized and existing political institutions are particularly unresponsive to the movements' challenge, left-libertarian parties have moved closest to a logic of constituency representation. Where these conditions are absent, parties have developed a less unique organizational form. Third, variations in the patterns of competition in party systems remain one important factor influencing the organization and strategy of left-libertarian parties. Where they are able to influence the formation of government, left-libertarian parties are pulled more toward a logic of party competition than where they are in a weak competitive position as opposition parties.

Research Design and Methodology

A more detailed description of the comparative design and research procedure of this book appears in the appendix; here I confine myself to listing some basic research premises and strategies. My research is based on a two-pronged empirical comparison, not a methodologically questionable contrast between the ideals of left-libertarian participatory politics and the empirical realities of the Belgian and West German ecology parties. On the one hand, comparison of Agalev, Ecolo, and the Greens serves to extract common features of left-libertarian parties that can be contrasted to the structure and strategy of conventional socialist, liberal, and conservative parties in Belgium, West Germany, and other European countries.[3] On the other hand, I analyze the differences among the three ecology parties and even among their subunits in order to explore the variability of left-libertarian politics and the logic according to which activists influence the parties' dynamic. My theoretical framework seeks to account for both similarities and differences among left-libertarian parties as well as differences between them and their conventional competitors.

Three considerations led me to choose the Belgian and West German ecology parties to explore the impact of the crisis of participation and of left-libertarian challenges on contemporary party systems. First, in both countries ecology parties represent left-libertarian politics in comparatively pure forms. The parties do not derive from older parties which then turned toward left-libertarian objectives, such as Scandinavian or Dutch left-socialist and even centrist parties. If left-libertarian parties develop a new form and strategy of interest intermediation between civil society and state, this thrust should be most clearly articulated by the new ecology parties, although other left-libertarian parties, of course, should display similar traits.

Second, since the early 1980s the Belgian and West German ecology parties have won a considerable number of votes and are playing an increasingly important role in each country's party system. The West German Greens established themselves as a major political force, receiving 8.3 percent of the vote in the January 1987 national elections. In Belgium the Flemish Agalev and the Walloon Ecolo won 6.2 percent in 1985 and 7.1 percent in 1987 in national parliamentary elections. The parties' extensive involvement in electoral campaigns and legislative decision making over the past five to eight years makes it possible to study the effect of participation in conventional political institutions on the parties' commitment to a radically new form of mobilization and political strategy.

Third, Belgium and West Germany offer interesting contrasts on key variables that may shape the internal process and the external strategy of left-

---

3. It would be desirable, of course, to establish common properties of left-libertarian parties on a broader base than three cases. For the sake of detailed empirical investigation, I have not pursued this strategy. Nevertheless, my findings on the Belgian and West German ecology parties match quite well with the fragmentary evidence on left-libertarian parties in other European countries (cf. Kitschelt 1989).

libertarian parties. Left-libertarian movements are more mobilized in West Germany than in Belgium, the Belgian parties were more readily accepted as legitimate contenders by their competitors, and the parties' competitive position in the contest for government control varies across and within the two countries. These theoretically significant environmental conditions allowed me to explore similarities as well as differences in left-libertarian politics.

The most important source of my study is 134 interviews I conducted with party activists in Belgian and West German regions and cities in 1985. I selected a multiplicity of research sites in order to examine ecology parties in varying contexts. The party militants I interviewed include municipal councilors, party employees, members of state and national executive committees, and parliamentarians at the state and national levels. The interviewees were chosen to reflect the variety of militants' experiences, views, and positions in the party organization. Each interview lasted from one to four hours.

At each research site I used a wealth of other data sources. Most important were the minutes of party meetings and local and regional magazines and newsletters for party members. In a very few instances I was also allowed to examine local membership files. Another important resource were local newspaper reports about party activities which are collected with great diligence by most party units. Finally, observation of party meetings helped me to check and expand my knowledge of party procedures.

Plan of the Book

Chapter 1 is an analysis of the conditions facilitating the rise of left-libertarian parties in Western democracies. My aim here is to show that the Belgian and West German ecology parties are but two examples of left-libertarian parties that have arisen in a number of West European countries with similar socioeconomic and institutional environments. Chapter 2 fleshes out the theoretical logic for reconstructing party organization and strategy in general and applies the model to the case of left-libertarian politics.

Chapter 3 recounts the brief histories of the Belgian and West German ecology parties and surveys their programs. Chapters 4 through 9 comprise the book's empirical core. I have chosen a "bottom up" approach, beginning with grassroots activism, working my way up through the organization, and finishing with the alliance strategies of ecology parties. This sequence of themes captures the phenomenological perspective of an activist who enters a party, gets involved in local politics, expands his or her interests to national politics, runs for office, deals with political mobilization in the party's environment, and chooses party strategies.

In this vein, the fourth chapter examines the careers and motivations of individuals who join ecology parties. Chapter 5 explores the involvement of basic party units in local politics and their links to the regional and national party organization. Chapter 6 analyzes patterns of communication and control in party decision making and is particularly concerned with the interplay between the formal and the informal role of party organs such as conferences, executives, parliamentary groups, and individual politicians. Chapter 7 focuses on the recruitment of militants to party office and, more importantly, elected office. Chapter 8 analyzes the linkages between ecology parties and their external movement constituencies to determine how closely the parties are tied to their political and cultural milieu. Chapter 9 turns to the strategic controversies within ecology parties and analyzes the internal and external conditions that influence strategic choice. The concluding chapter summarizes the book's main points and explores some of the broader consequences of left-libertarian politics for contemporary democracies.

1 | Left-Libertarian Parties in Western Democracies

In contemporary democracies, political stability and change are intimately linked to developments in the party systems.[1] For at least two generations prior to the 1970s, most democratic party systems were structured along such stable patterns of societal cleavage as class, religion, ethnicity, and center/periphery relations.[2] Since the 1960s, however, electoral dealignment and realignment have undermined this continuity (Beck, Dalton, and Flanagan 1984a). New political demands have spawned new parties cutting across established cleavage structures.

Probably the most significant new development is a cohort of left-libertarian parties. These parties first appeared in Scandinavia, France, and the Netherlands under New Left labels and competed with the established communist and social democratic parties. More recently, in Austria, Belgium, Switzerland, and West Germany, ecology or "green" parties have attracted considerable electoral support. Since the late 1970s the programmatic outlook and electoral constituencies of New Left and ecology parties have begun to converge.

Left-libertarian parties oppose the priority given to economic growth in public policy making, an overly bureaucratized welfare state, and restrictions placed on participation which confine policy making to the elites of well-organized interest groups and parties. They favor imposing limits on the

---

1. This chapter draws heavily on Kitschelt (1988a).
2. Lipset and Rokkan (1967), who made this argument about European party systems, are concerned with the representation of societal cleavages in party competition, not with the relative strength of particular parties. Party labels may change even where the same political alternatives are incorporated. Critics and supporters of Lipset and Rokkan's argument are mistaken in testing the persistence of cleavages by the electoral stability of individual parties, as do Maguire (1983), Rose and Urwin (1970), and Shamir (1984).

institutions that modern conservatives and socialists prefer for allocating social costs and benefits: markets, because they orient human preferences toward the pursuit of material commodities, devalue social community, and endanger the supply and protection of nonmarketable collective goods, such as an intact environment; bureaucracies, because they subject individuals to centralized controls, establish a hegemony of professional expertise undercutting political participation, and organize social interaction according to impersonal rules. From the left-libertarian point of view the formal rationality and efficiency of markets and bureaucracies deprives people of choosing a lifestyle that maximizes autonomy and solidarity.

All left-libertarian parties share a similar socioeconomic and cultural profile of voters. While there are no systematic studies of left-libertarian electorates covering all Western democracies, surveys show that left-libertarian voters are from the younger, well-educated middle classes, are employed in human services (teaching, health care, social work), have left-of-center political convictions, subscribe to "postmaterialist" values, and sympathize with environmental, feminist, and peace movements.[3]

Left-libertarian parties have an impact only if they receive a significant level of electoral support, so the circumstances under which they achieve it need to be explained. It is difficult, however, to choose a single and universally applicable criterion for judging when parties are electorally significant. Since left-libertarian parties vary in age and are often less than a decade old, averaging their past electoral performance is of limited use. Moreover, a criterion of electoral relevance should not be too stringent because even a small percentage of the vote may often shift the balance of power in an election and determine chances of government formation. For this reason, I have classified those left-libertarian parties as significant which have at least once between 1980 and 1987 received more than 4 percent of the vote in a national parliamentary election.

Table 1 shows that left-libertarian parties in ten West European democracies have at least once surpassed the 4-percent level of voter support. Eight of these are included in the analysis; Luxembourg and Iceland are too small to count as comparable cases.[4] In Denmark, the Netherlands, Norway, and Sweden, left-libertarian parties have predominantly New Left or left-socialist roots.[5] In Denmark and Norway, they originated in the late 1950s and 1960s,

---

3. Electoral analyses of the Scandinavian New Left parties are provided by Andersen (1984), Logue (1982: chaps. 6 and 8), and Thomas (1986). For France, see Boy (1981) and Vadrot (1978). For West Germany, compare Bürklin (1985a; 1987) and Veen (1984). Several countries are covered in Müller-Rommel (1985a and c).

4. Surveys of New Left and ecology parties can be found in Baumgarten (1982), De Roose (1984), Florizoone (1985), and Rüdig (1985a and b; 1986).

5. On the Danish New Left, see Hansen (1982), Logue (1982), and Lund (1982); on the Netherlands, read Gerretsen and Van der Linden (1982) and Jacobs and Roebroek (1983); on

Table 1
Left-libertarian parties in Western democracies: best performance, 1980–1987

Countries with significant left-libertarian parties
(support greater than 4 percent of the vote in at least one national election in the 1980s)

Austria (A)	The Greens	4.6%	(1986)
Belgium (B)	Agalev (Flanders) and Ecolo (Wallonia)	7.1%	(1987)
Denmark (DK)	Socialist People's party	14.5%	(1987)
Iceland	Women's party	5.0%	(1983)
Luxembourg	The Green Alternative	5.2%	(1984)
Netherlands (NL)	Green Progressive Accord (PPR/PSP/CPN)	5.7%	(1982)
Norway (N)	Socialist People's party	5.4%	(1985)
Sweden (S)	Left Communist party	5.4%	(1985)
	Center party	12.4%	(1985)
Switzerland (SW)	The Greens	4.8%	(1987)
	Progressive Organization	3.5%	(1987)
West Germany (FRG)	The Greens	8.3%	(1987)

Countries without significant left-libertarian parties
(support up to 4 percent of the vote in all national elections in the 1980s)

Parties or proto-parties exist

Canada (CND)	Green Party of Canada	—	(no contest in national election)
Finland (FI)	Greens	4.0%	(1987; 1983: 1.4%)
France (F)	Ecologists	3.9%	(first round of the 1981 Presidential election)
	Greens	1.2%	(1986 parliamentary election)
Ireland (IRE)	Comhaontas Glas/Greens	—	(no contest in national elections)
Italy (I)	Radical party	2.5%	(1987)
	Green lists	2.9%	(1987)
Japan (J)	Green party	—	(declared only)
New Zealand (NZ)	Values party	0.2%	(1984; 1975: 5%)
Spain	Green party	—	(declared only; no independent participation in elections)
United Kingdom (UK)	Ecology/Green party	1.1%	(in districts contested in the 1983 election)
United States (US)	Citizens's party	0.1%	(presidential elections 1984)
	New World Alliance	—	(no contest in national elections)

No parties declared
Australia (AUS)
Greece
Portugal

languished in the 1970s, and found new vigor in the 1980s as they developed left-libertarian programs and profiles of voter support. In the Netherlands, New Left parties gained strength in the late 1960s and 1970s. Yet their efforts to embark on a left-libertarian transformation have proved less successful than in Denmark or Norway, because they have faced stiff competition for left-libertarian voters from the traditional Dutch socialist party and from a new moderate center-left liberal party, the Democrats '66. The Democrats '66, like a small Norwegian liberal party that has tried a similar strategy, are not included in Table 1 because their program and electoral support are not confined to left-libertarian constituencies.[6] Sweden, finally, is unique because two established parties—the formerly agrarian Center party and the Communist party—moved toward the left-libertarian agenda and stemmed the growth of newly founded left-libertarian parties. Although these parties have not entirely renounced their traditional clienteles and ideological affinities, on the whole they must be included in the left-libertarian party cohort.[7] In Switzerland two new parties represent more moderate and more radical left-libertarians. The Greens draw the bulk of their support from western Switzerland, while the Progressive Organization is strong in the northern cantons of Basle and Lucerne. Under the umbrella of the Austrian Greens a similar ideological differentiation takes place, combining two previously competing "green" and "alternative" lists. The German Greens, and to a certain extent Agalev and Ecolo in Belgium, also combine New Left and moderate ecological roots.[8]

Table 1 lists thirteen countries that have no electorally significant left-libertarian party. Some have parties or proto-parties that have so far remained below the threshold of electoral significance introduced above. Fairly close to the threshold of left-libertarian representation has been France. Here left-socialist parties, such as the Unified Socialist party and a number of Trotskyist

---

Norway, see Hansen (1982) and on Sweden, Kitschelt (1983; 1986), Nelkin and Pollak (1980), Rubart (1983), and Zetterberg (1980). Left-libertarian strategies in Norwegian and Swedish centrist-liberal parties are discussed in Elder and Gooderham (1978).

6. The Norwegian liberals, unlike the Swedish Center party, barely cleared the 3 percent electoral threshold in 1981 and finally lost their parliamentary representation in 1985 (Modeley 1986). They thus represented less of a threat to the Norwegian left-socialists than the Democrats '66 did to the Dutch New Left. For the electorate of the Dutch Democrats '66, compare Irwin and Dittrich (1984).

7. In Kitschelt (1988a) I considered Sweden, together with Switzerland and France, as cases with "borderline" significant left-libertarian parties. Since the Swedish and Swiss left-libertarian parties, however, can be explained in terms similar to those of other countries, I have counted them here as true cases. France, on the other hand, is now counted as a country *without* a relevant left-libertarian party because its institutions proved unfavorable to a sustained left-libertarian party mobilization (discussed later).

8. Müller-Rommel (1985c) emphasizes the existence of *a more* New Left and *a more* moderate ecological type of left-libertarian party. In Belgium Ecolo in particular draws upon a more moderate clientele for reasons I explain in Chapter 3.

and Maoist groups, gained a respectable electoral following in the 1960s and early 1970s, though they have now virtually disappeared. In fact, the French ecologists were the first to enjoy some modest success in local and regional elections in the 1970s, but their performance in all National Assembly elections has been disappointing; one exception was an ecology candidate who received almost 4 percent of the vote in the first round of the 1981 presidential election.[9]

In Italy, as in France, New Left parties participated in elections in the 1970s and 1980s, yet none has surpassed the 4-percent level. The libertarian Radical party managed to collect 3.5 percent in the 1979 parliamentary election but has seen its voter support decline since then. In the 1980s various Green lists have participated in local and regional elections with modest success.[10] In the national election held in June 1987, this loose alliance received 2.9 percent of the vote and parliamentary representation for the first time. Among the remaining countries one other left-libertarian party has won parliamentary seats without surpassing the 4-percent level: the Finnish Greens, an alliance of local lists which received 1.4 percent of the vote and two seats in the 1983 national elections. In 1987, however, the party managed to win 4 percent of the vote and thus may be included in future counts of significant left-libertarian parties.

At least three other countries had left-libertarian parties contesting elections between 1980 and 1986. The New Zealand and British parties were in fact the first ecology parties in the world, but they covered only a limited range of left-libertarian themes. The New Zealand Values party gained over 5 percent of the vote in the mid-1970s but was then displaced by another third party, the Credit party, which is not primarily left-libertarian (see James 1978). The British left-libertarian party—initially called the People's party (1973), then the Ecology party, and finally the Green party—experienced several ups and downs, regroupings, and splits but has never gained much electoral support, nor does it embrace a comprehensive left-libertarian agenda (see Rüdig and Lowe 1986). As in New Zealand, another third party, the liberal/social democratic alliance, has absorbed but not given much prominence to left-libertarian themes and constituencies.

In Canada, Ireland, Japan, and Spain, left-libertarian parties have been founded but have received insufficient support. In Australia, Greece, and Portugal, left-libertarian parties did not even exist in the 1980s, unless one counts the splinter parties of the radical left still wedded to a predominantly

9. Detailed information on the French New Left and ecology parties are provided by Garraud (1979), Leggewie and de Miller (1978), Nicolon and Carrieu (1979), Nugent (1982), and Nullmeier and Schulz (1983), Parodi (1979), and Vadrot (1978). The most comprehensive study of the Unified Socialist party is Hauss (1978).

10. Background information on the Italian New Left and ecology parties can be gathered from Leonardi (1981), Langer (1983; 1985), McCarthy (1981), Potter (1982), and Spiss (1985).

traditional socialist/redistributive political agenda, although they have recently made efforts to appeal to left-libertarians.

I have included ten of the thirteen countries without significant left-libertarian parties in the comparative analysis. Greece, Portugal, and Spain were dropped because their transition to democracy is too recent; an initial exploration, moreover, showed that they share none of the attributes that facilitate the rise of left-libertarian parties in other countries.

Explanations of Left-Libertarian Politics

About half of the eighteen most important Western democracies have electorally significant left-libertarian parties. In the other half these parties are weak or nonexistent. Any attempt to explain this variance can rely on three different theoretical arguments. First, structural explanations identify basic economic, social, and cultural changes in advanced capitalism as the source of the new preferences and demands.[11] Not the breakdown of institutions that occurs in economic and political crises but the success of modern industrial economies and attendant sustained increase in material affluence generate new demands that cannot be satisfied within existing economic and political institutions. For structuralists, economic growth, transformations in a society's occupational profile, and changes in values and lifestyles are the key causes and preconditions of collective mobilization.

Critics have argued that structural change theories leave out political institutions and power relations and therefore cannot explain the timing, form, or intensity with which new demands are articulated (see Melucci 1985:792). While the economic and cultural transformation of modern societies explains *why* left-libertarian demands may burst into the political arena, only political institutions and power relations explain *how, when,* and with *what* political effect these demands articulate themselves. The actors' skills, resources, and capacities for rational calculation, as well as the broader institutional structures they can utilize, are decisive in explaining the timing, organizational form, and strategy of collective mobilization.[12] Explanations emphasizing resource mobilization and political opportunity structures focus on variables such as the relative power and organization of classes and interest groups in society, the nature of party systems, policy-making institutions, and party control of executive power.

Both theoretical approaches stand in contrast to a third line of reasoning

11. The most important and sophisticated theoretical contributions to the structural analysis of left-libertarian demands are Bell (1973; 1976), Habermas (1975; 1981), Ingelhart (1977), Offe (1983; 1985), and Touraine (1973; 1978). Although their substantive explanations differ considerably, they follow a general "standard causal pattern" to which all structural analysts subscribe.

12. This argument has been developed in the literature on social movements under the label of "resource mobilization theory" and a "polity theory" of collective mobilization. Cf. Gamson (1975), McCarthy and Zald (1977), and Tilly (1978).

commonly labeled "breakdown" or "relative deprivation" theory (cf. Gurr 1970). Based on a psychological frustration-aggression argument, relative deprivation theory predicts collective mobilization when social institutions cannot deliver the benefits actors expect from them. For breakdown theorists, economic crisis and dislocation in particular create favorable conditions for collective mobilization.

I argue that a combination of structural change and resource mobilization theories provides the most satisfactory explanation for left-libertarian parties. The former highlights necessary background conditions of party formation. But only the latter, by examining favorable political opportunities and resources, defines sufficient conditions for the creation of left-libertarian parties. As I have discussed elsewhere (Kitschelt 1988a and b), the relative deprivation theory contributes comparatively little to our understanding of left-libertarian politics.

Structural and resource mobilization theories are best tested by correlating the existence or absence of electorally significant left-libertarian parties with the independent variables that each of the two perspectives finds relevant. The small number of countries ($N=18$) and problems of collinearity among relevant independent variables severely constrain possibilities for a statistical analysis. I define the dependent variable as a dummy (significant left-libertarian parties exist = 1; other cases = 0). Three measures of association between independent variables and the presence of left-libertarian parties are given. If independent variables are interval-scaled, I use linear regression analysis (Pearson r's). Since the dependent variable is a dummy, I also employ a loglinear regression model (LOGIT) to provide a statistical significance test for the correlations examined.[13] Finally, I cross-table independent variables dichotomized around the median with the left-libertarian party dummy variable and calculate the ratio of cases that are correctly classified in the resulting two-by-two tables as a "coefficient of reproducibility" (CR). In addition to this rather general comparative analysis of all eighteen countries, I provide a more detailed discussion of Belgian and West German left-libertarian party formation for each variable discussed in this chapter. This information should provide the necessary background for understanding the position and orientation of Agalev, Ecolo, and the Greens in their national contexts.

My empirical indicators are at the macro-level. They presuppose microfoundations that cannot be explicitly tested in this chapter because adequate comparable data are lacking. Better data about the socioeconomic position and values of left-libertarian voters alone would not provide adequate microfoundations. Data are needed on voters' strategic choice and electoral preference schedules in light of different party constellations and policy-making institutions.

13. I will not discuss loglinear regression coefficients because they are more difficult to interpret than linear regression analysis.

Social Change and Party Innovation

Modern welfare state capitalism was made possible by an unprecedented period of economic growth, affluence, and institutional stability. But according to theories of postindustrial society, this success generates new demands and discontents. Left-libertarian movements and parties perceive new technological risks to human life and the natural environment, bureaucratic restraints on individual autonomy and self-organized collectivities, and limits to democratic participation. At the same time, rising standards of education, individualization of lifestyles, and greater social and cultural mobility have made citizens more aware of these grievances. Theories of postindustrial society argue that the growing tension between citizens' demands for autonomy and participation on the one hand and the increasingly comprehensive and complex hierarchies of social control on the other lead to the formation of left-libertarian parties.

If postindustrialism theories are right, more individuals in affluent countries should develop strong preferences and capacities for pursuing left-libertarian goals and thus promote the formation of left-libertarian parties. If we take 1980 per capita incomes as a baseline,[14] the average income in countries with sizable left-libertarian parties is significantly higher than in countries without them (Table 2). The correlation is a strong .71, and 15 out of 18 cases are correctly classified. Austria, France, and the United States are the only anomalies.

Both Belgium and West Germany are correctly classified. Closer examination shows that a correlation between levels of affluence and ecology party support holds true among and within the two countries. In the national elections in Belgium and West Germany in 1987, the ecology parties received 7.1 percent and 8.3 percent respectively. Within Belgium, the Flemish per capita Gross National Product (GNP) was 18 percent ahead of Wallonia's by 1979 (McRae 1986:79). While the Walloon ecology party Ecolo started at a higher level of electoral support than the Flemish Agalev in the early 1980s, by 1985 Agalev had caught up with Ecolo and in 1987 received a larger share of the electorate. Agalev's initial disadvantage was due to the timing of building its party organization. While Ecolo ran in most Walloon constituencies in the early 1980s, it took Agalev until 1987 to build an extensive organization covering all areas of Flanders.

Within West Germany as well there is a definite relationship between affluence and the Green vote at the aggregate level. If we regress electoral support for the West German Greens in state and national elections from 1981

---

14. I have consciously chosen income levels in a year preceding the "peak performance" of left-libertarian parties up to 1987. Moreover, the 1980 exchange rates are more representative of the actual purchasing power and standard of living in countries with different currencies than are later exchange rates. The dollar and dollar-pegged currencies had just recovered from a low without yet being overvalued.

Table 2
Left-libertarian parties and per capita income, 1980

	Income greater than $11,000 per capita		Income less than $11,000 per capita	
Significant left-libertarian parties exist	B	(11,816)	A	(10,251)
(Average = $13,109)	DK	(12,952)		
	FRG	(13,305)		
	N	(14,019)		
	NL	(11,851)		
	S	(14,761)		
	SW	(15,922)		
No significant left-libertarian parties exist	F	(12,136)	AUS	(10,129)
(Average = $9,240)	US	(11,364)	CND	(10,582)
			FI	(10,440)
			I	(6,906)
			IRE	(5,193)
			J	(8,873)
			NZ	(7,441)
			UK	(9,335)

Coefficient of reproducibility (CR) $= 1 - \dfrac{\text{N of mistakes}}{\text{N of cases}} = .83$

Pearson's r: .71

Significance level (LOGIT regression) p ≤ .04

Source of data: OECD (1982).

to 1985 on the per capita income of West German states, the association between income levels and electoral support is significant.[15] Figure 1 illustrates this link. Other variables such as industrial structure, extensiveness of party organization, and competitive position of the parties in each state may explain the remaining variance.

While economic affluence is thus a fairly reasonable predictor of successful left-libertarian party formation, other indicators proposed by postindustrial theories fail to reveal significant associations. The size of the tertiary occupational sector in the eighteen democracies is not associated with significant left-liberation parties.[16] Similarly, the relative size of the student population in advanced education shows no link to party formation.[17]

15. Autocorrelation between the levels of Green electoral support within each German state over several elections might make the association look stronger than it is. But given the small number of cases and the limited purpose of this analysis, I have settled for a simple bivariate calculation.

16. The Pearson r coefficient is .1 (not significant) and almost half of the cases are falsely classified. See Kitschelt 1988a: table 3.

17. I take the number of college students per 100,000 inhabitants as a measure of educational advancement in the eighteen countries. This measure is not associated with left-libertarian party formation. Data are provided by UNESCO (1984).

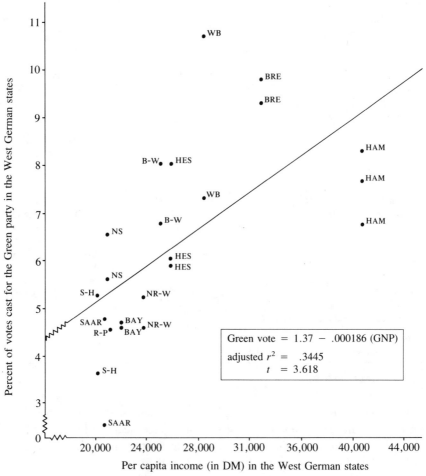

Key: S-H = Schleswig-Holstein; SAAR = Saarland; NS = Niedersachsen; R-P = Rhein-
land-Pfalz [same result in two elections]; BAY =˙ Bayern; NR-W = Nordrhein-Westfalen;
B-W = Baden-Württemberg; HES = Hessen; WB = West Berlin; BRE = Bremen; HAM =
Hamburg.

Source of income data: Statistisches Bundesamt 1984.

Figure 1. Relationship between per capita income in the West German states (1980) and the
Green vote in state and national elections (1981–1985)

Theories of postindustrialism further maintain that with increasing economic affluence economic redistribution loses its prominence on the political
agenda, and postmaterialist values of self-actualization and political participation come to the fore (cf. Inglehart 1977; 1987). If this is so, postmaterialist
values should bring about the emergence of left-libertarian parties. Although

we lack data on all eighteen democracies, we can test this proposition against a sample of six. A common measure for the advance of postindustrialism in a country is the difference between the percentage of survey respondents who express postmaterialist and those who express materialist values. If we average annual surveys for 1976 through 1980 for three countries with significant left-libertarian parties (Belgium, the Netherlands, and West Germany), materialists outweigh postmaterialists by 21.8 percent.[18] In the three countries without significant left-libertarian parties (Britain, France, and Italy) the corresponding difference is 30.0 percent. In the latter three countries, the inflation rate was much higher than in Belgium, the Netherlands, and West Germany and depressed support for postmaterialism (Inglehart 1985). Once we correct for this external circumstance, postmaterialist commitments in both groups of countries are too similar to provide a reasonable explanation of left-libertarian party formation.

Inglehart (1984b:62) and Dalton (1984b) argue that value change does not instantly translate into electoral realignments. Still, this does not explain why the apparent "lags" between value change and party realignments differ from country to country. Theories of postmaterialism either do not use reliable measures of value change or underrate the importance of changing cognitive capabilities, rational calculation, and institutional opportunities and constraints as determinants of collective political action. At best they account for changing individual orientation, preference, and capability of engaging in collective protest. But they do not sufficiently predict the conditions which lead to the formation of left-libertarian parties.

Political Institutions and Power Relations

Groups making left-libertarian demands choose the most effective and efficient strategies for putting their issues on the political agenda. Because forming social movements or political parties requires more effort, skill, and imagination than employing existing channels, rational activists attempt to build new vehicles of interest representation only when traditional organizations fail to respond to their demands. They can do so, however, only if they have the resources and opportunities as well as the motivation. Thus, significant left-libertarian parties appear only when the *unresponsiveness* of existing political institutions coincides with favorable *opportunities* to displace existing parties.

One institutional arrangement that makes the rise of left-libertarian parties more likely is the welfare state. Comprehensive entitlement programs and transfer payments protect the material well-being of most citizens from the

18. Data are calculated from Abrahamson and Inglehart (1986), tables 2 and 7.

risks of the business cycle and labor markets. This "safety net" not only generates a subjective sense of economic security and shifts people's attention to issues not related to income and material security but also frees people's resources for the pursuit of a left-libertarian policy agenda.

Welfare states encourage left-libertarian mobilization in another sense. They organize many social services (education, social welfare, health care, and the like) within bureaucratic institutions. Nonmarket services in general, and the bureaucratic provision of social services in particular, have given rise to intense consumer dissatisfaction, which in turn has fueled left-libertarian demands for a decentralized, consumer-controlled reorganization of public services (Hirschman 1981:39–41). Table 3 shows that indeed there is a strong positive association between comprehensive welfare states and the existence of significant left-libertarian parties. Again, the number of anomalies is very small.[19]

The strength of welfare states is the result not only of economic development but also of political struggles led by centralized interest groups and bureaucratized mass parties, particularly parties of the socialist left.[20] It is these political organizations that often block the access of left-libertarian demands to the political process. The resistance is especially strong where traditional agents of social change—labor unions and socialist parties—are involved in centralized policy bargaining and frequently participate in government.

In capitalist democracies the power of labor is based on a centralized, comprehensive organization of workers (see Schmitter 1981). This form of interest representation has enabled labor to engage in corporatist elite bargaining with business and political parties and has constrained consideration of left-libertarian demands in two ways. In terms of policy-making procedures, new, less well-organized interests are rarely recognized by the dominant corporatist interest associations and parties. And in terms of policy outcomes, business and labor build compromises around economic and social policies diametrically opposed to left-libertarian demands: the imperatives of industrial growth and bureaucratic regulation. When a coalition of producer interests dominates policy making, left-libertarians resort to new and disruptive vehicles of interest representation.

As a rule, business groups and conservative parties are resolutely opposed to left-libertarian demands for a more egalitarian, participatory, and ecological society. Unions and labor parties, in contrast, share with left-libertarians a

19. The figure understates the exceptional social and economic security that Swiss citizens enjoy, thanks to Switzerland's broad company-organized social security system and unique position in the world economy. Compare Schmidt (1985).

20. The strength of the combination of these forces has been stated most convincingly by Castles (1982), Flora and Heidenheimer (1981), Schmidt (1982), and Uusitalo (1984).

Table 3
Left-libertarian parties and social security expenditure, 1979–1980 (percentage of GNP)

	Expenditure greater than 19%		Expenditure smaller than 19%	
Significant left-libertarian parties exist	A	(21.4%)	SW	(12.8%)
(Average = 23.3%)	B	(24.5%)		
	DK	(26.2%)		
	FRG	(23.0%)		
	N	(19.8%)		
	NL	(27.6%)		
	S	(31.2%)		
No significant left-libertarian parties exist	F	(25.5%)	AUS	(11.6%)
(Average = 16.0%)	IRE	(20.6%)	CND	(14.8%)
			FI	(18.0%)
			I	(16.3%)
			J	(9.8%)
			NZ	(14.1%)
			UK	(16.9%)
			US	(12.2%)

CR = .83
Pearson's r: .61
Significance level (LOGIT regression) p ≤ .03

Source of data: ILO (1985).

mistrust of markets and a commitment to greater solidarity in social organization. For this reason, labor corporatism is one key to understanding the emergence of left-libertarian parties. As labor organizations are drawn into corporatist interest intermediation, they become preoccupied with tangible short-term material benefits to their constituencies rather than profound institutional change in capitalism. As their objectives narrow, they sever actual or potential ties to the left-libertarian agenda. It comes as no surprise, then, that throughout the 1970s labor unions showed sympathy toward left-libertarian goals, such as phasing out nuclear power, only in a few noncorporatist countries (France, Japan) and opposed them in most corporatist countries.

Indeed, most of the countries Schmitter (1981) identifies as having medium or high levels of corporatism, such as Austria, Belgium, Denmark, the Netherlands, Norway, Sweden, and West Germany, have significant left-libertarian parties.[21] Among countries with little labor corporatism, only Switzerland has important left-libertarian parties. Corporatism is strongly linked to low strike rates as a result of compromise between centrally con-

21. Only Finland, with a medium level of corporatism but no significant left-libertarian party, falls outside this pattern. The growing strength of its Green party in the 1987 election, however, shows the impact of corporatism here too.

certed capital and labor organizations. The importance of labor corporatism for left-libertarian party formation can thus be demonstrated also by the high negative correlation between levels of strike activity and significant left-libertarian parties ($-.78$; see Table 4). Only a single case—Japan—is classified in the wrong cell. The importance of labor corporatism is, of course, linked to other variables such as the size of countries (Katzenstein 1985), the degree of ethnic pluralism (Lijphart 1977b; 1984), and the rigidity of electoral cleavages (see Powell 1986:38). But none of these circumstances leads to association with left-libertarian parties anywhere nearly as strong as that of strike frequency and party development.

The close link between systems of interest intermediation and highly organized left-wing parties capable of controlling government policy has usually been underemphasized in the literature on corporatism.[22] Corporatism prevails where socialist and social democratic parties have often held government office. Because leftist governments follow a course of moderate social change and support a compromise between capital and labor around the objectives of economic growth and high employment, they are unavailable for voicing left-libertarian demands.

Whether and when left-libertarians respond by forming their own parties depends on patterns of party competition. They usually prefer socialist to conservative parties because they share with socialists at least a commitment to economic redistribution. Left-libertarian voters support a new alternative only if defection from the socialists will not automatically promote a conservative government. Moreover, as long as the traditional left is in the opposition, it is able to gloss over the conflict between pro-labor and left-libertarian demands, appealing to both constituencies and thus preempting the rise of an effective new party. When a socialist opposition party appears strong enough to wrest power from a conservative government in a forthcoming election, left-libertarians will be especially hesitant to support a new party.

Conversely, three conditions favor left-libertarian parties. First, where divided bourgeois parties do not really pose a threat to a hegemonic left in government, left-libertarians may see little cost in abandoning the socialist parties. Second, long socialist government incumbency may dampen left-libertarians' hopes that socialist governments can meet their demands. Third, where traditional left parties are very weak and permanently confined to the opposition, left-libertarian voters have nothing to lose by abandoning them (cf. Pinard 1975).

In light of these conditions, the formation of left-libertarian parties is least likely where left-wing parties have recently come to power or are highly competitive opposition parties hoping to take over the government after the next election. Various empirical measures of the relative strength of socialist

22. Lehmbruch (1979 and 1984) and Rokkan (1966) must be exempted from this criticism.

Table 4
Left-libertarian parties and strike activity (working days lost per 1000 employees in the labor force, 1965–1981)

	Loss less than 260 days/year		Loss more than 260 days/year	
Significant left-libertarian parties exist	A	(10)		
(Average = 61)	B	(156)		
	DK	(148)		
	FRG	(28)		
	N	(28)		
	NL	(22)		
	S	(95)		
	SW	(1)		
No significant left-libertarian parties exist	J	(71)	AUS	(427)
(Average = 439)			CND	(707)
			F	(278)
			FI	(358)
			I	(840)
			IRE	(484)
			UK	(375)
			US	(411)

CR = .94
Pearson's r: − .78
Significance level (LOGIT regression) p ≤ .05

Source of data: ILO (1983), quoted in Cameron (1984).

parties, of right and left party cohesiveness (Castles 1982; Schmidt 1982), and of party fractionalization (see Dodd 1976) yield no significant correlation with the existence of significant left-libertarian parties, yet the duration of socialist government participation in the 1970s clearly does (Table 5). Where traditional left parties have held power for prolonged periods of time, they normally have pursued policies contrary to left-libertarian expectations, eventually eroding their base of support among this group of voters.

Socialist government participation also explains the timing of left-libertarian party formation. New Left precursors of today's left-libertarian parties were formed in the late 1950s and 1960s only in countries with frequent socialist governments and a divided political right, such as in Denmark, the Netherlands, France, Norway, Sweden, and Switzerland. These new parties were revived or strengthened at the end of the 1970s if socialist or social democratic parties also had held office for most of the decade.[23] In countries

23. Thus, the Scandinavian New Left parties made considerable electoral progress, while the French and Dutch New Left parties stagnated or declined throughout the 1970s. The increasing bipolarity of the French party system and the rise of the socialist opposition party contributed to the decline of the Unified Socialist party.

Table 5
Left-libertarian parties and major socialist/communist party government
participation (months in government, 1970–1980)

	Participation more than 61 months		Participation less than 61 months	
Significant left-libertarian parties exist (Average = 100.3)	A	(132)	NL	(52)
	B	(90)		
	DK	(97)		
	FRG	(132)		
	N	(85)		
	S	(82)		
	SW	(132)		
No significant left-libertarian parties exist (Average = 29.8)	FI	(122)	AUS	(35)
	UK	(62)	CND	(00)
			F	(00)
			I	(00)
			IRE	(51)
			J	(00)
			NZ	(36)
			US	(00)

CR = .83
Pearson's r: .74
Significance level (LOGIT regression) $p \leq .03$

Source of data: Keesing's Contemporary Archive 1970–1980.

where the right was well organized and prevented socialist control, left-libertarian parties emerged only in the late 1970s, after long periods of left government participation; they now carry the "Green" or "ecology" label. This rationale explains the cases of Austria, Belgium, and West Germany.

The tradeoff between New Left and ecology parties in all countries but Switzerland suggests that the two types are members of the same political family. Where New Left parties have won significant electoral support, ecology parties have been less successful even when they appealed to voters who were ideologically more moderate. Moreover, in Norway, Sweden, and the Netherlands these moderate libertarians are already served by center-to-left liberal parties complementing the New Left. Conversely, most successful ecology parties have appeared in countries without sizable New Left or center left-libertarian parties. While the New Left has embraced the ecology agenda, most ecology parties have accepted the libertarian and anticapitalist spirit of the New Left.

In addition to the attributes of party systems and governments discussed above, electoral systems may influence the formation of new parties (Harmel and Robertson 1985; Lijphart 1984: chap. 9). Indeed, none of the five countries with plurality voting systems (Australia, Canada, New Zealand, the United Kingdom, and the United States) has a significant left-libertarian party, while most countries with qualified proportional electoral rules do (with minimum thresholds of parliamentary representation in the neighborhood of 4 or 5 percent). Yet the correlation between voting systems and left-libertarian parties is not very neat, since at least five countries with proportional representation do not have significant left-libertarian parties. In the French case, for instance, the shift from a majoritarian to a proportional electoral system had no influence on the ecologists' support in 1986 compared to 1981. Conversely, in countries with plurality voting, third-party challenges around other than left-libertarian issues have occurred and have sometimes attracted a considerable share of the votes. Even in a plurality system, voting for new and small parties may be rational if voters believe a new party can displace the established contenders in the long term, or expect that the major parties will change their policies if a critical percentage of voters defects to a new alternative.

The overriding influence of electoral laws on the formation of left-libertarian parties could be proved only if these parties failed to appear in countries with favorable social and institutional circumstances but unfavorable electoral laws. Such a case does not exist. All countries with plurality voting systems are heavily overdetermined by other conditions that preclude the rise of left-libertarian parties. They are mostly less affluent, have less comprehensive welfare states, lack labor corporatism, and have experienced only short periods of socialist rule. Thus, although plurality voting laws do create an impediment to left-libertarian parties, this factor should not be overemphasized.

Left-Libertarian Movements and Parties

Any account of left-libertarian party growth would be incomplete without an examination of the major role of social movements. The anti-nuclear power movement in particular was a crucial catalyst in the late 1970s and early 1980s. Such movements indicate the intensity of left-libertarian demands and resources in a country. They also reveal that the new demands cannot be pursued through established parties and interest groups. Moreover, the practices of left-libertarian movements reflect a country's political culture, expressed in common beliefs about political participation, tolerance for opposition to cultural deviance, and the legitimacy of political protest and cultural innovation.

Protest against nuclear power is only one of the left-libertarian activities that grew out of a broad infrastructure of environmental, feminist, peace, student, and neighborhood movements. In many countries, however, anti-nuclear movements became the symbol and rallying point for left-libertarian activism in the late 1970s and in several instances led directly to the formation of ecology parties. The limitations of movement protest convinced many participants that they had to confront the political elites in the arena of electoral competition. For this reason, in Western democracies the scope and intensity of anti-nuclear movements should be studied in relation to left-libertarian party formation.

The significance of the nuclear controversy is difficult to determine because cross-national data on the mobilization of opposition to nuclear power are confined to qualitative comparisons or to inventories of case studies (for example, Gyorgy et al. 1979; Mez 1979). Ideally, opinion polls, the incidence of mass demonstrations against nuclear facilities, and politically motivated delays in nuclear licensing procedures would measure the strength of anti-nuclear movements. In practice, we must rely on informed judgment about the intensity of conflict in each country (Table 6).

The relative size of a country's nuclear energy program would be an obvious explanation for levels of conflict, but this logic does not generally apply. Belgium, Britain, Canada, Finland, Italy, and Japan had extensive nuclear programs but did not experience intense national controversy in the 1970s. Conversely, Austria, Denmark, and the Netherlands had modest plans but nevertheless were marred by conflict. With the exception of the United States, which sustained a fairly intense nuclear power controversy from the early 1970s on and drew international attention to the issue, no other country without left-libertarian parties witnessed a strong mobilization against nuclear power. Only France is difficult to classify. Here, an initially intense anti-nuclear movement in the mid-1970s triggered the participation of ecologists in local and regional elections. Later, government repression, the opposition Socialist party's attempts to co-opt anti-nuclear activists, and the movement's complete lack of policy impact quelled the mobilization of collective protest (Kitschelt 1986).

There is some evidence that socialist government participation intensified the nuclear conflict and also precipitated the growth of left-libertarian parties. Since conservative parties have always been firmly committed to nuclear power, anti-nuclear activists hoped that left parties would listen to their demands. In fact, where socialists were continuously in the opposition during the 1970s, as in Japan and France, they did distance themselves from nuclear power. When they were in government, however, their concern with economic growth and employment usually prevailed over the pleas of anti-nuclear activists.

Nevertheless, the link between left government participation, nuclear conflicts, and left-libertarian parties is far from perfect. The United States, with no leftist party, has a relatively intense conflict, and many Democrats and Republicans in Congress opposed nuclear power. Belgium and Finland imple-

Table 6
Left-libertarian parties and the nuclear power controversy, 1975–1980

	Intense Nuclear Conflict	No Intense Nuclear Conflict
Relevant left-libertarian parties exist	A	B
	DK	N
	FRG	
	N	
	S	
	SW	
No relevant left-libertarian parties exist	US	AUS
		CND
		FI
		IRE
		I
		J
		NZ
		UK

CR = .83

mented ambitious nuclear power programs under socialist governments but avoided marked conflicts. Idiosyncratic factors, such as whether plants were built before the nuclear controversy, whether they drew international attention in the mid-1970s, or whether they were near large urban areas, have an independent effect on the intensity of anti-nuclear mobilization.

To sum up, the nuclear power controversy in the 1970s contributed to the emergence or strengthening of left-libertarian parties but was certainly not the sole determinant. It roughly indicates, but does not fully represent, the broad scope of cultural and political left-libertarian activities in the "incubation" period of the new parties and the link between institutional settings and the rise of left-libertarian politics. For this reason, it is worth examining political structures and social movements more comprehensively in the two cases this book focuses on, Belgium and West Germany.

Institutional Setting and Left-Libertarian Movements in Belgium and West Germany

West Germany and Belgium both incorporate most of the features that stimulate left-libertarian opposition. They have centralized economic interest groups, corporatist bargaining, and tightly structured bureaucratic parties. Regional, state, and national governments often include the socialists, who unify all relevant forces of the traditional Left. The executive branch of the

Belgian and of the West German state is firmly tied into the party-led networks of interest intermediation.

Political scientists have called both West Germany and Belgium "party states" or "particracies" because in them well-organized, cohesive parties provide the medium through which interest groups, legislatures, and the executive branch interact in the process of policy formation.[24] Political clientelism and proportional representation of the established parties in the career bureaucracy are common. Parties wield considerable control over the mass media, the judiciary, and educational institutions. Moreover, they provide important channels for interest groups to participate in policy making.

Both West Germany and Belgium have two-tiered systems of interest-group representation. Business, labor, the professions, and the churches enjoy privileged access to policy-making arenas and are closely associated with the executive and the established parties through regular communications, interlocking leadership positions, and organizational linkages. Consumer groups, women's associations, environmentalists, neighborhood groups, and many other "public interest groups" fall into a second tier. Because these groups have comparatively low levels of formal organization and lack elites who can make binding commitments on behalf of their constituencies, party politicians and public officials give them little credibility. They are further disadvantaged by the fact that they crosscut cleavages represented by the major parties. Organizationally and ideologically, then, the demands articulated by public interest groups and related social movements are expressed outside the perimeter of what can usually be accommodated by a policy style based on inter-elite bargaining.

In Belgium the interorganizational networks of interest groups, social service organizations, political parties, and even quasi-state agencies are called "pillars."[25] Each of the three major party families (Catholics, socialists, liberals) has a network of pillar organizations. Although these pillars originated as self-defense organizations for particular social groups at a time when Belgium was torn by sharp class and religious conflicts, the organizational might and the material incentives these networks still control have kept them alive even at a time when ideological polarization has declined and political compromises have reduced class and religious conflicts (Billiet 1984).

24. In the more recent literature, see especially Billiet and Huyse (1984), Ceulers (1981), Dewachter and Clijsters (1982: 209–13), and DeWinter (1981) for Belgium, and Dyson (1977; 1982), Katzenstein (1982; 1987), and Narr (1977) for West Germany. The "party state" perspective is criticized by Heisler (1974: 186) for Belgium, and Haungs (1973) for West Germany. While these authors claim that the role of parties in policy making is limited, they underrate the penetration of the state by party functionaries and the cohesiveness of the major "state parties."

25. On interest group intermediation in Belgium compare Bundervoet (1983), Ellemers (1984), Huyse (1983; 1984), Lorwin (1971), Molitor (1978), and Van den Brande (1987).

Interest intermediation in West Germany is less governed by party/interest group pillars than in Belgium but close interorganizational linkages among parties, interest groups, and state agencies do exist.[26] In addition to major business organizations and unions, the professions and religious welfare organizations enjoy the most direct access to public policy making. Here, too, an exclusive system of interest representation has created barriers for new groups trying to get access to the policy-making process.

In both countries the state executive has little autonomy vis-à-vis political parties and organized interests. In West Germany cooperative federalism limits the range of innovation to compromises among only the most entrenched interests (Lehmbruch 1978; Scharpf et al. 1976). In Belgium the ethnolinguistic conflict between Flemings and Walloons led to a constitutional reform creating a para-federalist state, further complicating political consensus building among the different pillars.[27] In both countries the complex networks of federal control relying on coordination through parties and interest groups are vulnerable to obstruction by veto powers and often bring about immobility and paralysis in policy making rather than cooperation.

Given the relative decentralization and weak autonomy of the Belgian and the West German executive, centralized parties are the main agents for cohesion and stability, making these countries "consociational" or "centripetal" democracies (see Lijphart 1977b; 1984). The parties rely on their active membership as pools of political talent channeled through long-lasting careers to positions of leadership and responsibility. The party leaderships are usually supported by coalitions of moderate activists, many of whom also belong to the interest groups with which a party is directly or indirectly affiliated. Aside from occasional rank-and-file revolts, party leaders have the capacity to organize broad intraparty compromises on policy and strategy. Their power derives from a combination of party office, ties to powerful interest associations, leadership in parliamentary party groups, and, if the party is governing, executive office.

The parties' internal centralization facilitates the formation of government coalitions because intraparty opposition can be disciplined. And given the generally centripetal competition for uncommitted voters in the center of the political spectrum, all major parties can coalesce with one another, including the parties of the Left. Yet entrenched party hierarchies are insensitive to the articulation of new demands that represent minority positions. For this reason, during the 1970s the left-libertarians were unsuccessful in making their voices heard within the socialist parties of both countries.

Although Belgium and West Germany share basic features of the party state

26. I am relying especially on Alemann and Heinze (1979), Dyson (1982), and Offe (1981).
27. On constitutional reform and the federalist solution to the ethnolinguistic conflict see especially Fitzmaurice (1983: chap. 4), Lijphart (1981), and McRae (1986) and Molitor (1981).

such as interest intermediation and intragovernmental policy coordination, substantial differences in their political cultures and systems of party competition have influenced the development of their respective left-libertarian parties. In general, West Germany is characterized by more polarization among parties, a more adversarial political culture, and a higher mobilization of left-libertarian movements than Belgium.

Belgium is the only European party system that incorporates at least three cleavages in its party system: religion, class, and language.[28] Since the 1970s, the three traditional liberal, socialist, and Catholic parties have split into separate Francophone and Flemish organizations. A Flemish nationalist party, the Volksunie, receives a substantial share of votes. So Belgium's fragmented party system makes it unlikely that a new contender will dramatically alter the strategic position of existing parties or their options for coalition building. Since the new contender does not pose a threat, existing parties adopt a more conciliatory stance toward it than in a more bipolar system in which a small number of votes for a new party may alter the balance of power dramatically. Moreover, new parties can gain parliamentary representation without a large following or dramatic shifts of voter support. Owing to the varying size of the Belgian multi-member electoral districts, the threshold of representation varies from 2 to 33 percent, with an average of about 4 percent (Leonard 1983:149–50). Thus, both institutional rules and the behavior of established parties result in tolerance of new parties. In turn, this tolerance may reduce the level of hostility new parties express toward existing political institutions and actors.

In West Germany the situation is different. For close to twenty years the electoral picture consisted of a large Christian conservative party, the Christian Democratic Union (CDU/CSU), a large moderate leftist party, the Social Democratic Party (SPD), and a much smaller liberal party, the Free Democratic Party (FDP), together receiving 97 to 99 percent of the vote in the 1972, 1976, and 1980 elections and revolving primarily around class and religious cleavages.[29] Given the close competition between the two major parties, any new party could easily upset the balance of power and thus was attacked vigorously by the established parties. In the late 1960s this happened to the neo-Nazi party, which posed a threat to both Christian Democrats and Liberals, and in the 1980s to the Green party, which benefited primarily from the defection of Social Democrats. At the same time, the German 5-percent threshold of electoral representation requires that a new party attract a consid-

28. The historical formation and the structure of the Belgian party system are discussed in Hill (1974), Lorwin (1966), Urwin (1970), and Zolberg (1977; 1978).

29. Political cleavages in German voting behavior are analyzed in Baker, Dalton, and Hildebrandt (1981) and Pappi (1977; 1984). Of course, an analysis of sociological cleavages leaves out very important strategic bases of voting behavior, e.g., responding to a government's economic policy performance.

erable following, a requirement bound to change the relative power of existing parties. These two conditions make it harder to form successful new parties in West Germany and also fuel the antagonism between old and new.

As a consequence of restrictive electoral rules, intense polarized competition between the major parties, and their elites' hostility toward any new competitor, the West German Greens came into existence only after a long period of high left-libertarian movement mobilization. In contrast, the Belgian parties Agalev and Ecolo began to develop at a lower level of left-libertarian movement mobilization and encountered fewer obstacles in gaining parliamentary representation.[30]

Compared to Belgium, the greater scope and intensity of left-libertarian social movements in West Germany in the 1970s was primarily due to differences in political institutions, social cleavages, and cultural orientations. In addition, economic affluence may have had a slight independent impact on cross-national and intranational variations of left-libertarian movements. West Germany is somewhat wealthier than Belgium, and in both countries left-libertarian movements are usually more vocal and varied in the prospering metropolitan areas, such as Hesse and Hamburg in West Germany and the Flemish urban region between Antwerp and Brussels in Belgium.

In Belgian politics the ethnolinguistic conflict of the 1960s and 1970s, the relative decline of labor corporatism in the 1970s (Van den Brande 1987), and the fragmentation of the party system convinced political elites to react more flexibly and tolerantly to new challenges than they had in earlier decades. Moreover, Belgium's small size, the sharp conflicts around multiple cleavages in the past, and a long democratic tradition had instilled a climate of compromise which made "combat governments" unimaginable (Zolberg 1978:132), reduced the appeal of radical parties, and moderated the mobilization of left-libertarian movements.

Belgian politics was tottering on the brink of ungovernability during the first postwar decade (Huyse 1980), but the class and religious compromises of the late 1950s ushered in a period of calm. The freeing of previously channeled political energies, however, gradually intensified the language conflict (Van Haegendorn 1981:31). The Flemish movement was driven by cultural protest against Francophone domination, whereas the Walloon backlash was initially inspired by economic concerns of a declining region whose citizenry wished to participate in Flanders's increasing affluence (Mughan 1979).

In the late 1960s the regional-linguistic cleavage overlapped at its peak with emerging left-libertarian demands for social decentralization and democratization (Lijphart 1977a:61–63). This is evidenced by the conflict over the

---

30. These contrasts between West Germany and Belgium are discussed in greater detail in Chapter 3.

division of the University of Leuven into a Flemish and a Francophone campus, a conflict that combined ethnolinguistic, anticlerical, and New Left concerns (Zolberg 1977:123–24; Jacobs and Roebroek 1983:20–21). Some sympathizers with left-libertarian demands were initially drawn to the ethnolinguistic parties, the Flemish Volksunie and the Rassemblement Wallon, although the Flemish party primarily appealed to conservatives and the Walloon party to socialists. Other left-libertarians supported Maoist and Trotskyist sects or the Communist party, which still played a modest though declining role in the old industrial centers of Wallonia. The Belgian socialists were initially unreceptive to left-libertarian demands and stayed close to their blue-collar constituencies.

Between 1953 and 1974 the number of demonstrations in Belgium increased dramatically, but their size declined. This change can be explained by the reorientation of protest movements away from class, religious, and ethnolinguistic cleavages toward left-libertarian issues.[31] Most of the left-libertarian activists participated in a plethora of independent local protest movements and initiatives.

Environmental protests against new chemical plants, harbors, roads, and canals increased, particularly in Flanders. The best-known conflict in the 1970s concerned the Duwvaart canal project, which would have cut through the only recreation area close to Antwerp (Peeters and Vermeiren 1980:62–75). Also in Flanders, a Third World movement, complete with shops and information centers, gained a large following. In Wallonia, Belgium's declining steel and coal region, however, environmental conflicts were more subdued. They focused on river control projects and protests against the expanding tourist industry in the Ardennes. Other activities included a neighborhood movement raising questions about urban planning and the quality of residential life, primarily in the Brussels region.

Two left-libertarian movements important in other countries never left a deep impact in Belgium: the anti-nuclear and feminist movements. Construction of Belgian nuclear power plants began in the early 1970s before the emerging American nuclear controversy drew international attention to this technology. Also, Belgium's dense siting of several nuclear plants at two locations reduced the number of targets at which the anti-nuclear movement could take aim. Only in Wallonia has the construction of nuclear power plants, across the Belgian border in France, stirred widespread resistance. Whereas in other countries nuclear protests could crystallize the left-libertarian groups around a common cause, in Belgium the absence of such mobilization has kept the movement sector relatively disjointed and weak.

Feminism has not gained wide support in Belgium, either. The issue of women's economic equality was already championed by socialist unions and

31. This interpretation is derived from findings reported in a quantitative analysis of Belgian protest events based on police records (Smits 1984).

parties. Mobilization around such feminist cultural and lifestyle causes as legalized abortion, protection from male violence, and lesbianism has been thwarted by Belgium's strong Catholic tradition. Belgium is among the few countries that did not liberalize abortion laws in the 1970s and 1980s. Given this isolation, many feminist groups have withdrawn from politics and focused instead on cultural activities since the late 1970s (cf. Jacobs and Roebroek 1983).

Smits's (1984) study of Belgian protest events reveals a regional imbalance in protest mobilization. As mentioned above, the incidence of demonstrations increased more in affluent Flanders than in Wallonia, where a precipitous economic decline gave class issues greater prominence. Other evidence confirms that the Flemish region is more conducive to left-libertarian protest. Surveys show that Walloons are more inclined to voice grievances through established channels of political participation than Flemings who are also more optimistic about the success of protest tactics (De Graeve-Lismont 1975: 519–20). In Wallonia, class voting is much more pronounced than in Flanders (Frognier 1975:480–81), where the socialist party has begun to court left-libertarian groups in addition to its working-class constituency (Mabille and Lorwin 1977:402). Finally, the peace movement protests in the early 1980s against the stationing of new medium-range nuclear missiles in Belgium also demonstrated the difference between Flanders and Wallonia. In Flanders especially vehement protests prompted the socialists to take a staunch position against these weapons, whereas the Walloon socialists remained noncommittal.

Thus, social, political, and cultural conditions in Belgium led to a rather subdued left-libertarian mobilization with only limited tendencies toward radical departure from the political order. In contrast, West Germany experienced a virtual explosion of protest activism and challenges to its political institutions after the relative lull of the 1950s, a decade marked by economic recovery and the integration of the social democrats into postwar capitalism and parliamentary democracy.[32] This lull, interrupted only by the movement against nuclear armament of the German military, set the stage for the eruption of the 1960s and 1970s. In the weak and fragile democracy of the 1950s conservative elites resorted to a predemocratic friend-foe rhetoric to create loyalty to the new order. Reminiscent of Bismarck's persecution of social democrats, opponents of the Christian Democratic government were treated as enemies of state and constitution, not as democratic competitors. While the social democrats were the victims of this demagoguery in the 1950s, many of them joined the same chorus against the New Left of the 1960s and the social movements of the 1970s.

The SPD expelled its own student organization, the Socialist German

32. Detailed analyses of the West German social movement sector from the 1950s to the 1980s can be found in Brand, Büsser, and Rucht (1983), Langguth (1983), and Roth (1985).

Student Association (SDS), when it refused to renounce Marxian socialism and participation in the Easter March disarmament movement of the early 1960s. Thus, the SPD involuntarily created the first effective New Left organization, detached from the party and free to gain mass support later in the 1960s (Briem 1976; Otto 1977). Events in the 1970s reaffirmed the friend-foe approach that German political elites continued to share. Reluctance to respect "opposition on principle" and to tolerate radical dissenters fueled a political polarization that led to the Radicalism Decree of 1972, enacted to remove from office civil servants with leftist convictions. Moreover, Christian Democratic and many Social Democratic politicians alike denounced the anti-nuclear and peace movements as communist front organizations.

The friend-foe rhetoric and harsh treatment of radical political critics reinforced the growing antagonism and polarization between the "establishment" and the libertarian left. Whether or not ostracizing radical dissenters contributed to the isolated incidents of terrorism throughout the 1970s (cf. Sack 1984; Steinert 1984), it certainly did help to create a "camp mentality" and solidarity among the many left-libertarian movements that later supported the Green party.

From the late 1960s onward, the SPD tried to absorb more moderate elements of the protest generation in its youth organization, the Young Socialists (Braunthal 1983: chaps. 4 and 5), but many left-libertarians participated in an informal New Left culture or in electorally unsuccessful Maoist or Trotskyist parties. Alongside these activities, the first of the so-called citizens' initiatives or citizens' action groups appeared in the 1960s. Concerned with local issues such as better urban planning, stricter pollution standards, and improved educational and cultural institutions, these groups attracted many supporters and activists (cf. Mayer-Tasch 1977; Rammstedt 1980).

In the early 1970s a feminist movement developed to press for legalized abortion. After a compromise abortion law was enacted, many feminists turned from politics to building women's self-help networks and a feminist subculture free of the sexism of everyday family and work life. Many have been guided by the vision of transforming sex relations, not merely equalizing men and women (Drewitz 1983; Schenk 1981).

Also in the 1970s, work cooperatives, service organizations, self-help groups, and communal living captured the imagination of many young people and constituted a loose movement for social and cultural transformation. Though the youths' specific goals are as diverse as the groups are many, they all share a desire to reshape the market economy in ways that allow working and living to be reintegrated (Bewyl and Bombach 1984; Huber 1980).

The intense public controversy over West Germany's nuclear power program brought many diverse political and cultural left-libertarian movements in contact with one another as the 1970s progressed. The anti-nuclear movement became a catalyst for intermovement cooperation (Kitschelt 1980; Rucht 1980). This fusion of protest groups and escalation of the nuclear issue into a national controversy succeeded because all established parties represented in parliament firmly supported the nuclear program, despite serious reservations shared by a large number of German voters. The SPD/FDP coalition government was unwilling to alter nuclear policy although both parties faced considerable internal opposition to it.

In the early 1980s the anti-nuclear movement fed into the emerging peace movement against the stationing of new NATO medium-range nuclear missiles in Western Europe, which built an even wider coalition that included groups outside the left-libertarian constituency (Mushaben 1985; Rochon 1988). Again, initially none of the established parties was willing to represent peace movement demands, even though surveys showed that a majority of the population supported them. The movement reached its peak in 1982–83 and has since declined. Nevertheless, in West Germany as in Belgium the waves of protest have left behind significant groups with common experiences, continuing networks of communication, and political visions that can easily be reactivated by new issues and demands. The German movements especially have generated a lasting infrastructure of communication centers and media activities, symbolized by the founding of an alternative daily newspaper, the *Tageszeitung* or *TAZ*, which achieved a circulation of about 50,000 copies in the mid-1980s. Although these groups do not constitute firmly integrated and closed subcultures, they do create a political atmosphere and disseminate symbols that have helped left-libertarian parties to flourish.

In summary, West Germany has developed a more mobilized and topically diversified social movements sector than Belgium. Environmental and industrial issues as well as sociocultural questions have attracted a large number of activists. West Germany's rapid economic recovery and growing affluence after World War II, its political opportunity structure promoting polarization between the established elites and an "alternative camp," and the political culture of elites still taking a friend-foe approach to dissent all contributed to a stronger left-libertarian mobilization than in Belgium. Nevertheless, the two countries share a wide range of facilitating conditions.

The Rise of Left-Libertarian Parties: A Synthesis

A simple model combining the five strongest predictors of left-libertarian party formation in eighteen Western democracies illustrates that structural, institutional, and precipitating conditions are closely intertwined (Table 7). Since the relatively high collinearity among the five independent variables rules out a meaningful multivariate analysis of their contribution, I have added up favorable and unfavorable conditions to a summary "bet" of how likely

Table 7
Variables that influence the presence of left-libertarian parties in the 1980s

	Per capita GNP		Social security expenditure		Strike activity 1965–1981		Left parties in government		Intensity of nuclear controversy		Odds for the emergence of left-libertarian parties
	High	Low	High	Low	High	Low	High	Low	High	Low	
Denmark	X		X			X	X		X		5:0
Netherlands	X		X			X	X		X		5:0
Sweden	X		X			X	X		X		5:0
West Germany	X		X			X	X		X		5:0
Austria		X	X			X	X		X		4:1
Belgium	X		X			X	X			X	4:1
Norway	X		X			X	X			X	4:1
Switzerland	X			X		X	X		X		4:1
France	X		X		X			X		X	2:3
United States	X			X	X			X	X		2:3
Finland		X		X	X		X			X	1:4
Ireland		X	X		X			X		X	1:4
Japan		X		X		X		X		X	1:4
United Kingdom		X		X	X		X			X	1:4
Australia		X		X	X			X		X	0:5
Canada		X		X	X			X		X	0:5
Italy		X		X	X			X		X	0:5
New Zealand		X		X	X			X		X	0:5

Combined CR = .87.

left-libertarian party formation is in each country. In four countries, all variables correctly predict party formation, and West Germany is in this group; in four other countries, four out of five variables correctly predict it, and Belgium belongs to this second group; in eight cases, the variables predict the absence of left-libertarian parties. Only two ambiguous cases remain: the United States and France. Here, socioeconomic variables strongly predict the presence of significant left-libertarian parties. In addition, in the United States the anti-nuclear movement left a deep impression, and in France the mobilization was intense though limited to a very short time period. But in both countries the political institutions and opportunities that triggered the formation of left-libertarian parties—such as labor corporatism and long-term socialist government participation in the 1970s—are missing.

Overall, the model's link between macro-societal and political variables is consistent with existing theoretical models of party formation.[33] Societal changes drive the transformation of citizens' wants, but these lead to the emergence of political parties only if political opportunities and constraints make it rational to step outside established channels of political communication, and if polarizing conflicts of high symbolic importance create the initial conditions for consensus about the nature and outlook of left-libertarian parties.

If we are looking for theoretical parsimony of the explanatory model only, the least ambiguous predictor of left-libertarian parties in the sample of all eighteen democracies is the level of strike activity. This variable predicts only a single case improperly: Japan. Theoretical parsimony, however, would be bought at the cost of ignoring the complex web of interacting conditions. Strike activity is only one indicator in a syndrome that includes economic development, social policy, corporatism, and left-party governments. The *interdependence* of these factors is probably more important than each factor individually.[34]

The explanatory model in Table 7 faces three limitations. First, because the independent and dependent variables are dichotomous, it cannot account for variations in the strength of left-libertarian parties once they exceed the 4-percent level of electoral significance. Yet a more fine-grained comparison of West German and Belgian socioeconomic, institutional, and cultural condi-

33. For the general study of social and political collective mobilization, Smelser (1963) has outlined an explanatory approach that combines social change, political opportunities, and precipitating conditions. For the analysis of party formation, Pinard (1975) has elaborated this model. Other useful contributions with a similar approach include Hauss and Rayside (1978) and Wilson (1980).

34. Charles Ragin (1987: chaps. 6–9) has made a fascinating proposal to use Boolean algebra in comparative analysis to model the interaction of independent variables contributing to an outcome, even if the number of cases is small. His proposal becomes more difficult to apply, however, the more possible combinations of dichotomized independent variables are not actually observed in empirical cases. In Table 7, for instance, the eighteen countries cover only ten of thirty-two different possible combinations among independent variables.

tions suggests reasons why the German Greens attract more electoral support than Agalev and Ecolo. In the future, with more data on electoral performance, it should be possible to regress economic and political conditions for left-libertarian support in a more sophisticated way than in this chapter. A more sophisticated analysis should also account for qualitative change in the party representation of left-libertarian demands over time. In Sweden, for example, many left-libertarians who endorse moderate environmentalist policies defected from the Center party in the 1988 parliamentary election and enabled a Swedish Green party, which had lingered in political obscurity since its founding in the late 1970s, to win parliamentary representation.

Greater sophistication in relating independent and dependent variables could possibly take care of a second limitation of the present analysis. I have identified exclusively indigenous determinants of party formation but neglected the effect of the international context and the diffusion of ideas. As left-libertarian parties gain prominence in a core set of countries with favorable internal conditions, diffusion might cause similar parties to appear in countries with less favorable conditions. For example, the Italian Greens won 2.9 percent of the vote in 1987, which if counted together with the Radical party means that left-libertarians there now surpass the 4-percent threshold.

A third limitation of a macro-level explanation is the absence of individual-level data that can test whether the motivational and cognitive implications of the macro-model are true. As long as these micro-foundations are missing, it will always be possible to make a case for alternative explanations of the left-libertarian phenomenon, such as a crisis or breadown theory. The most prevalent counterexplanation holds these parties to be responses of the educated younger generation in the 1970s and 1980s to the frustrations of tight labor markets and fierce competition for scarce positions in the political elite (Alber 1985; Boy 1981: 414–15; Bürklin 1984a; 1985a; 1987).

However, not only comparative macro-analysis of left-libertarian parties but also survey data on left-libertarian voters yield little support for the crisis model (see Kitschelt 1988a and b). In the 1970s the countries with significant left-libertarian parties have done economically as well as or better than their competitors in terms of growth, unemployment, and inflation. And demographic data showing that left-libertarian voters are young, educated, not overly wealthy, and without many traditional attachments (marriage with children, religious affiliation) and status goods (home ownership) can be interpreted as supporting either breakdown or structure theories, depending on the motivations and beliefs one attributes to those voters.

The Strategic Outlook for Left-Libertarian Parties

Macro-structural and resource mobilization theory leads us to conclude that left-libertarian parties are more than short-term "flash" and protest parties.

Instead, they result from a complex interaction of institutional and conjunctural factors and express a broad challenge to the existing networks of interest intermediation between state and civil society of which established parties are only one element. Breakdown theories predict the quick demise of left-libertarian parties as some temporary economic and political strains disappear.

On the other hand, the structural and political conditions on which left-libertarian electoral support is based are not necessarily permanent or irreversible. Explaining the *emergence* of political parties is one thing; explaining their long-term *persistence* is another. Even though left-libertarian issues apparently constitute a new *cleavage dimension* in modern politics, this cleavage will not necessarily spawn lasting independent political parties.

Left-libertarian parties are threatened by a number of actual and potential changes. The welfare state has come under attack in Europe; labor corporatism noticeably declined in the 1980s; and a renewed discipline of the marketplace may challenge the foundations of economic security and affluence on which left-libertarian parties rest (Offe 1987). Under such circumstances the dominant political agenda of Western democracies could shift away from the highly publicized left-libertarian issues so prominent in the 1970s and 1980s—ecology, energy, feminism, and nuclear armament—and reestablish an exclusive hegemony of economic-distributive politics.

In a sense, left-libertarian parties themselves pursue a political agenda that could erode the institutional underpinnings on which they have thrived. They fight the bureaucratic welfare state, labor corporatism, and the structural rigidities of "consensual" democracies. Although their vision of social change differs radically from that of conservative free-market ideologies, their attack on the post–World War II political and economic class compromise could unintentionally play into the hands of conservative political forces; if it undermines the organized power of labor, it may recenter the political conflict on distributive issues.

The outlook for left-libertarian parties also depends on the strategic moves of their competitors. Conservative parties can hardly become a threat, but in a number of countries socialist and social democratic parties have been ousted from government office in the 1980s. As opposition parties they have greater incentives and opportunities to blur the issues that separate their working-class supporters from left-libertarian constituencies and to present themselves as politically more effective advocates of left-libertarian causes than the left-libertarian parties themselves. Since left-libertarian supporters are predominantly educated, highly sophisticated individuals who are more likely to vote strategically than from blind loyalty to a party, this social democratic strategy may become a serious threat to the new parties.

Finally, the future of left-libertarian parties depends not only on conditions and competitors in their environment but also on their own strategic capabilities. In this respect, they face a difficult task. On the one hand, they must preserve the fluid, open organizational form and obstructionist quality that challenge the highly institutionalized corporatist welfare state and maintain the loyalty of their core constituencies. On the other hand, they must become effective political players in terms of both electoral appeal and impact on public policy. In parliamentary multiparty systems, effective politics usually presupposes a cohesive, disciplined party organization and a consistent, moderate political strategy that appeals to marginal supporters. Left-libertarian parties must resolve the conflict between a logic of constituency representation oriented toward the visions of their core party militants and activists and a logic of party competition adhering to standards of electoral success and external strategic effectiveness. The next chapter introduces a theoretical model explaining how political actors and conditions shape the choice of organizational form and strategy in left-libertarian parties.

2 | Organization, Strategy, and Elections

External circumstances such as economic development, labor corporatism, and extended leftist party incumbency in government facilitate the initial success of left-libertarian parties. Once a party has gained electoral momentum, however, its internal ability to develop a viable organization, a substantive political program, and effective strategies becomes equally decisive for its success. In this sense its leaders exercise considerable control over the party's future.

I propose a theory of party formation that reconstructs the selection of organizational forms, programs, and strategies from a set of feasible alternatives. The feasibility set depends on institutional constraints and opportunities as well as on activists' preferences and orientations. To simplify somewhat, parties choose from a continuum of options located between polar alternatives represented by a logic of constituency representation and a logic of electoral competition. A logic of constituency representation is inspired by the ideologies and political practices of core supporters. Faced with a tradeoff between breadth of popular appeal and ideological purity of policy and strategic stances, they prefer the latter. A logic of electoral competition, however, means adjustment of internal organization, program, and strategy to the conditions of the "political marketplace" to maximize electoral support.

While scholars have proposed many explanations as to why parties adopt a logic of electoral competition, they have made few efforts to understand "divergent" instances in which parties follow a logic of constituency representation. This chapter identifies some shortcomings of theories entirely concerned with the behavior of parties complying with a logic of electoral competition. I then propose a theoretical model to explain how parties choose between different logics of party formation. I employ the model to reconstruct the organizational and strategic choices between the two logics in left-libertarian parties. Finally, I extend the model by introducing what I call "perverse effects." Even if ideology rather than electoral efficiency is guiding party activists, the organizational, programmatic, and strategic dynamic of parties often leads to outcomes not anticipated or intended by the activists themselves.

Electoral Competition and Political Ideology

Beginning with the ground-breaking works of Ostrogorski (1902/1964), Michels (1911/1962), and Weber (1919/1958), scholars have explained party organization, programs, and strategies in terms of four variables: (1) ideology of the core constituency; (2) prerequisites and consequences of organizational coordination; (3) imperatives of the electoral marketplace; and (4) institutional constraints on party competition. These explanations are not necessarily incompatible and have been combined in complex theoretical constructs. In the final analysis, however, most classical party theorists have treated the imperatives of the electoral marketplace as the decisive determinant of party structure and strategy.

Early party theories recognized that at least initially political parties rely on social cleavages and popular ideologies, which shape their organization and strategy according to a logic of constituency representation. Weber (1919/1958), Neumann (1932; 1956), and Duverger (1954) distinguished between "framework parties" or "parties of individual representation" on the one hand and "mass parties" or "parties of social integration" on the other. Framework parties appeal to liberal-capitalist clienteles with an individualist spirit and mode of political action; they develop loose organizations with a small membership and are governed by elites of notables whose chief aim is to win political office. Mass parties are supported by class or religious constituencies who share collectivist belief systems and political practices; they build large, cohesive, bureaucratized organizations, choose stable political strategies, and are less willing to compromise their principles in order to gain public office. Today's empirical studies still find that a party's social cleavage base translates into a distinct form of organization, independent of the context of party competition in which it operates (cf. Lagroye and Lord, 1974; Janda and King, 1985).

Even early contributions to the party literature, however, argued that although ideology matters most in the initial stages of party formation, structural constraints on the behavior of parties determine organization and strategy later on. Forces beyond the intentions and control of individual party activists move political parties from a logic of constituency representation to a logic of party competition. Along these lines, Michels (1911/1962) sought to prove that all large membership parties require a hierarchical organization and eventually gravitate toward a defense of the political status quo, be they radical socialist, moderate, or conservative. The organization's size, the complexity of its tasks, and the incompetence or lethargy of its amateur members give rise to an internal division of labor and a corps of professional political leaders. These leaders in turn are most concerned with organizational viability and electoral success, independent of followers' political demands, because they are primarily interested in protection of their own political status and office rather than the ideology of the party's rank-and-file militants and core supporters.

Other scholars have explained the "end of ideology" in party politics by examining party competition in modern democracies (cf. Downs 1957; Duverger 1954; Kirchheimer 1966). They propose that parties dilute their ideologies and streamline their organizations in order to attract the vote of marginal sympathizers and capture a maximum share of the electoral market. When parties compete for the median voter they adopt broadly similar "rational-efficient" organizational forms, programs, and strategies.

Some scholars have added, however, that the nature of a rational-efficient party form varies according to institutional context, characterized by electoral rules, extent of state centralization, number of competing parties, and the presidential or parliamentary base of executive power (cf. Epstein 1967; Harmel and Janda 1982; Sartori 1976).[1] From this perspective, Michels' centralized and bureaucratic parties are rational-efficient vehicles of party competition only in countries with parliamentary government, a centralized state organization, and proportional representation.

Institutional theories of party formation share with general theories of party competition the basic postulate that patterns of electoral competition shape choices of organizational form, program, and strategy and may bring about a discrepancy between the ideology of its core constituency and its actual course of action. Yet these theories rarely detail how party activists bring about the shift from a logic of constituency representation to a logic of electoral competition. In other words, structural theories lack "micro-foundations" that explain how party activists respond to structural constraints and alter their behavior and organization. Existing proposals to provide micro-foundations of party theory yield some valuable insights but on the whole, as I will argue in this section, are unsatisfactory.

The least detailed conventional explanation for the overriding importance

1. Simple typologies of rational-efficient party organization tend to ignore the fact that complex historical and institutional conditions influence what efficient means. For instance, Wright's (1971) rational-efficient party model builds on mainstream American parties with loose cadre organizations, a model that would probably not be efficient in a parliamentary democracy with corporatist patterns of interest intermediation. Given these complications, I agree with authors who reject the possibility of an exhaustive typology of political parties (cf., e.g., Riggs 1968:45–46; Steininger 1984: 111; Wiesendahl 1980: 215–44).

of electoral competition in party politics builds on a theory of evolutionary learning. Parties adapt to electoral competition or face extinction. Learning may be a trial-and-error process in which only those strategies are retained that maximize electoral support.[2] Parties will gravitate toward essentially similar organizational patterns and strategies in the very pursuit of electoral success. But evolutionary learning theory falls short of a satisfactory explanation if we accept that human behavior is not merely random but also reasoned and purposive in light of preferences, opportunities, and constraints. Evolutionary theory tells us nothing about how activists reason about political strategy. Therefore, it cannot fully reconstruct the internal process of organizational and strategic change in parties.

A second argument for the importance of electoral competition to the behavior of parties cites the unique incentives of political entrepreneurship. According to Michels, individuals moving into leadership positions change their political preferences. They derive gratification no longer primarily from the party's shared ideology or from the support of its loyal following but from rewards outside the party (votes, recognition by political elites). Hence, party leaders gradually shift their strategy toward an optimum acquisition of internal and external resources, moving away from rank-and-file preferences (cf. Wellhofer and Hennessey 1974:297–305). This argument, however, insufficiently specifies the optimum point of party strategy on the continuum between courting the core constituency and maximizing votes. It cannot tell us why and to what extent the rank and file allow leaders to diverge from their position, because it provides no avenue to reconstruct the militants' political debates that shape the dynamic of strategy formation.

The theoretical literature on party dynamic proposes at least four different (but partially compatible) views of militants' outlook and behavior. In the first view, party members are considered to be "cooperative" and acquiescent to leadership's orientation toward a logic of party competition. Michels sees members as by and large lethargic with few claims to participation in party decisions. Moreover, decision making involves prohibitive transaction costs whenever the number of participants and of decision alternatives is sufficiently large. Members may leave decisions to political leaders simply because involvement yields too small a payoff.

Second, party leaders may be able to pursue a course different from what militants would welcome because they dispense selective incentives to the discontented. The rank and file like emotional identification with the leaders (Michels), who compensate followers indirectly with solidary and material gratifications rather than directly with policies that are consistent with militants' political demands.

---

2. Note that evolutionary theories need not specify a causal mechanism to bring about efficient outcomes other than random variation. Cf. Van Parijs 1982.

Third, party activists get involved under conditions of uncertainty and goal ambiguity and therefore contribute to a party even with little direct payoff. According to Schlesinger (1984:386–87), many of them are young and inexperienced with little information about the personal costs and benefits of party activism; others place a low value on their time because they have no definite job commitments or are engaged in occupations that grant a great deal of time flexibility. Activists recruited from the "leisure market" need no tangible policy payoffs to maintain their enthusiasm.

A fourth explanation claims that party leaders coerce members into following a political course different from that they would otherwise choose. This argument builds on the premise that activists are steadfast ideologues and insist on strategies that thwart leadership's efforts to maximize electoral support. According to Robertson (1976:39), activists have a more radical commitment to changing the world than the average voter or they would not go through the trouble of working in a party. Because activists will try to reverse leadership's stances, only oligarchy can maintain electoral orientation. The leaders need active members helping them reach the electorate, but they must not allow members to control the political agenda. For this reason, "the less power the members of a party have, and the stronger the leadership, the better its electoral chances." (Robertson 1976:43)

Alone or combined, membership lethargy, leadership incentives, uncertainty about the payoffs of activism, and coercive oligarchy are insufficient to explain the organization, program, and strategy of political parties. Empirically, the proposition that party leaders pursue systematically different and usually more moderate strategies oriented toward a logic of electoral competition underlies all four arguments. But we encounter the following inconsistencies: (1) Party leaders, or at least middle-level functionaries, are often more radical than party activists. (2) Conversely, parties usually include very sizable groups of activists who are neither passive nor radical. (3) In many instances neither the rank and file nor the party leadership are homogeneous groups that express diverging political tendencies.[3] Competition among party leaders may produce a convergence of opinion between rank and file and leadership.[4]

Theoretically, there are no a priori reasons why party activists should be more radical than the party leadership. Radicals may join because they are alienated from politics and wish to change society dramatically. But moderate

---

3. I provide empirical substantiation for these arguments in Chapters 4 and 5 and particularly 6, where I argue that only a specific segment of activists in "middle level" positions (conference delegates, members of steering committees, and administrators) is more radical than either the average party leader in elected office *or* the average rank-and-file militant.

4. This argument has been made by Lipset et al. (1956) about the relationship between the rank and file and the leadership of labor unions.

supporters may join to set the party on a course of incremental social change.[5] Opposition to radicalism may give rise to a "militant reformism"—insistence on gradual change or the status quo—which is at least as intense as the convictions of party radicals. Sartori (1976) argues that in multiparty systems where electoral support can be increased by either "centripetal," moderate or "centrifugal," radical strategies, the position of activists and party leaders is not determined by the goal of electoral success.

Conceptually, most existing theories of intraparty politics, particularly those in the rational choice framework, are flawed for three reasons. First, they treat the preferences of rank-and-file militants as an exogenous variable, rather than as part of a dynamic process in which militants respond to the external environment of party politics as well as to internal debates and coalitions. Rational choice theories assume militants' preferences but do not analyze the formation and nature of their preferences.[6] Second, they introduce party "leaders" and "followers" as homogeneous groups, rather than as diversified coalitions with a variety of orientations and preferences. Third, a priori postulates about rational strategies fail to analyze the actors' cognitive belief systems. Party activists may have not only different policy and electoral preferences but also diverging cognitive views of how these objectives and the strategies for reaching them are causally related. Consequently, it is usually uncertain and controversial which strategies and political programs maximize electoral support. Uncertainty about the consequences of political strategies and disagreement about policy programs within parties require a more sophisticated reconstruction of intraparty groups than a simple dichotomy of "leaders" and "followers" permits.

Because activists weigh policy objectives and electoral strategies, parties are not unambiguously "market based" organizations (Schlesinger 1984) with vote and office maximization as a fixed standard of success. Active members are expected to consider many potential objectives and strategies and choose among them in light of variable preferences and cognitive beliefs.[7]

5. In an attempt to integrate a Downsian model of party competition with a model of activists in political parties, Aldrich (1983) leaves it open whether people join parties from more radical or more moderate convictions. If people who are alienated stay outside, parties will be more moderate; if apathetic people abstain, party activists may be more radical than the average voter.

6. Rational choice reconstructions of intraparty politics often lay claim to only a "thin" conception of rationality, which foregoes investigation of activists' substantive ends and encompasses only the rational pursuit of those ends. But all rational choice theories in fact do assume a "thick" notion of rationality that (1) attributes specific objectives to actors and (2) claims that they behave in certain ways because they pursue these and not other objectives. For a discussion of notions of rationality, see Elster (1986). In his explanation of party behavior, Schlesinger (1984:385) intends to rule out psychological explanations and consideration of the actors' goals, but then goes on to declare that the inexperienced young who became party activists content themselves with selective incentives—certainly a strongly psychological argument.

7. Rational choice reconstructions of party behavior as adaptation to electoral imperatives (such as provided by Schlesinger 1984) assume that electoral competition clearly prescribes the

Discourse on policy and strategy is not governed simply by electoral vote maximization, because in most Western democracies parties have other tasks and powers than electoral representation. They are focal organizations in complex networks of communication between state and civil society and have many ties to political actors and organizations other than those provided by electoral competition. Most important among them are ties to interest groups and state agencies. In this sense, parties are often vehicles of interest articulation as well as interest aggregation (cf. Wright 1971:26). Such multiple linkages to other political institutions account for a goal diversity not reflected in the electoralist view of party politics.[8] The electoralist view ignores the fact that in many democracies parties are more than electoral machines.[9]

Structural and rational choice theories emphasizing electoral orientation fail to develop a dynamic theory of party change and diversity which could explain why parties sometimes diverge from a logic of electoral competition. For Schlesinger (1984:392–96), parties that move away from the maximization of electoral support are unexplained "aberrations" from the theoretical model. Robertson (1976:49–54 and chap. 5) attributes strategic variations entirely to external constraints on parties, such as their competitive position, while ignoring endogenous change in the distribution of beliefs and preferences. In such models it is difficult to see how activists actually translate perceived external constraints into intraparty collective action.

To conclude, imperatives of electoral competition often do not explain the empirical dynamic of party organization, program agendas, and strategic choice. As an alternative to the rational reconstruction of parties as dominated by leaders pursuing maximum electoral support, some behavioral studies have analyzed activists' political beliefs and orientations and arrived at a view of intraparty politics most succinctly stated by Eldersveld (1964). Parties are conflict systems with subcoalitions of activists advocating a variety of different strategies and goals. People join parties based on widely diverging motivations and incentives. Eldersveld's research challenges not only the simplistic leader/activist dichotomy, but also the image of party organization

---

criterion of success for political parties. Following Offe and Wiesenthal's (1980) critique of Olson (1965), one could say that rational choice theories short-circuit the problem of collective action. Collective preferences must be manufactured in the process of collective organization, they are not simply given.

8. In terms of modern organization theory (Scott 1981), one could say that the electoralist view of parties reconstructs them as "rational purposive" organizations, not as "rational" or "natural" systems pursuing a variety of goals and objectives in a complex environment. The view that formal organizations do not pursue a single goal but balance and negotiate a multiplicity of goals is not new, but was already expressed by Etzioni (1960) and Perrow (1961).

9. Not by chance, the literature emphasizing the electoral constraints on party strategy has employed the model of Anglo-Saxon party systems where parties are more divorced from nonelectoral systems of interest intermediation between state and civil society than in continental Europe.

and strategy created by rational reconstructions: parties are "minimally efficient systems" which suffer from structural weaknesses characteristic of voluntary organizations in general (cf. Horch 1982). They have little control over their members, employ small professional staffs, and rely on few resources to communicate with and coordinate activists in different segments and levels of the organization. For this reason, parties are not tightly coupled hierarchies with oligarchic control but loosely coupled networks of activists and subunits with more or less autonomy at each level of organization. Leaders must build often fragile and shifting coalitions across a multiplicity of support groups and cannot take rank-and-file support for granted.

Eldersveld's empirical research and theoretical conclusions are based on American party machines in the 1950s and certainly require modification and revision for application to West European parliamentary systems.[10] Moreover, the behavioral approach provides a "thick" description of party politics in unique settings, but does not yield more parsimonious and general hypotheses helping us understand the dynamic of parties in a variety of competitive party systems. It is therefore important to find a theory that combines the strengths of both behavioral and rational reconstructions of party behavior according to the following criteria: (1) It should explicitly recognize different purposes and motivations for joining and working in parties. (2) Yet it should also avoid being overly descriptive and inductive. (3) It should allow for a dynamic analysis of organizational, programmatic, and strategic change showing why parties switch from a logic of constituency representation to a logic of party competition and vice versa.

Choosing between Constituency Representation and Electoral Competition

When parties follow a logic of constituency representation, their organization, strategy, and programs are derived from the ideology of their core support groups in society. When they follow a logic of electoral competition, they adopt political stances that appeal to their marginal sympathizers in order to maximize electoral support. I explain the choice among the different logics in terms of the relations among three groups of activists in political parties: ideologues, lobbyists, and pragmatists. Taking a dynamic perspective, I argue that changes in party behavior occur when political conditions in the environment of a party affect the relative strength of each group and the internal coalitions they form.

---

10. Most European parties certainly have a stronger bureaucratic and hierarchical core than American parties. Still, their organizational structures are far less developed than those in private corporations or public administration. See Horch (1982), Rose (1974), and Wiesendahl (1984).

Actors and Objectives

Party activists take a position on the nature and salience of three objectives for their personal involvement in a party as well as for the party's overall politics. First, they must determine what the nature and the importance of *collective goods* are, what the party pursues through changing social institutions and life chances that affect most citizens. Activists who emphasize the provision of collective goods as the party's main objective stress the need for broad party programs and long-term strategies. Second, activists must decide the importance of the provision of *selective goods* for specific, well-defined electoral clienteles. They are here mostly concerned with their relationship to special pressure groups and the *strategic* and *tactical* gains on their behalf that can be made in policy making. Party activists must weigh and rank order the importance of collective and selective goods for a party's strategy and determine the relationship among both objectives. Under what circumstances can parties trade off demands for collective goods against selective goods in such situations as coalition formation with other parties? Third, they must assess what *internal gratifications* or *private goods* the party provides for its activists. Decisions on the provision of private goods affect the *organizational form* of a party. Activists may expect the organization to reinforce their purposive commitments, produce a sense of solidarity, and encourage the militants' participation.

Depending on the content, relative importance, and ranking of programmatic, strategic, and organizational concerns, we can construct three ideal types of party activists: ideologues, lobbyists, and pragmatists.[11] This typology replaces the more familiar dichotomy of leaders and followers. The party leadership has no independent fourth set of preferences. Whether party leaders are predominantly ideologues, lobbyists, or pragmatists depends on the distribution and coalition building among the three types, and the rules governing the contest for leadership.

Ideologues emphasize the party's pursuit of collective goods and see little value in the provision of selective goods. They perceive a tradeoff between piecemeal reforms benefiting narrow constituencies and the goal of comprehensive social reorganization.[12] Since parties can rarely achieve comprehensive social change in the short run and since ideologues reject most incremental policy reforms as counterproductive for their long-term objec-

11. My strategy of theory construction resembles Downs's (1967) analysis of bureaucracy. Downs first defines ideal types of bureaucratic actors and then explains organizational dynamics as the outcome of interactions between individuals with different preference sets under conditions of external constraints.

12. Ideologues have always argued against tactical reformism that it would undermine the pursuit of long-term, comprehensive change in society. An example is Lenin's (1902/1969) critique of the Mensheviks that social reform would further a limited "trade unionist" consciousness and put off revolutionary changes indefinitely.

tives, some other mechanism is needed to maintain their commitment to day-to-day political work. This device is the "private goods" the party organization provides to militants. The party reinforces commitment by ideologues when its organizational form creates a microcosm of the society the activists hope to realize eventually. For ideologues, party organization is a laboratory to explore new forms of social solidarity and decision making. Because the gratifications derived from organizational experiments are immediate and the collective benefits of comprehensive social change are likely to be realized only in the distant future, ideologues may be more concerned with the party's appropriate organization than with its long-term program. In any case, both the party's collective and its private benefits have greater significance for ideologues than do the provision of selective goods and incremental reform programs.

Ideologues constrain a party's flexibility in the choice of goals and strategies. They oppose alliances with other parties and make it difficult to diversify a party's appeal to new electoral constituencies. Internally, ideologues reject a flexible adjustment of party structures according to criteria of electoral efficiency and consider such reforms as efforts to betray the party's most cherished and noble goals. Thus, ideologues are most ardently committed to a logic of constituency representation and reject a logic of electoral competition.

Lobbyists consider the provision of selective goods delivered to specific constituencies to be a party's most important goal. Lobbyists give comparatively little thought to the relationship of a party's selective objectives to its comprehensive ones and often find the latter impractical and irrelevant. Lobbyists tend to choose strategies and tactics opportunistically. In negotiations on interparty alliances, they are willing to trade off policy objectives benefiting other constituencies as long as their party can make progress in redressing the grievances of the particular constituency they represent. When the party cannot mobilize enough support to provide the desired selective goods, however, they will value most the party organization as a guarantee of the party's honest support of their aspirations. Thus, lobbyists rank the provision of selective goods as the party's most important goal, followed by the organizational gratification the party can deliver. They attribute least importance to comprehensive party programs.

Lobbyists allow greater strategic flexibility than ideologues. As long as their party remains committed to the special interests lobbyists value most, they are willing to tolerate unorthodox interpretations of program and alliance strategies. Rigid insistence on the priority of specific policies, however, does limit a party's flexibility in adjusting to the preferences of marginal sympathizers or potential alliance partners. Lobbyists choose between the logics of constituency representation and party competition depending on the opportunities and constraints their pursuit of special interests encounters in a given situation.

Pragmatists give the party a relatively free rein in electoral politics. They value its pursuit of collective goods, yet see a productive relationship of mutual reinforcement between policies providing selective and collective goods. In contrast to ideologues, pragmatists view incremental piecemeal reforms as the path to long-term comprehensive change. Because they treat selective policies only as means to more comprehensive objectives and reject special interest demands as ends in themselves, unlike lobbyists they hold no particular social reform or benefit to a constituency group as sacrosanct and exempt from adjustment to voter demands and bargaining with potential allies. Since pragmatists emphasize external practical policy achievements, they show least appreciation for the exclusively internal incentives a party organization can provide its activists. In fact, pragmatists are most likely to treat the organization purely as an instrument of external policy, not an expression of party ideology and solidarity. Pragmatists rank the party's pursuit of collective goods first, place selective goods second, and organizational gratification last. It is evident that they are most inclined to press for a logic of party competition.

If an activist can give high or low priority to collective and private goods and can choose either a radical, opportunistic, or moderate approach to the provision of selective goods, then ideologues, lobbyists, and activists constitute three of twelve preference sets represented in Table 8. Each ideal type of party activist also ranks the three objectives differently. These rankings are given in each cell.

In addition to the three main types of militants, Table 8 specifies three groups called near-ideologues, near-lobbyists, and near-pragmatists. The remaining six cells of the table, however, remain empty. This reflects the hypothesis that activists are *intellectually constrained* in the choice and rank order of collective, selective, and private goods. The typology proves its usefulness and the constraint is demonstrated, if indeed most activists in a party belong to one of the specified types of militants.

Empirically, ideologues, lobbyists, and pragmatists are characterized not only by distinct beliefs and orientations but also by their political careers and patterns of involvement. Ideologues are often a party's "organic intellectuals" (in the Gramscian sense) and emerge from the radical intellectual subcultures associated with it. Because they are primarily concerned with overall institutional change and the party's organizational politics, they seek national party and electoral office but shun all roles and tasks that involve small-scale incremental social reforms. They are hesitant to work for the party's local organization or as elected municipal councilors, but vigorously intervene in national debates. In leadership recruitment they believe that

Table 8
Styles of activism in political parties

	Collective goods important (broad view of party program)		Collective goods unimportant (narrow view of party program)	
	Private goods of the party organization		Private goods of the party organization	
	Important	Unimportant	Important	Unimportant
Radical strategy and tactics: Pursuit of selective goods undermines commitment to collective goods	Ideologues (1) party organization (2) broad program (3) selective policy success		Lobbyists (1) selective policy success (2) party organization (3) broad program	
Opportunistic strategy and tactics: Pursuit of selective goods, *no matter* what the commitment to collective goods		Near-Ideologues (1) broad program (2) party organization (3) selective policy success		Near-Lobbyists (1) selective policy success (2) broad program (3) party organization
Moderate strategy and tactics: Pursuit of selective goods reinforces commitment to collective goods		Pragmatists (1) broad program (2) selective policy success (3) party organization		Near-Pragmatists (1) selective policy success (2) broad program (3) party organization

political criteria such as a candidate's stance on broad programmatic, organizational, and strategic issues should be decisive ("politicized" recruitment style).

The political biographies of lobbyists typically include past and ongoing work in special interest groups and issue related movements belonging to a party's political orbit, such as unions, professional associations, public interest groups, or religious organizations. Lobbyists generally continue to devote more time to their work in interest groups than other party activists and get involved in party suborganizations, study groups, and committees that are of special concern for the constituency or movement they belong to. While more inclined than ideologues to participate in a party's local activities, they also have special appeal as candidates for national electoral office because they can represent well-defined external political constituencies. In the recruitment of political leaders, lobbyists prefer candidates running on their record as standard bearers and representatives of specific clienteles and social groups rather than those with broad ideological and programmatic commitments ("movementist" recruitment style).

Pragmatists, finally, are least likely to be involved in a party's subcultures and interest associations and have less political experience and awareness than the other groups when they first join. Pragmatists seek involvement in areas where practical accomplishments count most: local politics in municipal councils and regional or national legislatures; they are less inclined to run for purely internal party positions. When they compete for political office, they emphasize criteria of political professionalism, efficiency, and competence, including a candidate's voter appeal, familiarity with the technical aspects of specific policy areas, and personal reliability and integrity ("professional" recruitment style).

Table 9 summarizes the orientations of ideologues, lobbyists, and pragmatists as well as the empirical patterns of political activism I predict to be associated with each type of party militant. The distinction among different groups does not tell us yet (1) the relative strength of each group, (2) what coalitions may form among them, or (3) which group(s) will dominate the leadership. Table 9 reveals that in the triangular relationship between ideologues, lobbyists, and pragmatists, each pair of groups can form a coalition around a preferred issue—programmatic, strategic, or organizational—that defeats the third group.

If all groups are about equally strong and must rank the party's priorities in binary choices among alternatives, cycling majorities will occur.[13] A coalition of ideologues and lobbyists can defeat the pragmatists on the importance of the organizational purity of the party (private goods to members). This

13. In other words, Arrow's (1963) paradox, that no collective preference schedule exists that could lead to consistent democratic choices, occurs in this case.

Table 9
Three types of party activists and their political involvement

	Priorities among party objectives			Political career experience	Patterns of political involvement	Criteria of leadership recruitment	Overall style of politics and social change
	Collective goods	Selective goods	Private goods				
Ideologues	second priority	third priority	first priority	radical intellectual subculture	national party organization	"politicized" recruitment style	logic of constituency representation, radical change
Lobbyists	third priority	first priority	second priority	interest groups and social movements	emphasis on group activity outside party	"movementist" recruitment style	between logics of party competition and constituency representation
Pragmatists	first priority	second priority	third priority	little activism prior to party	local party sections	"professional" recruitment style	logic of party competition

coalition is most likely to impose a logic of constituency representation on the party. But if selective policy reforms are on the agenda, a coalition of pragmatists and lobbyists may defeat the ideologues and implement a logic of party competition. Finally, ideologues and pragmatists can agree on the overriding importance of comprehensive party programs against selective pressure group gains. This unlikely coalition would emphasize broad social reform without favors to special interest groups. Since it is difficult to envision the practicality of such an alliance, realistic choices boil down to the first two alternative coalitions (ideologues/lobbyists or lobbyists/pragmatists).

Since there is no dominant coalition of actors that would always win regardless of the issue to be decided, it cannot be determined in advance which orientation the party leadership will express. It is most likely that leaders represent the dominant alliances within a party. Leaders who cannot adjust to alliances or shape them as they wish will exit or force the dissenters to exit.[14] Leaders are not always more moderate (pragmatist) than the rank and file. Their orientation depends on intraparty coalitions and their ability to resolve tensions between the party's radical subculture, its special interest constituency, and the marginal voters to whom it may appeal. Thus party leaders remain critically dependent on intraparty coalitions, although their public prestige, visibility, and personal charisma may endow them with a certain power of blackmail over their party.

Strategic Situations and Intraparty Coalitions

Identifying types of party activists is not sufficient to explain or predict, in a given circumstance, the impact of a specific group or the emergence, dominance, and decline of intraparty group coalitions. To arrive at a theory of party dynamics, we must consider the *strategic situations* in which parties find themselves. The activists' skills and choices do matter, but strategic situations influence the relative strength of each group of militants as well as their propensity to enter coalitions and shape a party's leadership.[15] I describe strategic situations by three parameters which impact on the internal dynamic of political parties: (1) mobilization of the cleavage on which a party is based, (2) openness of a regime's political institutions to a party's democratic participation, and (3) a party's position vis-à-vis its competitors.

A social cleavage is highly mobilized when public opinions represented by a party are sharply polarized and sizable political subcultures, interest groups,

14. To come to this conclusion we are not compelled to assume fully democratic elections within a party. We must only presuppose that party militants have the right to entry and exit and "vote with their feet" if the leadership does not meet their approval. Theories of party oligarchy from Michels' time onward have generally downplayed the importance of exit to the orientation of political parties. A threat of exit may even bolster control over the leadership (cf. Hirschman 1970:83–85).

15. I follow the argument by DeNardo (1985: esp. chap. 1) that strategic choices make a difference in collective mobilization. Nevertheless, external constraints and opportunities mould the "feasibility set" of political options and influence the actors' preferences. Rational strategic actors thus cope with external circumstances in predictable ways.

and social movements crystallize around the cleavage. Parties representing sharply polarized cleavages attract ideologues and lobbyists, with pragmatists remaining marginal. The dominant groups form a coalition supporting a logic of constituency representation. The impact of cleavage mobilization on intra-party coalitions should surface both in longitudinal and in cross-sectional comparison. Over time, the intensification of cleavages attracts ideologues, while the decline or institutionalization of cleavages strengthens pragmatists who might be able to form a coalition with lobbyists. Across party units, in a party's strongholds of mobilization relatively more activists are ideologues than on the periphery where pragmatists prevail.[16] Cleavage mobilization thus affects intraparty politics in two ways, first through differential recruitment of ideologues, lobbyists, or pragmatists into the party, and second through the politics of intraparty coalition building.

A second, related external condition shaping internal party dynamics is the *responsiveness of political regimes* to new demands and to parties represent-ing new cleavages.[17] Where existing elites are willing to permit a party's participation in the process of policy deliberation and show some responsive-ness to its demands, the party will attract pragmatists committed to incremen-tal reform within the existing institutions. Inside the party, pragmatists will attempt to build intraparty coalitions with lobbyists.

Conversely, the more intransigently a regime resists a new party's demand for recognition, participation, and policy impact, the more likely the party will be dominated by an alliance of ideologues and militant lobbyists. In a "closed" opportunity structure, pragmatists have little credibility in the eyes of most lobbyists because the chances that an incremental reform strategy will succeed are remote. Under these conditions pragmatists represent only a small segment of the membership. The personal costs of entering an "outlaw" party, such as social stigma, exclusion from employment, or state harassment, are so high that only the most committed and alienated radical ideologues and lobbyists will join.[18]

16. Socialist parties as well as Catholic and rightist parties may illustrate this dynamic. In Germany's social democracy before World War I, for instance, the industrial centers around Berlin and in the Ruhr area were dominated by radical activists, while most activists in the southern German periphery advocated a moderate party course (Schorske 1955). As the class cleavage is institutionalized and pacified, radical ideologues abandon socialist parties which in turn come under the domination of an alliance of labor union lobbyists and electorally oriented pragmatists.

17. In the literature on social movements, many authors have emphasized the links between the responsiveness of political regimes and the mobilization and strategy of challenging new movements. Compare Eisinger (1973), Kitschelt (1986), and McAdam (1982).

18. Again, socialist parties show how regime repressiveness shapes intraparty coalitions. Even Michels (1911/62:132 and 178) observed that the outlook of party leaders depends on the political opportunity structures they encounter. For a broader theoretical reconstruction of working class strategy compare DeNardo (1985:154–87) and Kitschelt and Wiesenthal (1979). Insightful empirical comparative analyses supporting the general argument are provided by Katznelson and Zolberg (1986) and Lipset (1983).

For democratic regimes, electoral rules, the relations between interest groups and party elites, the effective number of competitive parties, and state institutional structures (such as the centralization of public administration, the autonomy of the courts, and the influence of legislatures over policy-making) affect the openness of a regime. As a rule of thumb, plurality voting laws, corporatism, administrative centralization, and semi-autonomous legislatures and courts contribute to the closure of a regime.

A third condition affecting intraparty coalitions and external party strategy is a party's *electoral competitiveness*. A party's competitive position refers to the probability it will win government office and/or influence public policy. If that probability is high, the party is in a hegemonic or monopoly position; if it is low, the party is in a marginal position. In either case, competitiveness is weak because the party's fortunes do not really depend on electoral performance. A party is in a strong competitive position, however, when small differences in its electoral support affect its chance of participating in government and significantly influencing public policy. In two-party systems, competitiveness is high when the electoral support of the major contenders is very close. In multiparty systems, competitiveness is a concept more difficult to operationalize (see Strom 1984; 1988).

In general, the competitiveness of a party is a function of (1) the level and change rate of its electoral support, (2) the fragmentation of the party system, and (3) the number of feasible government coalitions that exclude the party. Electoral competitiveness increases the more a party's share of votes is growing, the fewer parties effectively compete, and the fewer options are feasible to form governments without its support. As a party's power to form alliances with other parties or to exercise influence over government policy grows and it gains a pivotal position in a party system, it attracts more pragmatists and lobbyists in anticipation of incremental reforms and satisfaction of special interests.[19] Under these circumstances, pragmatists and lobbyists can persuade activists of the advantages likely to follow from an electoralist strategy. In contrast, when the party is in a weak, marginal competitive position, ideologues will be relatively more numerous than pragmatists or lobbyists and command the more convincing arguments that an electoralist strategy has a low marginal yield. Where a party is in a hegemonic position and does not need to fear competitors, pragmatists are numerous, but so are ideologues. Since the party is not in danger of losing its monopoly, ideologues argue that radical policies realizing a party's ultimate program are feasible.

Cleavage mobilization, institutional rigidity, and a party's competitive

19. These hypotheses are well known in the literature. Sartori (1966) makes the argument that in fragmented systems parties have fewer incentives for pursuing a centripetal policy (or logic of party competition) than in less fragmented bipolar systems. Similarly, Robertson (1976:140), among many others, highlights the proximity of relative support for competing parties as an important dimension shaping party strategy.

position do not always pull parties in the same direction of internal coalition building and strategy formation. There are conditions under which conflict within parties is likely to intensify (Table 10). Intraparty conflict will be intense particularly where high cleavage mobilization and institutional rigidities push a party toward a coalition of ideologues and lobbyists and a logic of constituency representation, yet its strong competitive position pulls it toward a coalition of lobbyists and pragmatists and a logic of party competition.

It would be easy to analyze the trajectory of most political parties in terms of the four configurations represented in Table 10. The German Social Democratic party, for instance, found itself in a weak competitive position faced with high cleavage mobilization throughout most of the German Empire (upper left cell). Then in the Weimar period it achieved a stronger competitive position (upper right cell). In the early Federal Republic its competitive situation was weak when cleavage mobilization was declining (lower left cell). In the 1960s its competitiveness increased and it ended by pursuing a strategy of alliance building and "realism" (lower right cell).[20]

Cleavage mobilization, institutional rigidity, and a party's competitive position are essentially the variables Kirchheimer (1966) used to explain the emergence of "catch-all" parties that pursue a logic of party competition. Catch-all parties arise when sharp cleavages decline and parties have access to and impact on major policy-making arenas, arriving at a strong competitive position. Yet outlining the theoretical argument implicit in his account also shows that catch-all parties are a contingent outcome of constellations that may vary across parties, whole party systems, and time periods. Whereas Kirchheimer suggests an "equilibrium model" in which all major parties gravitate toward the catch-all model, my approach seeks to account for the continuing diversity of political parties and even the reversibility of development toward the catch-all model. Moreover, it provides a micro-logic of party dynamics from the perspective of political actors which is by and large missing from Kirchheimer's account.

My theory also differs from a life cycle interpretation of political parties, which suggests that parties always start out with a logic of constituency representation in order to carve out a loyal clientele, then move toward a logic of party competition as they age and mature (Robertson 1976: 128 and 132). Like Kirchheimer's account, Robertson's model cannot explain the diversity of paths parties have taken and the possibility of reversal from moderate to radical strategy. Moreover, life cycle theories shed little light on the external conditions or the internal micro-foundations of strategic change in political parties.

20. Of course the applicability of the model is not confined to the longitudinal study of a single party but can also be applied in a cross-sectional analysis of party strategies in different political systems.

Table 10
Orientation of parties between constituency representation and party competition

		The party's competitive position	
		Weak	*Strong*
Cleavage mobilization and institutional rigidiy	High	*"Fundamentalism"*: logic of constituency representation	*Internal conflict and polarization*: logic of constituency representation versus logic of party competition
	Low	*"Demobilized fundamentalism"*: low conflict and gradual waning of the logic of constituency representation	*"Realism"*: adoption of the logic of party competition

So far I have treated cleavage mobilization, institutional opportunity structures, and electoral competitiveness as independent variables influencing the internal balance of power in parties and their external strategies. To turn the theory I have sketched into a model that truly reflects the dynamic interaction between parties' environment and their internal choices, one especially critical variable is still missing: policy performance. Voters hold parties responsible for their decision whether or not to participate in governments. In either case, both a party's core constituencies and its marginal sympathizers evaluate the success of a strategy in light of the policy consequences they attribute to the party's actions. Empirical studies reveal excessively complex, diverse, and even contradictory links among the organization, strategic stance, government control, policy performance, and electoral support of a party. I therefore offer only a few very general hypotheses that illustrate ways of creating a dynamic link between a party's internal and external processes.

If an intraparty coalition of pragmatists and lobbyists appeals to marginal voters, supports alliances with other parties, and appears to affect public policies in ways endorsed by its electorate, it will (1) attract more marginal voters and (2) demobilize its radical core constituencies through incremental reform policies. Within the party, the demobilization of core constituencies, policy success, electoral support, and the moderate intraparty coalition constitute a "virtuous circle" which strengthens the bond between lobbyists and pragmatists. Most parties able to cling to power for extended periods have experienced this virtuous circle. The Scandinavian social democratic parties and also many Christian democratic and conservative parties in continental Europe immediately come to mind.

Conversely, if a dominant moderate coalition fails to deliver policy results and loses voter support, it antagonizes marginal supporters, radicalizes its core constituencies, and leads to a replacement of that coalition by one of ideologues and lobbyists. While the party's electoral competitiveness decreases, its loyal external constituencies become more radical, reinforce radicalism inside the party, and further its electoral decline.[21] This downspin may come to a halt when the party is reduced to its hard core supporters or when the collapse of its electoral support is blamed on the new intraparty coalition of ideologues and lobbyists. As long as a radical coalition stabilizes and increases voter support, however, it will prevail over its intraparty challengers.

Figure 2 summarizes my theoretical reconstruction of the variables that interact in a party's choice between a logic of constituency representation and a logic of party competition. My main focus is on the links between conditions of party activism (cleavage mobilization, opportunity structures, and the parties' competitiveness), internal party coalitions, and the choice of party organization, program, and strategy. I pay less attention to the dynamic interaction of party strategies with electoral outcomes and with the parties' policy performance, because ecology parties in Belgium and West Germany have emerged too recently to examine the long-term interplay between party strategy, policy impact, and electoral performance. Thus I confine myself primarily to a cross-sectional comparison of the external conditions and internal alliances that influence their logics of party formation.

In this section I have proposed a theoretical framework for studying the dynamic of political parties that diverges from the existing literature in one important respect. Most studies treat parties as purely "rational systems" in which the participating agents combine their demands and pool their resources to pursue electoral office as the overriding and uniting objective. In contrast, I treat parties as elements in a broader network of political interest intermediation and claim that ideology and beliefs can influence the structure and strategy of party politics. In the language of contemporary organization theory, I treat parties as open, rational, and natural systems.[22] Their collective choices are influenced by the norms, ideologies, and cognitive beliefs that characterize different groups of party militants and sympathetic outsiders and are rooted in the mobilization of social cleavages. Organizational "mythologies" (Meyer and Rowan 1977) may not fully reflect the reality of party politics, but they have real consequences for the collective dynamics of party organizations. In this sense, ideologies and images make an impact on parties, particularly if external circumstances are favorable.

21. Examples for this vicious circle of party politics are many West European communist parties, above all the French and Spanish parties, and the British Labour party. In all these cases moderate strategies ended in defeat and a radicalization of (shrinking) core constituencies which in turn alienated moderate party activists and changed the balance of power within the parties.

22. I am indebted to Scott (1981:20–22) for this formulation. The use of organization theory in the study of political parties, however, has mostly remained at the conceptual level and has rarely moved to substantive hypotheses and empirical research. For a critical review see Janda (1983).

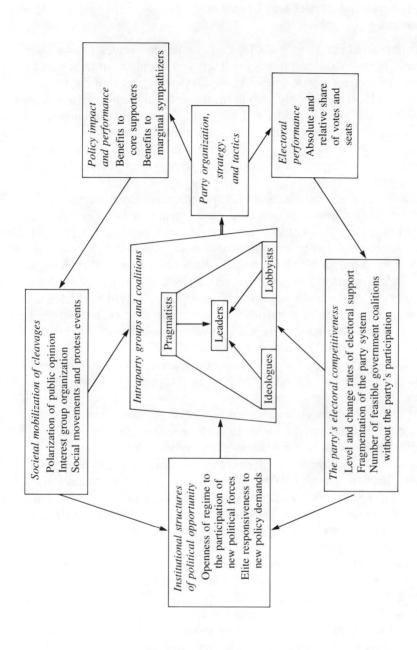

Figure 2. A theoretical model linking the internal and external politics of parties

Left-Libertarian Parties and Logics of Party Formation

If left-libertarian parties follow a logic of constituency representation, their program, organization, and strategy will set them sharply apart from existing parties. This orientation is particularly prevalent in areas where the left-libertarian cleavage is highly mobilized, the political institutions are unresponsive to the new demands, and the parties are in a weak competitive position. Since the established parties in northern Europe rely on declining cleavages such as class, religion, or urban-rural divisions and are highly competitive in centripetal or consociational party systems, they adhere to a logic of party competition.

As a consequence the organizational, programmatic, and strategic differences are smaller among conventional parties than between them and their new left-libertarian competitors. Conventional parties thus provide the benchmark against which left-libertarian parties can be measured. Their programs are concerned primarily with economic distributive issues. They have an extensive and intensive party organization with local subunits as the bottom of a hierarchical structure of command with an articulated division of labor and professionalized staffs of party functionaries. Under their centralized direction, regional and national party leaders usually combine party, legislative, and often executive office in government. Most conventional parties rely on coalitions of pragmatists and lobbyists which pursue moderate strategies in order to win political office by attracting the support of marginal sympathizers.

The common features of established parties are attributable to the institutional rules and patterns of competition in most northern European party systems. Proportional representation, multi-member electoral districts, and parliamentary government strengthen central coordination and internal cohesiveness. Since in contrast to plural voting systems every vote counts toward parliamentary seats, mass membership—the "organizational encapsulation" of the electorate (Wellhofer 1979; 1985)—has assured parties of reliable electoral turnout. Multi-member districts and parliamentary government facilitate and require organizational centralization. At the same time, stable leadership and internal discipline assure the continuity of a party's strategies and objectives, a guarantee especially attractive to marginal supporters for whom voting is only meaningful and rational if the party of their choice follows the course set before an election and endorsed by their vote.

Moreover, the bureaucratic mass party model is reinforced by the parties' crucial role in interest intermediation between centralized economic interest groups and the political executive. Interlocking elites and dense linkages of parties to interest groups facilitate policy compromise and increase a party's capacity to govern. Further, a bureaucratic mass party provides a reliable, stable mechanism for recruiting leaders and enables the party to penetrate the state bureaucracy, thus increasing its leverage in the policy process.

Finally, bureaucratic mass parties in parliamentary regimes with centralized interest groups and proportional representation are able to engage in longer-term political strategies. The relative stability of policy-making networks, electoral support, and organizational base allows them to treat political competition and cooperation as iterative games involving compromise and short-term sacrifices in exchange for long-term advantages. Centralized mass parties are able to develop a certain collective rationality because they can make "detours" in the pursuit of political objectives and thus address the problem that collective goods can be attained only if individual interests are somehow subordinated to a long-term collective strategy.[23]

In contrast to conventional parties, left-libertarian movements and parties are unlikely to solve collective action problems through centralized, hierarchical, and formal organization. Instead, they try to recast the role and dynamic of parties as intermediaries between citizen and state. Unlike class, religious, or ethnic conflicts, left-libertarian movements revolve around a multiplicity of issues and situations not limited to one single political arena or overriding controversy. Left-libertarians fight the "submission of subjectivity" under centralized agencies of economic and political control (Foucault 1983:213). They oppose what they see as the "cage" into which public bureaucracies, private corporations, and professional experts try to fit all spheres of life, and engage in a multitude of decentralized, local conflicts which rarely erupt into a single large-scale confrontation.

Most left-libertarian issues fall into two broad categories. First, social movements concerned with a "politics of space" protest against the subjection of human or natural resources and physical space to the imperatives of economic growth and the accumulation of political power. Environmental protection, appropriate technology, disarmament, and urban planning are typical issues addressed by these movements. The second kind of movement expresses a "politics of social identity," which calls for protecting and recreating an autonomous cultural definition of individual and collective lifestyles and personal conduct as opposed to the definition of "normal" behavior by experts in the "helping" professions and the male-dominated culture of most work organizations. Feminism, self-help groups of clients in "people processing" organizations (hospitals, welfare agencies, and the like), cooperative enterprises, and consumer-controlled social services represent the politics of social identity.

Movements of social identity reject centralized organization probably more

---

23. The notion of rationality as the ability to make detours is developed in Elster (1979). For labor unions, the organizational correlates of collective rationality have been discussed by Lange (1984). This argument can be extended to parties as well.

unequivocally than groups concerned with the politics of space. For activists calling for cultural change and an autonomous choice of lifestyles, interpersonal relations free of formalized controls and hierarchies constitute an end in itself. Groups concerned with the politics of space, however, demand external collective goods that can be produced only by centrally enforced collective decisions (pollution standards, technical regulations, new energy or transportation systems, and the like). Such groups voice opposition to bureaucratic institutions but are more likely to emphasize the need for efficient organization in pursuit of their objectives.[24] In areas where the left-libertarian cleavage is highly mobilized, both types of movements exist. In areas with lesser mobilization the politics of space prevails. I show throughout this book that variations in the scope and intensity of left-libertarian movements affect the organization and strategy of ecology parties.

The multiplicity of issues and objectives held by left-libertarian activists accounts for the absence of a shared comprehensive ideology. Left-libertarian movements are characterized by a *negative consensus* that the predominance of markets and bureaucracies must be rolled back in favor of social solidarity relations and participatory institutions. But they do not subscribe to a common analysis of the predicament of modern society nor do they endorse a shared positive utopia, defined by a clear image of the institutions a new social order should realize. More typically, left-libertarians develop ideas and demands for reorganizing individual spheres of social life without placing them within a comprehensive ideological framework (Nelles 1984). The aversion to centralization and hierarchy also translates into a rejection of authoritarian "master thinkers" and overarching ideologies. Contrary to the conventional expectation that a decline of ideology contributes to an acceptance of the status quo, left-libertarians show that ideological diversity may reinvigorate social criticism.[25] The absence of ideological unity in turn is an impediment to the emergence of a broad-based, coherent political organization.

A diverse, fragmented social base further accounts for the diffuse, participatory, and decentralized nature of left-libertarian politics. It is true that many supporters of left-libertarian movements are educated professionals in the personal service sector (education, health care, psychological counseling, welfare services, urban planning). These strata enjoy relatively high economic standards of living and job security which tend to reduce the salience of distributive economic issues for them. At the same time, their intellectual sophistication enables them to detect qualitatively new deprivations in contemporary societies which relate to the left-libertarian agenda. Nevertheless,

---

24. A distinction similar to that of politics of space and politics of social identity has been developed by Rucht (1986). Rucht also notices different organizational practices in each strand of left-libertarian protest mobilization.

25. I have shown elsewhere that ecological activists develop widely varying ideas about desirable social institutions (Kitschelt 1984). In Chapter 3 I sketch briefly how a similar ideological uncertainty and openness characterizes left-libertarian parties.

these strata lack a sense of identity and consequently an identifiable class interest. Most of their demands concern intangible and indivisible collective goods that do not advantage middle-class constituencies.[26] Moreover, individuals in the new intellectual stratum are cross-pressured; as professionals employed by the large economic and bureaucratic institutions, they tend to endorse measures promoting economic growth and the stability of existing institutions within the framework of a market economy and administrative management. Yet as consumers, as urban residents, and as clients of social services, improving their quality of life may depend on limiting bureaucratic control and institutional growth. What emerges is a cultural contradiction between an ethic of self-denial and discipline in the work process and an ethic of enjoyment and autonomy in the sphere of consumption.[27] Since individuals experience this ambiguity and contradiction in their daily lives, it is not by chance that representatives of the new intellectual stratum can be found at the forefront of *both* proponents and opponents of left-libertarian demands.[28]

In contrast to other social cleavages, left-libertarian politics thus cannot build on broad "natural" collectivities with shared experiences, well-defined interests, and a single visible adversary. The differentiation of life spheres and individualization of biographies in modern bureaucratized market society have eroded collective identities and spontaneous solidarities (Beck 1983). When social solidarity can no longer be derived from the material conditions and antagonisms of society, but must be manufactured by the participants in the process of collective mobilization itself, creating comprehensive protest organizations becomes a formidable task. More than any previous social mobilization, left-libertarian struggles are in the first place "consciousness-raising" events, involving a process of clarifying the cognitive and normative grounds on which collective demands can be based.[29]

26. Using Hardin's (1982:69–72) language, these goods are "nonfungible," because the costs of their production and the benefits of their consumption cannot be determined in terms of the same measuring scale.

27. I am following here Daniel Bell's (1976) formulation of the problem. Similar arguments have been made by Touraine (1973) and earlier by Bergmann et al. (1969) and Offe (1969) who diagnose a horizontal discrepancy of life chances between the privileged and politically well organized "productive" sector and the hard to organize "consumptive" sector of modern society.

28. To borrow Wright's (1985:43–51) terminology, salaried professionals are located in "contradictory class positions." But while Wright sees the contradiction primarily between control of the production process and lack of ownership in the means of production, I would emphasize more the contradiction between the role and interests of salaried professionals in work life and in the sphere of consumption.

29. Offe and Wiesenthal (1980) argue that the marketplace defines the interests of business more clearly than those of labor and gives the former a natural advantage in the class conflict. While business can monologically act on their interests, labor must produce these interests dialogically. This argument would apply with even greater force to left-libertarian demands. Compared to both producer groups, the normative and institutional grounds for defining collective consumer interests are considerably more ambiguous.

The nature of the stakes, ideas, and actors involved in left-libertarian struggles also shapes the *selective incentives* collective mobilization employs to induce participation. In principle, voluntary associations may rely on purposive, participatory, material, and social incentives as well as belief in the legitimacy of authority over their members' behavior.[30] The left-libertarian aversion to market exchange (economic gain) removes material incentives as a viable commitment mechanism and may, for instance, explain the small size of environmental movement organizations (Hardin 1982: 101–24). Absence of natural social solidarities and disaffection with hierarchy also remove legitimate authority from the list of potential incentives. The nature and diversity of goals and ambitions left-libertarian activists express, however, make it improbable that purposive, participatory, and solidary incentives alone can bring about a cohesive organization. Since the activists' motives are directly tied to the organization's purposes and participatory decision procedures, left-libertarian groups enjoy little flexibility for modifying their objectives in order to attract more supporters, establish alliances with other groups, or strike compromises with political adversaries. Internal changes of organizational purpose or external bargains with allies through goal compromise may precipitate the defection of activists or the instant replacement of the group's public representatives. Left-libertarian movements rely on incentives and organizational structures that rule out disciplined strategic behavior.[31]

The stakes, ideas, actors, and incentives involved in left-libertarian struggles thus stand in the way of building large, hierarchical, solidary movement organizations. Organizational form and strategies are closely intertwined with the objective of undermining social regulation by centralized corporate and state organizations. In this sense, the *medium* of collective mobilization in left-libertarian movements becomes part of their *message*. These movements tend to rely on loose networks of grassroots support with little formal structure, hierarchy, and central control. They herald self-actualization, participation, and social solidarity and are engaged in what Gusfield (1981:322) called a "quickening of actions, the change of meanings, and the understanding that something new is happening in a wide variety of places and arenas," political and cultural practices clearly separated from efforts to build large instrumental

30. Olson's (1965) original economic theory of collective action did not include a range of incentives broad enough to reconstruct participation in voluntary interest associations (cf. Horch 1982; Moe 1980). As discussed in Chapter 4, my typology of incentive mechanisms follow Knoke and Wood (1981: chaps. 3–5) and is originally derived from Clark and Wilson (1961).

31. In this sense, Piven and Cloward's (1977) statement is correct that movements avoid compromises and co-optation if they engage in disruptive action. I am less convinced of Piven and Cloward's reverse statement that negotiations and strong movement organizations *always* end in cooptation. Piven and Cloward's generalization discounts that compromises may be rational. It also does not account for the opportunity structures and ideologies that may maintain radicalism even if strong organizations exist.

organizations of collective interest representation. Six organizational properties appear to be particularly characteristic of left-libertarian social movements.[32]

1. There are no barriers to membership; formal requirements such as
   membership cards, dues, endorsement of an ideology or a probation
   period are absent.
2. Citizenship rights in the movement are primarily exercised through
   "presence" and participation at gatherings, not through representative
   institutions.
3. Organizational statutes are rudimentary or nonexistent. There are few
   formalized decision procedures.
4. There is little division of labor and activists are "amateurs" who change
   their tasks and roles frequently.
5. Elite positions are severely circumscribed in authority and tenure.
   Spokespeople and public representatives of the organization are rotated
   frequently.
6. Activists show little organizational loyalty or attention to the goal of
   organizational maintenance.

If left-libertarian parties follow a logic of constituency representation, they
model their own internal organization on that of the ideas and practices of left-
libertarian movements. They adopt a fluid process of internal participation
that avoids fixed hierarchies and formal procedures. Decision making is
decentralized, and party activists hold formal leadership positions for brief
periods at a time. Leaders engage in a continuous exchange of information
with both rank-and-file militants and activists in left-libertarian movements
and can be recalled at any time. The parties keep themselves open to new ideas
and demands and base their decisions on discussions rather than on preferences of party elites.

The left-libertarian logic of constituency representation expresses an ideal
of "amateur politics" which is analyzed in Wilson's (1962) seminal study on
amateurism in the club movement of the American Democratic party in the
late 1950s. While older socialist visions of party democracy tried to reconcile
the impossible, for example mass participation with a centralized, cohesive
organization,[33] amateur politics comes close to the left-libertarian spirit of

---

32. The characteristic organizational form of new social movements was first analyzed by
Ash (1972), Freeman (1975: chap. 4), and Gerlach and Hine (1970). Relevant later elaborations
include Case and Taylor (1979), Donati (1984), Gundelach (1984), Mansbridge (1980), Melucci
(1985), Oberschall (1980), Rothschild-Whitt (1979), and Rucht (1984a; 1986).

33. This contradiction is particularly acute in the writings of Rosa Luxemburg (1971) and led
to Lenin's (1902/1969) odd notion of "democratic centralism."

participatory involvement *without* a strong party apparatus.[34] In the United States, the amateur spirit has been expressed inside the existing decentralized and highly fragmented political parties. On the other hand, as discussed in the first chapter, in a number of European countries the centralized structure, bureaucratic process, and strategic outlook of traditional parties eventually forced left-libertarian amateurs to form their own parties. Under such circumstances left-libertarians have a better chance of articulating their logic of constituency representation than in countries where they form merely undercurrents in a two-party system.

Perverse Effects: Unintended Outcomes of Party Activism

In all human interaction, the link between individual intentions and collective outcomes is uncertain. The joint actions of many individuals often bring about consequences which are neither anticipated nor welcomed by anyone. Raymond Boudon (1977) has called these unintentional outcomes "perverse effects:" actions that from the perspective of a single individual appear desirable and rational, but that when pursued collectively lead to undesirable or irrational outcomes for all.

The problem of perverse effects is primarily rooted in two common misperceptions social actors fall prey to.[35] First, they underestimate the *resources* needed when scaling up what is a rational course of action for an individual to that of a large collectivity. To commuters the private car may seem faster than a bus, but because road space is scarce, a collective shift to the automobile slows rather than speeds the movement of traffic. Similarly, a prisoner's dilemma game poses a situation of scarcity in which the players have resources neither to communicate with one another nor to enforce cooperation. Finally, the "anarchy" of the marketplace may seem a less efficient form of economic coordination than planning, but planning often generates prohibitive transaction costs removing whatever efficiency gains it promised.

Misperceptions of actors' *true motivations* are a second source of perverse effects. Individuals may hold different preference schedules than observers commonly attribute to them. In this sense, the failure of collectivities to act on shared objectives derives not only from the difficulty of coordinating a large

---

34. This is what Hofstetter (1971) calls the "procedural" dimension of amateurism. It is distinct from a "strategic" dimension which concerns the willingness of activists to sacrifice policy objectives in order to win elections.

35. I do not argue here that these two misperceptions exhaust the range of "perverse effects" in human societies. Failure to recognize tradeoffs between objectives, for instance, may be neither reducible to resource scarcity nor to the false attribution of motivations. Elster's (1985: chap. 8) admirable reconstruction of Marxist ideology can be read as an exercise in uncovering the sources of perverse effects.

group of individuals (resource scarcity), but also from the individually rational preference to free-ride rather than to contribute to a collective good. The
absence of cooperation appears perverse only to observers who do not realize
the ranking order of the actors' preferences. Moreover, in many circumstances, individuals may be unable or unwilling to reveal the preferences on
which they act. The choice of preferences may be driven by *meta-preferences*
or "second order volitions" (Hirschman 1981:71) which are inconsistent with
the actors' stated intentions. For instance, individuals may advocate participatory procedures as the most consensual and legitimate method of collective
choice, but really hope that such rules impair collective agreements and
protect the individual's freedom from collective intervention. In this case, a
meta-preference for personal autonomy, not a concern with consensus and
legitimacy, determines the overt support of participatory decision rules.

A famous example of unintentional, perverse effects in formal organizations is the vicious circle of bureaucratic control Crozier (1964:187–98)
discovered in French nationalized firms. By closely supervising and regulat-
ing the shop floor, managers intended to improve workers' productivity.
Instead the rigidity and inefficiency of the production process increased.
When managers intensified their efforts the problems grew more acute.
Crozier shows that the managerial staff misperceived workers' motivations
and the resources needed for social control from the top. The overt language of
motivation that governed management and the shop floor—material self-
interest, duty, and fear—did not uncover the pride in autonomy, status, and
self-directed workmanship guiding the workers' behavior, especially that of
the specialists controlling critical areas of information. At the same time,
management did not command the resources for depriving the shop floor of all
control over the work process, forcing it to pass information up the hierarchy
and centralizing all decisions.

In the literature on political parties, Michels' (1911/62) "iron law of
oligarchy" is the most prominent theory of perverse effects.[36] Michels shows
that even in leftist labor parties, which use the language of participation and
democracy, oligarchies will emerge. He argues that large organizations with
complex task structures lack the resources to coordinate the preferences of
large numbers of party members. Instead, division of labor, hierarchy, and
professional experts become the devices parties must use to reach decisions.
At the same time, most party members will not commit the resources to
politics (time, money, physical and intellectual energy) required to make
democracy work. Thus, *transaction costs* and *membership lethargy* impede
party democracy. I call this argument Michels' "weak" theory of oligarchy.
Michels also maintains that advocates of party democracy misperceive the

36. The best reconstruction of Michels' argument is probably Wippler (1984).

true motivations of political agents. The masses long to identify with political leaders. The leaders, in turn, are driven by personal greed and a desire for social status and political power, not by altruistic concern with the party's collective goals. As a consequence even in radical parties leaders abandon the quest for fundamental social change and develop a preference for the political strategy that maintains their privileged position. This argument is what I call Michels' "strong" theory of oligarchy: *elite control* permitting leaders to impose goals that differ systematically from those of the rank and file.

Michels' theory of perverse effects in political parties, however, has a number of shortcomings. While he devotes only the first two chapters of his book to the more innocent bases of organizational stratification (transaction costs and mass apathy), more than two-thirds of his study examines the "dictatorial appetites" of party bureaucracies and leaders (Michels 1911/ 62:147). Michels' "strong" theory of oligarchy as elite control has proven more controversial than his "weak" theory.[37] Michels underrates forces such as elite competition, which mitigate a simple polarization of powerless but radical mass base and conservative but dominant leadership.[38] At times he subscribes to an anarchist or syndicalist reading of political parties according to which radicalized masses are misled by leaders coopted into a country's political elite.

In the first place, this view neglects the realities of mass conservatism even among socialist party members after the turn of the century (Groh 1973).[39] Furthermore, parties have weak sanctions for disciplining their members and rely primarily on purposive incentives. Hence, without taking a substantial loss of members, it is difficult to remove a party's course too far from what grassroots supporters are willing to endorse. Michels also tends to vastly overstate the development of party bureaucracies (Lehnert 1979). Even in contemporary mass parties, there are limitations to bureaucratic structures, not only because of their volunteer base but also because of the nature of their tasks (Wiesendahl 1984). Modern organization theory predicts that complex, uncertain, and shifting environments discourage organizations from developing rigid bureaucratic structures.[40] Thus, neither what Michels describes as the end of oligarchical control (conservative policies advocated by entrenched

37. For critical appraisals of Michels' theoretical argument, see especially Eldersveld (1982:158–161), Hands (1971), Lipset (1962), and May (1965).

38. Michels (1911/62:108 and 172) mentions elite competition in parties, but never discusses the theoretical significance of this observation for his broader theory.

39. In this sense, Lenin's (1902/1969) emphasis on reformist "trade unionist" consciousness among the rank and file of working class mass organizations is more realistic than Michels' theory. Sources show that Michels was indeed indebted to syndicalist thinking at the time of writing *Political Parties* (cf. Cook 1970:782).

40. See, e.g., structural contingency theories of organization, such as Emery and Trist, (1965), Perrow (1972), Scott (1981), and Thompson (1967).

party leaders) nor the means to that end (party bureaucracy) always reflects the reality of party politics.

Michels' "strong" theory of oligarchy is not only an artifact of academic research but also suggests an interpretation of social reality which is frequently employed as a guide to analyzing action by left-libertarian party activists. A distortion or gross simplification of the internal life of political parties based on a simplistic dichotomy of conservative party leaders and radical followers and improper attribution of activists' motivations, it generates its own perverse effects. Ideally, left-libertarians use Michels' strong theory of oligarchy as a *self-destroying prophecy,* telling parties which forms of organization to avoid in order to achieve an open participatory organization. For two reasons these applications of Michels' theory lead to perverse effects. First, the motivational premises of the strong theory of elite control concerning the disposition of party leaders and followers are inadequate. Second, the left-libertarian application of Michels' ideas is one-sided and ignores the fact that Michels also identified technical problems of resource scarcity, both in the transaction costs of the decision-making process and in the limited contributions of party members, as causes of weak forms of party oligarchy, which centralize political authority in a representative leadership.[41]

Left-libertarian ideologues in particular interpret political reality in terms of a cognitive frame derived from a distorted interpretation of Michels' strong theory of elite control. The perverse effects that occur when a one-sided view of Michels' strong theory becomes a guide to practical action furnish not only evidence against some elements of his theory, but also clarify why left-libertarian politics may diverge from *both* a rational-efficient and a fluid-participatory party model, even when activists intend to follow a logic of constituency representation. For the West German and Belgian ecology parties this book highlights four classes of perverse effects.

Misperceptions of rank-and-file activists' motivations. Radical left-libertarians assume that human beings have a strong desire to participate in collective decision making, underrating apathy and the absence of political motivation as formidable obstacles to political action. As a consequence they ignore the need for selective incentives. This misinterpretation goes a long way toward explaining the narrow base of activists in left-libertarian parties, the often tense interpersonal atmosphere in party meetings, and the high turnover rates among party activists, particularly in the centers of left-libertarian mobilization (Chapter 4).

41. In Part 5 of his book, Michels (1911/62:307–29) discusses some of the recommendations anarchists and syndicalists especially have made to prevent the formation of oligarchies, such as plebiscites within parties, job rotation, and low pay for party functionaries. He also discusses the perverse effects these measures bring about because they ignore resource scarcity in parties and the actual motivations of political actors as foundations for oligarchy.

Misperceptions of rank-and-file activists' resources for political involvement. The practice of left-libertarian politics is based on the belief that if all party members have the *right* to participate in all decisions, the transparency of the organization will bring about democratic politics. This assumption ignores the unequal *resources* that activists can marshal. Unless rights and resources are equalized, activists with the most potent resources will dominate the political process.[42]

Misperceptions of organizational resources for coordinating political action. Organizations must allocate time and money for communication and decision making. Left-libertarians often disregard the need for a rational allocation of these critical resources in the party organization. They represent decision making as a synoptic rational collective choice in which ends are deliberated and efficient means to pursue these ends are chosen, while in reality political decision making follows a model of incremental muddling through or of disjointed, erratic choices which are best reconstructed by a "garbage can" pattern of decision making (Cohen et al. 1972). In practice, left-libertarian parties are fragmented, compartmentalized "stratarchies"[43] in which different levels and party organs are relatively independent from one another and often governed by rival bands of politicians. These patterns of organization and decision making tend to limit the parties' external strategic capacities because of their inability to develop a continuing dialogue with their constituencies and to make consistent choices of strategy vis-à-vis competitors and potential allies (Chapters 5 through 9).

Misperceptions of leaders' motivations. Because a party leadership with wide-ranging rights and responsibilities is assumed to follow narrow material self-interests and to betray the rank and file, left-libertarian parties have tried to minimize the formal powers of their leaders to the extent that party officials operate in what can accurately be called a "culture of mistrust." At the same time, party leaders are deprived of the means of effective administration and information processing (full-time appointments, staffs, and the like) in order to undercut their ability to control the parties. As a consequence many militants are unwilling to assume party office and those who do are often unrepresentative of the rank and file. In place of accountable formal authority, unaccountable informal leaders dominate the parties and decision-making power emigrates to those positions, particularly in the parliamentary groups that control resources beyond the parties' reach. What takes place in left-libertarian parties is an inversion of Crozier's vicious circle of hierarchical control. The weakness of accountable leadership undercuts coordination and

42. See, e.g., Weber (1968:948–52), who attributed the rise of a political elite from an initial structure of grassroots democracy to the unequal distribution of resources and capabilities in politics.

43. The notion of stratarchy was first introduced by Eldersveld (1964) to describe U.S. parties that, according to his findings, fit neither the models of party oligarchy nor those of party democracy.

communication. This outcome in turn reinvigorates efforts to control the leadership and restrict its political authority, thus magnifying the problem.

Left-libertarian social movements encounter similar problems, but perverse effects tend to be more noticeable in party form, because parties operate under different institutional constraints and opportunities than movements. First, parties tend to be more *durable* than movement organizations. Permanent organizations require that members develop a relatively strong commitment to participation and are more likely to develop some kind of division of labor and role differentiation. These features cast dilemmas concerning the routines of organizational decision making into much sharper relief than in temporary movement organizations which ride cycles of upswings and downswings of public attention. Second, parties are concerned with a *multiplicity of objectives and policies* rather than a single goal or policy typical of movements. Whereas movements often frame their demands as a negation of existing policies, parties are more likely to present constructive alternatives. To meet this challenge parties need more resources in the decision-making process and tend to employ functional differentiation of organizational units and division of labor.

A third difference is a consequence of this organizational durability and goal complexity. Parties often engage in *strategic action,* that is the purposive, rational pursuit of objectives in a sequence of steps that may include detours and incremental approaches. Fourth, parties compete in the *electoral marketplace* and are exposed to a different logic of action than merely representing the interests of their core constituencies. The electoral contest reinforces the propensity toward permanent party machines and differentiated task structures in European party systems. At the same time, the status of electoral office introduces an element of hierarchy and inequality of political resources among left-libertarian party militants that is difficult to counteract by organizational measures within the parties themselves.

In a nutshell, perverse effects and the challenges posed by traditional forms of political organization are much stronger for parties than for movements because the former operate in a more highly institutionalized and constrained environment. Competition in an electoral marketplace makes it difficult for left-libertarian parties to pursue a logic of constituency representation and generates perverse effects. Left-libertarian parties may be guided by ideology and policy, but the results of their efforts may often fail to reflect the intentions of the political actors. Under certain conditions these perverse effects trigger organizational learning and adaptation to a logic of party competition.

Conclusion

In this chapter I have argued that external political circumstances and internal coalitions explain how parties decide between pursuing a logic of constituency representation and a logic of party competition. I have contrasted my argument to that of existing approaches which tend to reduce this choice to a conflict between radical rank-and-file activists and moderate leaders. These views are misleading because they do not reflect the diversity of militants and leaders and cannot explain why the balance of power between moderates and radicals may shift over time.

For the empirical study of left-libertarian party politics in Belgium and West Germany, three hypotheses follow from the theoretical framework I have developed in this chapter. First, left-libertarian parties will pursue a logic of constituency representation where (1) social mobilization of the left-libertarian cleavage is high and where (2) existing elites vigorously oppose the new party's claims to participation in the political system. In these areas the share of ideologues among party activists is relatively high compared to that of lobbyists and pragmatists, and ideologues are likely to join in a coalition with lobbyists. In Chapter 1, I described how left-libertarian social movements are more mobilized and incumbent political elites more antagonistic to left-libertarian challenges in West Germany than in Belgium. Hence, my theoretical model predicts that conditions are more favorable to a logic of constituency representation in the West German Greens than in the Belgian Agalev and Ecolo.

The second hypothesis is that left-libertarian parties are likely to experience intense internal conflict over party organization, program, and strategy where the left-libertarian cleavage is highly mobilized, and simultaneously where the parties find themselves in a strong competitive position in the party system. In this situation the differences among ideologues, lobbyists, and pragmatists are sharply accentuated and intraparty factionalism is common. Again, these conditions are more likely to arise in West German rather than Belgian ecology parties.

Third, the logic of constituency representation is most likely to be beset by perverse effects in ecology party organizations located in areas where there are many left-libertarian social movements and where ecology parties are in a strong competitive position. As a consequence, perverse effects should be more significant in the Greens than in Agalev or Ecolo.

In spite of these variations *among* and *within* ecology parties, however, all left-libertarian parties express central tendencies that set them apart from their conventional competitors who predominantly follow a logic of party competition. In a sense, left-libertarian party organization and strategy are shaped by a unique set of ideas and vision of politics. But the prominence of perverse effects shows that the parties' political practice does not directly reflect their militants' political discourse. For this reason, the subsequent investigation focuses more on the actual behavior of left-libertarian parties and militants' experiences than on left-libertarian theoretical discourse.

3 | Founding Ecology Parties

Political Entrepreneurs and Social Movements

In the West German and Belgian ecology parties growth has followed a common pattern (Table 11). During the initial "incubation phase" local and regional electoral lists emerged for the sole purpose of contesting a single election, with little thought given to building lasting party organizations. In both countries the 1979 European elections marked the beginning of a second phase, that of "agenda setting." Because voters are more likely to support a new party in a secondary election than in the principal national contest, party founders seized the opportunity to prove the ecologists' electoral viability (cf. Reif 1984; 1985). The second period was marked by factional battles between different ideological groups and individual political entrepreneurs. Once the parties had won some initial parliamentary representation in the early 1980s, they entered a third period in which they began to institutionalize their organization, program, and strategy. This process was accompanied by a realignment of party factions. Since then, party debates have revolved around the relationships between competitive strategy, linkages to left-libertarian movements, and electoral representation.

In both countries regional politics has shaped the internal political alignments and external strategy of the emerging ecology parties. Not only in Belgium where each linguistic community has its own independent ecology party, but also in the case of the West German Greens, regional party organizations have developed diverse coalitions of activists and political strategies. Given this decentralized development, the national ecology parties are often nothing but a reflection of the momentary impact of different regional groups. In West Germany, this dynamic contrasts with the more nationalized structure of conventional parties.[1]

1. In Belgium, of course, the established socialist, Christian, and liberal parties have also divided themselves into more or less independent Flemish and Walloon organizations since the 1970s.

Table 11
Stages in the development of ecology parties in Belgium and West Germany

	Agalev	Ecolo	Die Grünen
"Incubation" period of party formation	*1976–1979* First electoral participation in national elections	*1974–1978* Independent local ecology lists participate in national elections	*1977–1979* Independent, local, and state lists participate in local and state elections
"Agenda setting" period: struggles over political composition of the parties	*1979–1982* Loose work group Agalev, initial electoral success in the 1979 European elections and the 1981 national election; formal separation from the revival movement Anders Gaan Leven	*1978–1981* Party formation, factional struggles between Brussels and Namur party sections, electoral success in the 1979 European elections and the 1981 national election	*1979–1982* "SPV Die Grünen," factional struggles between right and left over control of the proto-party after initial success in the 1979 European elections; founding of Die Grünen in January 1980
Electoral consolidation and strategic debates in the parties	*1982–present* Gradual electoral growth in the 1985 and 1987 national elections, internal strategic diversity, but little factionalism	*1981–present* Stagnation of electoral support near the 1981 level; small leftist faction leaves the party in 1986	*1982–present* Electoral success in state and national elections; realignment of party factions around fundamentalists, realists, ecosocialists, and ecolibertarians

Agalev: The Flemish Ecology Party

The Flemish ecology party Agalev grew out of the Catholic revival movement Anders Gaan Leven (Live differently), founded by the Jesuit priest and teacher Luc Versteylen.[2] Originally, Versteylen rallied his movement, centered in a suburb of Antwerp, around the idea of a lifestyle built on "voluntary simplicity" and a rejection of values associated with industrial society, such as competition for income, status, and power (see Agalev 1981:29–30). The movement always had goals broader than ecological ones; a main aim was to defend the "new poor," among whom Versteylen included children and the elderly, the sick and infirm, linguistic and immigrant minorities, the clients of public social services, and residents of polluted and decaying suburbs (Agalev 1981:15).[3]

Versteylen created a communications center in an old brewery building, soon added a small publishing house, and eventually founded an alternative school in which he taught the pedagogic principles of his philosophy. To reach out beyond Antwerp, Versteylen created meditation groups, Dagelijkse Doeningen, in several Flemish towns later on. Beginning in 1973 he involved his followers in environmental protests, the most famous of which aimed at halting plans to build a canal near Antwerp to link the Maas and Schelde rivers. Here, as elsewhere, Versteylen and his group employed a theatrical, colorful, happening-like protest style they copied from the Dutch left-libertarian movements of the 1960s and 1970s. His group founded the "Green Bicyclists," Groene Fietsers, a group that introduced Belgium to the bicycle demonstration.

In the same vein, Versteylen treated his first forays into the realm of organized politics as an extension of the "playful action" model. In the 1974 parliamentary elections and the 1976 local elections, Versteylen endorsed "green lists" of candidates who ran on the tickets of traditional parties but were known to support his movement's principles. Disappointed by the policies the "green" candidates pursued once elected, Anders Gaan Leven activists ran on independent Agalev tickets in the parliamentary elections of 1977 and 1978, receiving 0.3 and 0.7 percent of the vote in the province of Antwerp. The lists had a temporary character, and the decision to adopt the acronym Agalev itself symbolized the playful, aesthetic appeal of the movement; it was meant to be a parody of "meaningful" party names and was expected to leave people confused as to whether it was an organization of Turkish immigrants or Russian dissidents (Agalev 1981:7).

2. The history of Agalev is sketched in greater detail in Agalev (1981), Buyle (1985), Leroy (1980; 1984), Peeters and Vermeiren (1980:110–20), Stouthuysen (1981:223–93; 1983), and Versteylen (1981). Other information relies on interviews with party militants.

3. Without being educated in the modern neo-Marxist social sciences, Versteylen thus intuitively built upon what Offe (1969) described as the new disparity between production and consumption sectors in advanced capitalism.

But with the electoral list's modest success, the temporary Agalev work group soon began to develop a life of its own no longer inspired by Versteylen alone. The salience of environmental issues and growing popular disaffection with the coalition government of all major parties, struggling unsuccessfully to determine the status of the Brussels region in the quasi-federalist Belgian constitution, helped Agalev attract a different breed of activists. These were men in their 30s and 40s, often with experience in political organizing, who sensed the fledgling party could add something new and important to Flemish political life. In contrast to Versteylen's emphasis on self-reform and cultural change, these activists were more concerned with institutional change through comprehensive environmental regulation, egalitarian economic redistribution, and European federalism.

As a consequence of Agalev's respectable showing in the 1979 European elections, 2.3 percent of the vote in Flanders, 2.64 percent in the university town of Ghent, and 3.6 percent in Agalev's home base of Antwerp, the Work Group Agalev was founded as a permanent proto-party, although binding decisions were still made by the groups and assemblies of the broader movement Anders Gaan Leven.[4] Not surprisingly, tensions and mistrust began to build between the Agalev work group and the movement's charismatic founder, Versteylen, who remained committed to the ideal of an informal, cultural movement inspiring self-reform rather than instrumental political action. Versteylen and many movement participants opposed the separation of politics from cultural change and eventually criticized the political activists' demand for a party statute as de-Agalev-ing (''veragaleffing'') Agalev, the takeover of ''electologists'' rather than of ecologists (Versteylen 1981:36–61).

Militants in the proto-party, in turn, showed almost unanimous distaste for Versteylen's political approach. They considered his strategy and program to be naively apolitical, and they rejected his charismatic leadership style, which they held incompatible with the party's demands for a participatory, egalitarian society. Because of its close links to Versteylen's movement, the Work Group Agalev was still viewed with mistrust by other movement groups in Flanders, such as the Union of Opponents to Nuclear Power (VAKS). When in 1981 Agalev organized a conference with Flemish environmental groups on the strategy to follow in the following year's local election, the participating movement organizations gave Agalev a limited endorsement but did not actively support it.

Agalev's political position changed dramatically, however, when the Belgian government collapsed in the fall of 1981. In the October 1981

4. Luido Dierickx, a leading member of the Agalev work group and deputy in the Belgian parliament since 1981, welcomed electoral participation in 1979. Although he still opposed forming a party, he hastened to qualify his statement by adding ''certainly not a party in the traditional sense of the word'' (Dierickx 1979:38).

elections Agalev received 3.8 percent of the Flemish vote, with more notice-able electoral inroads in the metropolitan regions of Ghent-Eeklo (4.5 percent) and Antwerp (6.1 percent). This success allowed the party to enter the national parliament with two deputies and, in the ensuing months, to separate the party from the movement, to overcome resistance to formal statutes at a May 1982 conference, and to build a party organization with specific internal decision procedures and membership dues.[5] At the same time, the party's success caught militants in ecological movement organizations off-guard, though relations between them and Agalev began to improve when the party distanced itself from Versteylen's revival movement. In any event, Flemish social movements were not strong enough to generate a political alternative to Agalev (cf. Jacobs and Roebroek 1983:48–49).

Since 1982 the institutionalization of the party has progressed apace. This is evidenced by electoral successes in the local elections of 1982 (5.7 percent of the vote), the European elections of 1984 (7.1 percent), and the national parliamentary elections of 1985 and 1987 (6.1 and 7.3 percent). The party organization now covers most of Flanders, representing a rather wide spectrum of opinion but with little organized factionalism or clearly identifiable political wings. Most militants in "hard core" New Left organizations, such as Maoist or Trotskyist parties, have preferred to remain outside the party. Moreover, Agalev has been spared from sharp internal conflicts because it has always been an opposition party in a weak competitive position and thus has not been faced with hard strategic choices about coalition building and policy compromise. While it appears that a large majority of the militants are pragmatists, there exists a significant minority of lobbyists and ideologues.

Ecolo: The Walloon Ecology Party

In Wallonia Ecolo's roots go back to the Francophone party Rassemble-ment Wallon (RW).[6] In 1972 RW lost activists who wanted to be more than an ethnolinguistic single-issue party. They endorsed a broader program that included a federalist political structure, grassroots democracy, and elements of socialist planning, founding a new organization, Démocratie Nouvelle. In 1975 the key activists of this new group together with the Belgian ornithologi-cal association and other movements decided to found a Belgian section of the international ecology association Friends of the Earth. Its highly politicized French section, Amis de la Terre, not the American parent organization,

5. This process involved intense conflicts with many activists coming out of Versteylen's movement. As one leading proponent of party statutes I interviewed recalled, "I tried to win support for the statutes by saying that they would only be temporary and could be revised annually, although I knew very well that they would develop a life of their own and would be very difficult to change once implemented."

6. Mahaux and Moden (1984) reconstruct Ecolo's development. Again the interviews conducted for this study serve as a supplement.

served as the model for the Belgian effort.[7] The emerging ecology party in Wallonia in turn created a movement organization.

The Walloon section of Amis de la Terre soon became active in elections by fielding temporary electoral lists in individual cities and districts such as Namur and Liège, but did not organize a political network that operated between elections. In January 1978, however, an assembly of environmentalists founded Ecolo as a proto-party. Another meeting in August of the same year resulted in a program, inspired by the ideas of Amis de la Terre. This development led to personal struggles among the most influential political activists and their followers in the organization. Eventually the militants in the Namur section of Ecolo, favoring a more coordinated, federalist party structure, prevailed over their competitors in the Brussels Ecolo group. The conflict split the Brussels section of Amis de la Terre. In the national elections of 1978 and 1981 each faction fielded separate lists in Brussels, but the Namur group, aided by its wider organizational network all over Wallonia, clearly prevailed.

Ecolo won a surprising 5.1 percent of the vote in the 1979 European elections (and 7.7 percent in the *arrondissement* Namur). Encouraged by this success, in March of 1980 a conference of all militants passed a party statute and charged the core activists with preparing an electoral program, which was approved shortly before the 1981 parliamentary elections. In these elections Ecolo received 6 percent of the vote in the Francophone area of Belgium and two seats in the Belgian Chamber of Parliament. Because of its earlier party formation, Ecolo performed better than Agalev in the 1982 local elections (7.1 percent) and the 1984 European elections (9.9 percent), but gained few votes beyond its 1981 base in the 1985 and 1987 parliamentary elections (6.2 and 6.5 percent). Compared to Flanders, the relatively less favorable circumstances for left-libertarian politics in Wallonia—less economic affluence, weaker left-libertarian movements—was reflected in the party's electoral performance.

The disappointing electoral returns in 1985 precipitated a conflict in Ecolo. As a consequence of the worse than expected performance, Ecolo's leaders embarked on negotiations with the Catholic/liberal Walloon regional government which held exactly 50 percent of the parliamentary seats and was interested in broadening its support through a limited agreement with Ecolo. A small leftist faction, primarily rooted in the Brussels Ecolo section, stood up against the leadership based in Namur and Liège. When the latter prevailed, many radicals as well as one deputy of the party's parliamentary group exited

7. Militants in the Belgian Amis de la Terre, for instance, complained about the narrowness and low level of political awareness typical among their American associates. See Olivier Deleuze and Gerard Wilgros, "Friends of the Earth: Un congrès mou," *L'Ecologiste*, no. 26 (November–December 1980):30.

from Ecolo and formed a leftist alternative which gained a few votes in the 1987 elections. Despite this conflict, Ecolo's leadership has received broad support within the party. The party includes a more limited range of political opinions than Agalev and, due to the relative weakness of left-libertarian movements in Wallonia, also has fewer ties to social movement constituencies. Most of its activists support a pragmatic course in organizational, programmatic, and strategic respects.

The Greens: West Germany's Ecology Party

Both Belgian ecology parties emerged from or founded a single movement organization. In the more complex and mobilized West German social movement sector, however, the formation of the Greens involved more heterogeneous, varied coalitions of groups and political entrepreneurs.[8] Here, as in Flanders, many movement activists initially opposed the founding of an ecology party. Political entrepreneurs with differing programs and ideologies acted as catalysts for building viable coalitions of activists and voters that gradually emerged from an evolutionary process of innovation, selection, and retention of successful new party alliances. Although I first sketch the development of the party as a whole, it is crucial to realize that the individual Green party units in the West German states have varied origins and continue to crystallize around different organizational forms, programs, and strategies. As a general rule, these differences can be traced back to the strength and scope of left-libertarian movement mobilization in each state.

To simplify somewhat, a right wing, a centrist, and a New Left support group vied for control of the Green party as it emerged after 1977, when the first local electoral lists appeared.[9] In the incubation phase of the party (1977–1979), most of the Greens' local and regional precursors were dominated by centrist and even a few right-wing politicians, whose disagreements with the established parties were limited only to the ecology question. As in Belgium, the second phase of party formation began with the 1979 European election campaign. Militants of all tendencies discussed the possibility of presenting a new ecology party in that election, particularly since West German party law provides lavish government compensation for electoral expenses for parties winning as little as 0.5 percent of the vote. What emerged was a provisional Green electoral alliance dominated by conservative and center/left ecologists and a very few New Left militants, called "The Other Political Association:

8. Within the large body of literature on the history of the Greens see especially the empirically comprehensive account of the party's early development by Klotzsch and Stöss (1984). The analytically clearest piece is Bolaffi and Kallscheuer (1983). Other useful materials can be found in Brun (1978), Hallensleben (1984), Langguth (1984), Lüdke and Dinne (1980), Mettke (1982), Reents (1982), Stöss (1980), and Troitzsch (1980).

9. Bolaffi and Kallscheuer (1983:71–72) further break these groups down into seven subgroups, a distinction I disregard here for the sake of simplicity.

The Greens'' (Sonstige politische Vereinigung (SPV), die Grünen), which went on to receive 3.2 percent of the vote on election day (Horacek 1982).

Many radicals had hoped they could eventually win electoral support for a leftist electoral list separate from the Greens. But the SPV developed a momentum they found unstoppable. In order to receive state campaign subsidies the SPV had to register as a party. These funds, in turn, would enable the SPV's organizers to build a national communication network far superior to what the fragmented regional leftist organizations could hope to achieve. For this reason, at conferences in Offenbach (November 1979) and Karlsruhe (January 1980), delegates from the constituent Green local and state protoparties discussed the formal creation of the new party, *Die Grünen*. In these meetings, the New Left turned out in force to make up lost ground. Its representatives clashed with conservatives and centrist activists over whether membership in the new party should be exclusive or compatible with membership in other political associations. The Left favored a permissive stance in order to preserve its own organizational identity outside the Greens. A compromise was finally reached that allowed the decision on membership to reside with the state party organizations, at least for a transition period.

Once the party had been founded, conservative and rightist activists soon dropped out, because their authoritarian ecologism proved incompatible with the libertarian and egalitarian conceptions of the center-left and the Left. The electoral performance of independent right-wing ecology parties also showed that the ecological right, apart from a few well-known figureheads, had little mass following and could deliver few votes. While the right disappeared from the Greens, the far Left, especially former militants in the New Left splinter parties, affiliated with the Greens in large numbers. These factions gradually lost their political identity as new programmatic and strategic issues and debates emerged within the Greens and superseded old divisions between a Marxist left and a libertarian center in the party.

In the mid-1980s four political tendencies were associated with pragmatist and ideological positions in the Greens. On the pragmatic side, realists and ecolibertarians to varying degrees called for the pursuit of a logic of party competition and emphasized a moderate reformist program. Ecolibertarians valued a fluid, decentralized party organization more than realists, who placed more emphasis on the efficiency and cohesiveness of the party. The main factions representing the ideologues were fundamentalists and ecosocialists. Both groups called for far-reaching, dramatic policy ruptures but differed in their assessment of the party organization and specific ideological questions. Fundamentalists were firmly committed to an open, loose, and informal party structure akin to the mobilization of left-libertarian movements, whereas ecosocialists were less inhibited about treating the party organization as an instrument for effecting social change. In the view of party militants, realists and fundamentalists were stronger than ecosocialists and especially ecolibertarians. In addition to the four wings there was a large centrist camp of activists who belonged to no tendency; often these had joined the party after involvement in left-libertarian movements and thus in many ways approximated the ideal type of "lobbyist." This group did not organize a communications network until 1987.

The realignment of Green intraparty divisions and strategic issues is closely linked to the growing electoral success of the Greens. After an electoral campaign dominated by close competition between the social/liberal government and the Christian democratic opposition, with 1.5 percent of the vote in the 1980 federal elections the Greens remained far below the 5 percent needed to enter the West German parliament. In 1983, however, after the collapse of the SPD/FPD government, many former supporters of the Social Democrats switched sides, helping the Greens win 5.6 percent of the vote and twenty-seven seats in parliament. In 1987, finally, the party gained 8.3 percent of the vote and forty-two seats in parliament. Again, most of the votes came at the expense of a Social Democratic party in disarray, caught between a labor union wing strictly opposed to the lure of left-libertarian politics and a reformist wing advocating competition with the Greens on ecological issues.

Behind these general trends in the national Green party, however, are dramatic differences in the development of the Green state party organizations. Here we find at least four different political alliances that reach back into the founding years of the first proto-parties and relate directly to the relative strength and composition of the left-libertarian movement sector in each state. In states with strong left-libertarian movements that engage in both the "politics of space" and the "politics of social identity," the dominant coalitions are comprised of ideologues and lobbyists. This is true primarily in the city-states of Hamburg, West Berlin, and, to a lesser extent, Bremen.

In large less urbanized states with a more limited left-libertarian movement sector mostly confined to the politics of space, the moderate realists and lobbyists are much stronger. This configuration prevails in Baden-Württemberg in the southwest and in Lower Saxony. A mix of both models can be found in North Rhine–Westphalia and Hesse, states with both urban centers of broad left-libertarian activism and more peripheral areas with movements articulating the politics of space. Finally, there are four states at the periphery of left-libertarian politics where the Greens have rather vague political profiles, but are generally dominated by pragmatic activists (Bavaria, Rhineland-Palatinate, Saarland) or influenced by a highly mobilized state party nearby (Schleswig-Holstein close to Hamburg). To give a sense of the internal variations in the Greens, I briefly review the development in three states where I conducted most of the interviews and in which the parties build on different configurations of left-libertarian movement activism: Hamburg, Baden-Württemberg, and Hesse.

In the Hamburg state elections of 1978 a "Colored List" (Bunte Liste) already received a respectable 3.5 percent of the vote. It was supported by numerous local social movements and neighborhood initiatives but dominated by cadres of the Communist League, a Maoist New Left party. This electoral alliance outdistanced a rightist ecology grouping that managed to capture only 1.0 percent of the vote. After 1978 most activists in the Colored List returned to their preexisting party and movement affiliations and the electoral alliance became dormant. When a Green state party organization was founded in 1979, most leftist activists did not join and still held out hopes for a pure socialist alternative to the conventional parties. Before the next state elections in 1982 these groups founded a loose Alternative List (AL) as a competitor to the Greens, although the Hamburg Greens themselves were closer to socialist ideas than the Greens in any other state. Because a split of AL and Greens would have brought the electoral defeat of both lists, after long negotiations they joined forces and received 7.7 percent of the vote running as Green Alternative List (GAL). The Social Democrats lost their majority in the state and negotiated with the GAL to form a joint government, but both GAL and SPD failed to agree on a common program.

In renewed elections in December 1982 the Social Democrats regained their absolute majority, whereas the GAL stabilized their electoral support with slight losses at 6.9 percent. Since 1982 the Hamburg party has remained in the hands of a radical coalition of fundamentalists and ecosocialists. In 1986 elections again led to severe losses for the Social Democrats and gains for the GAL, now receiving 10.4 percent of the vote. But because of the renewed unwillingness of both sides to form a joint state government, new elections became necessary again in which the GAL was forced to give up all its previous advances and fell back to 7.0 percent, while the Social Democrats gained enough votes to form a government with the Liberals.[10]

With the increasing success of the Greens since 1982, hopes in the Hamburg AL gradually vanished that a pure New Left party could displace the Greens. Eventually, the AL dissolved in the fall of 1984 and recommended that its followers join the Greens. A similar transformation took place in West Berlin and Bremen. In West Berlin an Alternative List remained victorious over the Green state party, but eventually decided to affiliate with the Green national party. It gained 3.7 percent in the 1979 state elections, 7.2 percent in 1981, and 10.6 percent in 1985, but never got into a strong competitive position because the Social Democrats lost heavily and a Christian Democratic/Liberal coalition won a clear majority of the votes.[11] In Bremen a precursor of the Green party was the first ecology list in West Germany to

10. The strategic implications that led to this sequence of events are discussed in detail in Chapter 9.
11. On the history of the Berlin AL see Hoplitschek (1981), Schaper (1984), and Sellin (1984).

enter a state parliament when it received 5.1 percent of the vote in 1979 (cf. Willers 1982). An Alternative List backed by the city's New Left challenged the center-left Green state party, but was decisively beaten in the 1983 state elections. As a consequence the Bremen Greens embarked on a more moderate course and reached the 10-percent threshold in the 1987 state elections.

The best examples of moderate Green state parties are in Baden-Württemberg and Lower Saxony. In each case protests against nuclear power, new freeways, airport expansion, and acid rain were crucial for rallying support to the new party. In both states party ideologues have been mostly confined to university towns and metropolitan centers, but have never dominated the state parties. In Baden-Württemberg conservative ecologists played an important role in the early process of party formation, but they were soon displaced by center-left activists calling for social change beyond ecological protection. After Bremen in 1979, the Baden-Württemberg Greens in 1980 were the first state party to gain legislative representation. In 1984 they went on to improve their share to 8 percent of the vote. In Lower Saxony electoral outcomes fell into a similar range in the 1982 and 1986 state elections. In both states the Greens face a conservative government majority and, particularly in Baden-Württemberg, weak Social Democratic competitors. In this environment, internal programmatic and strategic conflicts have occurred but have not reached the intensity and divisiveness typical of states with strong centers of left-libertarian mobilization.[12]

Somewhere at midpoint on the continuum, with Hamburg and Baden-Württemberg as polar cases, are the Hessian Greens. They rely on left-libertarian movements more mobilized and varied than in Baden-Württemberg and face a highly competitive Social Democratic party, but also have large pockets of weak support, particularly in northern Hesse. The Hessian party benefited from the spectacular controversy over the extension of the Frankfurt airport in the early 1980s, which rallied a large coalition of local residents in the neighborhood of the airport and political militants from Frankfurt to oppose the project.

Initial efforts to build a Green party in Hesse led to three competing lists participating unsuccessfully in the 1978 state elections. By 1982, however, a single Green party then dominated by ideologues from the Frankfurt region managed to garner 8 percent of the vote in that year's state election and force the governing Social Democrats to negotiate with the Greens or go into opposition. As in Hamburg, these negotiations failed, but the Greens lost heavily in the ensuing state elections of 1983, arriving at only 5.9 percent of the vote. Because the Social Democrats could not regain enough support to form a government by themselves, the Greens were faced with the choice

---

12. For the development of the Green state parties in Baden-Württemberg and Lower Saxony compare also Beddermann (1978), Hasenclever and Hasenclever (1982), and Mombaur (1982).

between government and opposition for the second time in a row. Having been punished by the electorate for not choosing an alliance with the Social Democrats after the 1982 elections, the Hessian Greens undertook a dramatic reversal of strategy leading to a toleration of a SPD minority government and, finally, to a coalition with the Social Democrats. In the course of this change, militant Green ideologues were displaced by an intraparty alliance of lobbyists and pragmatists. The government coalition collapsed when the Social Democrats pulled out in March 1987, but the Greens went on to increase their electoral share to 9.4 percent in the subsequent state elections.

This capsule history of the Belgian and West German ecology parties since their inception shows that each party and subnational party unit operates in a unique environment. The degree of left-libertarian movement mobilization, as well as of the parties' competitive position, has significantly affected each party's path. In West German centers of left-libertarian social movements such as Hamburg and Hesse party sections are home to a raucous factionalism. This is much less the case in areas of weaker social mobilization such as Baden-Württemberg and Flanders, let alone Wallonia or some of the peripheral German states (Bavaria and Rhineland-Palatinate being the best cases). At the level of national institutions, the adverse climate for nonconformist political activism in West Germany and the constraints of its electoral system promoted a broad coalition of libertarian, ecologist, and New Left forces in the Greens, while the Belgian ecology parties cater to a more clearly circumscribed clientele which excludes parts of the New Left, evidenced by Ecolo's split in 1986. Finally, the potential and actual strategic importance of the German Greens for forming government majorities fuels intraparty conflicts, as it did in Hamburg and Hesse, an importance unparalleled by the Belgian parties with much weaker competitive positions in their party system.

Electoral Support for Ecology Parties

The linkage between left-libertarian party formation and political context also surfaces in an examination of the parties' electoral support. Similarities and differences between regional and national party support can be analyzed in terms of (1) individual characteristics of left-libertarian voters, (2) the social ecology of districts and regions with high and low left-libertarian electoral support, and (3) the response of voters to strategic moves by left-libertarian parties.

There is little doubt that a new "educational class" (Bürklin 1984a:79; 1987) of young and well-educated citizens supplies the bulk of ecology party voters in Belgium and West Germany.[13] In occupational terms, more white-

13. The socioeconomic composition of sympathizers with the Belgian ecology parties is analyzed in Defeyt (1985), Deschouwer and Stouthuysen (1984), and a survey by the Belgian polling institute INUSOP (*Le Soir,* March 14, 1984). West German data can be found in Berger

collar employees and professionals support ecology parties than workers, yet for two reasons the propensity to vote for an ecology party does not rise with income. First, the group with on average the highest earnings, self-employed businessmen, shows very little inclination to vote for ecology parties.[14] Second, most left-libertarian voters are still in the early stages of their earnings life cycle because they are predominantly under thirty, although the parties have also made headway among those thirty to forty years old.[15] The young unemployed represent a significant, though rarely overproportional share of ecology party voters. Education and age may also explain why left-libertarian voters tend to have no religious affiliation.[16] In West Germany more men vote for the Greens than women, but among voters younger than thirty-five the reverse is true.[17] In Belgium as many or more women support Agalev and Ecolo than men.[18]

Within this broad profile of party activism, there are, however, some significant differences between Belgian and West German ecology voters (Table 12). Agalev and Ecolo voters tend to be somewhat older, less educated, less often having a high status occupation, less postmaterialist and less leftist than their West German counterparts.[19] Moreover, the link between postmaterialism and leftism is not as strong in Belgium as in West Germany (Savage 1985). The data suggest that the institutional and cultural context of left-libertarian politics in both countries influences voting behavior. In West Germany the more recent experience of democratization may still contribute to a sharper generational conflict and elite intransigence vis-à-vis new chal-

---

et al. (1983; 1987), Bürklin (1985a; 1987), Feist et al. (1984), Fogt and Uttitz (1984), Müller-Rommel (1984a), and Veen (1984).

14. Probably for this reason Swyngedouw and Billiet (1988:28) come to the conclusion that Agalev voters are culturally much richer than materially and find few Agalev voters among the professional and managerial occupational group.

15. The association between age and party preference is established in Defeyt (1985) and Deschouwer and Stouthuysen (1984) for Belgium, and in Berger et al. (1987), Bürklin (1985a), Fogt and Uttitz (1984), and Schmidt (1984) for West Germany.

16. For West Germany, compare Berger et al. (1983:180), Bürklin (1985b:472), and Schmidt (1984:5). Similar Belgian trends are reported by Deschouwer and Stouthuysen (1984:13–14).

17. In the 1983 national election 5.9 percent of the men and only 4.9 percent of the women voted for the Greens (Statistisches Bundesamt 1984:88). In 1987 the ratio was 8.3 percent (men) to 7.7 percent (women), but among 18–24 year olds, it was 14.5 percent (men) to 16.5 percent (women) and among 25–34 year olds 16.9 percent (men) and 17.9 percent (women) (Berger et al. 1987:262).

18. In Agalev there appears to be no gender related difference (Deschouwer and Stouthuysen 1984:9), while about 60 percent of Ecolo's sympathizers are women (Le Soir, March 14, 1985).

19. Socioeconomic and political differences are highlighted by Swyngedouw's (1986) and Swyngedouw and Billiet's (1988) analysis of vote switching to and from Agalev. In the 1988 national elections, Agalev won most votes from people previously abstaining or supporting small leftist parties and also gained a considerable amount from the Flemish nationalist party Volksunie and the Christian democrats; but it won from the socialists just about as many votes as it lost to them.

Table 12

Profile of Belgian and West German ecology party voters, 1980–1984

	Supporters of the West German Greens	Supporters of the Belgian Agalev and Ecolo
Age		
under 35	82.6%	71.9%
over 35	17.3%	28.1%
	(N = 455)	(N = 284)
Education		
low education	37.3%	41.9%
high education	62.6%	58.1%
	(N = 455)	(N = 284)
Value Orientation		
materialists	5.2%	16.8%
mixed orientation	35.8%	56.8%
postmaterialists	59.0%	26.4%
	(N = 425)	(N = 280)
Ideology		
left	20.7%	5.0%
moderate left	50.0%	30.0%
moderate	24.4%	50.6%
moderate right	4.2%	13.6%
right	0.7%	0.8%
	(N = 378)	(N = 243)

Source of data: Müller-Rommel (1987), based on Eurobarometer 16–22.

lenges and may explain why ecology voters place themselves more on the left than in Belgium. Because measures of postmaterialism are very sensitive to actual levels of inflation and unemployment, findings must be interpreted with caution (cf. Inglehart 1985). Belgium's economy performed significantly worse than West Germany's in the early 1980s and that, rather than fundamental cultural differences, may be reflected in the lesser Belgian postmaterialism.

The sociocultural composition of the left-libertarian electorate explains geographical variations of voter support across electoral districts and regions. Green parties perform above average in metropolitan areas with a preponderance of service sector employment and large universities. Agalev's and Ecolo's strongholds are in the corridor between Brussels and Antwerp and in the university towns of Ghent, Ottignies, and Namur. The Greens do very well in most major metropolitan areas. In both countries ecology parties perform below average in strong working-class districts where there is widespread socialist support. In Belgium this affects Ecolo's vote in the old steel and coal belt from Mons and Charleroi to the suburbs of Liège.[20] In a similar vein, the Greens have been unable to make strong gains in the working-class towns of the Ruhr area and in the Hamburg and West Berlin working-class districts.[21]

In rural areas ecology parties in both countries receive many fewer votes than in metropolitan centers, except where social movements concerned with the politics of space, for example opposition to nuclear facilities or other industrial projects, are mobilized.[22] In general, rural areas lack a dense infrastructure of left-libertarian movements and cultural activities as well as a large pool of voters with the typical Green socioeconomic profile. This may partially explain differences of ecology party support in Belgium and West Germany. West Germany has more metropolitan regions that are highly mobilized, while Belgium has more dispersed, semirural small communities, a pattern reaching back to the rural industrialization and even the medieval economy of the Low Countries (cf. Katzenstein 1985:168–69). Hence, Belgium has fewer left-libertarian social movements and a relatively smaller share of ecology party voters residing in metropolitan areas (Müller-Rommel 1985c:495).

At first glance the regional and national electoral support of Agalev, Ecolo, and the Greens seems not to reflect variations of movement strength and territorial organization. Comparing the 1983 West German national elections (5.6 percent Green voters) and the 1985 elections in Flanders (6.1 percent) and Wallonia (6.2 percent), there almost appears to be an inverse relationship between economic affluence, urbanization, and left-libertarian movement mobilization on one hand and electoral support for ecology parties on the other.[23] By 1987, however, national election outcomes show the expected positive association between affluence, movement mobilization, and electoral support: 8.3 percent for the West German Greens, 7.3 percent for the Flemish Agalev, and 6.5 percent for the Walloon Ecolo. Now national and regional electoral outcomes are consistent with the hypothesis that ecology parties are stronger in centers of left-libertarian movement activism.

20. In Liège itself Ecolo initially did well, presumably because it collected a large number of protest votes. This is not surprising because the city was bankrupt and in financial receivership under state oversight authorities.

21. In the twelve electoral districts of the Ruhr area, the Greens received an average 6.6 percent of the vote in the 1987 national election, compared to an average of 7.5 percent for the state of North Rhine–Westphalia and 8.3 percent for all of West Germany. Electoral analyses that show the failure of the Greens to make headway in working class neighborhoods are Schmollinger (1983) and Müller-Rommel (1983:103).

22. The link between environmental mobilization and rural voting was first analyzed by Rönsch (1980). For instance, in the district including the site planned for the West German nuclear waste repository, Lüchow-Dannenberg, the Greens received 9.7 percent of the vote in the 1987 national election and only 7.5 percent in the state of Lower Saxony.

23. Almost the same inverse relationship applies in the 1984 European elections: Greens, 8.2 percent; Agalev, 7.1 percent; Ecolo, 9.9 percent.

In the mid-1980s, however, in addition to left-libertarian cleavage mobilization and national political institutions, another contextual variable also began to affect ecology party support, that is, competitive position and strategic behavior. Because left-libertarian voters are young and very well-educated, they have little party loyalty and are especially likely to vote strategically. As in the cases of Hesse and Hamburg described above, they punished the Green state parties when the latter failed to seize opportunities to form government coalitions with the traditional left parties. In a similar vein, the relatively disappointing performance of Green parties in a number of other state elections (North Rhine–Westphalia, Saarland, and West Berlin in 1985, Lower Saxony in 1986, and Schleswig-Holstein in 1987) is attributable to the parties' failure to take a clear position on an alliance with the Social Democrats before elections in which both parties together stood a realistic chance of winning a majority. In regions where ecology parties are confined to the opposition, strategic choice (or the failure to disclose definite strategic commitments before elections) appears to have little impact on the vote. This is the case not only in West German states on the periphery of the left-libertarian cleavage (Bavaria, Rhineland-Palatinate, Baden-Württemberg) but also in Flanders and Wallonia.[24]

Electoral support for ecology parties in Belgium and West Germany thus reflects the impact of all three contextual variables I expect to make a difference in the parties' internal dynamics. High cleavage mobilization is related to the socioeconomic profile of the population in a political unit and affects electoral support positively. Institutional and cultural differences across countries influence the radicalism of a party's voters (postmaterialism, leftist commitments). And parties in a strong competitive position become increasingly vulnerable to voter dissatisfaction if their strategic choice differs from that of the majority of their electoral supporters.

Party Ideologies and Programs

In this section I briefly develop three propositions and then discuss their consequences for ecology party programs: (1) left-libertarians lack a comprehensive interpretation of modern society which builds on a closed, deductive ideology; (2) they expand on the values of the bourgeois revolutionary era (liberty, equality, and fraternity); but (3) they do not offer a definite vision of the institutions that can implement these values in a libertarian and egalitarian society.[25]

While left-libertarians see grave deficiencies in all industrial societies,

24. Ecolo's (slim) chance of forming a regional coalition with the liberal and Christian democratic parties in 1985–86 does not fully count as a strong competitive position. See the discussion in Chapter 9.

25. To my knowledge no thorough review of ecology party programs has been published and this section does not fill this void. For a broader sociology of knowledge approach to ecological

whether capitalist or socialist, they disagree about the causes and potential remedies for these problems. For many left-libertarians the weaknesses besetting East and West indicate not only a failure of liberal and socialist ideologies but also the impossibility of organizing society based on any unified ideology. Party militants often declare that a comprehensive program of social change is impossible at this time (Lambert et al. 1982:544) and reject all-encompassing intellectual systems. The *Communist Manifesto,* for instance, represents a way of thinking and problem solving of a bygone era (Schmid 1983:47). Thus, many left-libertarians believe we live in an era of ideological pluralism. Yet this perspective indicates neither an endorsement of the existing social order nor a renunciation of political protest, as past sociologists had expected from an "end of ideology." Left-libertarians find it preferable to develop more tentative programs of social change than provided by existing ideologies. This lack of a coherent ideological foundation was succinctly captured by one Green parliamentarian from Hamburg, who said about his and his colleagues' political reasoning in the state legislature: "In speeches on the floor of the Hamburg House of Representatives, Green parliamentarians freely choose humanitarian and liberal, socialist and utilitarian, juridical or anarchist arguments to defend a proposal or reject that of another party."

In the preambles to the party programs of Agalev, Ecolo, and the Greens, four overriding values are introduced: economic harmony (more equality and social security), political harmony (more participation and consensus), social harmony (more solidarity, but also tolerance for individuality), and ecological harmony (compatibility of society and biosphere). Yet these values of the French revolution, appended with a commitment to ecological compatibility, do not lead to principles that would help ecologists identify specific social institutions necessary to achieve these goals. Private property, contractual relations, and the marketplace were the bedrock of liberalism; socialism called for replacing them by political planning and collective decision making; and anarchism sought to bypass them entirely with informal primary groups. In contrast, left-libertarians are unwilling to make a blanket commitment to any single set of social institutions. The cognitive and normative ambiguities of their politics come to the fore in their inconsistent and wavering positions when confronted with three basic questions of political theory to which liberalism, socialism, and anarchism give comparatively clear-cut answers.[26]

theories of society compare especially Touraine et al. (1980) and my own studies on political arguments in the evaluation of energy technologies (Kitschelt 1984). By attributing Green programs and ideologies to "German exceptionalism" and cultural uniqueness, American interpretations of the Greens (e.g., Kvistad 1987) often overlook the fact that most of the Greens' agenda, for instance radical democracy, appropriate technology, egalitarianism, state regulation of industry, and protection of civil liberties can be encountered in the programs of other European left-libertarian parties, including Belgium's.

26. For the sake of brevity, I have avoided extensive references and substantiation for each element of ecological thinking and that of its equivalent in liberalism, socialism, or anarchism.

These ambiguities surface in sharp disagreements among ecologists, but are also reflected in the ideological pluralism many of them support.

The three questions are common to all great political ideologies. First, a *theory of the self* determines what dispositions, drives, and aspirations human beings have and what conception of freedom follows from these orientations. One position endorsed by most anarchists and socialists and also supported in many left-libertarian discourses is that human beings have objective needs which enable us to separate them from "false," manipulated desires. A theory of objective needs leads to a positive conception of freedom: humans are free if they create institutions that enable them to realize their true needs. On the other hand, many left-libertarians support liberal assumptions about individuality and freedom of choice and dispute both a cognitive theory of true needs and a normative theory of positive freedom, holding instead that individuals are the sole judges of their own ends. Hence, individual autonomy is an overriding value of social organization. Institutions should be based on a negative conception of freedom enabling individuals to pursue whatever goals please them as long as they do not infringe on the reciprocal freedoms of their fellow citizens. Thus, a cognitive theory of objective needs clashes with a voluntarist theory of individual choice and human autonomy. In concrete policy decisions this makes it difficult to determine when and to what extent collectives can legitimately constrain individual autonomy through coercive control.

Second, all great political ideologies are concerned with principles of allocating scarce resources and a notion of social *justice*. For liberalism, principles of justice are essentially satisfied by procedural criteria according to which all those resource allocations are just that result from a free, noncoercive exchange among individuals. In contrast to this procedural notion of justice, socialism and anarchism subscribe to a substantive conception of justice and equality of life chances for all members of society. They call either for a central collective choice mechanism to generate a just society or a decentralized redistributive system of sharing based on compassion, altruism, and empathy. Because left-libertarians often do not subscribe to the superiority of any single criterion of justice, their policy proposals waver between central government regulation, market-based liberalism, and communitarian self-organization.

A third problem of political ideology concerns the relationship between *knowledge and politics*. Most optimistic are socialists who believe in the possibility of a scientific knowledge of society that empowers us to make

---

Just as Unger (1975) reconstructs an ideal liberal discourse not subscribed to completely by any liberal theorist, my brief sketch is not meant to reflect any individual theorist's thinking comprehensively.

planned, large-scale institutional changes to bring about the desired outcomes. Liberalism is more skeptical and supports the fallibilist view that because of our limited knowledge about society only an incremental logic of piecemeal reform and trial-and-error change is desirable. Anarchism is even more pessimistic about the possibility of organized social change and suggests that individual self-reform and self-reliance are the only ways to change society for the better. Left-libertarians in general and ecologists in particular again waver among the three positions. Because biological ecology teaches that ecosystems are complex, interdependent, and self-regulating, party activists often subscribe to a holistic philosophy of social change which calls for macroscopic, comprehensive social interventions. The science of ecology, however, also teaches skepticism about our ability to change society, for the consequences of even small interventions in ecosystems are nonlinear, difficult to anticipate, and fraught with unwanted side effects. Left-libertarians advocate no single position, vacillating between more optimistic and more pessimistic views of our knowledge and capacity to change society.

What appears from the perspective of conventional ideological systems as an intellectual weakness of left-libertarian thinking is often affirmed as a strength by left-libertarians themselves. Instead of advocating simple and singular solutions to the problem of justice and the choice between markets, bureaucracies, and solidary groups, they call for a new *equilibrium* between the three forms of social organization (cf. Agalev Werkgroep Economie 1984:20).[27]

The impossibility of developing comprehensive, logically consistent ideologies surfaces in the additive and disjointed character of ecology party programs. Rather than delineating principles of institutional choice, they quickly jump to very detailed outlines of specific arrangements and measures in individual policy areas. Such programs concern the supply and consumption of energy, the expansion of public transportation, the conversion of agriculture to biofarming, the reduction of air and water pollution, a redistributive labor market policy, more job satisfaction and more democratic participation in the economy, and empowering traditionally disadvantaged groups in society, such as women, youth, retirees, ethnic minorities, and homosexuals.

The economic and social policy proposals ecology parties have presented in numerous programs highlight the lack of a unifying comprehensive vision of society.[28] Consistent with a liberal view of socioeconomic institutions, some

27. A similar view is expressed in Berger and Kostede (1983:22–27) and in Pfriem (1985). Theoretically, these considerations are similar to Habermas's (1985) call for a new balance between the spheres of instrumental and communicative action.

28. The range of proposals is reflected in the following publications primarily written by party activists: Beckenbach et al. (1985), Berger, Müller, and Pfriem (1982), *Das Argument*, Sonderheft 164 (1984), Opielka et al. (1984), and Projektgruppe Grüner Morgentau (1986) in

party programs call for only indirect interventions in the free play of markets to foster ecological and social objectives, such as antitrust laws, support of small business, a repeal of subsidies to large corporations, pollution fines, or a resource tax to levy a scarcity rent on exhaustible raw materials. In addition, a gross revenue tax on corporations, frequently proposed to impose a heavier burden on capital intensive industries than lighter service industries, is envisioned to create incentives for investments promoting structural change toward less polluting, more labor-creating businesses, and a postindustrial economy.

More clearly socialist perspectives surface in a host of other economic and social policy proposals aiming at direct political influence over investment decisions and redistribution of economic resources. A broadening of the base of income and corporate taxes, for instance, is thought to be capable of financing new social policy initiatives and an "ecological reconstruction program" that would rebuild the physical infrastructure of modern society (energy and transportation systems, urban development, environmental protection). To take another example, displacing entrepreneurial authority over investment decisions by a consumers' and workers' democracy figures high on the ecologists' wish list. Finally, some even call for the socialization of key industries (banks, energy companies, major industrial polluters) as a precondition for ecological transformation of industrial society.

Communitarian proposals enter socioeconomic programs of ecology parties in several ways. Special protection and aid is proposed for nonprofit cooperatives in production and services. And individuals should find more opportunities to build decentralized networks of self-help outside the public sector or private enterprise. Moreover, the provision of a minimum income for all members of society, regardless of whether they work or not, should enable individuals to choose whether they wish to be gainfully employed. A minimum income would compel business to pay higher minimum wages and reduce the supply of labor, but increase autonomous household activities outside the market economy.

In general, economic policy debates in ecology parties have been more successful in proposing new substantive objectives for economic change than in designing institutional mechanisms and instruments for realizing them (Bergmann and Krischausky 1985; Sik 1985). Moreover, the ideological ambiguities of ecological politics often give rise to intractable disputes among party activists about the importance and priority that should be attributed to different innovative proposals. The actual mix of policy demands entering into party programs varies significantly depending on internal political coalitions.

West Germany, and Agalev Werkgroep Economie (1984), Agalev (1985b), Ecolo (1985b), and *La Revue Nouvelle*, 41 (April 1985), no. 4, for Belgium.

Not surprisingly, the most radical socialist and communitarian programs are passed in the strongholds of left-libertarian politics such as the Hamburg or West Berlin Greens, though the North Rhine–Westphalian and Hessian Greens have also accepted some radical programs. In areas with less left-libertarian mobilization, as in Baden-Württemberg, the party program is more moderate. At the federal level, Green programs are often the result of compromises forged among various party factions and tendencies, particularly in the area of social and economic policy (see Die Grünen 1983).

Agalev's (1985a) economic program is characterized by a variety of socialist, liberal, and communitarian elements. Ecolo's (1985b) program is more liberal market oriented than that of the other parties. The difference between more socialist/redistributive and more liberal programs also surfaces in the parties' proposals for a minimum income for each citizen, regardless whether he or she is working. While many Greens advocate a minimum income costing about 40 percent of West Germany's gross national product, a study group in Ecolo proposed a model which would amount to about 20–25 percent of the Belgian GNP, or little more than today's social expenditures.[29]

Tensions among liberal, collectivist/socialist, and communitarian/anarchist principles are articulated in most programmatic debates within ecology parties. Some activists deplore the lack of agreement on specific policy strategies, but others attribute little value to ideological unity. Because the working of markets, bureaucracies, and communitarian networks involves many tradeoffs between values and preferences, it is difficult to commit left-libertarian parties to a single vision of a better society. Moreover, the emphasis on democratic openness rules out hierarchical solutions to conflicts among political visions. In this sense, ideological pluralism and controversy in ecology parties is a vital aspect of their logic of constituency representation. Ecology parties express new ideas, but create no closed, comprehensive doctrine.

Conclusion

Both the Belgian and West German ecology parties have gone through similar stages of development and institutionalization. They draw their support from similar electoral constituencies, primarily young, educated, urban, and secular voters. All three parties are involved in essentially similar policy debates, lack coherent ideological principles, and develop programs in a disjointed, incremental fashion.

The development, electoral support, and programs of the Belgian and West German ecology parties provide some evidence to suggest that external politi-

29. See Opielka (1985) for the West German debate and *La Revue Nouvelle*, 41 (April 1985), no. 4, for a variety of contributions on the Walloon debate.

Table 13
Variations in the environmental conditions influencing ecology parties

	Left-libertarian cleavage	Competitive position of ecology parties	
		Weak	Strong
Political elites and institutions unresponsive to left-libertarian demands: West Germany	High mobilization	national Greens Hamburg GAL (1983/86 and 1987–)	Hesse (1982–1987) Hamburg GAL (1982; 1987)
	Low-to-medium mobilization	local Greens in Frankfurt	local Greens in Bielefeld, Freiburg, Munich, Tübingen
		Baden-Württemberg Greens most small town Green part sections	many counties and small cities in North Rhine Westphalia or Hesse
	High mobilization	local politics in the Brussels, Ghent, and Ottignies sections of Agalev or Ecolo	no case
Political elites and institutions somewhat responsive to left-libertarian demands: Belgium	Low-to-medium mobilization	Agalev in Flanders (medium mobilization) Ecolo in Wallonia (low mobilization)	Ecolo in the Walloon regional assembly (1985–)
		most local party sections in Belgium	Ecolo Liege Agalev in small communities of Schoten and Meise

cal conditions influence their internal structure and decision making. The development of ecology parties in areas where the left-libertarian cleavage is highly mobilized led to more conflicts among tendencies and factions than in areas with less mobilization. Similarly, the programmatic outlook of individual parties is influenced by the environment in which they operate. Cleavage mobilization, national political culture, and institutions, and the choice of party strategy in a strong competitive position also influence the parties' electoral performance.

The interaction between external conditions and internal coalitions in ecology parties can only be studied systematically if the settings vary. For this reason I have chosen parties and subnational party units which combine different levels of left-libertarian movement mobilization, elite openness, and party competitiveness (cf. Table 13). Most West German Greens interviewed for this study come from the state party organizations of Baden-Württemberg, Hamburg, and Hesse, each of which is characterized by a different external opportunity structure. Within Belgium the potential for variation is much more limited since the left-libertarian cleavage is mobilized nowhere near as highly as in West Germany and since Agalev and Ecolo are generally not in a strong competitive position. Nevertheless, the comparison of the West German and Belgian parties can shed light on both differences and universal patterns in the development of left-libertarian politics.

4 | Getting Involved

When Ulli decided to join the Hamburg Greens in the early 1980s, he was already an experienced student politician. He knew a great deal about the politics of agenda setting and debate in exhausting party meetings and had developed a practiced persistence in getting his way. He finds this experience has helped him become an active and effective participant in Green party meetings. Margret, now an unemployed teacher, came to the Freiburg Greens through experience with feminist consciousness-raising groups in the 1970s, and she entered the party to show "that politics can gain a different quality through the participation of women."

But the New Left and feminism are not the only routes leading to ecological politics. Ulrich, a Green municipal councilor from Stuttgart, formerly a theologian and now a professional gardener, had participated in environmental groups before he joined the Greens in 1980. He had briefly been a member of the SPD, but was repelled by the party's anonymous atmosphere and bureaucratic procedures. Fritz, a biologist working for the Frankfurt Zoo and a Green municipal councilor, joined the Greens in the late 1970s because he saw no other way to create an effective pressure group for protecting the environment. Erik, an Agalev activist from Ghent, is a retired chemical engineer who became concerned with the environmental consequences of modern industry and joined the party in 1981. Johan from Brussels took yet another route into Agalev. He was generally interested in ecology issues while studying languages, but decided to participate only when he chanced upon an opportunity to work full time at Agalev's Brussels office to perform his service as a conscientious objector to the military draft. He now intends to remain in the party secretariat after this two-year service is completed.

These six activists were chosen at random and illustrate the vastly different political backgrounds and experiences members bring to ecology parties. All six express distinct hopes and aspirations that inspired their entry into the party and maintain their activism. The parties can reinforce this activism only if they find ways of satisfying at least some of these diverse aspirations. Continued activism, therefore, presupposes a correspondence between members' motivations and the parties' incentives. I call the interaction between individual motivations and selective incentives *commitment mechanisms*.[1] I distinguish five commitment mechanisms, derived from organizational incentives theory.[2] First, parties attract activists on the basis of shared goals and reinforce this commitment by affirming and realizing these objectives. Second, parties provide avenues of participation that reassure militants that their contribution makes a difference. Third, parties create a social atmosphere that promotes solidarity and social integration among activists seeking personal ties and a sense of community. Fourth, parties may provide material resources (such as patronage) to appeal to activists attracted by the prospect of material gain (status, income). Finally, a party may create doctrines and rituals that lead activists to believe in the legitimacy of its collective procedures and the authority of its policy and leadership.

A party's commitment mechanisms are not freely chosen but depend on the range of aspirations and ideologies each member expresses and the institutions and resources the party employs to cultivate them. I argue in this chapter that the Belgian and West German ecology parties appeal to a limited number of left-libertarian activists because the parties operate from a narrow basis of motivations and provide few organizational incentives that reinforce political involvement. The unintended outcome of a participatory vision of left-libertarian party organization is actually a surprisingly restricted participation.

I proceed in three steps. First I analyze the social background and political careers of the 134 Agalev, Ecolo, and Green activists I interviewed. My findings must be interpreted with the caveat that I am relying not on a random sample of all activists but on a core group of continuously involved militants, most of whom hold party and elected office. Their background careers shed some light on the possible motivations and aspirations activists hold as they enter ecological politics. In the second part of this chapter I explore the

1. I am building here on Kanter's (1972:61–74) notion of "commitment mechanism" for the two-way process matching the individual's dispositions to contribute and the collective's efforts to satisfy and shape these expectations. Because of the difference between 19th century communes (in Kanter's case) and 20th century parties, my substantive typology of commitment mechanisms differs from hers.

2. Beginning with Clark and Wilson (1961), numerous typologies of organizational incentives have been introduced. Knoke and Wood's (1981) typology appears most practical for the study of voluntary associations because it places special emphasis on participation as an incentive distinct from purposive and social incentives. Of similar importance is Knoke and Wood's proposal to separate purposive incentive from legitimacy, or the belief in the generalized authority of an organization in guiding its members' actions, at least within a limited zone of authority.

activists' orientations and the party's organizational commitment mechanisms more directly. At that point I also make an effort to distinguish ideologues, lobbyists, and pragmatists in each party and to show each group's relative strength in relation to external circumstances. Then I discuss the parties' low membership enrollment and high turnover as major consequences of constrained commitment mechanisms.

The Careers of Ecology Party Activists

While a reasonable amount of information about left-libertarian voters is available, the same cannot be said for party activists. One would expect, however, that activists are recruited from that spectrum of the electorate which has the highest propensity to support left-libertarian parties: young, highly educated, urban professionals in the public service sector. Indeed, the limited evidence bears out this expectation. Left-libertarian party members tend to be very young compared to the average age of activists in established parties. Almost all available data show that the majority of members and activists is under 35 years old (Table 14). The average age lies somewhere between 34 and 38 years, whether one examines the age distribution of all party members in a district (rows 6 and 7) or of various subgroups of activists with special offices and tasks (rows 1 through 5). Belgian and West German ecology parties are very similar in this respect.

Information on the educational background of left-libertarian activists can be inferred from job descriptions.[3] Most activists are highly educated; they have at least some college education and often hold an advanced university degree (Table 15). Only in the Freiburg Greens does the percentage of party members with university degrees deviate from the normal range, primarily because an extraordinarily large number of university students belongs to this party district.

Occupational data on ecology party members and activists are not only sparse, but pose the additional problem that job descriptions are difficult to categorize or interpret. Again, however, the robustness of the findings suggests that even with varying definitions of employment categories the basic picture would not be altered much (Table 16). The highest percentage of party members and militants indicates employment in the public social service sector, primarily in education. Only among the Freiburg Green party members are students a more numerous group (column 5). More volatile is the percent-

3. In the data sources on Green militants in Baden-Württemberg and Freiburg, the job descriptions are precise enough to know in most instances whether a position requires a university degree or not. Where job descriptions do not reveal minimum educational levels, I have interpreted them in the most conservative way as not requiring university education, thus biasing my findings against the obvious hypothesis that left-libertarian parties attract highly educated people.

Table 14
Age of party activists in the Greens, Agalev, and Ecolo (in percentages)

	Under 25	25–34	35–44	45–59	60 and older	Average age
1. Green interviewees (1985)	3%	47%	29%	14%	7%	37.6 100% (N = 86)
2. Agalev and Ecolo interviewees (1985)	—	38	44	13	6	38.5 100 (N = 48)
3. Green district candidates in the North Rhine–Westphalian state election (1980)	20	41	21	11	6	34.5 100 (N = 150)
4. Green district candidates in the Baden-Württemberg state election (1984)	6	49	31	9	3	36.0 100 (N = 121)
5. Participants at Agalev and Ecolo preelection party conventions (1985)	8	44	34	10	4	35.9 100 (N = 255)
6. Members of the Wiesbaden Green district party (1984)	6	62	16	6	9	35.1 100 (N = 95)
7. Members of the Freiburg Green district party (1985)	18	49	20	6	8	33.7 100 (N = 262)

Sources: own survey (rows 1 and 2); Green state secretariat, North Rhine–Westphalia (row 3); Green state secretariat, Baden-Württemberg (row 4); Kitschelt and Hellemans forthcoming (row 5); *Grüne Hessenzeitung*, Vol. 4 (1984), No. 9: p. 27 (row 6) and Green district party secretariat, Freiburg (row 7).

Table 15
Educational accomplishments of party militants (in percentages)

	University degree	University or college attendance	No university education		
1. Green interviewees (1985)	62%	20%	19%	100%	(N = 86)
2. Agalev and Ecolo interviewees (1985)	75	17	8	100	(N = 48)
3. Green district candidates in the Baden-Württemberg state election (1984)	65	7	27	100	(N = 121)
4. Participants at Agalev and Ecolo preelection party conventions (1985)	44	33	23	100	(N = 255)
5. Members of the Freiburg Green district party (1985)	23	46	32	100	(N = 262)

Note: In rows 3 and 5, educational accomplishments were inferred from the militants' occupation. The figures may understate the actual level of educational achievements to some extent.
Sources: see Table 14.

Table 16
Occupations of ecology party militants (in percentages)

	Green interviewees, 1985	Agalev and Ecolo interviewees, 1985	Agalev and Ecolo conference participants, 1985	Baden-Württemberg Green election candidates, 1984	Members of the Freiburg Green district party, 1985
1. Educational sector, social services, media	31%	31%	36%	45%	16%
2. High school or university student, military or alternative civil service	9	8	8	7	46
3. Political functionaries[a]	13	15	4	b	b
4. Business/liberal professions/entrepreneur	23	25	12	26	7
5. White-collar employee	9	4	19	15	15
6. Blue-collar worker	2	2	3	2	7
7. Unemployed	6	6	5	5	6
8. Retiree, homemaker	6	8	8	—	6
9. No data/missing cases	—	—	5		4
	99%	99%	100%	100%	101%
	(N = 86)	(N = 48)	(N = 250)	(N = 121)	(N = 257)

a. full-time party employees, except parliamentarians
b. data unavailable
Sources: see Table 14.

age of activists and members who hold managerial or professional positions or are self-employed. Among interviewees for this study and among the Baden-Württemberg candidates for the 1984 state elections they represent the second largest group (columns 1, 2, and 4). Among Agalev's and Ecolo's militants attending the 1985 party conventions and among Freiburg party militants they represent a smaller group outnumbered by white-collar employees (columns 3 and 5). In general, white-collar and especially blue-collar workers are under-represented compared to their share in the overall adult population in Belgium and West Germany. In three samples party functionaries constitute a small but noticeable share of militants (columns 1 to 3). The unemployed, homemakers, and retirees make up the remaining balance, but do not amount to a very large group. On the whole the occupational profile of party members and activists confirms the expectation that left-libertarians are predominantly drawn from the ranks of salaried professionals. It provides little support for the argument that an economically deprived segment of the middle class and students with few job prospects form the parties' backbone of supporters.[4]

The age, educational, and occupational distribution of self-libertarian activists is consistent with the expectation that ecology parties represent a post-industrial middle stratum. Most studies of political participation in contemporary democracies have found positive links between higher education and high status occupation and political participation, though not with youth (cf. Barnes and Kaase 1979; Verba and Nie 1975). Given the activists' social background, therefore, we can presume they express a high demand for political participation. Thus, the socioeconomic profile of party members and activists suggests one hypothesis about activists' motivations for joining left-libertarian parties. Participatory commitment mechanisms are likely to be critical for attracting and maintaining their contributions to ecology parties.

The militants' social background is probably a less important determinant of party involvement than the political experiences they accumulated before associating with the party. In their biographies militants usually recount three areas of early political involvement. Many had participated in activities and organizations of the New Left, ranging from demonstrations, discussion circles, and student associations to some of the more doctrinaire New Left Maoist, Trotskyist, and communist splinter parties formed in the late 1960s. A smaller group had been involved in conventional political parties. Although a few militants came from the Christian democratic and liberal parties, most of these transferals took place from the socialist and ethnolinguistic parties (Belgium) or the Social Democratic party (West Germany). Left-libertarian

---

4. It is true that some of the party functionaries did not have steady employment before they were hired by their party. But even if we add some of the functionaries to the number of unemployed, we barely reach the average level of unemployment that prevails in Belgium and West Germany.

social movements, primarily environmental and feminist movements, but including civil rights, Third World, and urban planning (neighborhood) movements constitute a third area of engagement. In a number of instances, militants who had been involved in traditional parties or the New Left participated in left-libertarian movements next. Movement activism usually represents the last stage before joining ecology parties.

Based on the three areas of political activism preceding party involvement and using a residual category for those who had not participated in politics beforehand, we can reconstruct the career paths of the interviewees (Figure 3). The percentage of contributions to left-libertarian movements is somewhat higher in West Germany than in Belgium. A considerably larger share of Green activists had been involved in the New Left and traditional parties than in Agalev or Ecolo. Conversely, for almost a third of the Belgian militants, participation in the party organization was their first major political experience, while the same is true for only 10 percent of the West Germans.

The difference between the two countries can be interpeted in terms of levels of left-libertarian cleavage mobilization. In areas with highly mobilized left-libertarian cleavage, more activists tend to come from the New Left and social movements. Conversely, in ares with low cleavage mobilization, activists are more likely to lack political experience. At the national level, the higher West German mobilization of left-libertarian movement is reflected in the activists' greater political experience, whereas Belgian activists have been somewhat less involved in social movements and to a significant extent lack political experience preceding party membership.

At the subnational level, the impact of cleavage mobilization can be tested by dividing the activists into groups in areas (counties, cities) with high or low left-libertarian mobilization. High mobilization regions are characterized by both above-average electoral support for left-libertarian parties and evidence provided by the interviewed militants that left-libertarian movements revolving around the politics of space and the politics of identity have been important in their region. Where one or both of these conditions are missing, left-libertarian mobilization is moderate or low.[5] Left-libertarian cleavage centers are usually metropolitan areas with large liberal arts oriented universities.

In Table 17, I have divided ecology party militants into four groups according to what political experience their biographies reveal to have played the most important role before joining ecology parties. West German party militants in areas with high left-libertarian mobilization are much more likely to

5. A complete list of the locales from which the Belgian and West German militants I interviewed come is given in the Appendix. Obviously, there are some debatable cases. For instance, Stuttgart, Antwerp, and Liège all show an above average electoral performance for ecology parties, yet I have classified them as areas with medium mobilization because in the view of party militants they lack a broad culture of left-libertarian protest.

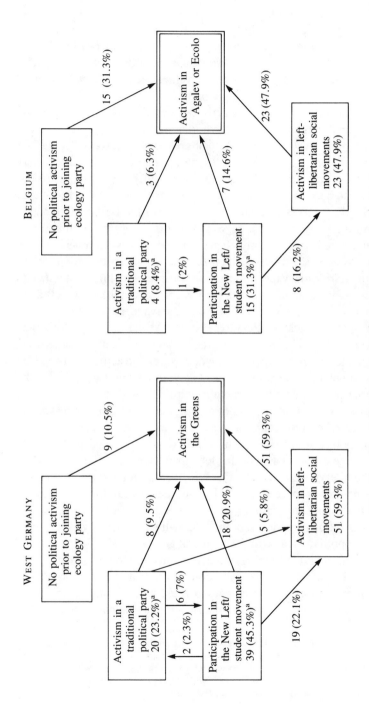

Figure 3. Political careers of party militants in Belgium and West Germany

a. Overall number of all activists who had been involved in a type of political activism at one stage of their political biography.

Table 17
Political career experience of party activists in Belgian and West German areas with high and low left-libertarian cleavage mobilization (in percentages)

		Political career experience					
		New left (and left-libertarian movements)	Left-libertarian movements only	Conventional party membership	No activism before joining ecology party		
West German Greens							
Mobilization of the left-libertarian cleavage	High	53%	28%	15%	4%	100%	(N = 47)
	Low	15	36	31	18	100	(N = 39)
	All Greens	36	31	22	10	99	(N = 86)
Belgian ecology parties							
Mobilization of the left-libertarian cleavage	High	58	21	5	16	100	(N = 19)
	Low	14	38	7	41	100	(N = 29)
	All Agalev and Ecolo	31	31	6	31	99	(N = 48)

have New Left backgrounds, often combined with movement participation, than elsewhere (Table 17). Interviewees who were only active in left-libertarian movements, belonged to conventional political parties, or lack political career experiences are more numerous in the areas with low or moderate cleavage mobilization.

In both countries militants' ties to the left-libertarian subculture of political organizations and movements are greatest in areas of high cleavage mobilization. As Table 17 shows, nationality has little effect on this association. Yet Green militants in areas with low left-libertarian mobilization tend to come more frequently from conventional parties (31 percent), while Agalev and Ecolo militants in similar regions are more frequently political novices (41 percent). Overall, the lower intensity of left-libertarian mobilization in Belgium translates into a somewhat less politicized past for Agalev's and Ecolo's activists.

In terms of the theory outlined in Chapter 2, two mechanisms can explain the link between individual political experience and the local party setting: recruitment and representation. In areas where movements are highly mobilized, it is more likely that experienced individuals will join ecology parties. Moreover, experienced activists are more likely to be chosen as municipal councilors, party executives, and parliamentarians, the pool from which interviewees in this study were drawn.[6]

The Mainsprings of Party Activism

Students of party involvement have always found it difficult to determine the motivations and rewards of those who contribute time and energy to parties.[7] Unobtrusive measures that can reveal true motivations do not exist. The unreliability of direct investigation of commitment mechanisms is illustrated by the finding that militants usually attribute very different motivations for party activism to themselves than to other party members (Eldersveld 1964: 302). Given these difficulties, in my report on interviews with Belgian and West German ecology party militants I explore the nature of commitment mechanisms indirectly through a content analysis of their political biographies, relying not only on what they say about their sincere intentions, but also on an interpretation of the logic of the situation they faced.[8] Moreover, I base

6. In Chapter 7 I explain that for winning party or electoral office political experience matters most in centers with left-libertarian mobilization.

7. Some of the hazards of motivational analysis have been discussed in Kornberg et al. (1979:86–87) and Janda (1980: 126–32). Attempts to analyze motivations for joining and contributing to parties are Eldersveld (1983), Falke (1982:96–110), Hauss (1978: chap. 6), and Kirkpatrick (1976). The limited usefulness of these measures is discussed by Greven (1987:58).

8. I am influenced here by Boudon's (1984:58–59) view that the "rationality of an action can be revealed and interpreted only if the structure of the situation is known in which an individual is placed."

my account on the ways militants describe the party's atmosphere, the membership, and general reasons for turnover, increase, and decline of participants.

Purposive and Participatory Motivations and Orientations

All the militants I interviewed expressed a strong personal concern with the parties' political goals and wished to help shape them. Because of the nature of the interview sample, it would be surprising to find activists who were not concerned with political purposes and chances for participation. What is more interesting, however, is the nature of the purposive and participatory commitments the activists support. In Chapter 2, I distinguished three ideal types of party activists based on the nature of their beliefs and the priority they attribute to party objectives, strategy, and organizational form. These three dimensions enable us to reconstruct the purposive and participatory motivations of Belgian and West German party activists and provide initial insight into the group structure of ecology parties. The militants' view of party objectives and strategies reveals their purposive orientation. Their commitment to a more or less participatory form of party organization indicates the importance they attribute to direct rank-and-file control of the decision-making process.

Ecology parties possess no comprehensive ideological doctrine and program for social transformation, but militants have varying conceptions of programmatic concerns. Party activists have broad views of the parties' goals if they (1) use the language of modern liberal, socialist, and anarchist ideologies to explain their objectives, (2) actively employ right/left vocabulary to describe political conflict, and (3) express an interest in a wide variety of concrete policy areas in their own political involvement.[9] Conversely, they express narrow programmatic concerns if they lack all or most of these conceptual schemes for organizing their political beliefs and instead focus on a single policy area they address in more or less technical terms as a "problem fixer," without placing it in a broader field of political controversy.

Table 18 shows that representation of party objectives is linked to militants' political experience and location in areas with high or low left-libertarian mobilization. Broad programmatic conceptualizations prevail among activists coming from New Left or conventional party backgrounds. Narrow programmatic concerns are more typical of social movement activists or party members without previous political involvement. About two fifths of all ecology activists in areas with low and medium mobilization, but only one fifth in areas with high mobilization, express narrow purposes. Nationality makes

---

9. I have classified the activists' ideological conceptualizations of party goals based on a content analysis of the political objectives they stated in recounting their own political biography. Good elaborations of the methodology from which this "content analysis" of activists' beliefs is developed are provided by Klingemann (1979) and Putnam (1973).

Table 18
Breadth of perceived party objectives, political career experiences, and cleavage mobilization of Belgian and West German ecology party activists (in percentages)

	Broad view of party objectives	Narrow view of party objectives		
Political career experiences				
New left (and left-libertarian movements)	96%	4%	100%	(N = 46)
Conventional party membership	82	18	100	(N = 22)
Left-libertarian movements only	48	52	100	(N = 42)
No activism before joining ecology party	42	58	100	(N = 24)
All activists	69	31	100	(N = 134)
Cleavage mobilization and program orientation				
West Germany (Greens)				
Mobilization of the left- High	77	23	100	(N = 47)
libertarian cleavage Low	54	46	100	(N = 39)
All Green activists	69	31	100	(N = 86)
Belgium (Agalev and Ecolo)				
Mobilization of the left- High	84	16	100	(N = 19)
libertarian cleavage Low	66	34	100	(N = 29)
All Agalev and Ecolo	73	27	100	(N = 48)

little difference, once left-libertarian mobilization is accounted for. Sixty-nine percent of the Green activists and 73 percent of the Agalev and Ecolo activists are concerned with broad political goals.

All of these associations are to be expected. The New Left has always engaged in comprehensive discourse about the foundations of economic and political power. Similarly, activists who used to be members of conventional parties tend to be concerned with a wide range of topics, leaving these parties because of deep disagreement with their policies. Militants who have been active only in left-libertarian movements, however, more frequently express concern with a narrow rather than a broad program. In particular this applies to activists from environmental movements who often have drifted into the parties because they expected to pursue their cause here more effectively than in social movements. In some cases movement activists have been recruited to the parties' electoral lists without being party members (see Chapter 7).

A second dimension of purposive motivations for joining ecology parties concerns the activists' attitudes toward strategies of social change. Roughly speaking, one group favors incremental change and piecemeal reform, while the other believes in the importance of catastrophic ruptures and large-scale social transformations. The criterion distinguishing these outlooks is the degree of willingness to enter alliances with other political forces, especially competing political parties, with the objective of taking small steps toward realizing party objectives. Because many militants refuse to take a clear-cut position on this issue, the spectrum of views must be divided into "radicals" who call for sudden, fundamental change, "moderates" who advocate gradual reform, and "uncommitted" or "opportunistic" activists who intend to make up their minds on a case-by-case basis.

Table 19 shows how strategic position is linked to political career paths, left-libertarian mobilization, and the view of party objectives. Although New Left activists are most likely to be strategic radicals, they also include a considerable number of moderates. Radicalism is lower among social movement activists and conventional party members, and political novices are strategically most moderate. At the same time, the percentage of those who remain uncommitted is highest among social movement activists and political novices. As the second section of Table 19 shows, national affiliation and left-libertarian cleavage mobilization also make a difference in strategic outlook. Agalev and Ecolo activists are predominantly moderate, whether they are located in centers or peripheries of the left-libertarian cleavage, while Green militants are more radical, with the degree of radicalism clearly linked to the area in which they are active. Section three of the Table indicates that militants with a broad conceptualization of party goals tend to be either radical or moderate, whereas those with a narrow ideology are rarely radical, most frequently remaining uncommitted to any strategic position.

These patterns of strategic orientation can be explained in terms of the theoretical framework developed in Chapter 2. The militants' strategic positions depend on their political biography and objectives; these in turn are influenced by the circumstances of left-libertarian mobilization and the accessibility of political institutions to left-libertarian demands. The associations in Tables 18 and 19 begin to identify the types of activists I have described as ideologues, lobbyists, and pragmatists. Ideologues, with broad conceptualizations of party objectives and radical strategic commitments, are more common in West Germany, where political institutions are less open to left-libertarian demands, particularly in areas with high left-libertarian mobilization. Ideological predispositions tend to be shaped through extensive involvement in the New Left and, to a lesser extent, social movements. Pragmatists, in contrast, are more prominent in Belgium's more open political system and in both countries in areas with low left-libertarian mobilization. Pragmatists tend to be ex-members of conventional parties or political novices. In both instances they have had less exposure to the left-libertarian subculture than militants coming from the New Left or left-libertarian movements. Activists undecided about their strategic commitments, finally, tend to be lobbyists. A considerable share of uncommitted activists has been involved only in left-libertarian movements and has a narrow, issue-specific conceptualization of party objectives.

Whereas the militants' perception of the parties' key objectives and their

Table 19
Political strategy, political career experience, cleavage mobilization, and view of party goals among West German and Belgian party activists (in percentages)

		Strategic commitment			
		Radical	Uncommitted/ opportunist	Moderate	
Political career experiences					
New left (and left-libertarian movements)		43%	18%	39%	100% (N = 46)
Conventional party membership		32	13	55	100 (N = 22)
Left-libertarian movements only		19	36	45	100 (N = 42)
No activism before joining ecology party		8	29	63	100 (N = 24)
All activists		28	25	47	100 (N = 134)
Cleavage mobilization and program orientation					
West Germany (Greens)					
Mobilization of the left-libertarian cleavage	High	51	28	21	100 (N = 47)
	Low	26	31	44	101 (N = 39)
All Green activists		40	29	31	100 (N = 86)
Belgium (Agalev and Ecolo)					
Mobilization of the left-libertarian cleavage	High	11	16	73	100 (N = 19)
	Low	3	17	80	100 (N = 29)
All Agalev and Ecolo		6	17	77	100 (N = 48)
View of party objectives	Broad	36	14	50	100 (N = 92)
	Narrow	10	48	43	101 (N = 42)

strategic views highlight different purposive orientations, a third dimension of belief systems and motivation concerns their participatory commitments and view of the parties' organizational form. Militants differ over the significance of open, participatory, grassroots-oriented party structures. Responses to the following questions reveal the extent and nature of participatory commitments best. Should party executives be paid professionals? How often should electoral positions in parliaments rotate among different party representatives? Should party executives and parliamentarians be allowed to express policy positions not discussed by party conventions? Should formal membership or continuous participation be the criterion for having a say over party policy and strategy? How tolerant should the party be vis-à-vis internal disagreement, factionalism, and lack of solidarity and discipline in the pursuit of an objective?

The participatory view opts for minimum elite authority and maximum significance for the individuality and participation of each militant, while a more instrumental view emphasizes professionalization, organizational stability, and cohesiveness. In a nutshell, the participatory position calls for a logic of constituency representation, while the instrumental position is willing to make concessions to a logic of party competition. To keep the analysis comparatively simple, I have dichotomized the militants' views on the significance of grassroots participation.

Table 20 relates political career paths, nationality, and left-libertarian mobilization to more instrumental or more participatory views of party organization. Forty percent of the militants take an unambiguously participatory position, while 60 percent lean toward a more instrumental position. Former members of conventional parties are most inclined to support a more instrumental party form in both Belgium and West Germany. Participants in New Left protests and social movements take the middle ground; many call for a highly participatory party structure, but a majority favors a more instrumental party organization. Political experience, particularly in organizations striving to gain power, thus promotes a more instrumentalist view of politics even among New Left activists who want to democratize society. These activists have learned that a certain degree of organization, discipline, and internal control is necessary to pursue political objectives.

Among the West German Greens, activists who have participated only in social movements and those with little political experience prior to joining the party are especially committed to participatory organizational forms. The high level of left-libertarian movement mobilization in West Germany translates into strong support for participatory objectives. In Belgium, on the other hand, where left-libertarian cleavage mobilization is more subdued, militants with movement or no political experience insist with less vigor on a highly participatory party organization. Moreover, the second part of Table 20 shows

Table 20
View of the party's organizational form, political career experience, and cleavage mobilization among West German and Belgian ecology party activists (in percentages)

		Highly participatory view	More instrumental view		
Political career experiences					
West Germany (Greens)					
New Left (and left-libertarian movements)		42%	58%	100%	(N = 31)
Conventional party membership		32	68	100	(N = 19)
Left-libertarian movements only		63	37	100	(N = 27)
No activism before joining ecology party		55	45	100	(N = 9)
All Greens		48	52	100	(N = 86)
Belgium (Agalev and Ecolo)					
New Left (and left-libertarian movements)		40	60	100	(N = 15)
Conventional party membership		—	100	100	(N = 3)
Left-libertarian movements only		27	73	100	(N = 15)
No activism before joining ecology party		20	80	100	(N = 15)
All Agalev and Ecolo		27	73	100	(N = 48)
Cleavage mobilization and program orientation					
West Germany (Greens)					
Mobilization of the left-	High	49	51	100	(N = 47)
libertarian cleavage	Low	46	54	100	(N = 39)
Belgium (Agalev and Ecolo)					
Mobilization of the left-	High	37	63	100	(N = 19)
libertarian cleavage	Low	21	79	100	(N = 29)
All activists		40	60	100	(N = 134)

that cleavage mobilization makes a more pronounced difference in views of party organization in Belgium.

Having reviewed the party militants' programmatic, strategic, and organizational outlook, we can now determine the relative strength of ideologues, lobbyists, and pragmatists in the Belgian and West German ecology parties by combining the three dimensions. Ideologues, lobbyists, and pragmatists are ideal types of activists with specific clusters of attitudes and preferences. If most of the West German and Belgian ecologists can be described by these types, the categories are useful for the analysis of intraparty dynamics. Table 21 is designed to test this claim.

In ecology parties ideologues are militants who emphasize a participatory party organization, a broad program, and radical strategy. Of all activists, 16.4 percent fit into this category (cell A). Predominantly West German Greens, they are referred to in that party as "fundamentalists." A second group of "near-ideologues," amounting to 8.2 percent of the sample and again mostly German Greens, combines radical strategy with a broad political program, but a more instrumental notion of party organization (cell B). Upon closer inspection, these are predominantly Green activists with an orthodox New Left or left socialist party career and a continuing commitment to elements of a socialist program, strategy, and organization. In the Greens they are called "ecosocialists."

Lobbyists have narrow programmatic concerns and attribute great importance to strategy, but waver between radical and moderate positions and give party organization considerable significance (cell G). Together with the "near-lobbyists" who attribute little significance to a participatory organizational form (cell H), lobbyists account for close to 15 percent of those interviewed.

Pragmatists value broad programs and moderate strategies and take an instrumental approach to party organization. If we include "near-pragmatists" with a narrow conception of political objectives, 44 percent of all activists are pragmatists (cells J and L). In this group, the Belgian activists interviewed are overrepresented, with 67 percent of them being (near) pragmatists, while only 31 percent of the Greens fall into the same category. These Greens call themselves "realists."

Ideologues, lobbyists, and pragmatists and their close relations represent 50 percent of the cells in Table 21 but 84 percent of the militants, leaving only 16 percent of the militants for the remaining six cells. This distribution suggests that ideologues, lobbyists, and pragmatists are empirically crucial types of party activists with characteristic beliefs and orientations.

Combinations of strategic, programmatic, and organizational views not covered by the three main types are less important. Only cells E and I with 8.2 percent of the militants deserve further interpretation. They include activists

Table 21
Styles of Activism among Green, Agalev, and Ecolo party militants

	Collective goods important (broad view of the party program)		Collective goods unimportant (narrow view of party program)	
	Private goods of the party organization		Private goods of the party organization	
	Participation important	Participation unimportant	Participation important	Participation unimportant
Radical strategy and tactics: Pursuit of selective goods undermines commitment to collective goods	(A) Ideologues ALL: 17.3% (N = 23) G*: 24% (N = 21) A/E*: 4% (N = 2) "fundamentalists"	(B) Near-ideologues ALL: 8.2% (N = 11) G: 12% (N = 10) A/E: 2% (N = 1) "ecosocialists"	(C) ALL: 1.5% (N = 2) G: 2% (N = 2) A/E: —	(D) ALL: 1.5% (N = 2) G: 2% (N = 2) A/E: —
Opportunistic strategy and tactics: Pursuit of selective goods, *no matter what* the commitment to collective goods	(E) ALL: 6.7% (N = 9) G: 5% (N = 4) A/E: 10% (N = 5)	(F) ALL: 3.0% (N = 4) G: 3% (N = 3) A/E: 2% (N = 1)	(G) Lobbyists ALL: 11.1% (N = 15) G: 16% (N = 14) A/E: 2% (N = 1)	(H) Near-lobbyists ALL: 3.7% (N = 5) G: 5% (N = 4) A/E: 2% (N = 1)
Moderate strategy and tactics: Pursuit of selective goods reinforces commitment to collective goods	(I) ALL: 1.5% (N = 2) G: — A/L: 4% (N = 2)	(J) Pragmatists ALL: 32.1% (N = 43) G: 23% (N = 20) A/L: 48% (N = 23) "realists"	(K) ALL: 2.2% (N = 3) G: — A/L: 6% (N = 3)	(L) Near-pragmatists ALL: 11.9% (N = 16) G: 8% (N = 7) A/L: 19% (N = 9) "realists"

a. Green activists only
b. Agalev and Ecolo activists only

with moderate or uncommitted strategic views valuing comprehensive political programs and participatory party organization. In the Greens this group approximates a small tendency that has been labeled "ecolibertarians."

To validate the usefulness of the typology of party activists one final time, we can link near-ideologues, lobbyists, and pragmatists to the environmental and biographical background that renders each type important (Table 22). Ideologues come from the New Left and/or left-libertarian social movements and are especially prominent in areas with high left-libertarian mobilization. Pragmatists are characterized by the opposite traits, while lobbyists represent an intermediate group recruiting itself mostly from the ranks of activists in left-libertarian movements and political novices. To make the group analysis of ecology parties more realistic, I illustrate each main type of party activist with a few political biographies.

Ideologues and ecosocialists draw most of their supporters from the New Left of the 1960s and 1970s. They also attract a considerable number of activists from traditional parties, primarily from the left fringes of socialist and social democratic parties. Bernd, a 37-year-old Hamburg lawyer, is a representative "fundamentalist." He was marginally involved in the student movement and later participated in various New Left groups, but could never settle on any one of them because they were too sectarian for his taste. In the 1970s he helped found a tenants' association in the Hamburg region. Bernd was at first repelled by the Greens and their initially narrow concern with ecology, but he joined in 1980 when he realized that the new party served as an antidote to the sectarianism of the Hamburg Left and provided a new progressive vision. Bernd remains firmly committed to a radical strategy and rejects efforts to make the party an electoral fighting machine. Another fundamentalist is Myriam, a teacher and Ecolo militant from Liège in her late thirties, who belonged to Maoist groups in the early 1970s and then drifted out of politics. Later, she became involved in organic agriculture and was recruited into the party because of her ecological engagement. She still expresses a broad commitment to a socialist-feminist world view and strongly criticizes efforts to moderate the party's strategy and rationalize its organization.

The ecosocialist career and outlook is exemplified by Rainer, a 38-year-old sociology student and activist in the Hamburg Greens. He became politically aware in the late 1960s under the influence of the student movement and soon joined a Maoist party, the Kommunistischer Bund. In the late 1970s his party sent him to another city to build an alliance among movement groups that would use the banner of ecology and anti-nuclear activism, but were controlled by his party. When these efforts failed, he joined the Alternative List in Hamburg and only in the mid-1980s, with great reluctance, became a member of the Greens. He favors a radical strategy and party discipline. For that reason, he continues to work for what is left of his cadre party, too.

Table 22
Types of party activists, mobilization of the left-libertarian cleavage, and political career experiences (in percentages)

		Ideologues and near-ideologues	Lobbyists and near-lobbyists	Pragmatists and near-pragmatists	
Cleavage mobilization					
Mobilization of the left-libertarian cleavage	High	45%	18%	38%	101% (N = 56)
	Low	16	18	66	100 (N = 57)
All activists		30	18	52	100 (N = 113)
Political career experiences					
New Left (and left-libertarian movements)		59	5	29	
Conventional party membership		21	5	19	
Left-libertarian movements only		18	60	29	
No activism before joining ecology party		3	30	24	
		101	100	101	
		(N = 34)	(N = 20)	(N = 59)	

Lobbyists mostly represent militants whose dominant political experience has revolved around a specific left-libertarian movement. We also find among their ranks a significant number of novice activists who lack any appreciable prior political experience. Paul, a 38-year-old journalist and militant in Agalev Antwerp, is representative. Before joining the party, he had long been active in local environmental conflicts in the Antwerp region. He also participated in a traditional nature protection association in Belgium, the King Baudouin Foundation. In trying to combine his environmental concerns and journalistic profession, he soon became embroiled in a series of controversies over newspaper columns he had written that were critical of official environmental policy. He initially opposed Agalev because he thought the party had imposed itself on the ecology movement in Flanders and only in 1983 did he begin to participate in Agalev. He values a decentralized, participatory organization and is reluctant to endorse a single political strategy.

Pragmatists and moderate lobbyists, finally, are the largest group among the Green, Agalev, and Ecolo militants and show a fairly balanced distribution of career paths. These "realists" draw more activists from traditional parties and from the pool of political novices than the other groups. Yet they still get considerable support from people with past New Left involvement or a commitment to social movements. Hubert, for instance, a 31-year-old instructor at the University of Marburg, was involved in the tail end of the student movement, then briefly joined the SPD, but soon became dissatisfied and began to participate in a libertarian loose New Left network. He belongs to the founding members of the Marburg Green party section and favors a political course aimed at building an effective party capable of pushing German politics toward a gradual implementation of the Green program.

A similar outlook is endorsed by Norbert, a 58-year-old retired postal worker who lives in a small town south of Frankfurt. He joined the socialist youth organization in 1946 and belonged to the SPD's left wing between 1959 and 1980. In the 1960s he participated in the Easter March movement, developing sympathies for Maoism and the unorthodox Left. During a surge of protest against the extension of the Frankfurt airport in his neighborhood, he left the SPD in 1980 and helped build the local Green party organization. In Agalev, Dirk, a 26-year-old member of the national party executive, also supports a pragmatist view of ecological politics. He was a student at Luc Versteylen's Catholic high school and participated in a few actions of the Anders Gaan Leven movement, but had joined the Agalev work group, the precursor of the party organization, by 1981. Although he originally opposed an electoralist strategy, he is now firmly committed to a moderate party course and criticizes radical positions as well as Versteylen's charismatic leadership of the revival movement Anders Gaan Leven.

To conclude, the analysis of purposive and participatory orientations in ecology parties has yielded three findings. It has shown the utility of disaggregating party activists into subgroups. Variation among their orientations and aspirations is too wide to permit meaningful interpretation of party behavior as a result of a leaders-and-led dualism. Moreover, my analysis has illustrated an association between external conditions (cleavage mobilization, national institutions) and the relative strength of intraparty groups. Mechanisms of recruitment and representation explain this linkage between context and individual disposition. Finally, the analysis is a first indication of the central political tendencies in the Greens, Agalev, and Ecolo. While the Greens are more likely to press for a "pure" left-libertarian program, organizational form, and radical strategy, the Belgian parties are more moderate.

Purposive and Participatory Incentives

Although ecology party activists express a broad range of commitments to the goals and participatory procedures of their parties, the actual process of politics in the parties is frequently a source of great disappointment. Many interviewees feel that the parties' immersion in the routine details of policy submerges the "big picture" of ecological politics. The pace of party activism is increasingly set by the agenda of established political institutions such as city councils or legislatures. Militants worry that the tyranny of attending to innumerable decision problems and legal details erodes the enthusiasm for left-libertarian programs and ideas that have provided the driving force of mobilization in the years following initial electoral success.

Tom, a Green municipal councilor, believes the party has shifted from concern with policy content to a fixation on strategy and organizational structure. "We tend to be more concerned now with *how* to do things than with *what* should be done," he says. Olivier from Ecolo Brussels notes that his party is losing its playfulness and utopian idealism; his colleague Pierre deplores the disappearance of celebrations and extraparliamentary activities which used to reinforce a common sense of purpose. Thomas, a Green municipal councilor from Stuttgart belonging to the more utopian and ambitious wing of his party, finds that as an elected party representative he frustrates many of his fellow militants by excessively legalistic and technical arguments about the feasibility of policy change.

Wilfried from Agalev Brussels laments that often people join to discuss concrete issues but are repelled by the dry, abstract, and technical level of many of the debates. Criticizing these expectations, Heinz from the Wiesbaden Greens observes that many enter the party as a "political community college" and are disappointed when it fails to live up to this model. Ecology parties raised hopes for social and political change they have great difficulty reconciling with their modest practical accomplishments. Raymond from Ecolo Liège finds that "for activists who want to change the world, it is difficult to settle for changing this street." And Frederic in Brussels general-izes that, "we are a little group doing not very interesting things." As many observe, intellectuals especially are easily put off by technical debates about small steps of political change and disdain taking care of the mundane details of local political business. Women also tend to dislike the technical debates in party meetings and get involved primarily only when gender issues come to the fore. As one women activist from the Berlin Alternative List argued: "It's my experience that many more women join a discussion when a district or area group debates women's issues than when the discussion conerns other is-sues. . . . The uninteresting topics, the repulsive discussions take away the enjoyment of politics and the engagement that women seek much more than do men."[10]

Whether activists like it or not, the instances that provide the most powerful reinforcement of purposive motivations are electoral advances. Although many activists tend to downplay the role of elections, the pride and celebra-tions after victory at the polls as well as the searching debates and internal party conflicts after defeat give testimony to the importance of electoral performance even for those activists who advocate a nonelectoralist logic of constituency representation.

A number of interviewees attribute the growing gap between the objectives and the realities of party politics to "generational" changes among party militants.[11] In Agalev and Ecolo activists note that early participants who viewed ecology as part of a new lifestyle have disappeared because the party could not meet their needs. Since around 1982, militants with little political experience and limited interest in radical programmatic questions are said to have shaped a new political style. In the Greens, ideologues joined relatively early on and now often feel threatened by what they perceive as the rapid entry of pragmatists, an influx they attribute to the party's electoral success and, in some German states, its actual or potential competitive strength. Green ideo-logues argue that different generations are set apart by ideological, stylistic, and strategic disagreements. According to the most common reconstruction of the party's development, activists from left-libertarian movements and the New Left dominated the party in the early 1980s, attracting more pragmatic militants with moderate and ill-defined political concerns after the big elec-toral successes of 1982/83. Gertrud from northern Hesse states that "now many people enter the party as a party, not as the representative of definite political concerns." Others assert that new members tend to be apolitical and to show little interest in the national direction of the party. While pragmatic

10. "Quotierung—quo vadis? Zwei Jahre Quotierung in der AL Berlin. Gespräch mit Sabine Fischer und Angela Schäfers," *Tageszeitung,* October 18, 1985.

11. The concept of generation refers to groups defined by a common set of formative political experience, rather than by age or life cycle. For different notions of generation, see Fogt (1982).

new members may be more attuned to changes in practical activities of the party, they often clash with some of the older militants who have a more ideological or single-issue commitment.

But a number of militants also observe a different tendency among recent joiners. They express a more spontaneous, concrete and less theoretical, abstract commitment to politics. This "anarchist" spirit easily alienates them from the routines of daily party politics and makes them withdraw from the party altogether. Especially in Hamburg, where an ecosocialist faction clinging to remnants of Marxism dominates the party, activists notice the gap between the established core group and the more expressive and emotional politics popular among recent joiners. Günther claims the latter have a more moral than a political-economic view of politics. And Thomas, emphasizing the influence of anarchism on his own views, states that "abstract concepts don't count with the young."

These assessments of new members are not necessarily inconsistent. Novices often subscribe to an "expressive" understanding of politics but only those who accommodate to the technicalities and routines of party politics stay on. In addition to the recruitment of new members, pragmatists have gained strength in ecology parties also through socialization and learning. In a number of instances, former ideologues or lobbyists have taken a pragmatic turn. Wolfgang and Heinrich, close friends and activists in the Freiburg Greens, recall they initially felt committed to a radical strategy and political program but through their involvement in local politics have become de facto moderates trying to reform society in small steps.

Despite these observations, however, the trend toward pragmatism is by no means certain. In Freiburg or Hamburg, for instance, which are left-libertarian strongholds, the party still attracts a continuing influx of ideologues and maintains a radical spirit. Pragmatists, however, have gained a dominant position in ecology party sections located in areas with low left-libertarian mobilization, such as the less metropolitan areas of West Germany and much of Belgium.

The frustrations of participation I have discussed so far are due to the immersion of parties in an established institutional setting of electoral rules, legislatures, bureaucracies, and governments. They illustrate the clash between militants committed to a unique ideology-based logic of constituency representation and institutional settings forcing ecology parties to adopt some elements of a logic of party competition. Yet, ironically, there is another even stronger force that makes it difficult to maintain purposive membership commitments: the parties' internal rules and efforts to keep their policies and strategies directly responsible to the rank and file bring about consequences the militants have not intended.

Militants experience the "perverse effects" of an open, participatory party organization as a discrepancy between their rights of participation in the parties and the resources they can bring to bear on political involvement. The decision-making regulations in ecology parties allow anyone to participate in any party meeting with a right to be heard and influence the decision, if not also to vote.[12] Ecology parties rely on a radically egalitarian and participatory set of *rules* and *rights* for each party member. These rules are blind, however, to the fact that activists' *resources* for exercising their rights, such as time, information, rhetorical skill, political experience, and the self-confidence to speak before a large audience, are distributed unequally. In a sense, the same objection that democratic theory has turned against an open, pluralist polity can be turned against participatory intraparty decision making: if the rules grant political access to anyone but the resources are unequally distributed, the pluralist choir sings with an upper-class voice (Schattschneider 1960). The most resourceful activist can set the political agenda and dominate the decision process.

The objection that unequal resources lead to unequal chances of participation is ubiquitous in all three ecology parties. Usually those who complain are people with more limited political resources and local activists, primarily of a moderate strategic and programmatic bent, who feel that a less representative, more resourceful group of activists can dominate the overall outlook of the party. Günther from the Hamburg Greens says that he is one of the few core activisits with several children and a full-time job giving him little disposable time to attend to political business. His commitments prevent him from participating in important debates and informal meetings and, in his view, limit his political influence compared to that of people with more disposable time and fewer social obligations. Marita from the Hessian Greens fears that "politics takes over too much within the party" and observes the frustration of many party members who feel there are too many occasions "where one has to be present if one wants to make an impact on the party."

Similar complaints are common even in Agalev and Ecolo, where ideological differences are less divisive. Herman from Agalev Antwerp suspects that "eternal students" and unemployed intellectuals are in the process of taking over the party because they can invest so much more time in political activism than others. Pierre from Ecolo Brussels talks about the rise of a "political class" within the party. In a similar vein, Seppe from Agalev Leuven feels that leadership is exercised informally through resourceful individuals. And Michel from Namur declares that influence is a function of time spent in party meetings.

12. One restriction is that the right to cast a vote in a decision process may depend on membership in a corporate organ (party conference, executive, parliamentary group, etc.). But power is often exercised more through the presence and political rhetoric of activists than the formal right to vote.

These militants realize that under conditions of resource constraints there is a tradeoff between participatory openness and political equality. Less openness and a more tightly structured system of representation and delegation with the authority and legitimacy to exclude from deliberations activists who may have the time for politics, but no mandate from their party membership, might equalize chances of influencing policy. This dilemma is expressed well in the statement of a former West Berlin parliamentarian of the Alternative List: "There is a contradiction that we have not yet solved. On the one hand, in the name of grassroots democracy, we do not really accept any authoritative decision level. On the other, this creates free spaces for political decisions as a consequence of which political decisions are not made by elected militants, but by informal circles, by certain people who sit down together."[13]

To overstate the problem slightly, a party with flexible opportunities for participation and no restraints on the activities of the most resourceful tends to become a Hobbesian world of inequality and anarchy; the fittest and most powerful, a group of "political entrepreneurs" who devote their life to politics, survive to dominate the parties. This Hobbesian world contributes to another source of frustration with political participation, an inconsistent, chaotic decision-making process in which resolutions rarely gain binding force for any length of time. Because authority to make decisions is dispersed and vested with those present at particular meetings, activists who lose a vote routinely try to reverse the decision whenever a low turnout of their opponents offers them an opportunity to prevail. Because decision procedures are fluid, the rules of decision making themselves become the object of countless controversies. Many activists feel that such "meta-debates" about decision rules, in which politicians with skill, experience, and tenacity excel, drive the deliberation of concrete policy matters out of party meetings and weaken purposive and participatory commitments. At one party conference of the Baden-Württemberg Greens, a speaker received warm applause for his description of Green party conventions as a form of torture which discourages activism and erodes party membership.[14] Concern with the uncertainty and shifting nature of decision rules is widespread, but probably most sharply articulated by militants who have a professional background in administration, law, or economics. Particularly in the Greens, activists complain, in the words of Kurt from Hamburg, about the "incomprehensible labyrinth of work groups and party institutions" in which it is difficult to determine when and how decisions have been reached.

In a nutshell, ecology party activists experience all the frustrations of collective decision making Hirschman (1981:92–120) describes in his study

13. Interview with Cordula Schulz, member of the West Berlin parliament, *Stachlige Argumente*, no. 27 (July–August 1984), 14–15.
14. Cf. *Grüne Blätter*, 4, no. 5 (May 1984), 5.

of private and public pursuits. Militants expend untold hours on reaching small decisions, siphoning off political enthusiasm. Decisions depend on chance factors such as the turnout of militants, the timing and sequence in which proposals are presented, and the social atmosphere that prevails at the meeting at the precise moment when a decision is made. And since decisions are easily revised, if not reversed, ecology parties sometimes run into the problem of revolving majorities when the same issue is subject to repeated votes.

Overall, the frustrations of participatory decision making are felt more intensely where ecology parties are polarized around ideologues and pragmatists. As later chapters show in detail, this is more often the case in the centers of left-libertarian cleavage mobilization, at the state or national rather than the local level of party organization, and in the West German Greens than in Agalev and Ecolo.

Solidary Commitments

Even though purposive and participatory commitment mechanisms are clearly most important for attracting militants to and keeping them in ecology parties, social atmosphere, the normative and personal bonds among activists, is an important factor in sustaining activism.[15] As Toon from Agalev Leuven says, "a party is not a social club, but people *are* looking for the psychological level." The language of solidarity, community, and conviviality plays an important role in ecological politics, yet the social base and patterns of intraparty interaction impede the development of a culture of solidarity.

Small size and location of party sections in the peripheries of the left-libertarian cleavage favor the development of solidary ties. Such groups are engaged in continuous face-to-face interaction and experience few ideological or strategic divisions. This facilitates more diffuse social relations beyond the realm of strictly political topics. Green militants in Hamburg and Frankfurt report that in particular the smaller suburban party sections that are somewhat removed from old cores of left-libertarian activism develop an integrative social climate in which politics is associated with personal friendship. Moreover, in less mobilized areas more interviewees mention solidarity commitments and personal ties to people who were already party activists as reasons for joining their party. This is particularly important in Agalev and Ecolo, while German Greens rarely emphasize the role of social contacts.

In ecology parties women constitute a somewhat higher percentage of members than in the established German and Belgian mass parties and more

15. Most studies find that solidary incentives are less important for joining than for maintaining party activism. Compare Conway and Feigert (1968) and Mayntz (1959:79–80). For this reason, parties and other voluntary organizations often create social commitment mechanisms. See Lammert (1976:79), Valen and Katz (1964:69), and Wilson (1962:166–68).

often demand solidary commitments. In Ecolo and Agalev women represent about one quarter, and in the Greens about 30–35 percent. Among the interviewees women tend to have less prior political experience and are more likely to mention personal contacts as an entrée to the parties.[16] Younger women often became politicized first in feminist consciousness-raising groups, where they developed a critical approach to male-dominated, instrumental, and competitive styles of political interaction. Margret from Freiburg, for instance, emphasizes that as a feminist she would drop out of politics were it not for the close human interaction in her local party organization, particularly with other women. Many women's groups in the Greens have established rules excluding men because they believe men infuse a competitive, instrumental spirit into the group process that erodes social solidarities.

In the larger party sections in the centers of cleavage mobilization, solidary ties are most difficult to establish. They usually flourish only in political cliques and subgroups of activists who have often known each other for a long time, have worked together in other political organizations before joining their party, and now represent cores of political tendencies or factions. Interviews with militants in the Hamburg and Frankfurt Greens in particular revealed such cliquish patterns of solidarity. Clique solidarity, however, also encourages the most extreme personal attacks against intraparty opponents outside each informal group and makes it impossible to build more general party solidarities. Lucas from Bonn bemoans the lack of a "personal interest in the individual human being" in his local party organization which is divided into rival cliques and groups who lack any respect or civility toward one another. Internal loyalty to cliques, according to Lucas, undermines the foundations of party unity and solidarity and violates the dignity of the individual militant.

As a consequence, particularly in centers of left-libertarian mobilization and more so in West Germany than Belgium, ecology parties are unable to build firm solidary commitments. One reason is that left-libertarian parties are dominated by intellectuals who have strong purposive and participatory motivations that routinely lead them into political clashes. Such conflicts are all the more likely because intellectuals prefer to shift the focus away from more concrete, immediate, and practical political tasks to broad strategic and policy choices that are bound to generate controversy. Intellectuals also value the social life of the party less than working-class and less educated party activists, who may lack the skills to articulate policies and participate in strategic decisions but enjoy the solidarity and status parties provide.[17] Intellectuals usually have their own personal networks of communication outside the party,

16. Similarly, Kornberg et al. (1979:200) found that women in Canadian parties have more personal motives for joining than do men. They also seek more emotional gratification and bonds from party work (ibid., 206).

17. In working-class parties, therefore, solidarity is particularly important for maintaining activism (cf. Denver and Bochel 1973; Jenson and Ross 1984). On the link between social involvement and class see also Barnes (1967: chap. 9) and Eldersveld (1964:296–97).

cultivate a libertarian and individualist lifestyle, and look outside the party for a sense of community and status. For instance, Olivier, an agronomist and long-term Ecolo activist, and Tom, an economist and writer with numerous connections in the West German New Left, both insist on a clear separation of the realms of friendship and party activism.

The large and relatively anonymous party meetings in the centers of left-libertarian cleavage are the sites of the most direct conflicts between leaders of various factions and groups. As Alexander, a Hamburg Green, states, many militants come to the meetings not for the social climate, but for the chance to pick a fight with a representative of a different party wing. Two groups find it especially difficult to cope with this situation: new, young party members and women. As early as 1981 the charismatic leader of Anders Gaan Leven, Luc Versteylen, warned that Agalev's transformation into a party would leave it "without women, without youth, without inspiration." (Versteylen 1981: 60). This problem is on the minds of Agalev and Ecolo activists but it appears to be more severe in the German Greens where political polarization inside the party is more pronounced.

Cliquish politics and the conflictual climate in many Green party sections create the highest social barriers for newcomers.[18] For this reason, the social and political gap between "generations" of militants and local party sections continues to grow (Bühnemann et al. 1984:89). According to Winfried from Stuttgart, the Greens can no longer claim to be the party of youth. Dress, political culture, and social networks separate them from those under 25. On the occasion of his 40th birthday, Tom from Frankfurt observed that Green activists who attended were divided into a group of his old friends and a group of younger activists. To Tom this is the symbol of a new division in the party.

In all three parties activists have begun to worry about the "ghettoization" of the active membership, as Lucas from Bonn phrases it. The parties appear to be failing to reach beyond a hard core of 30- to 40-year-olds who were involved in the movements and New Left organizations of the 1970s. Among recent joiners, only the most robust, instrumental activists with a thoroughly pragmatic outlook have the psychic predisposition to survive. Olivier from Brussels fears that Ecolo now attracts "tougher" people who can persevere in a hostile, competitive climate. These "politicos" are, in the words of a Hessian Green parliamentarian, "socialized into an organization," not socialized by a movement.

In a similar vein, there are indications that the percentage of women activists is stagnating, if not falling off.[19] Certainly ecology parties have

18. See Kurt Edler, "GAL Strukturen und Aktivistentreffen," in Die Grünen/GAL, *Einladung zur Landesmitgliederversammlung am 29./30. 3. 1985,* 3–4. Similar problems in Ecolo are observed by Lannoye (1985:51).

19. In the Freiburg Greens, the share of women fell from 43 percent of the members in the last quarter of 1982 (*Badische Zeitung,* November 26, 1982) to 37 percent in March 1985 (member-

always had problems attracting and retaining women. Many feminist militants report that their friends and acquaintances in women's groups have refused to join the party because of its social climate. Brigitte from Ecolo Liège finds that women do not see a party as an avenue for realizing a convivial lifestyle and therefore stay out. Marita from Hesse also had to accept that her friends preferred to remain outside the Greens because they perceive the personal confrontations in the Greens as even less bearable than those in other parties. A number of activists argue that these conditions have also affected the enthusiasm of those women who decided to get involved in ecological politics. Theo from Liège observes that the technicalities of local politics have discouraged women. Monika from the Frankfurt Greens has found that women are likely to drop out of the party because of the intense conflicts among its wings. In fact, some of the women activists refuse to recruit other women into the Greens because they deem the level of intraparty conflict intolerable.

In practice, a competitive, conflictual political style is apparently not the privilege of men. A number of Green feminists observe that the party's general patterns of interaction are also replicated in women's groups.[20] Strategic and programmatic disagreements cross gender divisions and women intellectuals engage in an individualist, libertarian approach to settling party controversies similar to that of their male colleagues.

The importance militants attach to solidary commitments shows again that although ecology parties may be driven by purposive and participatory concerns, the outcomes of party politics makes many uneasy. Where the left-libertarian cleavage is most highly mobilized and the largest share of activists emphasizes a logic of constituency representation, ecology parties are least likely to create solidary incentives. Rather than increasing participation and social commitment, concern with the parties' purpose and decision-making structure makes it difficult to address the militants' demand for social solidarity. Generally, activists from the periphery of the left-libertarian cleavage report less difficulty in attracting young entrants and women, less noticeable generational splits, and a more convivial social climate. Their party sections are politically more homogeneous, but socially more diverse, while party locals in the centers tend to be socially homogeneous, but politically diverse, with different cliques and groups of intellectuals fighting over party procedures and strategies.

---

ship file of the Freiburg party organization). Between January 1983 and the spring of 1985, only 30 percent of the new members were women.

20. See Hermans (1984:101 and 104) on women's groups in the Berlin Alternative List and Margret Sennekamp, "Persönliche Eindrücke vom Bundestreffen der Grünen Frauen in Bielefeld (August 1983)," *Immergrün,* no. 17 (September 1983), 6–7.

Material Commitments

Militants in any political party rarely admit to material or status motivations as driving forces of their involvement, while nonmembers routinely attribute material motivations to them (Kornberg et al. 1979:65). As a variation on this theme, in ecology parties many ideologues attribute material motivations to their pragmatist or lobbyist opponents. Conversely, moderates say either that status and material advantages play a role for all activists regardless of political attitude, or claim that few activists get involved for material reasons.

In light of the activists' political biographies, it is most likely that patronage and status-seeking play a relatively minor role. Even among the unemployed, students, and party functionaries I interviewed, 28 percent of my sample, few individuals had actively pursued a professional political career. In two instances functionaries were hired before they had even joined the party. In other cases unemployed activists had embarked on New Left politics and essentially renounced a secure occupation long before the ecology parties came into being. Moreover, given the parties' unpredictable internal decision modes and limited number of attractive positions, no rational decision maker motivated by status and material gain would find work for an ecology party a promising avenue to success.

Better than second-guessing the militants' true aspirations would be to assess the probable significance of material commitment mechanisms by examining the parties' resources and control over patronage. In many parties militants deny the importance of material commitment mechanisms, yet the parties' ample control of patronage belies these assurances.[21] But ecology parties have few patronage opportunities in the public sector. In Belgium, where the politicization of public employment is particularly high, a number of militants worry that Ecolo's and Agalev's disadvantaged position in fact deters sympathizers from joining. In the Greens, too, influence on public employment, even at the local level where the party often participates in municipal governments, is very limited. Hence, ecology parties can only provide jobs as party employees, staff members of parliamentary parties, and parliamentarians themselves. Jobs in party secretariats are neither prestigous nor highly paid.[22]

21. Wilson (1962:200–225), for instance, found that in the Democratic Club Movement patronage was very important, although the Clubs' ideology looked down upon material incentives. Members of the major West German parties routinely deny the importance of material motivations for party membership (Falke 1982: chap. 3), but the great potential for party patronage in public administration casts doubt on the sincerity of these claims. In the Christian Democratic party, 22.8 percent of all functionaries and elected officers are state officials (Schönbohm 1985:239). The party has even devised a software system for monitoring the promotion of its members in the public sector.

22. Party secretaries have a low social status throughout Western party systems. Compare Barnes (1968:110–12), Lohmar (1963:62), and Kornberg et al. (1979:12).

Elected office in parliament comes with high status and modest pay, since parliamentarians in all ecology parties have to return part of their salary to the party. Moreover, given regulations on tenure in elected office and, at least in the Greens, the changing fortunes of different party wings that affect employment opportunities for aspiring candidates, building one's professional future on politics is a high-risk undertaking. Josef, a Green activist from Lower Saxony, claims that he finds precisely the high risk of becoming a professional politician in a party which essentially shuns professional politics attractive and adventurous. This view, of course, is a far cry from Michels' image of the security-seeking bureaucratic politician in modern mass parties.

Although well-paying political staff positions in ecology parties are few, it is true that the German Greens receive generous public compensation for campaign expenses and state funds to employ a considerable staff aiding their state and national parliamentary groups. But in the mid-1980s even the Greens filled a total of no more than 450 paid positions, including state and federal parliamentarians, their staff, party secretaries and employees, and employees working for Green municipal councilors and city governments. Although the Greens are the largest West German "alternative entrepreneur," they employ a mere 1.1 percent of their approximately 40,000 members. By West German standards, Agalev and Ecolo in Belgium are poor, since the state bestows very little direct or indirect financial aid on political parties. Here, too, less than 2 percent of all members are employed by the party or serving in paid political office, although the membership is very small.

For ideological and institutional reasons, therefore, patronage and other material incentives cannot play an important role in attracting ecology party militants. Only for a brief period when the parties scored their initial electoral success did it appear very easy to get a prestigous elected office or well-paid staff position. But as the parties mature and rely more on a pool of proven activists with clear political positions, the lure of material incentives appears to be weak. In fact, I argue in subsequent chapters that ecology parties have created a reward structure with so many disincentives to ambition that they cannot fill potentially important positions at the local or national level with able activists.

Organizational Legitimacy as a Commitment Mechanism

An organization enjoys legitimacy when its members accept its decisions as authoritative and final even if they personally disagree with them (Knoke and Wood 1981: chap. 5). Compliance and legitimacy in a voluntary organization can derive from its history, procedures, programs, and leadership. Legitimacy is related to Hirschman's (1970: chap. 7) notion of loyalty to an organization. Loyalty and legitimacy presuppose a belief in the supremacy of the association over the individual, a sense of collective identification and organizational patriotism which is not confined to rational calculations of one's benefits from contributing to the collective.[23]

The only bases of legitimacy and authority ecology parties rely on are democratic procedures of participation and a correspondence between the purposes endorsed by individual militants and the parties at large. Ecology parties can appeal neither to a long tradition or mythical origin nor to charismatic leadership nor to a particular efficiency in producing desired outcomes as grounds for the legitimacy of the organization. As a consequence, militants attribute very little meaning and authority to the party as a collective. This narrow sense of organizational legitimacy, together with the libertarian individualism of most militants explains why organizational patriotism is all but absent.[24]

Although the interviewed militants all belong to the core group of Belgian and West German party activists, they often harbor great mistrust of their own party as a vehicle of political mobilization. It was almost a ritual at the beginning of many interviews that militants would distance themselves from the party. A member of the Green national executive, for instance, declared he is only "formally a member of the party and feel[s] no inner party loyalty." Winfried, a Green state parliamentarian from Stuttgart, found that "many cannot come to terms with the party form. There is a diffuse anti-party affect." In this vein, Agalev's representative in the European parliament sent a letter to the party executive stating he would like to leave the organization because he does not believe in the value of party membership.

Many interviewees sense that the left-libertarian revolt against party politics is a factor in hostility toward ecology parties themselves. This anti-party aversion appears in two different forms. One sentiment is a populist rejection of the divisiveness of parties, building on a desire to be "above parties" and project an organic image of society. This sentiment is particularly widespread in areas where left-libertarian mobilization is low. Here, particularly in small municipalities, nonpartisan traditions of local politics prevail that even ecologists are reluctant to undermine.[25] Moreover, left-libertarian movement activists, particularly in movements concerning the politics of space, often cannot

23. If "loyalty" were conceived as the aggregate function of purposive, participatory, solidary, and material commitments, one would neglect the importance of cognitive and normative beliefs regarding the legitimacy and position of the organization in the broader political system.

24. The absence of concern for the preservation of the collective party organization is also one of the features that characterize the American Democratic party "amateur politician." See Soule and Clark (1970:896) and Kirkpatrick (1976:122, 139, 144–47). A West German study asking members of different parties what they would do if they belonged to a minority opposition in their party found that 37.5 percent of the Greens would leave, whereas only 12 percent of Social Democrats and 14 percent of Christian Democrats would exit their party (Greven 1987:73).

25. On the nonpartisan nature of German local politics outside large metropolitan areas see Zoll (1974:182–84) and Dolive (1976).

bring themselves to join an ecology party because they fear party involvement would politicize movements around broader objectives that could split a single-issue mobilization and undermine its effectiveness.

Hans-Dieter, an ecological activist from the Black Forest, originally was skeptical of the Greens because he was opposed to intraparty factionalism and felt ecology is beyond left and right political positions. George, an Ecolo activist from Namur, also seized on the slogan "We are neither left nor right, we are in front," popular among politicians without New Left sympathies, yet involved in ecology movements, in both the Belgian and West German parties. He, as well as many other Belgian militants, points to the divisiveness and sectarianism of the "small left" as an example of what ecologists must avoid and calls for ecologists to place themselves beyond traditional party divisions. All three activists are opposed to a conflictual style of politics.

A second anti-party sentiment stems from the anarchist or syndicalist view that any party organization will subvert the struggle for a decentralized, egalitarian society by introducing hierarchies of competence and command. This sentiment is often based on firsthand experience with traditional parties and the small, doctrinaire New Left sects of the 1970s. It is widespread in left-libertarian cleavage centers, particularly among party ideologues and lobbyists coming from movements concerned with the politics of social identity. The syndicalist position is close to the radical-feminist critique of the New Left. Very young militants are more likely to express affinity for an anarchist rejection of society. Although the small nonrandomized sample of party militants in my investigation rules out definite conclusions, it is nevertheless striking that five of the thirteen Belgian and German interviewees thirty years old or younger spontaneously mentioned anarchist influences on their thinking and an initially strong rejection of the party form. Older militants with similar anti-party sentiments base their views on their own unpleasant experiences with New Left organizations or conventional socialist parties. Jochen from Frankfurt recalls he joined the "sponti-scene," bohemian and anarchist groups committed to direct, disruptive protest politics, when he realized how the Social Democrats had co-opted all progressive elements trying to work inside the party. Brigitte says that her encounters with New Left groups in Liège were so repugnant that she lost her belief in parties as a vehicle of social change.

In light of the overwhelming importance Maoist and other sectarian New Left parties of the 1970s assigned to loyalty and submission to the party's authority, it is easy to understand why many ecologists with some exposure to these groups adhere to individualist and anarchist beliefs and mistrust binding organizational rules of collective decision making. There are, however, some militants, especially among the ecosocialists in West Germany, who still view their involvement in New Left parties in a positive light and often practice elements of their communist organizational ethic inside their new party. Because they believe in collective discipline and the authority of the party, they are noted for their willingness to perform unrewarding, laborious administrative jobs and to campaign for the party, two tasks many other militants with less organizational loyalty despise. In West Berlin, for instance, cadres of the Maoist KPD kept the Alternative List alive when others abandoned it after the 1979 West Berlin elections and the poor Green showing in the 1980 federal election (Schaper 1984:60). Similarly, militants of the Hamburg Communist League provided the continuity between the 1978 Colored List and the formation of a Green state party in 1980 (cf. Langer and Link 1981).

Other more pragmatic militants have began to rethink the perception that, as Jochen from Frankfurt characterizes it, "nothing of how the other (parties) present themselves can be correct." Kurt from Hamburg hopes that activists will begin to appreciate the "value of an organizational body." And Willi from Stuttgart expects more activists with an "organizational psyche" will join. Myriam from Liège also says she wants to see party members accept personal responsibility for making sure that they abide by collective decisions.

On balance, however, these are minority positions reaching a limited audience, particularly in the left-libertarian centers of cleavage mobilization. Here, militants with New Left background or involvement in the politics of social identity, who are prominent among party ideologues, reject all efforts to increase the binding character of party commitments. Because the Greens are located in an environment where left-libertarians are generally more mobilized, anarchist and syndicalist antiparty resentments are more widespread than in Belgium.

Membership Growth and Turnover

Because of left-libertarian sympathizers' limited motivations for joining a party, as well as the parties' limited incentives reinforcing activism, ecology parties develop weak and contradictory commitment mechanisms. Left-libertarian purposive motivations are plentiful but easily disappointed by the slow progress parties make in realizing their objectives. Similarly, activists express great demand for participation but the actual experience of party politics is often disenchanting and falls far short of many militants' aspirations to contribute to an egalitarian, direct democracy. Moreover, there are unavoidable tradeoffs among a disciplined, collective pursuit of the parties' purposes, an individualist celebration of participatory politics, and a communitarian spirit of solidarity and social conviviality. Yet many militants expect their party to realize each of these objectives. Finally, antiparty resentments also make it difficult to focus activists on party building; the party as a collective organization has little legitimacy in the eyes of the militants. In other words, left-libertarian parties call for a broadening of political participation, but actually discourage it.

In this section I interpret overall membership enrollment and turnover in light of the parties' commitment mechanisms. Because so few activists have feelings of organizational loyalty, they expend little effort proselytizing among potential party members. They expect others to join the party out of inner commitment, not in response to invitations. More importantly, many militants believe that parties are no longer the primary mediating agents between state and civil society and therefore do not want to syphon off political activism from social movements into the parties.

With these attitudes, ecology party militants attribute little significance to formal party membership. Many Green militants view membership cards as an anachronism. They prefer nonmembers who actively contribute to the party's work to members who do nothing but pay their dues. Especially in centers of left-libertarian cleavage, active nonmembers have virtually the same rights at local meetings as their card-carrying fellows. Not surprisingly, there is little incentive to pay dues. Many members pay little or nothing and the office of the local party treasurer is ridiculed as a petty and formalistic affair.[26] Members frequently resist efforts to collect dues or try to negotiate rates with the treasurer.[27] Conversely, in some instances, treasurers have embezzled party funds because militants paid little attention to the local use of party resources.

In areas with low left-libertarian mobilization in the Greens, and especially in Agalev and Ecolo, membership and dues paying is taken more seriously and organizational commitment is higher. In the Belgian parties, although the threshold of membership remains low, almost all activists are members; those who do not pay dues are automatically struck from the membership roll.

Compared to major Belgian and West German parties, the member/voter ratio in ecology parties has remained low. While the average ratio for conventional parties is 10 percent of the voters in Belgium and near 5 percent in West Germany, corresponding figures are in the neighborhood of 1.3 percent for the German Greens (1987) and about 0.5 percent for Agalev and Ecolo (1985).[28] Because Agalev and Ecolo, in contrast to the Greens, remove noncontributing members regularly from their membership list, their member/voter ratios may

26. In contrast, socialist parties and unions valued it as a key position for maintaining regular and direct contact between members and organization through house visits (cf. Schönhoven 1980:184).

27. See, for instance, the treasurer's report of the Cologne Green party organization. Kreisverband Köln, *Die Grünen Info,* October 1984.

28. The Belgian estimate was calculated based on 1973 membership figures (Rowies 1975:14) and the parties' average voter support 1977–1985. The German estimate was provided by Fogt (1984:105). The Green member/voter ratio relies on an estimated 40,000 members at the time of the 1987 election (over 3,000,000 voters). Agalev and Ecolo had about 2,000 members when they received over 380,000 votes in October 1985.

actually not be that much lower than that of the German Greens.

Since ecology parties pay less attention to enrolling a mass membership than conventional parties but emphasize political activism, it would be important to compare activist/voter ratios and activist/member ratios across parties. As I explain in the next chapter, there is evidence that, as in the established parties, the majority of ecology party members remains politically inactive. Hence, the activist/voter ratios, like the member/voter ratios, are also much lower in ecology parties than in conventional parties.

One possible cause of low member/voter ratios may be the ecology parties' recent origin and rapid electoral success. Yet membership appears to have leveled off in the mid-1980s even though electoral support has since risen. What remains as the most plausible explanation for low enrollment and activism are the ideological orientations of left-libertarian sympathizers and the parties' insufficient commitment mechanisms.

In Belgium, where the membership base of ecology parties is especially narrow, most of the militants I interviewed find this situation troublesome and are inclined to hold the weakness of commitment mechanisms responsible for the low enrollment. Some 31 percent feel that the anti-party bias among left-libertarians is key. An additional 21 percent believe that the parties' work is not concrete and practical enough to attract supporters. And 10 percent claim party sympathizers are disenchanted by the slow change ecology parties bring about. Militants also reason that a participatory party organization is too time-consuming for most people (34 percent), does not leave enough time for movement activism (8 percent), and is avoided because Agalev and Ecolo have no access to patronage in the Belgian public administration (12 percent).[29]

High turnover among a party's members is a sure sign of weak commitment mechanisms. Unfortunately, reliable data are available only for Ecolo's Brussels section and the Green district party in Freiburg, where the parties annually gain or lose about 15–30 percent of their members and sometimes more (Tables 23 and 24). Both areas are centers of left-libertarian mobilization and may have higher turnover rates than party sections on the periphery of the left-libertarian cleavage, because in highly mobilized areas organizational patriotism and solidary commitments are weaker and intraparty conflicts are stronger than elsewhere. Indeed, while in the Brussels region only 27 percent of the party members in the fall of 1985 had joined before January 1983, in the less mobilized Walloon areas 43 percent of the members in 1985 had supported the party for at least three years.[30]

29. The percentage figures exceed 100 percent because activists gave more than one explanation. Additional reasons difficult to classify were given by 29 percent.

30. Ratios were calculated from raw data provided by the Ecolo national secretariat, Namur. Comparable figures on other ecology parties are not available.

Table 23
Membership turnover in the Brussels region of Ecolo, 1982–1985

	Total membership in 1982	Remaining in 1983	Remaining in 1984	Remaining in 1985
Joined up to 1982	133	82	53	46
Joined up to 1983	—	289	154	124
Joined up to 1984	—	—	205	143
Joined up to 1985 (actual members)	—	—	—	185
Gain over previous year	—	+203	+51	+42
Loss over previous year	—	−51	−135	−62

Source: calculations by Pierre van Roye, Ecolo senator from Brussels in the Belgian parliament (1981–85).

Purposive and participatory commitment mechanisms are especially important for ecology parties. But since the parties often disappoint the militants' expectations and cannot provide additional social or material incentives to reinforce activism, let alone appeal to the legitimate authority of the party, party membership and activism are likely to be volatile. As a consequence, purposive motivations may pull new members into the parties, but their enthusiasm soon vanishes and gives way to apathy. Oscillations in the size of party membership parallel to the electoral cycle may indicate that ecology parties have difficulty converting new members who join because of purposive commitments into reliable contributors. This expectation is based on the premise that people step up support for a party in periods of heightened political awareness, such as electoral campaigns (cf. Kornberg et al. 1979: 104). Great electoral success in particular, or expectations thereof, should boost membership, while it stagnates or declines at other times.[31]

The Belgian ecology parties have followed a cyclical pattern closely aligned with elections. Agalev's membership reached a high of almost 1,000 after the 1981 national elections and the 1982 local elections, but had dwindled to about 750 members by 1984. Ecolo experienced a similar decline from an initial high of about 1,000 members in the early 1980s to a low of about 800 members in 1984. Both parties rebounded to approximately 1,000 members each between the June 1984 European elections and the October 1985 national

31. The interaction between electoral success and party membership development is a controversial one for scholars. Some studies, such as Kuhnle et al. (1986), Schönbohm (1985: 244–53), and Wellhofer (1985) find an association but see membership increases as antecedents of electoral success. Other studies of the West German Christian Democrats (Falke 1982:48–50) and of Western socialist parties (Bartolini 1983:195–98) find no relationship. Still other work on political interest associations reports that organizations gain members when they are threatened by a crisis (Hansen 1985).

Table 24
Membership turnover in the Green district of Freiburg, 1983–1985

	Membership in January 1983	Remaining in March 1985
Joined up to January 1983	210	124
Joined up to March 1985	—	263
Losses 1/83–3/85		−86
Gains 1/83–3/85		+139

Source: membership file, Green party district secretariat, Freiburg.

elections. When campaigns pulled the parties into the public limelight, membership picked up. The purposive commitments of new members, however, rapidly faded when parties did not provide sufficient other participatory and solidary incentives to stay. This interpretation matches the interviewees' observations. They often found that newcomers lack a solid political background, are swept into the party on a general wave of enthusiasm, and cannot cope with political business on a daily basis. One Belgian activist went so far as to recommend his party should admit only activists already experienced in protest movements and political involvement.

In the West German Greens cycles are less clearly discernable due to the rapid succession of state, national, and European elections. But here, too, membership declined after a quick start (November 1979–June 1980) when the party suffered big defeats in the June 1980 North Rhine–Westphalian state elections and the October 1980 national election (Table 25). With electoral success at the state and national level, membership growth picked up again in 1982, 1983, and 1984. In 1985 the party was defeated in several state elections and became embroiled in all-out factional conflicts, two developments which may have repelled potential entrants and led to a general levelling off of membership growth.

Although the Greens have not experienced an absolute drop in membership since 1980, the data suggest a significant association between electoral cycles and membership development. Membership increases in individual states support this conclusion. From late 1983 to the middle of 1985 only those state parties that faced state elections achieved considerable growth (column 8, Table 25: Baden-Württemberg, Hesse, North Rhine–Westphalia, and Saar). In Baden-Württenberg monthly gains averaged 255 new members during the 1983 national election campaign (January 1983–March 1983). In the ensuing fourteen months the rate fell back to an average of 58 net additions per month. The pace accelerated to 130 members per month in the second half of 1984 after a series of successful state and European elections.[32]

32. Monthly data on the Baden-Württemberg Green party membership were provided by the state party secretariat in Stuttgart.

Table 25
Membership of the Green party in eleven cities, November 1979–Spring 1985

	November 1979 (1)	December 1979 (2)	June 1980 (3)	May 1981 (4)	Fall 1983 (5)	Spring 1985 (6)	Change (%) 6/80–5/85	Change (%) 4/83–2/85
Baden-Württemberg	1273	2058	3760	3392	5000	6270	+67%	+25%
Bavaria	978	1441	2940	2565	6000	6350	+116	+6
Berlin (West)	37	548	820	(91)[a]	3000	3200	+290	+9
Bremen	26	98	220	151	330	350	+59	+7
Hamburg	102	734	1060	419[b]	1200[b]	2010	+90	(+69)[b]
Hesse	297	618	1060	1525	2900	4300	+306	+49
Lower Saxony	284	1229	2640	2088	3750	4230	+60	+13
North Rhine–Westphalia	685	1853	3860	3545	7000	8500	+120	+21
Rhineland Palatinate	99	288	660	743	—	1800	+172	—
Saarland	59	82	220	149	450	600	+172	+33
Schleswig-Holstein	159	707	1080	685	1400	1470	+36	+5
Total	2979	9656	18320	15352	3200	39100	+116	+24

Sources: columns (1) through (4): Klotzsch and Stoess (1983: 1582); column (5): Bundesfinanzrat der Gruenen 1983; column (6): press release of the Green federal party secretariat (September 1985).
a. The Green state party organization collapsed and was displaced by an independent Alternative List whose members later affiliated with the Green party.
b. Figures for 1981 and 1983 do not include members of the Hamburg Alternative List which was dissolved in 1984. Most of its members joined the Greens.

The strong growth of the Hessian Greens between 1983 and 1985 sheds light on the importance of the party's competitive position as a boost for party enrollment and purposive commitment mechanisms. In Hesse the Greens faced several state and national elections in succession and, more importantly, negotiated with the SPD about supporting a common government program. The prospect of an alliance with the SPD deeply split the party, prompting many pragmatists to join in order to help tip the intraparty balance toward a moderate alliance strategy.

We can compare the impact of cleavage mobilization and competitive party position on membership enrollment. The smaller the difference in electoral support between Christian/Liberal and Social Democratic party blocs, the greater the probability that left-libertarian parties decide which bloc will form a government. Their competitive position is strong when the two blocs are less than 5 percent apart, and moderate where they are 5 to 10 percent apart. Figure 4 shows that the capacity of the Belgian and West German state or regional ecology parties to grow is a function of both their electoral competitiveness and of the left-libertarian cleavage mobilization in an area.

Agalev and Ecolo, located in areas where left-libertarian mobilization is comparatively weak, also have low member/voter ratios, although as indicated above some of the difference in the Greens may be due to stricter ways of counting party members. Interestingly, in regions with strong left-libertarian mobilization, Green member/voter ratios have risen more than elsewhere, but are still no higher than the national average (Table 26). In fact, in mobilized areas the parties started out with a much lower member/voter ratio and caught up with other areas only in the mid-1980s.

In core areas of left-libertarian mobilization, electoral success and social movements should facilitate entry into the party and lead to higher member/voter ratios. Since this is not the case, I interpret low member/voter ratios as indirect evidence for the weakness of commitment mechanisms in left-libertarian party strongholds. In these areas intense antiparty sentiment, particularly among intellectuals, offsets whatever advantage party units may enjoy in recruiting sympathizers. Moreover, intraparty conflicts, a lack of solidarity, and the frustrations of participation are also likely to depress party membership. On the periphery, in contrast, membership has developed more gradually and is generally more stable. While this political environment provides less encouragement to join, party sections in these areas have stronger commitment mechanisms for keeping their activitists, such as a more convivial social atmosphere and greater priority given to substantive policy discussions over procedural battles.

Nevertheless, it is militants in areas with comparatively low left-libertarian mobilization who are most worried by low membership enrollment and have started developing ways to increase it. Party units in these areas tend to be

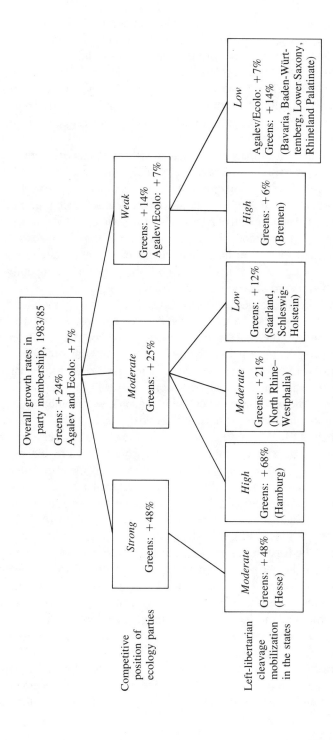

Figure 4. Impact of competitive position and left-libertarian cleavage mobilization on membership growth of the Belgian and West German ecology parties (% growth of members, 1983–1985)

Table 26
Member/voter ratios in Green state party organizations (as percent of 1983 Green voters and 1985 Agalev and Ecolo voters) and left-libertarian cleavage mobilization

		June 1980	May 1981	Fall 1983	Spring 1985	
	High	1.0%	0.4%	1.1%	1.7%	(Hamburg, Bremen)
	Medium	0.6%	0.6%	1.2%	1.6%	(Hesse, North Rhine–Westphalia)
Mobilization of the left-libertarian cleavage	Low (W. Germany)	0.9%	0.8%	1.5%	1.7%	(Baden-Württemburg, Bavaria, Lower Saxony, Rhineland Palatinate, Schleswig-Holstein, Saarland)
	Low (Belgium)	—	0.5%	0.4%	0.5%	(Flanders, Wallonia)

Source: see Table 23 on membership enrollment; German election data are reported in Statistisches Jahrbuch (1984), Belgian data in Institut National de Statistique (1985).

dominated by pragmatists who have a greater sense of organizational loyalty than most ideologues or lobbyists and are more committed to organizational efficiency and effectiveness than to a pure participatory party form. Pragmatists are also inclined to view a larger membership, even if most members remain inactive, as a source of financial support and a way to establish the party's popular democratic legitimacy. For example, two interviewees, Hans from the North Rhine–Westphalian Greens and Paul from Ecolo in Namur, argued that parties should value silent organizational supporters as well as activists. Both called for an intermediate level of supporters, between voters and activists, who make financial contributions but are not required to get actively involved in the parties' politics. Most ideologues and lobbyists in ecology parties reject this view of party membership as an adoption of the conventional mass party model.

As a practical step toward broadening membership support, Agalev, Ecolo, and some Green state parties such as the Lower Saxony Greens have started building educational foundations. These state-subsidized institutions offer courses and organize meetings on topics broadly relating to the parties' policy agenda. In the German Greens, some militants propose founding a "youth organization," which could count on substantial public subsidies and would reach beyond the party's core political generation to very young sympathizers.

As might be expected, these suggestions are anathema to most Green ideologues, who are committed to a pure organization of activists and suspect that the formation of mass organizations constitutes a critical step toward transforming ecology parties into conventional state parties. They oppose a youth organization because it would erode the party's claim to represent youth by assigning this task to a suborganization. They also fear that state-subsidized ancillary organizations will make the Greens increasingly dependent on the "party state" status quo and will create a conservative class of functionaries who live off politics.[33] Moreover, by closely emulating its electoral foes, the party would lose its symbolic distinction as an "anti-party" party which rejects the fusion of state and party politics as well as the corporatist networks of interest intermediation.

Despite these objections to new methods of membership recruitment, ideologues and lobbyists alike express deep concerns about the low level of activism in ecology parties. Many interviewees deplored the absence of a "shared political culture" or of a "cultural elaboration of the party," without quite knowing how to overcome it. The widespread belief in a fluid, decentralist party unfettered by a strong leadership inhibits the temptation to "engi-

---

33. The German Greens, in fact, filed a lawsuit with the West German Federal Constitutional Court in which they challenged the constitutionality of state financing for the established parties' political foundations eligible for state support. Yet after losing the case, many Green politicians have proposed models for building one or more such foundations affiliated with the Greens. As of spring 1988, this matter had not been resolved although the party was expected to come to a decision at one of the subsequent party conventions.

neer'' a committed, growing membership. Moreover, activists sense that more conviviality and party loyalty cannot be created by administrative fiat.

Conclusion

Motivations and selective incentives in ecology parties' commitment mechanisms clearly reveal the impact of left-libertarian ideology. Political purposes and participatory procedures are treated as the parties' most important concerns, while solidary commitments play a secondary role and material incentives or organizational partriotism are rejected outright by most activists. With this narrow range of incentives, ecology parties find it increasingly difficult to attract and keep members. In party sections, where purposive and participatory motivations are most keenly desired, the parties face the greatest impediments to realizing an open and socially supportive participatory process. Instead, factionalism, endless procedural debates, and intense interpersonal conflict frequently characterize the parties. As a consequence involvement in ecology parties stagnates and membership turnover is high.

Theories of voluntary associations explain why these unintended effects occur. Inclusive organizations that have very porous boundaries to their environment, low barriers to entry and exit, little authority over members, and no comprehensive ideology subscribed to by all members are capable of pursuing only that limited set of objectives which is endorsed by most members.[34] If groups or factions try to impose more ambitious and controversial goals on all members, opponents will leave and thus weaken the organization.

Left-libertarian parties are indeed voluntary associations with weak boundaries and little control over their members. Left-libertarian politics severely restricts the range of commitments individuals are willing to make to a party. Party members must approve only the barest outline of a common program, there are no meaningful entry and exit barriers, and material incentives or bonds of collective authority and legitimacy are all but absent. Yet at the same time party ideologues outline a very broad task structure, call for radical political strategies, and wish to treat the party organization as the laboratory for building a future democratic and solidary society. Given the activists' limited contributions to the party, their sense of individual autonomy, and the ease with which they can exit if they disagree with policies or procedures, these objectives cannot be attained. Instead of a solidary, participatory, integrated party, a disjointed party with considerable membership turnover and small cliques of political entrepreneurs engaged in rapidly shifting battles and coalitions emerges.[35]

34. My argument here is based on Curtis and Zurcher (1974) and Kanter (1972), as well as in many ways on Hirschman (1970).

35. Among American left-libertarian Democrats supporting the presidential bid of George McGovern in 1972, Kirkpatrick (1976:122) has hypothesized a similar organizational process:

Because there is a *scarcity of resources* owing to members' limited contributions and loyalty, ecology parties can do little to overcome these unintentional outcomes. Moreover, activists *misperceive the range and variability of motivations and aspirations* that keep people in the parties and require reinforcement by collective accomplishments. Libertarian impulses militate against the disciplined pursuit of collective purposes as well as the creation of an atmosphere of solidarity and conviviality among party activists.

Faced with this situation, ecology party militants have three choices. First, they can accept the unintentional consequences of the parties' political process and reconcile themselves to the imperfect reality of ecological politics. In practice, many activists across the ideological spectrum have come to choose this path. They endorse the pluralism of a conflictual political culture, with all the drawbacks for some of the goals they may value. Or second, they can give up elements of the libertarian view of party organization and build the party around a strong sense of collective identity and ideological unity which would allow them to broaden the range of purposes the party pursues. This is an option some pragmatists, but also some ideologues, especially among West German ecosocialists, appear to advocate. Third, militants may forego the "expressive" goals of the party organization (i.e. participation and social solidarity), maintaining the fluid, open structure but restricting goals to an instrumental pursuit of policy change and electoral success. This is obviously the conclusion many pragmatists have drawn. Whereas the second option tries to overcome the perverse effects of existing party structures by reaffirming the goals of left-libertarian constituency representation, pragmatists advocate a move toward a logic of party competition and call for a less demanding, more instrumental view of party membership.

In practice, ecology parties oscillate between all three options. Elements of the first and second option are particularly pronounced in centers of left-libertarian cleavage mobilization where ideologues carry the greatest weight. Elements of the second and particularly third option appeal to the predominantly pragmatic activists in areas with limited left-libertarian mobilization, and where ecology parties attain a strong competitive position. Throughout this chapter we have seen how the environment of left-libertarian cleavage mobilization affects the commitment mechanisms and orientation of ecology party activists. In areas with high left-libertarian mobilization, ecology parties come closer to a logic of constituency representation, but also encounter many perverse effects. Table 27 summarizes the contrasts that emerge between party sections in different political environments.

Limited evidence on left-libertarian parties in other countries suggests that

---

"The looser the organization, the less continuous the interaction, the faster the turnover, the more diverse the recruitment practices, the greater the opportunity for development of divergent role perception and for institutional change."

Table 27
Differences between commitment mechanisms and membership in areas with high and low left-libertarian cleavage mobilization

	High left-libertarian mobilization	Low left-libertarian mobilization
Political biography	frequent participation in the New Left of the 1970s	rare participation in the New Left of the 1970s
	frequent activism in social movements concerned with the politics of social identity	frequent activism in social movements concerned with the politics of space
	sometimes membership in conventional party	rarely membership in conventional party
Political orientations and motivations to join and contribute	predominantly broad conception of party objectives (same as low mobilization)	predominantly broad conception of party objectives (same as high mobilization)
	more radical or uncommitted strategic preferences	more moderate strategic preferences
	strong emphasis on participatory organization	weaker emphasis on participatory organization
	"syndicalist" anti-party bias	"populist" anti-party bias
Organizational (dis)incentives to maintaining membership commitment	intense internal conflicts over party objectives, organization and strategy	weaker internal conflicts over party objectives, organization and strategy
	low organizational loyalty	more organizational loyalty
	little social atmosphere in the local party units	more social atmosphere in the local party units
	generational segmentation of the party	no generational segmentation of the party
	high social barriers to the entry of new activists	lower social barriers to the entry of new activists
Development of membership enrollment	little significance of the formal membership role	more significance of the formal membership role
	many nonmembers active in party sections	few nonmembers active in party sections
	high turnover of members	lower turnover of members
	membership growth in response to strategic opportunities/strong competitive position	membership growth in the early founding phases of the party

the Belgian and West German experiences are not unique or merely an early stage of growing pains before developing into "normal" party forms geared to a logic of party competition. Weak organizational commitment mechanisms in left-libertarian politics have been observed in the Club Movement in the U.S. Democratic party in the early 1960s (Wilson 1962), the French Unified Socialist party of the 1970s (Hauss 1978), and the Dutch and Scandinavian left-libertarian parties of the 1970s and 1980s (Baumgarten 1982).[36] For all these parties high turnover is typical, as is the fact that they are unable to organize more than about 1 percent of their voters. As Wilson (1962:357) observed for American left-libertarians, the lack of a shared, solidary organizational culture in particular exacerbated the problem of commitment and organizational capacity.

All these features contrast with the motivational underpinnings and commitment mechanisms typical of the traditional socialist, conservative, and liberal parties of northern Europe. Although empirical studies are sparse, social solidarity, material commitments, and organizational loyalty play a greater role in conventional parties.[37] And member/voter ratios have not declined; in conservative parties, the ratio has dramatically increased over the course of the last two decades.[38]

Thus, overall, commitment mechanisms and member/voter ratios provide little evidence for a convergence of conventional and left-libertarian parties. Left-libertarian parties are unlikely to adopt the mass party model even where a logic of party competition affects internal patterns of participation and decision making. Most party activists subscribe to political ideas and aspirations which leave a distinctive imprint on commitment mechanisms and limit the parties' ability to attract contributors.

36. Hauss' (1978) study provides the greatest detail on commitment mechanisms. He found high dropout rates among activists exposed to intraparty conflict (p. 64–65), particularly among women and Catholics (p. 187), as young male, secular intellectuals begin to dominate the party, especially in Paris (p. 93); a less ideological climate in the provincial party organizations (p. 184); a lack of friendships or sense of loyalty to the party (p. 176); and a high annual turnover rate (p. 198).

37. In these parties, too, however, there are interesting differences between strongholds (or areas with a high mobilization of the cleavage on which the party is based) and peripheries. Compare Becker and Hombach (1983:92 and 97), Garwin (1976:370), and Lange (1975) on solidary commitments.

38. For changes in conservative party organization, compare Leonardi (1981) and Wertman (1981) on Italy, Van Haegendorn (1981) on Belgium, Kuhnle et al. (1986) and Selle and Svasand (1983) and on Scandinavia, Wilson (1979; 1980) on France, Falke (1982), Mintzel (1975; 1984), and Schönbohm (1985) on West Germany, and Layton-Henry (1983) on a broad set of conservative parties. Even in the United States it would be misleading to see a continuing decline of party organization (for a critique, see Eldersveld 1982:411–17).

5 | Acting Locally

The Ecolo section in a medium-sized town in eastern Belgium convenes on average twice a month. Eight and then ten activists gather in a pub after dinner. Most know each other well and their conversation almost imperceptibly drifts from personal matters to the official agenda of the day. There is no need for a formal chair or fixed procedure. On this particular evening they discuss ways to prevent the pollution of a local stream by a sawmill. Then they divide up assignments for the approaching national electoral campaign. This topic quickly turns the discussion into a familiar litany of lamentations about the shortage of activists and the party's poor financial situation. Toward the end of the meeting the Ecolo municipal councilor wants to talk about his initiatives in the upcoming city council debate about next year's city budget, but his fellow activists find this issue too technical and removed from their practical concerns. Finally, the section selects two activists to attend the next assembly of the district party yet does not get around to discussing the agenda for it.

The meeting of a large Green metropolitan party organization has an entirely different character. Although the party has recently begun to build suburban sections and work groups concerned with education, transport, women, and peace, the district assembly, convening once a month in the facilities of a Protestant youth organization, is still the main forum for party debates. Half an hour into the evening session about forty of the four houndred members are present. There are several subgroups engaged in animated conversation, but many participants appear to have few acquaintances. Members of the local party executive direct the meeting and have drawn up an agenda which is now supplemented by points members would like to raise. A number of announcements about meetings, activities, and organizational matters follows, among them the party treasurer's reminder that her party fellows should finally pay their dues.

The meeting first discusses the last state party conference about the party's recent electoral performance and its alliance strategy toward the Social Democrats. A handful of speakers repeatedly takes the floor to argue points with considerable rhetorical verve and, at times, polemic punch. Eventually, some participants submit motions to guide the party's strategy in the upcoming local elections as a result of which the governing Social Democrats are expected to become dependent on Green support in the city council. Following a further round of heated debate on whether a decision of this importance requires a qualified majority or a quorum of members, all motions are tabled and postponed to the next meeting. Many items on this evening's agenda remain but it is already past 11 P.M. and participants have begun to drift away. Originally, the district's Green parliamentarian in Bonn was scheduled to report on her initiatives to combat youth unemployment and further small workers' cooperatives, but this issue is canceled and the meeting is closed.

These sketches of two fictitious local party meetings are grounded in experiences familiar to most ecology party activists. They reveal different ways of setting political agendas and handling local party debates. As is true of most other European parties, ecology parties develop local sections rather than cells or committees as the basic building blocks of organization. In the countryside these sections are organized in individual villages. In larger cities the parties first created city-wide district organizations which were gradually supplemented by local neighborhood groups as membership grew and district assemblies became unwieldy. Moreover, they added a functional organization of work groups convening activists involved in particular policies or constituency groups. Nevertheless, the most important issues are still debated in the city district assemblies.

Local party organization can approximate one of three models within the broader framework of party structure. As elements of *simple hierarchies,* they may be governed by a small elite and subordinated to national party organs. Or, as basic units of *inverted hierarchies,* rank-and-file militants control political decisions and representatives directly from the local level. A third form of party organization, called *stratarchy* (Eldersveld 1964), involves relatively independent local, regional, and national party levels, each having their own elites and internal debates, connected by weak bonds of communication and control. Whereas both simple and inverted hierarchies are tightly coupled organizations with dense vertical and horizontal links, stratarchies are decentralized, loosely coupled, disjointed systems with elite fragmentation and a great deal of autonomy among suborganizations.

Although ecology activists often call for a participatory inverted hierarchy, the behavior of local party sections shows that the parties actually gravitate toward the stratarchy model. This is not only because of weak commitment mechanisms, limited resources for participation, and the divergence of political interests among ideologues, lobbyists, and pragmatists. The sheer complexity of political tasks municipal councilors or legislatures address also reinforces stratarchy. Militants must usually choose to focus their activities either on local or on national political problems and ignore many other important issues. Thus, while local party organization is indeed influenced by left-libertarian ideologies and visions, local politics nevertheless leads to unintended, "perverse" outcomes, which I illustrate in this chapter in three respects: the nature of participation in local sections, the role of local party executives and elected municipal councilors, and the communication among local, state, and national levels of the parties. As in the preceding chapter, the mobilization of the left-libertarian cleavage turns out to be a key to explaining varying patterns of political behavior in party sections such as the different style of local party meetings illustrated above.

Participation in Local Party Sections

It is difficult to assess the overall level of membership activism in ecology parties because militants may be involved not only in general meetings of local groups and district organizations but also in a variety of work groups, advisory committees, and social movements. Since the general meetings do make crucial decisions about personnel, policy, and strategy, they may serve as an indicator of party activism.

The Belgian and West German interviewees estimate regular participation in local section meetings at between 10 and 50 percent of the membership, with most estimates in the 20- to 30-percent range. Thus, the ratio of activists to members is not significantly higher than in traditional parties[1] and local ecology party sections reach only a small fraction of the parties' core constituencies. Green militants from sections and districts with less than 100 members estimate participation at an average of 35 percent. In medium-sized districts (100–200 members), the estimate declines to 30 percent and in larger organizations only an average of 20 percent frequent party meetings. Similarly, small Agalev and Ecolo districts with local groups ranging from five to twenty members have a higher regular turnout than the large organizations in Brussels, Liège, and Antwerp.[2]

Large districts are usually located in areas with high cleavage mobilization and weaker commitment mechanisms, more disincentives to participation

1. West German studies over the past thirty years report attendance rates ranging from 15 to 35 percent of the members. See Mayntz (1959:36–58), Lohmar (1963:40), and Becker and Hombach (1983:86).

2. Weak negative correlations between the size of party districts and the members' participation were also found in studies of the Italian and German socialist parties. Compare Barnes (1967:200) and Becker and Hombach (1983:82).

(anonymity, ideological conflict), and more alternatives to participation in general party meetings (work groups, movements). Where left-libertarian mobilization is low, however, party sections tend to be small, more socially rewarding, and often the only way to get involved in left-libertarian politics. For example, Marita, a Green activist, participated in a Frankfurt women's group before moving to a small Hessian town, where she soon discovered that the only outlet for left-libertarian politics was the local Green party.

Patterns of participation in ecology parties vary with the prevailing types of activists and levels of left-libertarian mobilization in a region. Pragmatists and many lobbyists are inclined to local politics and incremental social change. Ideologues, however, are concerned with national politics and usually less interested in local political involvement. These divergent orientations create a peculiar distribution of "localists" and "cosmopolitans" in ecology party sections.[3] In areas with low cleavage mobilization, most militants are pragmatic and localist and only the most active feel obliged to get involved in important regional and national affairs, such as in the nomination of candidates for elections or key strategic decisions. In left-libertarian cleavage centers, a division of labor between localists and cosmopolitans takes place. The localists attend to the political business in their own districts and go out of their way to avoid any involvement in state or national politics, while cosmopolitans employ the district party meetings and forums to discuss broader strategic issues.

My interviews revealed a great deal of mutual antipathy between localists and cosmopolitans. Young intellectuals with inclinations toward ideological politics, in particular, express contempt for the narrowness of local politics. In Hamburg, for instance, they rarely attend the local sections or district meetings, but dominate the Hamburg Green state assembly. Similarly, activists in Ecolo's Brussels district notice that people who participate in the suburban sections rarely appear at the district meetings and vice versa. Jürgen, a member of the state executive in the Baden-Württemberg Greens, has found that his district on the fringes of the Stuttgart metropolitan area is too localist to be able to discuss the broad lines of Green strategy and politics.

Localists have a similarly skeptical opinion of cosmopolitans. Guntram from Stuttgart asserts that local party and work groups on policy issues attract more practical and serious people who are dedicated to their work. Another Stuttgart Green militant calls the district assemblies where broad strategic controversies are fought out "meetings of pure chatterboxes." And Seppe, an Agalev member from Leuven, warns that the deep gulf between local activists and the thin layer of national party militants is bridged by only a small number of people combining both perspectives.

3. Of course, this terminology is borrowed from Merton (1968: chap. 12), but its meaning has been modified to fit the purpose.

Sometimes, the distinction between localists and cosmopolitans is so great as to lead to an outright organizational division. In Tübingen, a center of left-libertarianism, the Green district party caters to cosmopolitans and has experienced intense conflicts between pragmatists and ideologues. The bulk of the more pragmatic localists, however, works in the Alternative List, a joint local electoral arrangement of the Greens with a large number of local movement organizations. In the case of the Freiburg Greens, a moderate minority demanded that local sections should be separated by political wings.[4] And in the Flemish city of Ghent, just as in Ecolo Brussels, the inner-city Agalev group is more dominated by cosmopolitan ideologues, whereas the suburban groups are more localist and pragmatic. In general, however, the political stratification of local party sections is more typical of the German Greens than of Agalev or Ecolo.

Where the tension and separation between localists and cosmopolitans is strong enough, local party organizations often develop two groups of core activists. On the one hand, municipal councilors and party work groups are completely immersed in local activities. On the other, informal elites with offices in and/or strong ties to the state or national party influence the broader strategic debates.[5] Such divisions are very rare on the periphery of left-libertarian mobilization where most activists are oriented toward local politics and divorced from broader political deliberations.

Sometimes the electoral cycle and the parties' competitive position, however, pull large numbers of pragmatists and lobbyists with local concerns into national party debates. This usually happens when candidates for elections must be nominated and ecologists have a chance of gaining a strong competitive position. Pierre from Brussels recalls that an Ecolo district meeting on aspects of the party's program was attended by only sixteen militants, while a few weeks later 120 appeared in order to nominate the district candidates for the national elections. When the party is in a strong competitive position, strategic debates also attract many localists. Hubert from Marburg reports that while normally forty to fifty members attended party district meetings, this figure shot up to close to 100 when a local alliance with the Social Democrats, the first ever in the state, was debated. José notes a similar phenomenon in Ecolo Liège. During negotiations with the socialist party to form a joint city government, attendance at party meetings doubled.

Table 28 illustrates the importance of the party's competitive position for member turnout in the Frankfurt Green district assembly. From 1980 to 1983, when total membership was growing, a gradually declining percentage of

4. See *Badische Zeitung,* March 21, 1983.
5. Only in rare exceptions are the same individuals the main actors in local as well as state or national politics. Such an exception is Frankfurt, where Green municipal councilors have played important roles in strategic controversies at both the local and the national level.

Table 28

Participation in the meetings of the Frankfurt district party
organization of the Greens, 1979–84

Date	Participants	Total membership	Participants as a percentage of members (%)
11/1/79	25	30	83
4/15/80	34	*	43
6/25/80	30	98	30
11/18/89	24	*	22
5/5/81	23	*	20
8/11/81	36	120	30
8/17/82	52	*	27
3/29/83	61	*	27
5/17/83	38	250	15
9/6/83	38	*	15
10/4/83	49	*	17
10/18/83	85	*	29
10/25/83	70	*	24
11/8/83	87	*	29
12/6/83	70	*	24
1/3/84	46	*	15
1/10/84	26	*	9
2/7/84	65	*	20
2/21/84	65	328	20
5/29/84	47	*	13
10/28/84	143	415	35
11/19/84	160	*	38

*no data on overall membership enrollment available; percentage figures of member turnout calculated based on averaged trend in party membership development

Source: Minutes of the meetings of the Frankfurt Green district party, incomplete records.

members attended the district meetings. Suddenly at the end of 1983, however, attendance skyrocketed as the Hesse Greens began negotiations for lending support to the state's Social Democratic minority government. This strategic move triggered sharp factional conflicts and boosted the participation of pragmatists. At the district meeting of October 4, 1983, a motion opposing these negotiations was passed with 28 to 21 votes. Two weeks later, however, a greater turnout of pragmatists reversed the motion with 50 to 35 votes.[6] In a similar vein, participation surged at the end of 1984 when the party's ticket for the Frankfurt municipal election was nominated. Because of Frankfurt's

6. This information is taken from the minutes of the Frankfurt Green party district organization.

importance in the party, this test of strength between moderates and radicals had significance far beyond this region.

To sum up, participation in local and district party organizations is stratified along lines separating localists and cosmopolitans. These patterns vary depending on the area's cleavage mobilization and the electoral position of each party section. The stratarchal character of party organization is reinforced by the role played by local party executives and municipal councilors, to which I turn next.

Local Politics and Municipal Councils

Assemblies of all members have the highest authority in all local matters, yet local and district sections usually elect an executive or, where small, at least one secretary to run the day-to-day political business. Party statutes confine the role of executives to administrative tasks and, at least in the Greens, the office cannot be combined with that of a municipal councilor. No matter what the formal restrictions on their powers may be, rank-and-file militants often suspect the executives of trying to form an incipient elite. Particularly in the centers of left-libertarian cleavage, and here more in the Greens than in Agalev and Ecolo, resentment of hierarchies and executive privilege is widespread. The language of local party statutes, labeling executive organs something else, such as "speakers' council," "committee of representatives" or "coordination committee," symbolizes the opposition to strong leadership. Ecolo Liège must be credited for having invented the most obscure terminology in calling its executive the "structure permanente intermédiaire."

In practice, local executive office involves administrative toil, social hostility, and next to no political influence.[7] It is no wonder, then, that experienced party activists avoid the office. Members of party executives produce a collective good (organizational coordination), but do not receive any selective incentives (political influence, recognition, and the like). As a consequence members are elected as party executives who are often very young and have little political experience, ambition, or skill. Werner from south Hesse finds that "nobody in his right mind would volunteer for the district party executive." Benoit from Liège observes that the local executive never worked well and could never be filled with the statutory number of members. Other interviewees describe the local executives as "organizational miscarriages," a "rearguard of activists," or "collections of incompetents."

The weakness of local or district party executives, however, has important consequences for the parties' decision-making process. The focus for local

7. See, e.g., the complaints of a member of the Freiburg party executive in *Immergrün*, no. 7 (April 1982), 10. Most interviews confirmed the difficult position of local party executives.

party politics is the municipal councils and the activities of social movements. As we shall see, elected municipal councilors have decisive influence on the parties' council politics as well as communication with social movements. Strong executives with some power to direct the councilors would provide one instrument to counterbalance the councilors' control over the parties' local strategies. With weak executives, however, all depends on the involvement of the party rank and file in local affairs. Yet militants generally lack the time and energy to immerse themselves deeply in local politics and to gain the competence to supervise the councilors' work.

By default, then, municipal councilors become a local party elite that is rarely guided or constrained by rank-and-file input or party executives. Since the councilors are also free of oversight from state or national party organs, they constitute an almost independent group of decision makers in an organizational stratarchy, political entrepreneurs in a vacuum of control.

Quite naturally, the office of city councilor with its limited powers to effect small-scale changes in society is most attractive to localists, who are predominantly pragmatists and lobbyists. Although the sample of interviewees in this study is too small to draw definite conclusions, Table 29 illustrates that municipal councilors are recruited overproportionally from the ranks of pragmatists and lobbyists. In the German Greens the discrepancy between the orientation of municipal councilors and other interviewed groups (functionaries, state and national executives, and members of parliament) is greater than in Agalev and Ecolo where the tendency toward pragmatism is dominant at all levels.

The demand and supply of candidates for municipal office is the outcome of activists' political preferences and rational expectations about the political benefits they will derive from office. Contrary to common party mythology, ecologists serve their party not simply for either altruistic or narrow material motivations but in order to leave their political imprint on the parties' purposes and strategies. For this reason the attractiveness of municipal office increases where (1) local politics has a wide range of jurisdiction, (2) the number of inhabitants is very large, and (3) the ecology party is in a strong competitive position to influence council majorities and local policies. All three factors tend to increase the councilors' range of discretion and political impact.

Hence, small-town municipal council positions, often in areas firmly dominated by conservative parties, have little to offer in this regard. Here, Belgian and West German ecology party councilors face a restricted domain of political discretion. As a consequence in all but the largest cities ecology parties are able to fill municipal offices only with great difficulty. Even in a middle-sized Hessian university town like Giessen the Green district reported: "Although we have many members, only a small percentage is willing to engage as Green

Table 29
Strategic preferences and overall orientation of Green, Agalev, and
Ecolo municipal councilors and all other interviewed activists (in
percentages)

	Municipal councilors	All other activists
Strategic preference		
Greens		
Radical	15%	47%
Uncommitted	45	24
Moderate	40	29
All	100 (N = 20)	100 (N = 66)
Agalev and Ecolo		
Radical	—	9
Uncommitted	14	18
Moderate	86	73
All	100 (N = 14)	100 (N = 34)
Overall political orientation		
Greens		
(near) ideologues	15	42
(near) lobbyists	30	18
(near) pragmatists	40	29
none of the types	15	12
	100	101
Agalev and Ecolo		
(near) ideologues	—	9
(near) lobbyists	—	4
(near) pragmatists	79	62
none of the types	21	24
	100%	99%

politicians in uncompensated and indeed often thankless, but therefore time- and people-devouring local politics."[8]

In peripheral left-libertarian areas, party sections are small and often cannot find the candidates to present a full electoral slate. Usually the "hard core" of local militants volunteers for the municipal council, yet additional lesser known activists and sympathizers are often chosen to fill the electoral list. Many of them are ill-prepared to represent their party. Moreover, populist aversions to competitive party politics create barriers against office-seeking behavior. Christoph, from a small town in Baden-Württemberg, claims that people living in the countryside are unwilling to run for fear of antagonizing

8. *Grüne Hessen Zeitung*, 4, no. 12 (December 1984), 45.

friends and neighbors, a situation applying even to activists in environmental groups. In the small Hessian town of Usingen, for instance, the local citizens' initiative opposing a road project encouraged the Greens to run for local office. But they were unwilling to place any of their own members on the Green electoral list when the party could not find other volunteers. Very few women run on local ecology party tickets. Many women are not attracted to formal office, and the more ambitious ones prefer more visible electoral office at the state or national level.

In smaller municipalities the number of local elected offices is relatively greater than in large cities. Because of the small member/voter ratio in ecology parties, a large percentage of grassroots activists is recruited into municipal politics, even if electoral support is modest. In North Rhine–Westphalia over 1,600 Green municipal councilors, or close to 20 percent of all party members, were elected to 288 councils in September 1984.[9] Nationally, about 12.5 percent of Green party members (about 5,000) served in local elected office in the mid-1980s. In Belgium the equivalent figure is 5 percent but, unlike the Greens, Agalev and Ecolo are less willing to supplement their electoral lists with nonmembers and thus also experience a shortage of candidates for municipal office.

In areas with less left-libertarian cleavage mobilization, where pragmatists and moderate lobbyists prevail in the parties and are oriented toward localism, the involvement in municipal institutions cuts off whole party sections from broader debate in their parties. Jürgen, a member of the Baden-Württemberg Green state executive, bitterly complains that "gardeners, not politicians" run his local party organization. Mundane issues such as garbage disposal, environmental pollution, and traffic regulation dominate the local agenda. Another Baden-Württemberg activist remarked that after the last local election the local party organization essentially collapsed in her district because all committed activists had been elected to municipal councils and the county diet. The inability of ecology parties to attract militants becomes a keenly felt problem here, as this report from a Hessian party district demonstrates: "Arithmetically, it turns out that all Green and non-Green activists [in the district party organization] will be immersed in parliamentary work after the local elections. Necessary criteria which should be decisive for a nomination, such as qualifications, reliability, parity [between the sexes] or rotation [of representatives after one term in office] are, if at all, only formally discussed."[10]

Among newly elected municipal councilors enthusiasm for the office often wanes after a brief period of frantic activity, leading to high turnover among them. Although most activists in peripheral party sections are oriented toward

9. Compare *Grünes Info NRW*, 4, no. 12 (December 1984), 26–27.
10. *Grüne Hessen Zeitung*, 4 (September 1984), 20.

local issues, they dislike the technical nature of much work in municipal councils, are discouraged by usually conservative majorities rejecting their proposals, and prefer to focus on environmental and social protests outside institutionalized politics. Although rank-and-file activists usually ignore the details of what the party's municipal councilors do, there are rarely conflicts between party sections and their elected local representatives in the smaller and more peripheral districts of Ecolo, Agalev, and the Greens. There is a climate of mutual trust and informal consensus between the two groups. But municipal council politics often lacks the excitement that could reinforce commitment among councilors and activists as well.

In large metropolitan ecology party organizations located in areas with a dense left-libertarian infrastructure, recruitment for municipal office and relations between party activists and city councilors develop differently. Candidates for office are more plentiful and nominations are at times contested. Nominees are party members or sympathizers with a proven record in local work groups and citizens' initiatives, or belong to groups the party wishes to represent. Ecology parties continually make an effort to draw in women and to provide a balance in the age, occupational background, and social status of candidates. But even in left-libertarian cleavage centers, municipal councilors have a more localist, pragmatic orientation than the average activist and often express an aversion to the frequent ideological and strategic debates in their districts. They are relieved when they can concentrate on a tangible, concrete area of local politics and ignore what one councilor called the party's fruitless procedural debates in a political vacuum. Ernst, a Freiburg city councilor, confesses that he "gladly retreated from party politics" when he got a chance to do something practical as a councilor. Similarly, the Green vice mayor of Wuppertal, a large North Rhine–Westphalian city, told a journalist her thinking had not been shaped by political theories and she felt drained by the unending strategic discussions in her party district.[11]

Many city councilors find contacts with citizens' groups more rewarding and relevant to their local work than interactions with their own party. Michaela from Stuttgart says that "if the party activists see me once per half year, they are lucky." Josef from Bremen observes that antiparty feelings among city councilors prevent them from consulting the "party as party;" instead, they approach sympathetic movements and constituency associations. External groups, in turn, direct their demands and suggestions to the councilors rather than to party activists or local executives because only the councilors exercise effective influence over local politics. In this vein, Nicole from Agalev Leuven reports that her contacts with external groups were initially cool and reserved, but improved when she represented the groups' demands in the city council.

11. *Hannoveraner Allgemeine Zeitung*, April 11, 1985.

If municipal councilors keep up with their party, they frequently rely on party work groups concerned with local policy issues. These groups bring together localists who often have professional expertise in these areas (engineers, urban planners, social workers, and the like). In most municipalities, even in many highly mobilized districts such as Frankfurt or Freiburg, the pool of activists intrinsically motivated by local municipal council politics is too small to support an extensive grid of work groups. Instead there is usually one support group of activists and experts who work with the municipal councilors. Most of the time, however, the councilors are on their own, resenting the party for abandoning them in their local political dealings. They complain about receiving too few suggestions or tangible criticisms from their fellow activists. As Ernst from Freiburg phrases it, there is a "danger that the party will become superfluous in local politics. . . . Through their lack of participation in local politics, the grassroots activists force us to professionalize the municipal councilors." In the district of Wilmersdorf in West Berlin, municipal councilors of the Alternative List went on "strike" to protest against what they perceived as the inaction and intellectual "consumerism" of the party's rank and file (*Tageszeitung*, January 23, 1984).

Thus, in large metropolitan areas with a highly mobilized left-libertarian cleavage and a diverse party membership consisting of pragmatists, lobbyists, and ideologues alike, a wide stratification of party organization and decision making takes place. Many interviewees see a broadening gulf between pragmatic activists focused on the institutional city councils, locally oriented lobbyists emphasizing "direct action" in the urban environment, and the more ideological activists concerned with broader state and national issues. Local work groups reinforce this stratarchal segmentation because they tend to close themselves off from the local and district assemblies.[12] A clear division emerges between "experts" or "local issue specialists" on one side and "generalist" rank-and-file militants who attend the district party assemblies on the other.

Because of the disjointed, stratarchal participation in local party organizations, Green municipal councilors also extend their influence to the nomination of new candidates for city office. The few cases in which the Greens won enough votes to be represented on municipal councils for two successive electoral terms are instructive.[13] For want of qualified and motivated candi-

12. The work groups in the Cologne Green party, for instance, are not interested in sending representatives to the district steering committee (Kreisverband Köln, *Die Grünen Info*, October 1983, 30). Similar developments have been reported from the delegate's council of the Alternative List in West Berlin (see Zeuner in Bühemann et al. 1984:96–98) and on the relationship between the Hamburg work groups and the party organization.

13. I am relying primarily on the cases of Frankfurt, Gross-Gerau, Stuttgart, and Freiburg. Other examples would be Bielefeld and Tübingen. In all these cities the Greens scored early successes in the late 1970s and ran for their second term in elections held in 1983 through 1985. In Belgium Agalev and Ecolo contested only the 1982 municipal elections, while the subsequent elections of 1988 could not be considered in my study.

dates and in order to guarantee a certain stability of representation, municipal councilors often serve beyond one term, although rotation in office is usually encouraged. Moreover, first-cohort councilors have exercised influence over the selection of their successors. In Freiburg and Stuttgart they essentially handpicked the second generation of candidates from a pool of participants in party work groups on local politics and acquaintances in local movements. In Freiburg, a predominantly radical party district, and in Stuttgart, a more moderate one, these key individuals organized complete slates of candidates which then were officially acclaimed by the party. Ernst from Freiburg declares that "the list preparation did not leave much for the party meeting to decide."

In both cases rank-and-file activists grumbled about the recruitment process but endorsed the slates because the proposed candidates artfully balanced practical skills in local politics, representation of local constituencies, and different tendencies within the party. At a critical party meeting in Stuttgart, the municipal councilor who probably influenced the electoral slate more than anbyody else defended the proposed list in the following words: "Women represent about half the list, more women were not prepared to run. In the composition of the list, the following factors were especially taken into consideration: the policy areas of energy, social and cultural affairs, known social initiative groups, all tendencies of the party, disabled people, residents without citizenship, members of workers' councils—and each of you may find the 'prominent' candidates of your own."[14]

The stratarchal division of ecology parties is thus expressed in two patterns. In areas with low left-libertarian mobilization, entire local and district parties form self-contained units concerned with their own affairs, essentially detached from regional or national party organizations. In areas with high left-libertarian mobilization, the stratarchy articulates itself within the district parties themselves in the distinction of "localists" and "cosmopolitans" involved in separate discussion circles, work groups, offices, and party meetings.

In this environment the power of municipal councilors as an elite with great autonomy in local decision making derives from four sources. Most important is probably *self-recruitment*. Pragmatic localists with superior motivation and dedication to municipal affairs volunteer for these offices, while the more ideological cosmopolitans focus on national affairs. Localists in municipal councils are willing to make much heavier time commitments to local party affairs than any other group and hence have the competence and information to shape the parties' decisions.

A second source of power is the councilors' *positional advantages*. They not only get firsthand information on city affairs and interface with political adversaries and potential allies in other parties but also maintain more ties to

14. Minutes of the meeting of the Stuttgart Green district party on June 18, 1984.

local movement groups and enjoy more access to the mass media than all other activists. As I suggested before, the weakness of local party executives as a potential balance enhances the councilors' autonomy.

Third, the relatively *depoliticized nature of local politics,* often a nonpartisan affair with low-intensity controversies cutting across party lines, induces more pragmatic deliberations on local issues in ecology parties and strengthens the councilors' position. For this reason activists supporting radical strategies at the state or national level sometimes endorse a pragmatic, incremental local policy or alliance strategy (see Boch et al. 1981). Even in West German cities where the Greens and the Social Democrats cannot agree on supporting a joint government, municipal councilors still have maneuvering room and occasionally enter alliances with other parties to push through specific policy packages.[15]

Fourth, the position of municipal councilors is reinforced whenever they find themselves in *a strong competitive position* to make or break municipal council majorities. In many cities in Baden-Württemberg, Hesse, Lower Saxony, and North Rhine–Westphalia, favorable election results and intraparty coalitions between pragmatists and lobbyists have enabled Green municipal councilors to negotiate alliances with Social Democrats to run city governments. Some of these alliances have proven fragile, such as in Nuremberg and Munich. The main cause of failure is not necessarily defection on the part of Green city councilors and party activists, but the unwillingness of their Social Democratic alliance partners to honor agreements and treat ecology parties as more than "flash phenomena" to be exploited for short-term tactical gains.[16]

Owing to Belgium's more fragmented party system, Agalev and Ecolo have had fewer opportunities than their German counterparts to participate in the formation of local governments. And where they did join council majorities, such as in the villages of Schoten and Meise in Flanders, the fragmented party structure facilitated the defection of alliance partners, leading to the collapse of these coalitions within less than two years. A coalition between Ecolo and the socialists survived for a longer period only in Liège, with a party system more polarized around a right and a left block, although even here militants in both parties called for an end to the alliance (Beaufays et al. 1983).

15. In Freiburg, for instance, Green municipal councilors were nominated on a radical ticket, but in practice they have struck compromises with other parties in the city council on a number of occasions. In interviews they expressed a keen awareness of the discrepancies between their local initiatives and the radical strategic inclinations of many rank-and-file militants.

16. Only when both Greens and Social Democrats realize they are involved in an iterative game in which rewards depend on mutually cooperative strategies are coalitions more likely. In Marburg, for instance, a local red-green coalition that also included the liberals failed in 1981 (cf. Kleinert and Kuhnert 1982) but was revived after the 1985 local elections. I discuss the importance of iterative bargaining for internal decision making and external alliance strategies of ecology parties in Chapter 9.

The stratarchal organization of ecology parties thus must be interpreted in terms of the logic of the situation in which municipal councilors are placed. Councilors have superior resources and motivations for influencing local politics, while rank-and-file militants either are apathetic and uninterested in dealing with the councilors' work or support them from a pragmatic perspective. Ideologues with strong commitments to a participatory party organization, however, reconstruct the dynamic of local party organization very differently, as shown by the following two examples from the German Greens.

In the Cologne Green district party, a significant number of the most dedicated militants began to work in the municipal council in the fall of 1984 and thus dramatically depleted the party organization of activists with local interests. In order to fill this vacuum they founded an informal "Wednesday circle," intended to bring them together with other militants and enhance the parties' attention to local politics. Some party activists, however, immediately suspected the councilors of forming an exclusive elite of local decision makers rather than a forum for maintaining a linkage between elected party representatives and the rank and file.[17] Similarly, a report of the Stuttgart party executive shows that activists are likely to blame city councilors for too little responsiveness to and communication with the rank and file, but can propose no viable measures to solve the problem: "Within the party, [the separation of activists and municipal councilors] instills in the elected party representatives a consciousness of being above the party [*abgehoben*], of being the real movers and shakers, a consciousness the party tries to confront with procedural restraints [*Formalkram*] rather than programmatic work."[18]

As these examples suggest, party militants fear the councilors' autonomy and try to set bounds for it by imposing a panoply of procedural rules. In practice, however, these regulations do nothing to stimulate the rank and file's willingness to contribute to local politics. Moreover, additional rules and procedural oversights may have the unintended consequence of reducing the councilors' commitment. This, in turn, may give rise to more demands for procedural control of their dealings and more hostility within the party. A vicious circle develops in which party and elected representatives paralyze each other.

Antagonism toward municipal councilors similar to that illustrated by the Cologne and Stuttgart examples is rooted in beliefs about the working of party organization that are informed by Michels' "strong" theory of oligarchy. Party leaders are viewed as intent on furthering only their own selfish interests and as striving to reduce the rank and file's influence in order to subvert the

17. Compare Kreisverband Köln, *Die Grünen Info*, October 1984, 5, 32–34.
18. Kreisverband Stuttgart, Kreisvorstand, *Rechenschaftsbericht für 1983. Stadtbüro der Grünen Stuttgart.*

party's goals. This interpretation not only overstates the councilors' egoistic desires and fails to reconstruct the logic of the situation in which they gain autonomy but also leads to counterproductive, unintended consequences such as an atmosphere of mistrust and antagonism that paralyzes both councilors and militants. These perverse effects disprove the accuracy of a Michelsian syndicalist image of party organization.

From Local to National Politics

In the stratarchal organization of ecology parties, local pragmatists usually have little impact on state and national party policy. As we have seen, localists are relatively detached from what happens at other levels and thus are often underrepresented in state and national party organs. Even in local party groups and district assemblies, cosmopolitans usually control the agenda when state and national issues come up. The vertical stratification of ecology parties is reflected in the topics discussed at the local level, the contacts between local sections and national party representatives (executives, parliamentary groups), and the readiness of rank-and-file militants to attend party conferences.

In areas with weak left-libertarian movement sectors, party meetings revolve around local issues, campaign activities, and organizational questions. In an environment in which locally oriented pragmatists and lobbyists prevail, national party strategy or programs usually come up only before elections or major conferences. Similarly, the work of state or national parliamentarians stimulates little interest. Hannegret and Christa, Green parliamentarians from small towns in North Rhine–Westphalia and Baden-Württemberg, report they regularly meet with a circle of independent citizens to discuss their work rather than with their local party sections where little attention is paid to the broader questions of ecological politics. Belgian militants make similar observations in party districts outside such centers of left-libertarian politics as Brussels or Ghent.

More pragmatic interviewees in all parties question whether one should expect any different behavior from local militants: don't they have enough work attending to local politics? But local focus is a matter not simply of necessity but of political choice. Municipal councilors often justify their preference for local politics by comparing it with the abstract, sterile, and impractical character of state and national politics. Cosmopolitans in the Belgian and West German parties, however, deplore localism. In Agalev and Ecolo, these activists worry that local affairs will lead the rank and file to lose sight of a broader ecological vision and comprehensive strategy for changing society.[19] Green activists also complain about the parochialism of many party

19. For Agalev, see Toon Gazenbeek, "Haalt Agalev 1985?" *Blad Groen*, 4 (October 1984), 29–31, and for Ecolo, Raymond Yans in *Echos Logiques*, 5, no. 2 (1984), 19.

districts (*Kirchturmspolitik*). Christian, a radical from Hamburg, suggests that sociologists should study the ''backward consciousness'' of many Green local activists as a priority research area.

The weak ties between districts on the periphery of ecological politics and state or national party organizations are also reflected in the representation of these districts at state or national party conventions. Few localists turn out to these events. Where districts need to fill an allotment of delegates, they find it difficult to mobilize a sufficient number of volunteers. Peripheral party districts often are not only underrepresented but misrepresented. Because pragmatic localists are less likely to attend party conventions than ideologically or strategically oriented cosmopolitans, and because the shortage of volunteers rules out political discrimination among candidates, these districts often end up with delegations looking much more radical than the rank and file at large. Marita, a Green activist from a small Hessian town, observes that the same individuals always go to state assemblies or volunteer as delegates to national conferences, although they are not representative of her local party. As might be expected, pragmatists and lobbyists are more likely to report this distortion of democratic representation, although a number of Green ideologues admit it does occur. Some Agalev interviewees suspect that the 1985 congress on socioeconomic policy attracted more radicals than other conferences, but because of relatively broad pragmatic consensus inside Agalev and Ecolo the differential mobilization of pragmatists, lobbyists, and ideologues tends to be less pronounced than in Green party sections[20]

There is one exception to the differential mobilization of activists in national party affairs. In matters of very great importance, such as the nomination of candidates for state and national elections or the formation of government alliances with other parties, the more moderate localists suddenly mobilize and trespass on the cosmopolitans' turf. In these instances, delegates to party conferences more accurately reflect the overall distribution of political tendencies in a district.

In the centers of ecological politics, segmentation of localists and cosmopolitans runs right through the local party organization. District assemblies are often dominated by national political themes, but many interviewees complained these debates tend to be devoid of content. The meetings revolve more around alliance strategies and procedures of decision-making than substantive policy questions. In this regard, Green parliamentarians often remarked that rank-and-file activists demand their presence at district meetings and find many reasons to criticize their public demeanor, their access to the mass media, or their stance on the issue of rotating elected representatives but rarely discuss their substantive policy initiatives. Ideological concern with grassroots control fuels a vague resentment against ''higher-ups.''

20. This is also confirmed by data collected on conference delegates. Compare Kitschelt and Hellemans (forthcoming: chap. 5).

A significant number of state or national parliamentarians in the Greens, Agalev, and Ecolo have undertaken efforts to stay in touch with the local level: for example, through special study groups charged with preparing parliamentary initiatives. Moreover, in centers of left-libertarian mobilization, local factions often crystallize around supporting or opposing a parliamentarian. In other instances, however, contact between parliamentarians and local activists is sporadic. Andreas, who serves in the Baden-Württemberg state parliament, ended up working with independent environmental groups rather than his own party. Some parliamentarians argue they have too little time to attend party assemblies and meet rank-and-file militants. And in a few cases parliamentarians quite consciously ignore the local party organization because of political differences. Angelika from Hamburg finds that, "the district has always been too narrow for my concerns." Josef, a Green member of the *Bundestag,* resents the fact that in his district radicals are in charge, and so kept his distance. There is little question that state or national parliamentarians in Agalev, Ecolo, or the Greens rarely receive "imperative mandates" from their districts or regional parties asking them to pursue specific policies and initiatives in the legislatures. Instead, they have to set their own priorities.[21]

In centers of left-libertarian mobilization the large number of cosmopolitans, who are more willing than pragmatists to attend party conferences or serve as delegates, establishes a closer link between local party organizations and state or national party affairs. Interviewees generally sense that in such areas the choice of delegates reflects the distribution of opinions among rank-and-file activists fairly well, particularly where pragmatists and ideologues vie for control of a district organization. Delegates are often chosen according to their political leanings, establishing a minimum linkage between district and national politics. But even here delegates rarely receive detailed voting instructions from their constituencies, usually because of time constraints in local debates. Where open state or national conferences take place to which all party members are invited, the turnout of militants from centers of left-libertarian cleavage mobilization tends to be especially great. As in peripheral party districts, turnout at open party assemblies or care in choosing delegates increases when party conferences are scheduled to nominate candidates for national office or make difficult strategic choices in a strong competitive position.

Conclusion

The dynamic of local ecology party districts is shaped by the militants' libertarian, participatory ideas and aspirations and by such constraints as their

---

21. For a similar finding based on extensive participant observation in the Berlin Alternative List see Zeuner et al. (1982).

limited willingness to commit resources to party activism. Militants would welcome a tight coupling of rank-and-file, local, and national party elites, as long as it conforms to the model of an inverted hierarchy. Resource scarcity and the narrow incentives for participation, however, favor a stratarchal party organization. Moreover, the division of party militants into cosmopolitans and localists and the pervasive mistrust of leadership promote centrifugal tendencies, allowing levels and segments of the party organization to become relatively autonomous.

The resulting disjointed party organization increases the discretion of those militants who have the most time, resources, and dedication to immerse themselves in local, state, or national politics. Hence, each organizational level of an ecology party generates its own specialized functional elite, which occupies available party and electoral office but is essentially uncoupled from other intraparty elites and constituencies. In local politics pragmatic municipal councilors, by default, become the parties' "movers and shakers." Cosmopolitans with a generally more radical political outlook, however, establish the link to state and national politics. Thus, there appears to be a clear tradeoff between decentralization and democratic accountability in ecology parties. While the parties break up hierarchical command into a stratarchal pluralism, they do little to create a tightly coupled, comprehensive structure of democratic control.[22]

What this suggests is that ecology parties create too few incentives for militants to serve as bridges between levels and groups in the party, roles filled in conventional European parties by local executives and secretaries. In conventional parties, activists compete for these offices because they represent entry level positions in political careers which later on may be rewarded with moves up the ladder to more powerful office. Given their rejection of political professionalism and party careers, ecologists usually scorn this solution, ignoring the costs of rejecting career incentives. The prospect of promotion or reelection, however, is one of the most powerful incentives for keeping representatives responsive and accountable to their constituencies.

Although the features of stratarchy I have discussed appear across a wide range of Belgian and West German local ecology parties, they vary with the mobilization of the left-libertarian cleavage (Table 30). In highly mobilized areas stratarchal decentralization is pushed to the limit. Cosmopolitans and localists follow their own paths. On the periphery local organization is more integrated, but divorced from the higher levels of party organization. A comparison between the German Greens and Agalev or Ecolo can be explained almost entirely in terms of the difference in left-libertarian mobilization in each country. In general, Belgian party sections approximate the peripheral model of local party organization and are characterized by a more

---

22. The conflict between principles of decentralization and party democracy in the Greens has been emphasized by Zeuner (1983).

Table 30
Differences between local ecology party sections in areas with high and low left-libertarian cleavage mobilization

High cleavage mobilization	Low cleavage mobilization
larger party sections, but lower degree of participation	smaller party sections, but higher degree of participation
segmentation of activists on local or state/national party activism in the district party organization	most activists focus on the local level of party politics; few national activists, little segmentation in local sections
sufficient pool of candidates for municipal elected office	insufficient pool of candidates for municipal elected office
district assemblies discuss state/national party program, strategy, and organization regularly	district assemblies discuss state/national party program, strategy, and organization rarely and only before important decisions/conferences
choice of delegates to state/national conventions according to political criteria; district parties can fill all delegates' slots	choice of delegates to state/national conventions according to the availability of volunteers; district party can rarely fill all delegates' slots

pragmatic and nonideological spirit than Germany's. In all ecology parties the one factor that tends to overcome stratarchal decentralization is a party's competitive position. If it is strong, localists will get involved in state or national politics.

A brief comparison with local organization in conventional West European mass parties highlights the uniqueness of left-libertarian ecology parties.[23] In both groups of parties the ratio of active to passive members is approximately the same, but local sections in ecology parties clearly have more autonomy in choosing their agendas than those in other parties. Local activities in conventional parties focus on instrumental, organizational campaign questions, social activities, and speeches by party functionaries rather than on policy and strategy.[24] Although the local sections of conventional parties are far from being tied into a tightly coupled bureaucratic hierarchy as suggested by Michels, their local elites constitute a more clustered, interconnected core of activists who centralize all important decisions in a few personalities and maintain vital linkages to the state or national political level.[25]

23. Good studies of local party politics in West Germany are Becker and Hombach (1983), Lammert (1976), Mayntz (1959), Pumm (1977), Preusse (1981), and Raschke (1974). On Italy, compare especially Barnes (1967) and Lange (1975). For France, see Jenson and Ross (1984) on the communists and Lagroye and Lord (1974) on the Gaullist, socialist, and communist parties. For Britain, compare Brand (1973) and Layton-Henry (1976). For Belgium, see Obler (1974).

24. Compare Mayntz (1959:29), Preusse (1981:428), and Ronneberger and Walchshofer (1975:144–5).

25. On power structures in German local party organizations see Kühr (1974), Lammert (1976), Mayntz (1959:55–64), and Zeuner (1970:82–84).

In conventional parties the same people combine local party and elected office in municipal councils and thus move into a central position of influence. District party executives, often together with full-time functionaries, exercise considerable control over policy as well as the nomination of candidates for parliament.[26] Vertical communication between local districts and parliamentarians runs through the hands of the district executives who are continuously in touch with elected representatives (see Falke 1982:184–90). In most instances, the party leadership talks and the local members listen. While there is a fair amount of information and propaganda flowing from top to bottom, little information flows in the opposite direction.[27] In instances where factional conflicts strain the parties, the leadership is not shy about disciplining unruly party locals and districts (Raschke 1974).

Ecology parties, in contrast, inject a different organizational dynamic into the Belgian and West German party system. The individualism of activists such as municipal councilors, weak party organization, and stratarchal distribution of power across the party clearly diverge from the more integrated, hierarchical conventional parties. Ecology parties are influenced by a unique logic of constituency representation and party ideology, a logic that creates unanticipated perverse effects such as stratarchal dissociation of organizational levels and groups. Under certain conditions, local party sections succumb to forces pulling them toward a logic of party competition. At the local level a strong competitive position promotes a moderate alliance strategy. And as the parties' competitive position strengthens at the state or national level, more localists become involved in the choice of strategy and representatives, leading to a tighter coupling of local and central party debates.

26. According to Kaack (1971:504), about 40 percent of all German CDU party districts were controlled by a single individual, 20 percent were duopolies, and 40 percent were controlled by competing cliques.

27. See Lammert (1976:81), Lohmar (1963:39), Mayntz (1959:96), Preusse (1981:428), and Raschke (1974:149–223).

6 | Making Choices

A report by the Green federal parliamentary party perceptively states: "Essentially power is organizing communication, a process of mutual influencing through information and symbols."[1] Yet many militants maintain that communication is what the party does most poorly. Since the capacity to communicate translates into influence and influence contributes to power, most activists, regardless of their formal position within their party, sense they have too little power. Often it appears that the harder militants try to improve communication, the greater the difficulties become. Power is neither vested in an entrenched, unified elite nor in the grassroots but evaporates in a stratarchal organization unable to organize tightly coupled communications. As a consequence activists of all political tendencies are dismayed by the impenetrable labyrinth of boards and organs, the lack of dedicated activists at all levels, the inability of party conferences to decide important issues, the high turnover of functionaries, and the incompetence of party executives and steering committees in projecting a clear image of the party.[2] Even their members of parliament, to whom most militants attribute superior power and influence, grumble over their inability to catch the attention of the rank and file or of party

1. *Die Grünen im Bundestag,* no. 11 (1984), 16.
2. Internal party newsletters such as *Blad Groen* (Agalev), *Ecolo Infos* (Ecolo), and *Grüner Basisdienst* (the Greens) and those of each West German state party organization, e.g., *Grüne Hessenzeitung* (Hesse), *Grüne Blätter* (Baden-Württemberg), *Grünes NRW Info* (North Rhine-Westphalia), and *Stachlige Argumente* (AL Berlin) provide a gold mine of information on patterns of internal communication in ecology parties. See, e.g., Gabi Gumbel, Jürgen Maier, and Birgitt Schwarz, "Das Standbein wankt. Strukturelles und Grundsätzliches zum Landesverband," *Grüne Blätter,* 4, no. 10 (1984), 4–7, Hajo Kracht, "Wegweiser durch das grüne Labyrinth," *Grüne Blätter,* 4, no. 3 (1984), 17–19, and Benita Schulz, "Anmerkungen zur Struktur der Partei," *Grüne Blätter,* 4, no. 5 (1984), 26.

executives. Moreover, they often experience a lack of communication and cooperation within the parliamentary parties themselves.[3]

At a meeting of the Agalev party executive, a speaker expressed the predicament by saying "the people do not know what happens at the top [of the party], while the 'top' does not want to be a top."[4] And given the limited readiness of the rank and file to get involved, an Ecolo militant found that "often the impression of a certain loss of breath [*essouflement*] prevails, when [the party] is faced with the growth of new tasks and objectives."[5]

A thin flow of information across party levels and organs of representation characterizes a stratarchal division of power. Stratarchy prevents the centralization and bureaucratization of authority and at the same time is inimical to participatory control. Moreover, according to most militants' accounts, formal office and organizational status constrain their capacity to communicate, influence, and exercise power to a limited extent. When formal offices carry little authority and organizational procedures are inclusive and participatory, power is exercised by informal and unaccountable party elites: "Global result: Our concern with democracy leads to anti-democracy." (Lannoye 1985:51)

Power either remains diffuse or grows in undefined "cracks" of the formal party structure. Some militants herald this elusiveness and informality of power and control enthusiastically as the alternative to the rigid hierarchies so common among conventional Belgian and West German parties. Yet most of them strongly disapprove of the centrifugal dispersion of political control, the emergence of informal, unaccountable decision makers, and the rise of some political entrepreneurs and parliamentarians to central, influential positions; they see these results as an unintended, perverse effect undermining the parties' democratic legitimacy and the capacity to pursue its goals. Where left-libertarian mobilization and polarization with the established elites is high, as is the case with the West German Greens, stratarchal centrifugalism and perverse effects are most pronounced. Weaker left-libertarian mobilization and a strong competitive position lead to a tightening of communication and control in ecology parties.

Power in any political institution has a structural and a behavioral face.[6] Power derives from capacity to control and use information and other re-

3. See Dirk Schneider, " 'Einblicke in den Zellentrakt': Ein Klagelied mit verhaltenem Optimismus," *Grüne Hessenzeitung,* no. 11 (1983), 18–23, written six months after the Greens' entry into the German parliament.
4. Minutes of the meeting of the Uitvoerend Komite, April 27, 1983. *Blad Groen,* no. 24 (June 1983), 14.
5. Olivier Bribosa, "Rapport du Secrétariat Fédéral Sortant 1983/84," *Ecolo Infos,* no. 39 (June 16, 1984), 9–11.
6. For an application of the debate on conceptions of power to political parties compare Heidar (1984).

sources for desired ends. Control means the discretionary capability of acquiring and either disseminating or withholding information or resources in order to affect the behavior of other actors. It creates uncertainty for others.[7] The structural side of power concerns the resources vested in a formal position. The power of a formal political office depends on (1) frequency of its interactions with other militants and party officers, (2) resources (salaries, expense accounts) to provide time for politics, (3) access to political communicators outside their party (mass media, interest associations), and (4) sole formal authority over resource endowments. Moreover, the legitimacy of office and the willingness of members to accept an official's decision reinforces that power. Organizational statutes specify these structural elements of power only in part. The networks of communication, influence, and power are often hidden to all but the most involved and astute observers. Therefore, a better view of the actual control of resources and exercise of power in political decisions can be gathered from interviews with party militants.

Structural power is not everything, though. Actors must bring their resources and information to bear on political agendas and decisions. Here such elusive, intractable qualities as tactical skills, personal intelligence, energy, dedication to one's political mission, charismatic presence, and close bonds to networks of personal party associates become essential. These behavioral elements of power are most readily uncovered by studying the reputation of individual activists and observing actual decision making. If actors in positions with the greatest institutional control of resources and information regularly prevail—or are perceived as regularly prevailing—in a party's decision-making process, we may conclude that the structural bases of power are more important than a particular actor's skills and capabilities. Where outcomes vary with individual skills rather than institutional conditions, the reverse is true.[8]

In ecology parties only limited resources and control over information are vested in formal positions. Because they oppose bureaucratic hierarchical command, their officers have no right to exclude regular rank-and-file members from meetings of party executives or parliamentary groups or to withhold information from members. This makes it less likely that power is primarily based on the structural control of resources. Instead, party structure is designed to disperse and fragment power. Under these circumstances power concentrations depend less on positional authority than personal skill. More-

7. This notion of power has been developed in the sociology of organization particularly in the works of Crozier (1964), Hickson et al. (1971) and Thompson (1967).

8. This test presupposes some discrepancy between personal and positional power. Skilled individuals vie for the occupation of positions, reinforcing their personal power by institutional means. But, as I show in this and the subsequent chapter, personal and institutional power do not always converge.

over, even where positional rights and resources are a necessary condition for exercising party power, this potential is usually realized only if actors have the personal skills to take advantage of the opportunities they encounter.

The interplay of positional and personal power is reflected in the operation of party conventions, the party executive, and the parliamentary party groups I examine in this chapter. Agalev, Ecolo, and the Greens have similar organizational statutes with functionally equivalent party organs. For this reason I refer to party decision-making bodies in generic terminology rather than using the particular names of each one (see Table 31). The major difference between Belgian and German ecology parties is an additional state-level party organization in the Greens which Agalev and Ecolo, operating in a much smaller and more centralized political system, do not have.

At the local, district, state, and national levels for all three parties, party assemblies or conventions are the highest formal authorities deciding on organization, budgets, policies, and representatives. National conventions in Agalev and Ecolo and state conventions in the Hamburg, West Berlin, Bremen, and Hesse Greens invite all party members to participate and vote. In the other German states and at the federal level, the Greens convene conferences of delegates chosen by the local party sections. All other militants may attend these conferences but are not permitted to vote.

Between party conventions, state and national steering committees are the highest decision-making bodies in all three parties. In Agalev and Ecolo each party district chooses representatives to the national steering committee. In the Greens party districts select delegates to the state steering committees, and state conventions elect representatives to the national steering committee. In all ecology parties conventions also choose party executives at the state or national level who run the parties' day to day business and serve as their public spokespeople. In addition all ecology parties have arbitration committees resolving disputes over statutory provisions, and administrative employees who are hired and supervised either by the national steering committee (in Agalev and Ecolo) or by party executives (in West Germany).

Party statutes say little about the relationship between party organs and parliamentary representatives. Since I discuss the nomination process and the status of members of state and national parliaments in detail in later chapters, it suffices here to say that parliamentarians are expected to work with the rank-and-file party militants and to be accountable to party conferences.

Dilemmas of Collective Decision Making: Party Conventions

Party conventions elicit divided reactions from ecology party activists. Some of them praise the exceptional responsiveness of conventions to the prefer-

Function of party organ		Agalev	Ecolo	Greens	Generic terminology
Territorial division of the party organization and highest decision-making organ	Local	plaatslijke groep: ledenvergadering	groupe locale: assemblée locale	Ortsverband: Mitgliederversammlung	local party section: local members' assembly
	District	arrondissementelle geleding: ledenvergadering	groupe régionale: assemblée régionale	Kreisverband: Kreisversammlung	district party: membership assembly
	State	—	—	Landesverband: Landes(delegierten)konferenz	state party organization: state (delegates') convention
	National	landlijke geleding: kongres	parti fédérale: assemblée générale	Bundesverband Bundesdelegiertenkonferenz	national party organization: national convention
Territorial representation of the lower party units between conferences	District	—	Conseil de région (Brussels only)	Kreisausschuss (in large districts)	district steering committees
	State	—	—	Landes(haupt)ausschuss	state steering committees
	National	landlijke stuurgroep	Conseil de Fédération	Bundeshauptausschuss	national steering committees
Highest party representatives	District	secretaris	secrétaire	Kreisvorstand	district executive committee
	State	—	—	Landesvorstand	state executive committee
	National	uitvoerendes komite	Secrétariat Fédéral	Bundesvorstand	national executive committee
Arbitration committee		arbitrageraad	comité d'arbitrage	Bundesschiedskommission	arbitration committee
Administrative offices		sekretariaat	les ''permanents''	Landesgeschäftsstellen; Bundesgeschäftsstelle	state and national party secretariats

ences and demands of participants. Rules governing the setting of agendas, submission of motions, right to address the floor, and procedures of decision making prevent control by an elite orchestrating the proceedings and projecting a predetermined image of the party to the mass media. These rules make it possible for the conventions to discuss controversial topics openly and arrive freely at decisions that are often unexpected and surprising to participants and observers.

Many interviewees, however, argue that the existing procedures of decision making at conventions have led to serious problems with democratic rationality and legitimacy. Conventions are incapable of deliberating choices satisfactorily and often are unable to aggregate preferences into a broad consensus resolving an issue with a collectively binding and relatively permanent decision. Moreover, the composition of party conferences sometimes lacks democratic legitimacy because the participants are not representative of the parties' rank and file or external constituencies. In the view of these critics, the appearance of spontaneity at conferences is due to accidental factors such as the turnout of members or delegates, sequencing of agenda points, activists' receptiveness to emotional appeals, and intervention of charismatic political entrepreneurs in debates. Green militants are most inclined to mention these problems, while Agalev and especially Ecolo militants see a more directed and stable process of interest aggregation at their conventions.

Ecology parties usually set convention agendas in an interactive process involving their steering committees, executives, local groups submitting motions, and resolutions from previous conventions. As I noted in the preceding chapter, conference agendas influence the turnout of militants or delegates. The greater the militants' political resources and the more they are driven by ideological purposes and a cosmopolitan outlook, the more likely they are to discount the personal cost of the effort to participate in conventions and to value the benefits of political involvement. The young intellectual, the student and the professional without a family are most likely to bear the cost of time, money, and psychic energy expended in conferences. Organizational and less controversial programmatic issues lead to a low conference turnout, whereas preelection conferences with critical strategic decisions or the nomination of candidates for state and national elections boost turnout by attracting more localists and pragmatists. Only thirty-two members participated in an Ecolo national convention on a party charter,[9] but close to 100 attended a convention on economic policy and about 150 appeared at the September 1985 preelection conference. Similarly, Agalev's 1985 economic and preelection conferences brought together more militants than any preceding conference.

Where ecology parties are sharply divided into moderate and radical ten-

9. Cf. *Ecolo Infos,* no. 53, (March 1, 1985), 12–14 and Frederic Janssens, "Propositions pour la gestion interne," *Ecolo Infos,* no. 58 (June 1, 1985), 4–5.

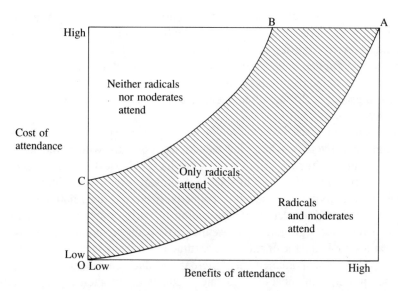

Moderates attend conferences in area enclosed by OMA.
Radicals attend conferences in the additional area enclosed by OCBA.

Figure 5. Indifference curves for attending party gatherings for two groups of party militants

dencies as is the case in many Green state parties, the outcome of convention votes will critically depend on the turnout of members or delegates. The more important the issues are, the greater will be the proportion of pragmatists and near-pragmatists attending conferences. A low turnout, as a rule, favors small groups of highly committed ideologues and lobbyists who are willing to bear the costs of attendance, even when benefits appear to be few (see Figure 5). At the aggregate level small turnouts give greater weight to metropolitan areas with high left-libertarian mobilization whence most ideologues tend to come.[10] In parties that are more dominated by areas with limited left-libertarian mobilization such as Agalev and particularly Ecolo, turnout makes little difference to the political outcome of conferences. In the highly polarized Green state parties, however, most interviewees, including the ideologues, agree that low turnout favors radical decisions at party conferences. I call this phenomenon "differential mobilization."

A few outcomes illustrate this relationship. A convention of 240 Hessian Greens held in June 1983, before that year's state elections, voted against an alliance with the Social Democratic minority state government, 130 to 110

10. The different political composition of party delegates from the center and periphery of a political cleavage is nothing new. In the German SPD at the turn of the century, the centrist party leadership relied most heavily on the moderate delegates from peripheral areas with low working-class mobilization, while radicals prevailed in Berlin and other centers of class politics. See Schorske (1955), esp. 136–45.

votes. After the elections, at conferences between the fall of 1983 and the fall of 1985, turnout at conventions debating Green alliance strategy increased to an average of almost 1,000 militants and all key votes were won by moderates favoring an alliance, with two-thirds majorities. Similarly, in Hamburg after the 1982 electoral victory of the GAL, and during the negotiations with the SPD to form a joint government, turnout at general assemblies of the Hamburg Greens increased and strengthened the moderate wing, although radical strategists still held a majority.

The discrepancy between radical conference participants/delegates and moderate rank-and-file activists is also evidenced by decisions on the issue of rotation, how frequently Green state and federal legislators should be replaced to avoid the formation of an entrenched party elite. In the mid-1980s national and state party conventions, for instance in North Rhine–Westphalia and Baden-Württemberg, routinely supported the radical proposal to rotate parliamentarians every two years in a four-year electoral term. Yet in a 1984 referendum among all North Rhine–Westphalian Greens, with an actual participation of 52 percent of the party members, the radical proposition was resoundingly defeated by a margin of three to one in favor of rotation after each electoral term.[11] Similarly, a large majority of Baden-Württemberg activists supported more lenient rules on rotation in a 1985 state-wide referendum.

Not surprisingly, ideologues strongly oppose intraparty referendums while pragmatists endorse them. As one radical militant argues, ''people who do not participate in the debates should not be asked to vote.'' Behind this theoretical argument, however, lurks a more simple, instrumental logic that is expressed in blunt terms by a Hamburg ecosocialist: ''Voters are to the right of the party members, party members are to the right of the activists. Since I would like to change people and politics, plebiscites cannot be a means of conducting Green politics.''

From the perspective of the pragmatists, this logic reveals a serious legitimation problem for party conventions. Can democracy be based on a small enclave of highly committed, resourceful individuals, or must it appeal to at least a broad audience within the political party itself, even though most members, and even many activists at the local level, have no time or inclination to get involved in national party politics?

The *differential mobilization* of intraparty groups in conferences affects not only pragmatists and ideologues but also lobbyists with very specific political concerns. Militants notice that people float in and out of conventions as policies and issues that interest them most are discussed. This enables lobbyists to get demands approved even if a majority of members or delegates is

11. Figures are taken from *Tageszeitung* (January 28, 1985) and *Kölner Stadtanzeiger*, January 28, 1985.

otherwise indifferent or opposed to their views. Wolf and Werner from the Hessian Greens observed at a party convention that feminist militants stayed only to pass a women's statute, and disappeared when other issues were discussed and voted on. In West Berlin a party convention passed a resolution to abolish cars in the city with 75 votes for and 72 votes against, even though 3,000 party members were entitled to voice their opinion. In a highly publicized incident at a North Rhine–Westphalian Green convention in 1985, a group of pederasts managed to pass a motion to abolish all laws protecting children from sexual relations with adults. The decision came at the end of a tiring round of program conventions and most delegates did not vote or were unaware what they were voting on. The resulting outcry of Green feminists and of the mass media, however, led to a quick reversal of the decision.

Because turnout and timing of decisions assume such overwhelming importance, a member of the Berlin AL writes that "state membership assemblies become the plaything of senseless factional interests. . . . Membership assemblies which are attended or not attended depending on their agendas are not able to be the expression of a continuous process of decision making among party members."[12]

The number of issues submitted to party conventions and the process of agenda setting frequently exacerbate the complications of democratic choice in ecology party conventions. All members, delegates, and local sections are invited to submit resolutions to the participants. Unlike traditional parties, ecology parties have no special screening commissions to rewrite or package the submitted motions. Thus, motions cannot be manipulated by party elites but burden conference participants with an overload of decisions. As a consequence many motions never go to the floor, left to be carried over from convention to convention or dealt with summarily by the party steering committee. Some militants fear that the neglect of rank-and-file motions in particular contributes to a sense of frustration among many local activists in the aftermath of conventions.

Several other factors reduce the time for policy deliberation at conventions. Debates are easily bogged down by discussions of issues with great emotional and symbolic appeal. At the Green national conference on the European elections in 1984, debate on the party's program never really got beyond the platform's preamble, which touched off intense debates about the role of multinational corporations in Europe. In a similar vein, Agalev's socio-economic convention in April 1985 was scheduled to debate a very large number of individual resolutions but focused on the highly symbolic questions of property rights in the energy industry and the schedule for shutting down nuclear power plants.

12. Peter Sellin, "Die Basisdemokratie verkehrt sich in ihr Gegenteil," *Stachlige Argumente*, no. 30 (January 1985), 6.

Emotional debates also enable activists with great rhetorical capabilities to sway a convention. Heinz from the Hessian Greens states that in conventions "politics simply depends on personalities who sell strategies." Grit, a radical militant from Freiburg, feels that "a few functionaries control the events." Also in Agalev, and particularly in Ecolo, there are complaints about the overwhelming influence of a select group of activists, though not as strident as in the Greens.[13]

Experienced militants have proven to be particularly adept at using decision procedures when controversies develop. They often engage in debates about procedures that are actually shadowboxing matches about substantive political disagreements. Thus, although ecology parties lack the strong guiding hand of national party elites and convention directorates, the inequality of personal skills spontaneously generates power differentials at conventions which lead to resignation or outbursts of hostility among less advantaged delegates. In the words of a delegate to a Baden-Württemberg state party convention, "The mass of delegates who are inexperienced in procedural matters helplessly surrenders to [militants skilled in debating conference procedures] and hopes desperately that the motions drafted by their locals will still be discussed."[14]

The parties' membership journals are full of irate letters and reports about the dominance of "political movers-and-shakers" [*Politikmacker*],[15] "old-left routiniers,"[16] and "rhetorically polished old functionaries."[17] A letter to the Hamburg membership journal categorically declares: "State party meetings have degenerated into podiums of analytical master thinkers [*Grosskörfe*]. . . . Apparently, they do not want to convince people, but to silence adversaries."[18] Political entrepreneurs, often with charismatic appeal, replace the formal authority of an elected or co-opted party elite.

Rank-and-file frustrations have triggered efforts to curtail the ability of prominent activists to take the floor. Since 1984 Green national conventions have instituted a lottery system from which an equal number of male and female speakers will be drawn to address the floor for a maximum of three minutes per speaker. Critics claim that now mediocre contributions, too brief for complex ideas, prevail in debates, while prominent party leaders congregate outside the convention hall. Says Josef, a Green activist from northern

13. For this criticism, see the debate at a meeting of the Ecolo steering group after the socioeconomic conference in the spring of 1985, "Compte-rendu du Conseil de Fédération," 17 Mai 1985," *Ecolo Infos,* no. 58 (June 1, 1985), 13.

14. Peter Dunkl, "Anmerkungen zur Basisdemokratie," *Grüne Blätter,* nos. 16–17 (December 1982), 21.

15. Alternative Liste Berlin, *Mitgliederrundbrief,* no. 19 (September 82), 10.

16. Ralf Fücks, "Wohin des Wegs? Anmerkungen zum Bundeskongress der Grünen," *Grüner Basisdienst* (December 1983), 49.

17. Margret Sennekamp, "Der andere Blick. Parteistrukturen aus der Sicht einer Frau," *Grüne Blätter,* 4, no. 6 (1984), 16–17.

18. "Leserbrief von Philippe," *GAL Rundbrief,* no. 3 (1984), 82.

Germany, "conventions are good for the rank-and-file militants to blow off steam, but not for operational decisions."

Rank-and-file resentment sometimes fosters a contrariness toward formal or informal party leaders which leads to lengthy discussions of details concerning the conduct of individual prominent speakers or matters of party finance managed by secretaries and executive committees. Rank-and-file militants are strongly opposed to providing more financing to the state and national party organizations.[19] The Greens in Lower Saxony went through three state conventions before choosing a financing scheme for their membership journal (*Tageszeitung*, May 17, 1985). At the June 1985 Green national party conference in Hagen, the treasurer's annual report received almost as much floor time as the debate about strategy and recent defeats in state elections. Strong resentment against political elites leads to an allocation of discussion time that disadvantages party policy and strategy.

As a consequence of time shortages, the overload of decision problems and the style of political debates frequently force conferences to make hasty decisions. Interviewees talk about "voting orgies" and "decision-making machines" which are set in motion when time is running out. Militants often do not know what they are voting on and the number of abstentions increases. Greens in particular observe that conventions have little capacity for arriving at clear decisions, often reverse themselves quickly, or support vague compromises. In North Rhine–Westphalia a 1984 conference initially endorsed a compromise resolution on alliance strategy with the Social Democrats after a day and a half of debate. Minutes later, the delegates agreed to amendments canceling out the first vote.[20] Similarly, the 1981 and 1984 preelection conferences of the Berlin AL were simply unable to decide among a host of alternative resolutions on party strategy. The votes were too close and too fluctuating to tell which side had won.[21]

Ecology parties thus face a number of obstacles to what many militants would consider a legitimately democratic, rational, decision-making process. There are two conditions under which these obstacles appear less severe. First, in areas with low levels of left-libertarian cleavage mobilization, the range of political opinions in ecology parties is narrower and open conflict at party conferences occurs less frequently. Moreover, militants are more willing to accept a structured decision-making process with guidance from a

19. For controversies in the Greens compare *Tageszeitung* (November 15, 1982) on the national party conference at Hagen and *Grünes NRW Info*, 3 (July 1983), 14 on the North Rhine–Westphalian state party. For Agalev compare *Blad Groen*, no. 21 (March 1983), 12.

20. See the report in *Tageszeitung* (December 18, 1984) on the convention at Niederaussem on December 15 and 16, 1984.

21. See Klaus Voy, "Abgestimmt und nichts entschieden," *Kommune*, 2 (December 1984), 35–36, Horst Eckert, report in *Stachlige Argumente*, no. 31 (March 1985), 4, and *Süddeutsche Zeitung* (January 28, 1985), 3.

conference executive committee. This is primarily the case in Agalev and Ecolo and some Green state parties on the periphery of the left-libertarian cleavage.

Many Belgian militants are dissatisfied with convention procedures, but emphasize that, due to the absence of strong antagonistic tendencies, most decisions are made with solid majorities. The low number of ideologues in the ranks of both Belgian parties reduces the potential for disagreement at conferences and increases willingness to accept a more regulated, centrally guided decision-making process. Both Belgian parties, for instance, prohibit agenda changes shortly before or during conventions; only issues that were announced to local party sections in advance can be raised. Of all parties, Ecolo's conventions are governed by the most relatively centralist party leadership. At the other extreme, in West German Green state parties where the left-libertarian cleavage is highly mobilized, agendas are the most malleable. Discussions focus more easily on procedural matters or ideologically highly charged questions, and decisions often remain ambiguous.

A second condition improving the democratic legitimacy of party conventions applies where ecology parties are in a strong electoral position. Hesse (1983–87) is so far the only case where a strong electoral position forced the Greens to face up to a hard choice on an alliance with a Social Democratic state government. Here, turnout at the crucial conferences was high, the feuding strategic factions received equal speaking time at the conventions, and decisions ran consistently along factional lines. In Hesse party democracy consists more in the appeal of competing party elites for the support of the rank and file than in a chance for all to participate in the debates. A strong competitive position makes militants more willing to commit themselves to more consistent, enforceable, and lasting choices and thus ultimately to support greater rationalization and more rigorous democratic legitimation of the decision-making process.

To conclude, open, participatory conferences without central direction or methods for aggregating preferences follow the model prescribed by the parties' logic of constituency representation. Yet they bring about unintended consequences some militants interpret as deficiencies in the rationality and legitimacy of decision procedures. The conclusion many militants draw from subscribing to a Michelsian image of party politics as controlled by self-interested elites creates perverse effects: the overload, if not displacement, of convention agendas and time-consuming debates about the political and financial conduct of party leaders. Often this very dynamic paralyzes effective decision making altogether and, for want of unambiguous party policies, increases the autonomy of parliamentarians and informal political entrepreneurs who interpret ambiguous decisions for a broad political audience inside and outside the parties. Efforts to adhere strictly to the left-libertarian logic of constituency representation actually promote the rise of unlicensed party spokespeople. In the emerging fragmented, stratarchal power structure, individual skills and charisma are a more important source of power than official position and procedure laid down by the party.

The Irrelevance of Organizational Structure

Unlike conventional West German and Belgian parties, the ecologists have almost completely emasculated the political role of party representatives and officials who carry on the day-to-day decision-making business between conventions in steering committees, party executives, secretariats, and party commissions. By design, party officials have few positional power resources; moreover, in the eyes of many militants they lack the political legitimacy to make or even propose important decisions. Officials find themselves caught in the middle between conventions and the parties' elected legislators. Despite all the shortcomings in decision-making capacity, the authority to choose definitive political strategies rests with conventions, while organizational resources and access to the mass media, important means to interpret and disseminate the parties' policies, are vested in the parliamentarians. Whatever power party officials do wield is based more on the personal skill, dedication, charisma, and reputation of individual office holders than on positional authority. The actual status of party officers in many ways realizes the intentions of militants calling for a nonbureaucratic, decentralized party structure but it also has curious and unexpected consequences. The role of party officers is contingent upon several external conditions. In areas of high left-libertarian mobilization, the antibureaucratic spirit affects the party apparatus most profoundly. Where cleavage mobilization is weaker, where political institutions are more conducive to the participation of ecology parties, and where the parties' competitive position is strong, party officers retain at least a semblance of power and influence.

Steering Committees

All three parties have steering committees at the state or national level, which convene delegates to discuss and decide party policy between major conventions. Steering committees meet relatively infrequently on a monthly or bimonthly basis and the officeholders are unpaid. This weak structural position gives them little weight in political deliberations and little mass media coverage. As a consequence delegate absenteeism and turnover are widespread, undermining the continuity of committee work. Few militants consider the committees effective and even fewer volunteer to serve on them. As a rule the steering committees latch onto administrative and financial oversight tasks but have little say over policy or personnel decisions. Angry because of their modest influence, steering committees frequently repeat the dynamic of goal displacement encountered in some party conventions: they project themselves as the guardians of grassroots democracy and retaliate against executives, secretaries, and parliamentarians they consider to be too influential with personal and political attacks and close examination of their political style and financial conduct.

Leo from Agalev finds that the steering committee is less a political organ than a petty regulator of administrative matters, unable to cope with broader political choices submitted to it by the parliamentarians or the party executive. "What we have presently is not a control of political priorities, but of ridiculous administrative procedures." An Ecolo militant states that his party's steering committee has not seen a political debate for months (Lannoye (1985:51). Committee members often have a reputation for low political competence and low continuity of political activism. As Gerard in Ecolo claims, they have "no memory and no continuity."

Most Green militants also hold steering committees in low regard. In this case, factionalism as well as institutional weakness work to their discredit, as they are dominated by the radical fundamentalist wing of cosmopolitan ideologues. In the eyes of many activists the legitimacy and credibility of state and national steering committees have seriously suffered because they have failed to represent different party wings. They attract people who, in the words of one Hessian parliamentarian, "are not elected to important offices, but have high ambitions." As a consequence steering committees are rarely taken seriously as policy-making bodies. Pragmatists claim the national steering committee is "a monolithic block of fundamentalists without function" and call for its abolition.[22]

Party Executives

In the Greens and in Agalev, and to a lesser extent in Ecolo, party executives suffer from the same deficits of positional power, legitimacy, and political influence as steering committees. Service on executive boards is honorary and limited to two consecutive terms of two years each. Meetings of the executive are held intermittently (weekly or biweekly). Executives usually direct a very small administrative staff barely able to keep up with the minimum requirements of administrative bookkeeping. Moreover, they have little access to the mass media or active support from the rank and file. Especially in the Greens, members of executives often sense they are received with hostility and suspicion by the grassroots militants. As one interviewed

22. "It [the Federal Steering Committee] is as time- and cost-intensive as it is ineffective. We therefore plead for the determined abolition of this organ which is characterized by arbitrariness and in which the often praised imperative mandate is not realized at all." (Ökolibertare Grüne 1984:57)

member of a state executive notes, "we have no grassroots, just the mistrust of the grassroots." And a former member of the Baden-Württemberg state executive declares: "I resigned from the managing executive because I no longer wanted to be kicked around by everyone and apologize all the time for being on the executive." For fear of being humiliated, party executives shy away from offensive political statements: "Better no press declaration than striking the wrong chord."[23]

Party executives often face a mountain of administrative work, with very few opportunities to communicate political messages. This situation has largely immobilized them and impaired their creative political role. As a result absenteeism, turnover, and low morale are the rule. A simple cost-benefit calculation drives many people to resign: "The enormous expenditure of time and personal energy required by continuous work in the state executive and the managing executive committee stand in no relationship to the results of this labor."[24] The high turnover rate, of course, makes life worse for those who remain: "The more members of the executive drop out, the greater is the work load for the remaining people."[25]

Party executives are embroiled in a vicious circle of mistrust and organizational deterioration (see Figure 6). Their weak structural position inspires few talented and purposive militants to seek the office. Axel from the Hamburg Green executive observes that "people want to steer the boat, but not row." The recruitment of often inexperienced or poorly motivated militants, in turn, weakens actual performance and creates even more incentive for leaving. Further, the short supply of candidates often makes it impossible to elect a committee that is politically representative of the rank and file. Because of their cosmopolitanism and concern with party organization, ideologues have the greatest propensity to run for executive office. Moreover, given that many rank-and-file militants do not consider the selection of executives an important political event, they are frequently chosen in conferences overrepresenting party ideologues.[26] Because executives enjoy little legitimacy, Green parliamentarians have little reason to take them seriously as guardians of party principle.

Many interviewees find this vicious circle shifts power in the Greens to informal groups and to charismatic individuals who steer clear of the unrewarding executive positions, remain without office, or aim at parliamentary

23. Michael Happe, "Ein Jahr im Landesvorstand. Anmerkungen zu einem dysfunktionalen Gremium," *Grünes Info NRW*, 4 (September 1984), vi.

24. Beate Orgonas, letter of November 8, 1983 to the state executive in Baden-Württemberg, Landesgeschäftsstelle Stuttgart.

25. Christine Muscheler, "Einige Anmerkungen zur bevorstehenden Landesvorstandswahl vom 27./28. 5," *Grüne Blatter*, no. 21 (May 1983), 5.

26. I contrast the choice of executives to that of candidates for parliamentary office in Chapter 7 and provide some data on the different political outlook of both groups.

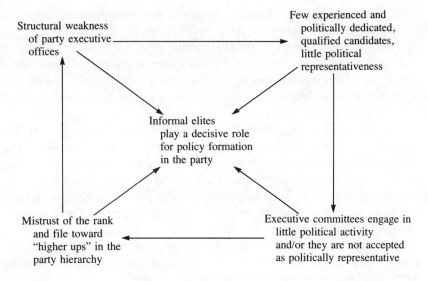

Figure 6. The vicious circle of executive office in ecology parties

seats. At a convention of the West Berlin Alternative List a participant read a list of militants who in his view enjoyed the highest real influence in the party, and asked them to run for the state executive but not one of them volunteered (Zeuner 1983:110).

The vicious circle of power, office, and accountability occurs more in Green state executives than the national executive in the Greens, Agalev, and Ecolo. Since the mid-1980s Green national executives have been practically professionalized because members receive "compensation for lost income" on days they attend to their office. In addition, the national party executive represents the party in televised election debates, enabling it to disseminate an image of the party to a very large audience. This has prompted stronger personalities from all political wings to run for the executive. Yet it remains dominated by the radical faction of the party, probably because it is elected at national party conferences to which ideologues turn out in greater numbers than pragmatists or lobbyists.

Nevertheless, compared to Green parliamentarians the national executive still suffers from decisive structural disadvantages in terms of staff support, access to the press, and political legitimacy in the eyes of both militants and the broader public. Because of these disadvantages and the executive's gener-ally more radical politics, many members of the executive frame their rela-tions to the parliamentary party according to the syndicalist version of Michels' oligarchy theory. They attribute to parliamentarians material and status motives and a willingness to be co-opted into existing political institutions. This perception has often led to tense relations between the executive and the parliamentary party, with the former trying to control the administrative and financial behavior of the latter, while rarely being able to discuss or direct policy initiatives or to present its own alternatives. Lucas, a member of the national executive for several years, observed that ''the federal executive seeks not to gain an independent voice, but to exercise narrow-minded control over the parliamentary party.''

Agalev and Ecolo party executives face similar constraints, though on a lesser scale. Belgian militants are less opposed to executives playing a creative political role. The greater institutional openness of Belgian politics and the lower level of left-libertarian conflict further soften criticism of party executives. Agalev and Ecolo executives also find themselves in a more favorable structural position vis-à-vis their parliamentary representatives, since the latter constitute a very small number of people and, accordingly, have more limited political weight than legislators in the Greens. Finally, the small size and regional division of the Belgian parties facilitate frequent meetings of executives and parliamentarians.

Nevertheless, Belgian activists also recognize intrinsic structural weaknesses in the amateur executive. It is difficult to find qualified candidates, and the reputation and power of party executives derive more from important personalities than from the office itself. In Agalev the generation of party founders initially dominated the executive. In recent years, however, turnover has been high and in the eyes of most interviewees political influence has declined. In Ecolo, in contrast strong personalities forming a core leadership continue to participate in the executive even while they do not formally belong to it. Interviewees distinguish between the ''official,'' elected and the ''officious,'' actually influential executives comprising the party's ''inner circle.'' Ecolo's actual power structure involves a degree of centralization and personalization of control that comes closer to that of conventional European parties than either Agalev's or the Greens'.

On the whole, the greatest barrier to strong ecology party executives which could act as an effective counterweight to large parliamentary party groups is the militants' commitment to a logic of constituency representation. Many militants prefer weak executives who are not entitled to formulate policies and strategies.[27] The unwanted consequence is an increase in the power of informal leaders and individual parliamentarians, and an evaporation of political power and coordination, thus reducing the parties' ability to mobilize and project clear strategies.

27. See for instance the controversy fought out in the Hessse executive committee: protocols of the executive meetings on April 8, 1983, and May 13, 1983, and Franz Josef Hanke, ''Aufstand im Vorstand?'' in *Grüne Hessenzeitung*, 3 (June 1983), 18.

Secretaries

Administrative secretaries are a third group of players in the ecology parties' executive organization. They are hired by the steering committee (in Agalev and Ecolo) or the executive (in the Greens) to run the party administration and accounting system, circulate information, publish membership newsletters, and prepare conferences. While most interviewees feel administrative employees should not meddle in political affairs, there have been some "strong" secretaries who have developed continuous ties to the mass media and political groups outside the party. In some cases, they have become power brokers within their own party by engaging in a meta-politics of agenda setting, channeling information, bringing party militants together, linking them to the mass media, and timing the decision process. The potential strength of party secretariats is rooted in the professionalization of the office, the permanency of political involvement making them always available to requests for political statements from the mass media or external political groups. Secretariats, however, are also vulnerable because they lack the political legitimacy of elected party office and can be removed by those who hired them.

Interviewees in the Hesse and Hamburg Greens rate the power of the state party secretariats low. In these areas where the left-libertarian cleavage is highly mobilized, charismatic political personalities at the helm of conflicting tendencies dominate the party and are very sensitive to the role of party functionaries. Under these conditions secretaries are careful to avoid antagonizing their employers. Thus, political polarization and a radical left-libertarian spirit reduce the power of secretaries, as is evidenced by the North Rhine–Westphalian and the federal Green secretariats. Both offices had strong secretaries in the first half of the 1980s but as controversies about the party's strategy and orgnizational form heated up they were replaced by more subservient administrative personnel.

As is the case with steering committees and executives, in areas with weaker cleavage mobilization secretaries play a greater political role. Interviewees agree that the Baden-Württemberg Green secretariat and even more so the Agalev national secretariat in Brussels have influenced party policy. The position of the Agalev secretary vis-à-vis a relatively weak party executive and parliamentary group has been strong over a number of years and has always been a matter of some controversy.

At first glance, Ecolo, clearly positioned on the periphery of the left-libertarian cleavage, represents an anomaly because activists attribute little political influence to its permanent staff at Namur (not to be confused with Ecolo's executive committee, called Secrétariat Fédéral). In this case, however, the existence of a closely knit network of party leaders revolving around the executive and the location of the party's headquarters in its stronghold of Namur has imposed political constraints on the administrative employees. Still, some members of the party's inner circle have called for instituting the office of a powerful elected secretary.[28]

To conclude, it would be a mistake to believe that secretaries in any ecology party exercise key influence over party policy and can subvert strong viewpoints in the rank and file, executive, or parliamentary groups. The secretaries' legitimacy and administrative tenure are too precarious to allow them to stray too far from the parties' mainstream.

Party Commissions

Aside from the institutions ecology party statutes specify, the West German Greens have at least one additional set of party organs with some influence, functionally organized work groups or commissions that focus on specific interest groups or policy areas. These groups are open to all members and originally attracted many lobbyists from social movements who wanted an organizational focus for their particular concern, such as the environment, women, gays, children, squatters, immigrants, the disabled, or cultural and social affairs within the party. The broad sector and great mobilization of left-libertarian social movements in West Germany may explain why work groups are more important in the Greens than in Agalev and Ecolo.

Although the number of Green state and national work groups is quite large, the militants interviewed attribute only limited power to them. Work groups meet irregularly, have high turnover, and rely on a small number of continuous contributors who are experts and lobbyists often with very little interest in the broader policies of the party. In Hamburg, for instance, interviewees claim that work groups had become increasingly homogeneous, cliquish, and oriented away from the other party organs. Because anybody can participate in work groups, and usually people with the strongest interest in a given policy area get involved, they have little democratic legitimacy in the party. According to Günther, a Green federal parliamentarian, "Those who show up vote. Federal work groups cannot represent the rank and file, they only convene people who have a lot of time." And another Green parliamentarian says of the gay rights work group: "I believe that the twenty or thirty people in the gay work group are as elitist as the Green federal parliamentary party."

In the mid-1980s the Green work groups on animal rights, gay rights, nuclear policy, and to a certain extent the one on social policy became launching pads for radical wings in the party, particularly at the national level. In these cases, activists in the ideologue camp have tried to use work groups to

28. For this conception, see *Ecolo Infos*, no. 55 (April 15, 1985), 8–9. The conflict in the party over its strategy toward the regional governing parties in Wallonia after the 1985 national elections led to postponement of organizational changes in the party.

push the parliamentary party toward a more radical course. The Green federal steering committee and federal executive, both heavily packed with ideologues, have tried to build up work groups as an instrument for checking the Green parliamentarians. In contrast, the purely lobbyist and expert work groups have generally been more cooperative with parliamentarians, especially those in state parties. Several Green state parliamentarians interviewed proudly declared that they "control" their work groups well, thereby increasing their own efficiency and expertise in parliament as well.

Clearly the most important functional interest representation in the Greens are the state and national work groups on women. They are a crossbreed of lobby, expert, and factional organizations. In most instances they convene feminists who are critical of any move toward a logic of party competition, whether through formalization and professionalization of the party apparatus or through moderate alliance strategies. In most cases, women's work groups have supported the radical wing in the Green party. In turn radicals have tried to promote their own control of the party under the cloak of women's rights by fielding likeminded female candidates for political office.[29]

Although women's groups have successfully pushed for women's rights within the party, such as formal rules of equal representation with men and a women's statute, some interviewees claim that many female militants do not support these work groups. These critics argue that the insistence on solidarity and community against what they perceive as male competition and aggression may be in fact only a thinly veiled pretext for repressing dissent against radical strategy within the women's own ranks. They fear that feminists may be unintentionally promoting a "totalitarian democracy" which ignores the fact that liberty is built on procedures guaranteeing tolerance for persistent disagreements and the right to engage in competition and conflict.[30]

The example of women's work groups illustrates the difference between the Greens, operating in an environment of relatively high left-libertarian mobilization, and Agalev and Ecolo located on the periphery of the new cleavage. In Agalev a women's group founded in 1982 decided, after a controversial debate, that men should be admitted to the group, something unimaginable in the Greens.[31] Since that time, the group has been relatively inactive. In Ecolo, a radical women's group was founded only in 1985, by militants from Liège and Brussels. The group calls for more women to be represented in the party

29. In this sense, Schöller (1985:88–89) discovered that the women who took over the executive committee of the Alternative List in Berlin in 1984 did not think of their activism as a feminist project but as a strategic move against moderates in the party who sought an alliance with the SPD.

30. For an experience with "totalitarian democracy," see Lore Michaelis, "Wandsbek-Frauengruppe mit Männerstrukturen," *GAL Rundbrief,* 4 (1984), 67.

31. See the minutes of the meeting of the *Werkgroep Vrouwen in Agalev* on March 4, 1982, in *Blad Groen,* 1, no. 6 (March 1982), 25–26.

leadership and claims to be a catalyst for feminization of the party.[32] But other women militants have attacked the group for its exclusion of men.[33] And the national party executive has refused to accept it formally as a party work group.[34]

In a nutshell, the positional power and legitimacy of the party apparatus is quite low in ecology parties. In centers of the left-libertarian cleavage this tendency is more pronounced than on the periphery. Where militants do attribute power to party officials, it is based on the office holder's personal abilities and charisma rather than institutional control of resources and information. Power migrates out of the realm of formal authority to informal groups of political entrepreneurs who sway a party's course with their rhetorical skill and personal following. This dynamic is the unintended consequence of the militants' efforts to create a tightly coupled, inverse hierarchy with democratic control through the rank and file. The party apparatus, unable to maintain a regular flow of communication between local party units and representative organs, produces a stratarchal fragmentation of power. And the weak political position of the party executives, as the grassroots militants' direct agents, in turn makes it difficult to hold to account those party agents that concentrate positional resources and attract strong political personalities: the parties' elected representatives.

Leadership by Default

The relationship among members of parliament, party apparatus, and conventions at the state and national level evolves along lines similar to those between municipal councilors and local party sections discussed in the previous chapter. By default, individual parliamentarians emerge as the central strategic players in ecology parties. Party conventions and executives provide weak guidance for the parties. At the same time, as paid, full-time political professionals with a staff, some access to the mass media, and a broad public audience, parliamentarians have a solid positional power base compared to that of party executives.

Moreover, parliamentarians are only indirectly controlled by their party because they are agents of numerous principals: They have been nominated by their local party section; they have been confirmed by the district party organization (in Agalev and Ecolo) or nominated by state party conventions to electoral lists (in the Greens); they should be responsive to district, state, or national party steering committees and party executives; moreover, they often

32. See the articles by Geneviève Cattiez, "Et nous les femmes d'Ecolo" and Myriam Kenens, "Pour une féminisme écologique," *Ecolo Infos*, no. 57 (May 15, 1985), 38–40.
33. See the letter by Irma Grosemans in *Ecolo Infos*, no. 60 (July 1985), 35.
34. Cf. *Ecolo Infos*, no. 59 (June 15, 1985), 9.

come from social movement organizations with which they still cultivate ties; finally, they have been elected by voters most of whom are neither party nor movement activists.

The very multiplicity of parliamentarians' dependency and accountability relations does not restrict their political freedom but rather increases it significantly. The interviewed parliamentarians indeed often wonder to which party organ they are really responsible: the local party sections? district and state assemblies? steering groups? party executives? or even the voters?[35] Olivier, an Ecolo parliamentarian, initially comments spontaneously that he feels responsible to his voters. But upon reflection he argues that the militants who nominated him and the party executive charged by the members with monitoring his activities were more important. If the preferences of voters, social movement constituencies, rank-and-file militants, and party executives differed, he would make up his mind on a "case by case" basis. The fragmentation of authority and control in ecology parties enables parliamentarians to pick and choose to which constituency they are loyal. And in light of the numerous intraparty organs and the vagueness and inconsistency of many convention resolutions, parliamentarians can deliberately misinterpret intraparty decisions and dismiss the legitimacy of party organs whose declarations run counter to their own views.

It would be mistaken, however, to conclude that the parliamentary parties are monolithic, centralized power blocks with clearly defined agendas and institutional interests distinct from those of the rank and file. Quite the contrary, a centrifugal dispersion of power also takes place within the parliamentary parties themselves. The deputies' experiences have shown them that individualism and disjointed activism are common in parliamentary groups. Strong libertarian convictions militate against a monocratic coordination of parliamentarians. The left-libertarian critique of hierarchical authority also pervades the parliamentary parties and preempts strong leadership.

The decentralized party organization and the prevailing styles of recruitment to elected office (see Chapter 7) create individualism and fragmentation of political control from the time parliamentarians are nominated. Ecology party deputies usually lack a common political socialization inside or outside the party. As one Green parliamentarian put it, "among us everything is represented, from chieftains in socialist organizations to religious zealots."[36] Individualism and heterogeneity of political experiences and ideologies have

35. For an example of these reflections, compare "Rapport du Groupe Parlementaire Ecolo," *Ecolo Infos, Numéro Spécial*, (April 23, 1983), 5–8.

36. See Dirk Schneider, "'Einblicke in den Zellentrakt'. Ein Klagelied mit verhaltenem Optimismus," *Grüne Hessenzeitung*, (November 1983) no. 11, 18–23. Page 19 quoted here. Instructive on the work of Green parliamentarians are also the annual reports of Die Grünen im Bundestag (1984; 1985) and Alternative Liste Fraktion (1984) as well as Die Grünen im Landtag von Niedersachsen (1984).

left an indelible imprint on the work styles of the parliamentary groups. The larger the groups are, the more fragmented their activities. For this reason the Green federal parliamentary party, the largest ecology party delegation in any European parliament, demonstrates a dynamic encountered on a lesser scale among Green state legislative groups and in Agalev's and Ecolo's joint parliamentary group.

The Green federal parliamentary group is divided into policy areas with specific "study circles" and informal cliques formed around personalities and factions. Deputies choose policy areas and parliamentary committee assignments according to personal and political inclinations, but must be elected by the entire group. In the first Green federal parliamentary party in the 1983–87 electoral term, deputies flocked to policy areas closely linked to the left-libertarian agenda, such as environmental, energy, transportation, and defense policy, but eschewed important political/economic matters such as taxes/finances, budgets, or economic affairs (Die Grünen im Bundestag 1985:11). Also at the state level, the business manager of the Lower Saxony Green parliamentarians observes that, "With the marked propensity towards individualism which is generally a characteristic of the Greens, there is also the inclination to work only on policy areas one enjoys and to avoid unattractive issues." (Die Grünen im Landtag von Niedersachsen 1984:50)

This work style results in a relatively uneven coverage of policy areas. In the Green federal party most bills, motions, and questions submitted to parliament concerned the deputies' preferred policy areas (see Langguth 1984: chap. 3). Similarly, Agalev's and Ecolo's legislative activities focused on peace issues, the environment, transport, health care, and democratic participation (see Agalev 1985b and Ecolo 1985c). The balance of policy areas covered by the legislative groups of ecology parties, however, is likely to shift and broaden with the participation of activists who have worked in ecology parties for an extensive period of time before being elected and are less likely to be lobbyists (see Chapter 7).

Ecology party legislators set political priorities in a disjointed manner and often encounter great difficulty in agreeing on or coordinating their activities. The study circles and experts among the Green federal deputies usually choose policies and hire staff personnel on their own. Green interviewees find that the circles are relatively isolated from each other and often issue public statements without prior consultation with the entire parliamentary party. Even within policy areas, parliamentarians develop independent initiatives. Coordination problems were exacerbated during their 1983–87 term by the decision to replace all parliamentarians by a group of alternates after half of the parliamentary term. While incumbents and alternates were expected to work jointly over the entire four-year period, this cooperation rarely materialized.[37] As a

---

37. See Zeuner (1985:14). I have given relatively little attention to the complex and intense debate about the issue of rotation and alternates in this study. See different evaluations of this

consequence of the disorganization and internal conflicts caused by the mid-term rotation, the Greens have abandoned the rule that parliamentarians are replaced every two years.

Even with rotations only once per term or every other electoral term, the individualistic, disjointed style of political work probably remains the single most important attribute of ecology party parliamentary groups. In this environment entrepreneurial skills and political creativity are rewarded by media exposure and attention within the party, while team players remain politically obscure. Hubert, a Green federal deputy, believes that the absence of organizational controls or social sanctions against individualism and antiauthoritarianism implies a refusal to organize collective political learning processes. He recalls that at the beginning of the 1983–87 legislative term, deputies still looked for a consensus on major initiatives, even if it was brought about by exhaustion rather than substantive agreement. Later on only individual initiative and success, meaning media coverage, counted. Success validated the correctness of a political initiative, even when its thrust was controversial.

Access to the mass media is key for a deputy's external influence and internal standing in the parliamentary party group. Many interviewees state that media presence is the ultimate measure of a deputy's power.[38] The executive leadership of the Green federal parliamentary group is confined to administrative tasks and has no prerogative to speak on behalf of the party. Hence, the mass media do not automatically turn to the group's formal leadership but to deputies, based on their personal reputation and the media's political inclinations. Individual deputies fiercely compete for media access; parliamentarians able to package personal charisma, eloquence, and political views diverging from the party mainstream can be assured of a disproportionate share of the media's attention. Because television and print journalists typically seek out politicians whose personality and nonconformist views fit into the media's frame for understanding politics as a drama staged by a few exceptional actors, there is an affinity between the ecologists' libertarian individualism and the media's own criteria of selecting newsworthy politicians. The media thus thrive on and reinforce political individualism in ecological politics.

Differential access to the mass media gives rise to endemic conflict among deputies. Interviewees suspect that some parliamentarians have developed

issue in *Die Grünen im Bundestag* (1984), 5, contributions in *Grüner Basisdienst,* July–August 1984), Henning Schierholz, "Rotation und kein Ende," *Grüner Basisdienst* (May–June 1984), 29–31, and, more optimistically, Halo Saibold, Axel Vogel, Wolfgang Daniels, and Eberhard Bueb, "Heinzelmännchen der Fraktion. Vier Nachrücker aus Bayern berichten über ihre Erfahrungen in der Bundestagsgruppe," *Grüner Basisdienst* (July–August 1984), 25–27.

38. Green state deputy Thilo Weichert warns that "within the state parliamentary party thinking in terms of effectiveness exists and the measure for effective policy is how frequently militants are mentioned in the mass media." Minutes of the Baden-Württemberg state executive meeting on December 15, 1984, Landesgeschäftsstelle Stuttgart.

ploys for routinely grabbing media attention.[39] Conflicts arise when deputies engage in spectacular activities without prior discussion with their colleagues, such as the 1983 peace demonstration by several Green parliamentarians in East Berlin. Moreover, highly visible foreign trips of parliamentary delegations (to Moscow, Washington, the Middle East, among others) have generated intense clashes among Green federal members of parliament.[40] Competition for media exposure in the Greens is not only a matter of personal rivalry but also of ideology. The radical faction claims the media prefer moderate Green spokespeople.[41]

Less well-known parliamentarians call for more solidarity and collective discipline. Others complain that a climate censoring ambition, individual creativity, and political effectiveness will condemn the parliamentarians to passivity.[42] This tension erupted for the first time in 1983–84 when some members of the Green executive in federal parliament who enjoyed close relations with the press used their position to make controversial statements on behalf of the party. This behavior quickly led other parliamentarians to challenge and replace this leadership by a group of women deputies. This event signaled not only the importance of women's issues for the Greens but also a widespread distaste for formal authority and for dominance of a handful of Green parliamentarians in the mass media. Subsequent Green parliamentary party executives have kept a low profile as technical moderators and facilitators of activities. Yet the new style has not undercut the influence of informal leaders within the party or the mass media.

It comes as no surprise that the deputies' individualism attenuates bonds between the party apparatus and parliamentary groups. Most of the deputies I interviewed rarely attend meetings of the executive or the steering committee and remain in the background at party conventions and in their local districts. In a party with weak formal structure and no professional political career tracks, organizational constraints or incentives that would encourage stronger bonds between legislatures and party constituencies, such as the chance to be reelected, are absent.

In their reflections on the nature of political representation, most interviewees support an individualistic and quasi-pluralist conception. They see themselves as spokespersons of mobilized constituencies inside or outside the

39. In a similar vein, Todd Gitlin (1980) found that New Left activists in the 1960s designed their strategies to get maximum media exposure.

40. Cf. Bernd Barutta, "Da gibt's Umgangsformen, da kannste nur mit dem Kopf schütteln," *Grüner Basisdienst*, (January 1984), 20–23.

41. Compare minutes of the meeting of the federal Green parliamentary party on December 6, 1984, when deputy Jürgen Reents complained that moderate Green deputies were receiving more media exposure than their radical colleagues and the members of the national party executive.

42. In this sense, the business manager of the Green federal parliamentary party criticized proponents of a more collectivist political style. See *Tageszeitung*, August 31, 1985.

party and adamantly oppose the idea that they should represent the parties' electorate. Typical responses were: "I can be responsible only to those who articulate themselves." "I cannot represent the interests of people who do not voice their own demands." "I cannot determine what voters want." "I would not want to talk to many of those who have voted for us."

While this interpretation of political representation often does not withstand critical scrutiny, it is evidence of the individualistic, espressive style of ecology parliamentarians. When pressed on the point that a commitment to mobilized constituencies has inegalitarian consequences because only the most resourceful, articulate social groups have a political say, a number of interviewees wavered and conceded that voters impose constraints on the party's and their own stance "in the final analysis." And in practice deputies often do follow collectivist principles of representation by voicing demands on behalf of weak, unmobilized, inarticulate social groups, whether foreign workers, the homeless, children, retirees, or even prostitutes. But only a minority of militants, primarily representative of the parties' pragmatist wing, outrightly endorse a collectivist notion of representation and responsibility to the voters.

My brief sketch of ecology party parliamentary groups has emphasized attributes that set them most clearly apart from traditional parliamentary party groups: an individualistic political style, a lack of hierarchical authority patterns within the caucus organization, open disagreements among deputies belonging to the same party in statements to the mass media, and an anti-collectivist notion of representation. While these features emphasize what characterizes the unique logic of constituency representation in ecology parties, as well as its unintended effects, forces exist which do push the parliamentary parties, to a lesser or greater degree, toward a more conventional mold.

First of all, because of the fully intended structural weakness of ecology parties, the thin links between deputies and rank-and-file organizations, and the ambiguities of choice in party conventions and other arenas, the key role of parliamentarians represents a de facto centralization of power, entrusting the formulation of the parties' policies to a small group of people, no matter how individualistically they act. Second, there is little doubt that the institutional environment of parliamentarism has affected the political behavior of ecology party representatives in a number of ways. While many of them originally perceived parliament as an ideal stage for attacking, disrupting, and ridiculing the existing political institution and as a storehouse of information about the inner workings of the system, they soon became immersed in the details of parliamentary work. Starting out from the conception of a "speaking parliament" addressing the nation, most deputies accustomed themselves quickly to the style of a "working parliament," in which much effort is invested behind the scenes in committees and detailed deliberation of administrative matters and legislation. As one member of the Green national legislative group declared: "Originally, we envisioned our work in Bonn more along the lines that we would not get engaged in parliamentarism very much. We saw the entire affair predominantly as acquiring information. We wanted to get more out of it than to contribute to it. That has developed very differently."[43]

In fact, Belgian and West German parliamentary groups have outperformed their competitors in industriousness and initiative. They take great pride in showing that they are better prepared on a wide variety of issues. In 1983 and 1984 the Green federal parliamentary group posed 81.4 percent of all questions to the government, initiated 54 percent of the "grand inquiries" (*grosse Anfrage*) leading to parliamentary debates, submitted 38 percent of the bills drafted by parliamentary party groups, and introduced 44 percent of the motions, although it represented only 6 percent of all deputies (see Ismayr 1985:315–19). A single Agalev deputy posed 1,603 questions to the government over a period of thirty months.

Ideologues in the parties interpret the acceptance of the parliamentary work style in a psychological framework: "The apparatus is swallowing us up." "Experience in these institutions social-democratizes us." "There is a risk of being corrupted by our status and material advantages." Pragmatists, however, reject psychological interpretations. They maintain that only credible policies will increase the parties' political weight vis-à-vis their competitors. They criticize the self-pitying and reductionist view that individual psychological weaknesses determine political behavior, and they endorse a more voluntarist, strategic, and instrumentalist view of the link between parliamentary means and ends.

The relative strength of the tendency to work within established parliamentary tracks appears to depend on the parties' political environment and on the ideological outlook of individual representatives.[44] In the Greens federal and some state parliamentary parties exhibit an individualist style and commitment to anticollectivist concept of representation more clearly than Agalev's and Ecolo's parliamentarians and Green state parliamentary groups on the left-libertarian periphery. Even within parliamentary groups, the most flamboyant, charismatic, and individualist parliamentarians tend to come from areas with high left-libertarian mobilization.[45]

Institutional context also makes a difference in the dynamic of parliamen-

43. Birgitt Arkenstette, quoted from Jäger and Pinl (1985:31).

44. In this sense, cultural socialization theories of parliamentary behavior (such as Badura and Reese 1976 or Searing 1986) do not take into account ideology and cleavage mobilization as counteracting forces.

45. Many examples come to mind of which I will mention only Olivier Deleuze (Ecolo representative from Brussels until his resignation in 1986) and Green politicians Thomas Ebermann, Joschka Fischer, Hubert Kleinert, Jo Müller, Otto Schily, Eckhart Stratmann, and Antje Vollmer.

tary parties. In Belgium, where the party system is less polarized, Agalev's and Ecolo's national deputies rarely challenge their colleagues in public, although individualism within their party is pronounced.[46] They are more willing to endorse a collectivist view of representation than their West German colleagues and they are more inclined to cooperate with their national party executive. The greater cohesion and centralization of the Belgian parties, particularly of Ecolo, translate into closer bonds between parliamentary group and party apparatus. The small size of the parliamentary group of course contributes to this process. Some Belgian interviewees believe the balance of power would shift in favor of the parliamentary group if it were to grow significantly.

The cohesion and political power of parliamentary groups are also affected by their competitive position. If a party is in the opposition, its parliamentarians feel little urgency to resolve internal conflicts and coordinate actions. But when they can make or break parliamentary majorities, deputies are compelled to conform to a single course or jeopardize the party's influence. The Hessian Green parliamentary party started out as a heterogeneous, disunited group. In October 1982 it could not agree on a common proposal for a strategy toward the Social Democratic minority government and decided that each deputy could present his or her own view at an upcoming party conference.[47] Work morale and cooperation among the deputies was low.[48] But in the face of indecisive party conventions and a weak state executive, the parliamentarians set out to define a joint political strategy. When they engaged in negotiations with the Social Democrats and were challenged by intense interparty opposition, the parliamentarians became, with only two exceptions, a cohesive, solidary group, able to plan its major initiatives in advance and commit itself to a consistent strategy.

In summary, parliamentarians in ecology parties reveal the influence both of left-libertarian ideas committing them to a logic of constituency representation and of considerable forces pulling them toward a conventional logic of party competition. The perverse effects of a weak, decentralized party and parliamentary group, exposure to parliamentary institutions and procedures, and a strong competitive position facilitate accommodation.

Conclusion

Guided by a syndicalist interpretation of Michels' ''strong'' theory of oligarchy, ecology party militants have by and large succeeded in guarding against

46. Conflict came into the open, however, about the parties' position on a socialist bill to liberalize abortion laws.

47. See the protocol of the meeting of the Hessian Green parliamentary party on October 28, 1982.

48. Complaints were raised about the high absenteeism at group meetings. See, e.g., the protocol of the January 25, 1983 meeting of the Hessian Green parliamentarians.

emergence of a formal hierarchical elite structure. Conventions are not controlled by a small executive committee and often lead to volatile outcomes surprising many participants. The party apparatus in steering committees, executives, secretaries, and work groups has little influence on the parties' political course. The image of spontaneity and fluidity, however, would be incomplete if one did not highlight four perverse effects that cause concern among most militants: (1) personalization of power, (2) inability to make decisions that live up to many militants' standards of collective rationality and legitimacy, (3) vicious circles of control and mistrust, and (4) dominance of parliamentarians in charting the parties' political course.

Organizational stratarchy does not rectify asymmetrical control of the party but only weakens its structural underpinnings. In a fluid organization power and influence move into a zone of informal communication and networking, where political entrepreneurs with wide personal power resources hold sway over conventions or parliamentary groups and over access to the mass media. Because *accountable* office holders have few positional resources for determining the parties' course, power is accumulated by *unaccountable* entrepreneurs through personal resources and abilities. Party militants widely recognize this dynamic as a problem. In cities like Hamburg and Frankfurt most interviewees agreed that the Greens are directed by a dozen or so informal leaders. In Ecolo the question "Who is most influential in the party?" repeatedly turned up the same five names.

A second perverse effect of the fluidity of decision-making procedures is weak rationalization and legitimacy of collective choice. Decisions often depend on chance factors such as the turnout at a particular meeting, the timing of the vote, and the framing of alternative options. With controversial issues, party conventions are haunted by Arrow's (1963) problem of cycling majorities. The lack of formal patterns of representation and the ambiguities of choice increase the influence of those who have the resources to attend most meetings as well as the power to interpret decisions with some political consequence. "We face the problem of having an unsatisfactory level of rationalization in our decision making which creates enormous freedom at the top of the party that can be asserted with rhetorical means in party conventions." (Hubert, from the Green parliamentary party in Bonn) As an Ecolo party executive put it, "We want open structures accessible to all; we have many meetings, and nobody can attend everything; we also lack clear rules when important decisions are going to be made; there is always the risk that decisions are made when one is missing." In sum, "In the party little is formalized, every decision can be revised at any time by a new majority— under the banner of egalitarian democracy. The Greens have not yet found a substantive system of representation, or any sustainable compromises. More and more, a certain type of politician comes to the fore. That is a young, unattached student or unemployed teacher who still has a little income so that he can travel around."[49]

From the perspective of a calculus of transaction costs that counts resource scarcity as a constraint on organizational choice, the number, speed, and complexity of decisions in a modern party rule out participation covering all important issues. To assure minimum standards of collective rationality and democratic legitimacy of choice, militants would have to install a formal system of representation and merge political office, accountability, and discretionary powers. But their ideological predilections keep them from accepting these correctives. This gives rise to a third perverse effect, an inversion of Crozier's (1964) vicious circle of control, here an ideology driven vicious circle of grassroots control. Whereas Crozier's management viewed the world through Weber's ideal type of bureaucracy, ecology party militants adopt a voluntarist interpretation of Michels' "iron law of oligarchy." In this interpretative frame, grassroots militants are seen as naturally radical whereas party leaders exhibit "accommodationist" tendencies. Hence, rank-and-file preferences govern the party only if formal authority is weak and leadership positions rotate frequently.[50]

Since party officials lack control of vital political resources and are met with hostility and mistrust, there are few incentives to serve in office. Power is exercised informally, party executives are politically incapacitated, influential entrepreneurs tend to avoid party office and run only for electoral office. The dialectic of formal party office and informal leadership is captured well by an Agalev party executive; "I had more influence as long as I had no office in the steering group and the executive committee; I could present myself as a grassroots activist; now I am subject to mistrust and efforts to supervise my behavior closely."

Personalization of power, rationality deficits of collective choice, and the vicious circle of grassroots control converge to contribute to the fourth unintended outcome, the autonomy of prominent parliamentary deputies. In the face of the ambiguity and questionable legitimacy of party resolutions, parliamentarians often make critical choices on alliance strategies and in representing their party to the mass media. In the parties' stratarchal, decentralized, and centrifugal decision-making procedures, power ends up in their hands by default and they often do not quite know what to do with it.

The extent to which ecology parties create decentralized, loosely coupled structures with unintended consequences depends on three by now familiar

49. Quotation from an interview with Joschka Fischer, Green federal parliamentary party, in Jäger and Pinl (1985: 111–12).

50. For especially stark examples of a voluntarist theory of oligarchy in the Greens see Arbeitsgemeinschaft Radikalökologisches Forum (1984) and Raphael Keppel and Jan Kühnert, *Manifest der Fundamentalisten,* Rothenburg and Wiesbaden 1985 (no publisher).

external circumstances. First, mobilization of the left-libertarian cleavage in the parties' environment affects their internal process in a number of ways which are summarized in Table 32. Second, political institutions and opportunity structures have driven the West German Greens more toward stratarchy in the party's organization than Agalev and Ecolo in Belgium. Finally, changes in a party's competitive position influence its structure. As the experience of the Hessian Green state party illustrates, a strong competitive position dramatically increases cohesiveness of the parliamentary party and centralizes political debates in party conventions around two competing factions, while the party apparatus (executives, secretaries, steering committees) remains without influence.

Without doubt, ecology parties differ from conventional parties most significantly in West German left-libertarian centers where ecologists are simultaneously in a weak competitive electoral position, as in West Berlin or Hamburg.[51] Nevertheless, even on the periphery of the cleavage ecology party organization remains very different. In conventional parties party executives guide, if not control, party conventions.[52] Party elites set and negotiate agendas far in advance. They usually schedule a disproportionate share of time for addressing the convention floor. A committee screens all motions and packages them into blocks that can be handled by a convention. Procedures are highly structured and decisions cannot be easily reversed. Delegates usually vote in political blocks and factions, and their leaders may negotiate compromises and alliances before or during a convention.

Similarly, the executive committees of the Belgian and West German mass parties are centers of power, particularly because their members frequently also hold electoral office, an accumulation of power prohibited in ecology parties. Executives are vital links in vertical party communication and exercise considerable control over local and regional organizations. At the same time, they connect the party apparatus to the parliamentary groups.[53] Highly cohesive party organizations go together with disciplined parliamentary parties (Ozbudun 1970). Individual members of parliament usually have little leeway to diverge from the party line, which is defined by the parliamentary leadership and party executives. Government parties usually enforce compliance of their parliamentary representatives (King 1976).

In one area, however, a convergence of conventional and left-libertarian

51. In Hamburg a weak competitive position was interrupted by brief interludes (December 82–June 83 and December 86–May 87) in which the party was in a strong competitive position vis-à-vis the SPD. Compare Chapter 9.

52. The German parties' convention management has been studied by Dittberner (1970), Günther (1979:110–19), Raschke (1974:135–41), and Steiner (1970). Probably the most detailed study on party conventions anywhere is Minkin's (1978) analysis of the British Labour party conventions.

53. The role of party executives is analyzed in De Winter (1981:75–84), Obler (1974), and Rowies (1975) for Belgium and in Mintzel (1975) and Raschke (1974) for Germany.

Table 32
Differences between the structure of ecology parties in areas with high and low left-libertarian mobilization

	High cleavage mobilization	Low cleavage mobilization
Conventions	little control by the central (in)formal party elites	some control by the central formal elites
	severe perceived deficits of rationality and legitimacy of conference decision procedures	moderate perceived deficits of rationality and legitimacy of conference decision procedures
Organs of formal representation	marginal role of steering committees in political decision making	ratifying and administrative of steering committees in political decision making
	little actual power of the party executive committees	more actual power of the party executive committees
	little communication of executives with rank and file; little cooperation with the parties' parliamentarians	little communication of executives with rank and file; more cooperation with the parties' parliamentarians
	intense legitimation problems of executives and steering committees: lack of political representativeness and effectiveness	moderate legitimation problems of executives and steering committees: politically representative but ineffective
	politically weak and challenged role of party secretariats	politically strong and unchallenged role of party secretariats
	numerous party work groups with expert, lobby, or factional orientation; strong feminist suborganization	few party work groups, mostly with an expert orientation to advise parliamentarians; weak feminist suborganization
Parliamentary party groups	larger number of representatives	smaller number of representatives
	internally fragmented and individualistic work style	internally more coordinated and collective work style
	externally weak connections to the party executives	externally stronger connections to the party executives
Prevalent ideology of party organization	the ideologues' view: "voluntarist" conspirational interpretation of the party structure	the pragmatists' view: effectiveness; party competition as imperatives to develop a formal structure able to manage the transaction costs of complex organizations

patterns of party politics appears likely. This is the relative dominance of parliamentary groups over party organization. Just as in conventional parties, ecology deputies often are the most influential politicians in their own party, a trend that has become increasingly pronounced, especially in the West German Greens. To understand this dynamic, our focus must widen beyond the unintended consequences of a decentralized, fragmented party organization to include recruitment procedures for parliamentarians. I examine this issue in the next chapter.

7 | Moving Up

In early January 1983, barely two months before the national elections in West Germany, the Green state executive in North Rhine–Westphalia approached the editors of an ecologically oriented journal on agriculture and biofarming to invite them to suggest a candidate for the Green electoral slate. Three days later Antje Vollmer, active in a farm youth organization and a Protestant pastor, decided to run. Within a week she introduced herself to the Green district party in the university town of Bielefeld and, together with three other militants, was accepted as a local candidate. She was also endorsed to run for a promising position on the party's state list. Ten days later at the state party convention she presented herself as an environmentalist working with young farmers to change agricultural practice and a single mother fighting against the prejudices of her church. As a result of her speech she was nominated to second position on the Green electoral slate (Vollmer 1984:6–9). This guaranteed her a "safe" seat when the party cleared 5 percent of the vote and won representation in the national parliament.

Four years later Vollmer was running for parliament again. Although she had been an ardent supporter of the party's two-year rotation rule for parliamentarians, she had decided to seek a second term in office. By now she was known as one of the party's most effective deputies and a sympathizer of its fundamentalist wing. The party convention nominated her as the lead candidate for North Rhine–Westphalia in the upcoming federal election. Several other parliamentarians also managed to get back on the party's state list in top positions.

Vollmer's political career illustrates important changes in the pattern of recruitment for legislative office both in the West German and the Belgian ecology parties. Originally, ecology parties idealized the amateur politician, one who serves for altruistic reasons in whatever office the party asks him or her to assume. This is not surprising since ecology parties attract intellectuals, a group quick to accuse professional politicians of turning into a business what they believe should be a matter of principle and ideology (Schlesinger 1965:1). Moreover, because ecology activists resent hierarchy and leadership, they also reject the well-known, high profile politician whose power undermines a participatory democratic party.

For this reason ecology parties initially followed a movementist recruitment style in which candidates for parliamentary office were selected on the basis of their movement constituency and the contribution they had made to left-libertarian protest. Party conventions would support candidates who had the right attributes—in terms of age, gender, occupation, and residence—and the right prior political affiliations, primarily in social movement struggles.

As we have seen in the preceding chapter, the loose, fluid, disjointed party organization endows parliamentarians with great discretion and authority to speak on behalf of the party to a broad political audience. Yet movementist recruitment does not assure that parliamentarians share the rank and file's political positions, nor that they have the skills to project a forceful party image in the public sphere. One way to cope with this problem would be to rationalize party structures and reduce the autonomy of parliamentarians. For ideological reasons, ecology parties have not pursued this path. If organizational structure and policy choice cannot be changed, however, at least the choice of personnel representing the party in key political institutions may be rationalized. By rationalize I mean undergoing a process in which a close link is established between the rank and file's preferences and what parliamentary representatives say and do. Movementist recruitment does not guarantee this rationality because ascriptive criteria and movement participation rarely reveal a militant's position on strategic questions of party policy. Hence, in ecology party organizations characterized by intense competition between ideologues and pragmatists, primarily in areas with highly mobilized left-libertarian cleavage, a politicized recruitment style has begun to emerge in which candidates are chosen based on their affiliation with political wings and tendencies. In areas with a weak left-libertarian cleavage and a dominance of pragmatists, in contrast, a professional recruitment style is developing which emphasizes a militant's loyalty to the party and his or her skills in presenting party views to a broader audience.

The gradual shift from movementist to politicized and professional recruitment styles goes together with a reevaluation of the problem of *political ambition* in ecology parties. No political party can do without ambitious individuals who promote its demands in the most effective way possible. Allowing too little ambition may be just as counterproductive as too much.[1]

---

1. Schlesinger (1965:2) writes: ''A political system becomes stable when it is able to control men's political ambitions. . . . A political system unable to kindle ambitions for office is as

The trick, then, is to design opportunities for and constraints on ambition that channel it toward the pursuit of party policy and electoral success. In the course of these efforts, ecology party militants have changed their original notions of political representation. Initially, elected offices went to people for what they *were* and what they had *experienced* in political struggles. Increasingly, however, the choice of political leaders is based on what candidates have *done* for their party and what they politically *stand for*.

Lobbyists who supported the movementist recruitment style stand to lose from changing styles, while ideologues and pragmatists ardently advocate the change. Ideologues expect new recruitment criteria to guarantee the faithful representation of the party purpose in the parliamentary arena. Pragmatists expect politicized or organizational recruitment to improve the link between parties and voters. Voters identify policies and programs with political personalities, whom they consider as a guarantee of party commitment to the strategy they support in voting.

Ideally, in order to analyze recruitment procedures we would have precise information about (1) the pool of candidates, (2) the decision makers, (3) the selection procedure, and (4) the attributes and orientation of the successful nominees. Unfortunately, in ecology parties data on all but the successful candidates are very hard to come by. For this reason I had to rely on fragmentary quantitative evidence as well as narrative accounts by my interviewees.

The Political Calculus of Ambition

Ambition and political careers depend not only on inner drives but also on institutions and opportunities. First of all, ambitious politicians have to consider the participants and procedures involved in the nomination process before they declare candidacy for an office. In ecology parties the participants are rank-and-file militants or convention delegates. As discussed previously, turnout tends to swell when candidates for elected office are to be nominated. Where parties are embroiled in sharp conflict between pragmatists and ideologues, high mobilization helps the pragmatists. A pragmatic politician has a much better chance of being nominated for elected office than of becoming a party executive because the selection process for the latter attracts fewer and more radical militants.

Second, ambitious politicians must consider the rules involved in the selection process. Where a slate of candidates is nominated according to individual runoffs with simple majority decisions, the majority of the assembly will fill

much in danger of breaking down as one unable to restrain ambitions. Representative government, above all, depends on the supply of men so driven; the desire for election and, more important, for reelection becomes the electorate's restraint upon its public officials. No more irresponsible government is imaginable than that of high-minded men unconcerned for their political future.''

all positions with candidates of its choice. However, block voting procedures in which several candidates are rank-ordered by the voters and nominated in a single vote give minority candidates a chance. In Agalev and Ecolo where factionalism is limited, simple majority rule prevails. Before the 1985 national elections the radical minority in Ecolo's Brussels district pressed for a block voting system, to get representation on the ticket, but it was overruled by the moderate majority and the national party leadership. In the West German Greens where there is more factional pluralism minorities have often successfully insisted on a block voting system, particularly in areas with high left-libertarian cleavage mobilization and nearly equally strong fundamentalist and realist wings.[2] In such cases party unity depends on the representation of all party wings.

Third, ambitious politicians must take electoral systems and the likely extent of support for the party at the polls into account when determining the odds of running for office. In Belgium's electoral system nominees run in multimember districts of varying size. To improve the proportionality of representation, disadvantaged small parties receive seats according to complex rules of compensation across districts. Because this makes the district actually winning a seat hard to predict, the number of candidates with some chance of being elected is much higher than the actual number of seats won. In Agalev and Ecolo the number of districts and the uncertainty of success leads to a fairly large number of promising nominations and thus reduces intraparty competition.

In contrast, the West German electoral system focuses small parties' chances on the state electoral lists, from which candidates move into parliament according to the percentage of votes their party receives in the state.[3] Here the nomination process is highly centralized and yields highly predictable outcomes, thus increasing the potential for conflict and competition among candidates.

Fourth, ambitious politicians must have resources they can employ to win office. Among them may be time, political experience, self-confidence, and social ties within the party. Hence, we expect that candidates are somewhat older and more frequently hold professional jobs than rank-and-file militants. Since direct data on the social composition of Belgian and West German ecology party activists and candidates are not available, I compare two subgroups to illustrate my point. Table 33 presents data on the age and

2. This happened for instance in the nomination of candidates for the 1985 state elections in North Rhine-Westphalia where the moderate minority successfully fought for a block voting system against the party's ecosocialist wing. Cf. *Tageszeitung* (February 2, 1985), 4.

3. An exception is state elections in Baden-Württemberg where candidates are nominated in single member districts and where underrepresented parties are given compensatory seats in those districts where they received the highest percentage of votes.

Table 33

Social composition of delegates to national party conferences and candidates for elected office in the Green state party organizations of North Rhine–Westphalia and Baden-Württemberg, 1980–85

	North Rhine–Westphalia			Baden-Württemberg	
	Delegates 1981 (1)	Candidates 1980 (2)	Candidates 1985 (3)	Delegates 1981 (1)	Candidates 1984 (4)
Age					
25 and younger	54%	25%	1%	45%	6%
25–35	31%	31%	48%	36%	55%
36–50	9%	25%	40%	10%	31%
51 and older	6%	13%	11%	10%	8%
	(N = 613)	(N = 151)	(N = 87)	(N = 444)	(N = 123)
Occupational background					
High school/university students/military service and conscientious objectors	47%	19%	12%	40%	7%
Professionals in teaching, social services, media	6%[a]	20%	36%	9%[a]	45%
Management, professions, entrepreneurs	9%	16%	15%	11%	26%
White-collar employees	17%	37%	15%	15%	15%
Blue-collar workers	11%	6%	7%	9%	2%
Unemployed, retiree, homemaker, no information	10%	3%	16%	14%	5%
	(N = 613)	(N = 151)	(N = 87)	(N = 444)	(N = 123)

a. teachers only

Sources: (1) Michael Seeland, Praktikumsbericht, Bundesgeschäftsstelle der Grünen, 1.9.–1.11.81; (2) Green state secretariat, North Rhine–Westphalia; (3) information folder for Green state party conference in North Rhine–Westphalia, Spring 1985; (4) Green state secretariat for Baden-Württemberg.

occupational background of delegates from North Rhine–Westphalia and Baden-Württemberg at a 1981 Green national convention. The table compares these groups to the constituency candidates in the 1980 North Rhine–Westphalian state election and in the 1984 Baden-Württemberg state election, as well as candidates for the Green state list in the 1985 North Rhine–Westphalian election. Given the nature of the German electoral system, Green constituency candidates as a rule have next to no chance of being elected in their districts, although they represent the pool of candidates likely to be willing to assume important office. Only those militants from this pool who are also nominated for the party's state electoral list (in North-Rhine–Westphalia) or run in one of the Green electoral strongholds (in Baden-Württemberg) have a realistic chance of being elected.

Delegates to the 1981 convention probably represented the hard core of activists who attend any national conference even when minor issues are being decided. They are very young and mostly still in school or university. Since most Green national party conferences in the 1980s tended to take radical positions, we can presume that these delegates overrepresent ideologues. In contrast, the candidates for the state elections tend to be older and more professional. We can only speculate that they may also represent less radical positions than the delegates. What these data at least suggest, however, is that different socioeconomic groups are attracted to electoral office than those that attend party conventions, particularly when conventions cannot make personnel decisions about electoral lists, as is the case with all Green national conventions.[4]

Gender and family status are two additional factors influencing willingness to run for elected office in ecology parties. Interviewees emphasize the reluctance of many women to seek office. Since the pool of women volunteers is relatively small and they quite naturally want to run for only the most effective jobs, meaning elected office, it is especially difficult to find women candidates for the less valuable party executives. In Agalev and Ecolo party executives are mostly men. In the German Greens many state executives set aside half of the seats for women, but often not all of these seats can be filled.

Many women do not want to participate in the highly confrontational, divisive setting of political appointment. And those with family commitments are less available than men. Hence, even for elected office the number of women candidates is often relatively small. In the North Rhine–Westphalian pool of candidates for the 1985 state electoral list, for instance, only 26 percent were women. Lack of political experience may also be a factor. Among the 1985 candidates in North Rhine–Westphalia, 55 percent of the

---

4. All candidates for the Green state lists are chosen in state party conventions, while federal conventions elect the national party executive and determine party policy.

men but only 35 percent of the women indicated a past affiliation with another party, labor union, or New Left group.[5]

Fifth, ambitious politicians must take into account the nature of the office they seek. They want to have influence on their party's policies and the opportunity to communicate with large audiences. As discussed in the previous chapter, in ecology parties positions on party steering committees and executives generally do not provide much political influence but electoral office does. The value of electoral office rises even further where parties might get into a strong competitive position as a consequence of elections. Yet ecology parties have introduced a number of constraints to reduce the attractiveness of electoral office at both the state and national levels. Parliamentarians must return a considerable share of their earnings to the parties. In Agalev and Ecolo deputies serve a maximum of two terms. Initially, the Greens restricted parliamentary office to two years, or half an electoral term. Since the mid-1980s, however, this rule has been relaxed and deputies can serve at least one full term. Rapid turnover of deputies was not only politically divisive within the party but also made it difficult to guarantee continuity and effective representation of the party's political demand in legislatures.

Time restrictions and financial obligations may deter materially motivated individuals from seeking political office, but not militants who strive for political power and influence. At least initially, therefore, other informal rules were meant to restrain ambition. In Agalev, for instance, people were asked not to present themselves as candidates for an office but to wait for others to field their names. This censorship of personal ambition and quest for office was particularly strong in the centers of the left-libertarian cleavage. In the search for nominees to the Hessian state parliament in 1982, the Frankfurt district party newsletter declared that "those who bring their own name into play have already disqualified themselves."[6] And Bernd from the Hamburg Greens notes that "people in the alternative scene cannot afford to appear as if they are eager to make a political career." Indeed, many representatives elected early in the party's history did not declare their own candidacy but were drafted by the party. Christa from a small village in Baden-Württemberg was urged to run for parliament by her local group. And Christian from Hamburg only considered nomination when a previous candidate failed to win endorsement from a majority.

In more recent years official pronouncements denigrating personal political ambition have become less credible and effective than at the beginning. The

5. Data are based on a file of curriculum vitaes and political autobiographies submitted by the candidates to the February 1985 Green party nomination convention in North Rhine-Westphalia.

6. Kreisverband Frankfurt, *Mitgliederrundbrief,* no. 27 (February 18, 1982), 9.

high demand for electoral office demonstrates this better than any other fact. While elections for party steering committees, state party executives, and even national party executives often attract fewer candidates than there are openings—or at least involve too few candidates to make the selection process truly competitive—nominations for state or national elected office attract many more candidates than there are positions to be filled (Figure 7). A fundamentalist member of the Green national executive deplored the fact that "outside the parliamentary party there are few people who are willing to get involved in politics."[7]

Evidence of the great demand for parliamentary office abounds. In North Rhine-Westphalia, for instance, close to 100 candidates vied for the ten to twenty top-ranking nominations on the Green party's list of candidates for the 1985 state election. In the Belgian *arrondissement* of Antwerp, the expectation that two or three Agalev candidates would be elected in the 1985 national election attracted more than ten candidates. Similarly, in Ecolo's Brussels district the number of candidates far exceeded the seats Ecolo expected to win.

A significant number of interviewees in all three parties no longer rejects ambition as immoral for left-libertarian activists. They defend the vanity and enjoyment or, as one militant put it, the "intense quality of the experience" that comes with the political limelight of a parliamentary mandate. Hans, a Green member of parliament, says that "the desire to show off is nothing bad, it is important for successful politics." Similarly, Olivier from Ecolo asserts that ambition is not reprehensible as long as it is constrained by the party. More radical militants in all ecology parties still despise ambition and suspect their moderate colleagues of having succumbed to motives of material gain and status seeking. Yet ambition is not the sole prerogative of pragmatists. Christa, who leans toward the Green fundamentalist position, expresses her disapproval of colleagues who have "tasted blood" and wish to continue their political career, yet she ended up running herself for a second term in parliament. Hendrik, another Green parliamentarian, speculates that ambition may be stronger in the Greens than elsewhere "because militants do not have to submit themselves to the sweat shop [*Knochenmühle*] of the party hierarchy for decades" before reaching a visible political position.

It would be false, however, to identify political ambition in ecology parties with the desire for lifelong professional political careers. Since direct questions about militants' desire to become professional politicians are unlikely to yield sincere answers, their professional background, opportunities, and political orientation can serve as a rough indicator of whether they are inclined to pursue a political career. These characteristics put the interviewees into three groups: amateurs, entrepreneurs, and functionaries.

7. Interview with Regina Michalik in Jäger and Pinl (1985: 158).

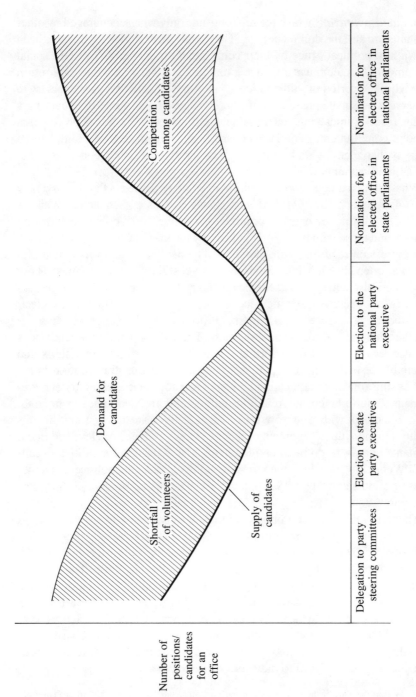

Figure 7. The calculus of candidacy: supply and demand curves for political office in ecology parties

Amateur politicians who have run for office only when encouraged by other militants are still the dominant type. They tend to be lobbyists who have been drawn into political office by their commitment to a specific cause or social movement. Amateurs usually have a regular career to which they will return after a limited period in paid political office. In their daily lives amateurs try to preserve a personal sphere free of politics. They spend some time earning a living from politics, but detest people fascinated by political power as a lifelong commitment. Women emphasize an amateur view of politics more strongly than men. In Schlesinger's (1965) terminology, amateurs have "discrete" political ambitions.

What is most unique about ambition in ecology parties is the rise of a new type of politician, the *political entrepreneur*. This person defies Weber's (1958:389) distinction between politicians who live "off" politics by drawing a salary and those who live "for" politics by means of accumulated wealth or of a profession requiring little attention. The new political entrepreneurs, in contrast, often have few financial resources yet still live "for" politics. These postmaterialist entrepreneurs dedicate their lives to politics regardless of whether they operate on the socioeconomic fringes of the welfare state collecting student assistance, unemployment insurance, or welfare checks, or whether they take an occasional odd job. The entrepreneur's influence does not necessarily derive from formal position but from individual skills and intangible resources such as personal charisma and a central location in the parties' informal communication networks and social cliques. Political entrepreneurs tend to be cosmopolitan in outlook and are ideologues *or* pragmatists. Lobbyists with a narrow range of objectives are rarely found in this group. No more than 25 percent of the interviewed Green, Agalev, and Ecolo militants qualify as political entrepreneurs. They resurrect a political "calling" Weber saw vanishing with the rise of the bureaucratic political machine. These politicians have, in Schlesinger's (1965:10) terminology, "progressive" ambitions.

The third and smallest group of ecology activists consists of *functionaries* who live "off" politics or would like to do so, but lack the skills, creativity, charisma, and psychological disposition for becoming political entrepreneurs. Functionaries pursue a political career in the occupational sense. They usually have no stable employment record, have often been out of work before getting a party job, or cannot easily return to their old profession after a full-term political assignment. In the party they shy away from controversy and are very concerned with the stability of the organization, an essentially conservative attitude quite widespread among the parties' professional staffs, regardless of whether they are inclined to radical or moderate positions.[8]

8. Within the staff of the Green federal parliamentary party, a strong though probably not dominant faction represents the demands of functionaries. By establishing a work council, staff

Functionaries lack a strong affinity to particular policy issues and tend to be ideologues or pragmatists. They would like to get or keep political office but do not expect to rise to prominence and influence in the party. In Schlesinger's terminology, functionaries have "static" political ambitions. Less than one fifth of my interviewees exhibited the characteristics of a political functionary.

These admittedly vague and preliminary estimates show that even within the core group of party militants who are municipal councilors, party executives, salaried employees, or elected representatives, the number of would-be political professionals is fairly limited. Most elected representatives consider political office as an exciting but temporary episode in their lives. Nevertheless, a significant number of Belgian and West German parliamentarians in ecology parties have sought reelection. Over 25 percent of the incoming 1987 Green members of parliament had either been members of the previous parliamentary group or had served in elected office at the state level.[9] In Agalev and Ecolo more than half of the parliamentarians serving from 1982 to 1986 ran for a second term. And in the Hessian Greens, where the state parliamentary party has become a cohesive group fighting against a fundamentalist minority in the party, most deputies in the 1983–87 electoral term intended to run for office again.

Recruitment Results

The results of the nomination process by which candidates are placed at the top of Agalev's, Ecolo's, or the Greens' electoral lists depend critically on the relative strength of and coalitions among groups of party activists. These in turn are linked to external conditions such as the level of left-libertarian mobilization, the responsiveness of incumbent elites to new parties' demand for participation and policy impact, and the parties' electoral position. In addition, we must take into account a certain process of maturation and learning over time which comes with the accumulation of experience in choosing nominees.

A movementist style of recruitment develops first, in the initial phase of party formation. In centers of left-libertarian cleavage and in cases where the parties are in a strong electoral competitive position, recruitment then tends to shift toward a politicized style. This is particularly true in the Greens. In areas

employees have engaged in trade unionist efforts to increase their job security beyond the end of the legislative term. Cf. "The Green Fear of Mass Dismissals," *Tageszeitung* (April 7, 1986). In my interviews amateurs as well as political entrepreneurs were adamantly opposed to granting parliamentary staff personnel long-term job security.

9. Precise figures on how many of the previously elected deputies tried to run for a second term and failed are not available. Fragmentary evidence suggests that less than half of the 1983 Green national parliamentary party group ran for office again.

with lower mobilization, particularly in Agalev and Ecolo, a style favoring intraorganizational, professional criteria begins to gain ground.

Movementist Recruitment

According to most Greens' recollections, a candidate's involvement in social movement activities initially was the most important criterion for being nominated for electoral office. A candidate who could credibly demonstrate *Betroffenheit,* a sense of being directly affected, bewildered, or shaken by a grievance and protesting against it in a social movement, impressed party conventions most. The sincerity and authenticity of one's past activism counted far more than ability to elaborate sophisticated arguments about party theory and strategy. Antje Vollmer's first nomination to the German parliament, recounted at the beginning of this chapter, nicely illustrates this pattern of recruitment. In the early 1980s many activists like her wound up on Green electoral lists even though they did not belong to the party. In the Greens, this is referred to as "open list" recruitment.

Agalev and Ecolo have recruited fewer nonmembers to their electoral lists from the very beginning and generally have given less weight to the criterion of movement activism. The smaller left-libertarian movement sector and the paucity of parliamentary mandates in Belgium—from 1981 to 1985 the parliamentary group had only nine members—make it difficult to accommodate many pure movement activists. Agalev's and Ecolo's core activists have always been further removed from movement organizations than the West German Greens. For this reason they put greater emphasis on professional recruitment, emphasizing long-term party affiliation and proven militancy in the party itself.

The movementist recruitment style that has prevailed in the Greens means that delegates and party members who participate in the nomination of the all-important state electoral lists will not prenegotiate their choices before party conferences or vote strategically. Other than encouraging people to run, party executives have very little say in the nomination process. They do not sound out candidates, nor do they propose full slates of nominees on which delegates may vote. Candidates usually introduce themselves to a broader party audience for the first time at the nominating convention itself and much hinges on their ability to project an image that elicits the delegates' support. Effective presentations typically refer to the candidates' movement activism. Previous tenure in political office, in the Greens or in any conventional party, is a political liability and can be used to impugn the candidates' amateur credentials. Similarly, a candidate's speech should be well-delivered yet not too rhetorically polished, lest it arouse the delegates' suspicions that they are dealing with a professional. For this reason candidates whose group affiliation and lack of political background guarantee their amateur credentials, such as most women, older, and less educated people with no previous party involvement, can count on the delegates' sympathies. By contrast, a candidate who emphasizes his or her proven political record runs the risk of violating the party's norms of amateurism: "If you have accomplished something, that will be turned against you. If you are competent, this will be turned against you."[10]

One reason why it often takes Green conventions a long time to nominate candidates for the state electoral lists is the large number of candidates who are unknown to most militants and must introduce themselves. A North Rhine-Westphalian Green convention took fifteen hours to select the first seven out of fifty candidates for the Green state list in the 1983 federal election.[11] In Hesse it took two days to nominate fourteen candidates for that election and three and a half days to determine the state list in the 1982 election.[12]

In the movementist recruitment process ascriptive criteria such as occupation, age, location of residence, family status, and gender often serve as indicators of candidates' representativeness of constituencies. The most important ascriptive criterion is clearly gender. The strong representation of women on ecology party lists is a statement of allegiance to the women's movement and to the transformation of sex roles in modern society. Moreover, having many women candidates on electoral lists is an important element of ecology party strategy vis-à-vis its electoral competitors. Conventional parties are still predominantly run by men, and presumably for men.

Although Agalev, Ecolo, and the Greens have equally emphasized recruitment of women, women have made the most headway in the Greens. In the party's first federal parliamentary party, one third of all parliamentarians were women. Between 1983 and 1985 all Green state parties adopted the principle that party and electoral offices should be filled equally with men and women. In the 1987–90 legislative term, twenty-five of the forty-two Green federal parliamentarians are women. There can be little doubt that the nomination of women has improved the Greens' public image, especially among young female voters. As Antje Vollmer's example shows, many women have discovered their political talent in the Greens and have played a decisive role in the party's politics.[13]

In Agalev and Ecolo the representation of women is less far-reaching and less institutionalized. In part this is because the Belgian electoral system often

10. Michael Vesper, administrative manager of the Green parliamentary party in the Bundestag, quoted in *Frankfurter Rundschau* (May 15, 1985).

11. *Tageszeitung* (January 24, 1983).

12. See the letter by Chris Boppel in Die Grünen Frankfurt, *Rundbrief* (April 1983).

13. In doing so, however, women risk becoming the target of feminist attacks in the party. Petra Kelly, a leading Green figure in the early 1980s, was accused by women in her party district of adopting male behavior because, in their view, she was too familiar with facts and knew too much. See Petra Kelly in *Tageszeitung* (December 17, 1982).

makes it impossible to predict in which district a small party will win a seat. Another factor is the weaker influence of feminism in the Belgian left-libertarian movement sector and in the ecology parties.

In the movementist recruitment style nominees represent social groups and activism on particular issues rather than comprehensive political programs. Delegates seek out candidates with political biographies and personal attributes that serve as symbols for attracting the support of external core constituencies. For this reason many interviewees see an exponential proliferation of selection criteria. The list of nominees should represent a multitude of social movements (environmental, feminist, alternative economy, peace, civil rights, self-help groups, and the like), young and old, both sexes, different social classes, and different areas of an electoral district. In traditional parties, party executives who propose "balanced" slates assure that multiple criteria of social representation are brought to bear on electoral lists.[14] Lacking central concertation, ecology parties engage in countless votes at party conferences, choosing from a bewildering variety of personalities. In this process chance factors such as the skilled timing of a candidacy at a certain stage of the selection often determine the fate of a candidate more than anything else.

Because the candidates' political stances and proven abilities play little role in this nomination process, a growing number of Green activists criticize movementist recruitment. Party regulars have learned by experience that a militant's social and biographic background is not always, or even frequently, a good indicator of a candidate's stance or effectiveness in furthering the party's viewpoint. Thus, the representativeness and democratic legitimacy of choices based on movementist criteria are called into question. After the selection of the Alternative List nominees for the 1985 elections in West Berlin, a militant criticized the arbitrariness of movementist nominations at the party's convention in these words: "The biological fact of being a woman is as little proof of one's personal character, political consciousness, and activism as is the insistence on being strongly affected [betroffen] by a particular grievance. Nor does the fact of being gay entitle one to a seat in the House of Deputies. Other people [at the convention] appealed to their local constituency groups, that is citizens' initiatives or groups which had approved their candidacy. But one would learn quite coincidentally from others that actually these grassroots organizations had ceased to exist."[15] Militants further complain that nobody knows what political strategy nominees chosen according to movementist criteria will pursue once they become deputies. In

14. See the instructive discussion in Obler (1974) for Belgium and Zeuner (1970) for West Germany.

15. Ilse Schwipper in a statement at the state party convention of the Berlin Alternative List on November 16 and 17, 1984. Reprinted in *Stachlige Argumente*, no. 30 (January 1985), 7.

1982 members of the radical wing in the Frankfurt Greens criticized movementist nomination of candidates for the Hessian state elections: "We object
to the fact that the majority of the Hessian Green grassroots activists have
uncritically chosen the people who over the course of the next four years will
have the task of making policy in the state according to Green principles."[16]

Particularly in strongholds of left-libertarian politics where conflict between pragmatists and ideologues has heated up in the mid-1980s, there are
signs that movementist recruitment is declining because it is unable to link
choice of a candidate to choice of a policy position. Party regulars are slowly
discovering that parliamentarians control vital power resources, such as access to the mass media, and exercise decisive influence over the party's
strategy vis-à-vis its competitors. Both radicals and moderates, therefore,
have struggled to rationalize the recruitment of parliamentarians and move
from an ascriptive, social notion of representation to a political and ideological one.

Politicized Recruitment

Political factions in ecology parties vie for control over the most important
offices, that of the parliamentarians. Where there are a great many factional
struggles, the nomination of candidates has increasingly become a competition between radical and moderate wings. Factionalism, in turn, tends to be
most active in centers of left-libertarian cleavage mobilization where many
individuals with political experience and broad programmatic concepts join
the parties, and where the parties are in a strong competitive position and are
being forced to choose coalition strategy.

In politicized recruitment all ascriptive attributes except gender rapidly fade
into the background. Movement activists who have not previously participated in the parties' political discussions now have less of a chance of being
nominated as open list candidates since it is impossible to readily identify their
position on intraparty issues. In a politicized recruitment process successful
candidates belong almost exclusively to the young, highly educated core
groups of pragmatists and ideologues. When the North Rhine–Westphalian
Greens nominated the state electoral list for the 1985 election, the twenty most
successful candidates were younger, more educated, and more likely to be
academics in the social service sector or students than the entire pool of
candidates (Table 34). They were predominantly drawn from Green strongholds, while most candidates from weaker regions (such as the Ruhr industrial
area) were unsuccessful. Most successful candidates expressed concern about
social and economic affairs but few about environmental policy. In a nutshell,
politicized nomination processes make lobbyists lose some of their clout while

16. *Grüne Hessenzeitung*, no. 5 (July–August 1982), 24.

Table 34

Successful and unsuccessful candidates for the Green state electoral list in the 1985 North Rhine–Westphalia state elections (in percentages)

	20 leading candidates	All other candidates
Age		
25 and younger	5%	—
26–35	70	40%
36–50	25	45
51 and older	—	15
	100	100
Occupation		
Academics in teaching, social services, politics	45	33
Students	15	10
Other professionals with university degree	15	15
White-collar employees	15	15
Blue-collar workers	—	9
Unemployed/not working	10	8
No information	—	9
	100%	99%
	(N = 20)	(N = 62)

young intellectuals with a broader strategic ideological or pragmatic outlook increase theirs.

Where factions and tendencies play a role at conventions, vote trading, prenegotiations about the support of candidates—or even the composition of entire lists—and strategic voting become commonplace. Politicized recruitment contributes to a rationalization of democratic representation by establishing a close correspondence between the preferences of active party constituencies and those of parliamentary nominees. Because pragmatists take a greater interest in the nomination of electoral candidates than that of party officers, they have more influence on the choice of delegates to conventions nominating candidates than to other conferences. Hence, it is likely that ecology party parliamentarians are on balance more moderate than members of party executives. For instance, in the Green federal parliamentary party elected in 1987 pragmatists clearly outnumber ideologues, although the latter control the party's national executive.[17]

Bearing in mind that my sample of activists is neither large nor randomized, we can gain some evidence for the different outlooks of party officers and

17. Fogt (1986) claims that later cohorts of Green parliamentarians are more radical than earlier ones. It is not clear, however, how he arrives at his classification of political wings in the party. That many parliamentarians emerge from the New Left is not by itself a reason to classify them as radicals, for as I have shown in Chapter 4, a substantial number of New Leftists has turned toward the pragmatist wing in ecology parties. Fogt's largest group is that of "other non-

Table 35
Political outlook of militants in party or electoral office (in percentages)

	(Near) ideologues	*(Near) lobbyists*	*(Near) pragmatists*	*None of the three types*
West Germany (Greens)				
Municipal councilors	15%	30%	40%	15%
State and national parliamentarians	38	21	31	10
Party executives	50	13	25	13
Administrative employees	50	13	25	13
All Greens	36	21	31	12
Belgium (Agalev and Ecolo)				
Municipal councilors	—	—	79	21
National parliamentarians	—	—	57	43
Party executives	11	6	67	17
Administrative employees	11	11	56	22
All Agalev and Ecolo	6	4	67	23

elected representatives from Table 35. In West Germany pragmatists are overrepresented among municipal councilors, while many ideologues are found among party executives and functionaries. Green state and national parliamentarians, however, roughly reflect the distribution of political sentiments in the overall sample. In Agalev and Ecolo, located in areas with relatively low left-libertarian mobilization, pragmatists dominate at all levels, although even here party executives and functionaries tend to be slightly more radical than elected officials.

With the rise of politicized recruitment, the criterion of being female has taken on a new significance in nomination procedures. In 1983 the Green state parties in which either ideologues or pragmatists were clearly in charge chose the fewest women for the party's parliamentary group. This was the case for areas both with strong left-libertarian mobilization and many party ideologues and with weak mobilization and predominantly pragmatic activists. However, in state parties with intermediate left-libertarian mobilization in social movements and intellectual subcultures, almost 50 percent of the nominees were women.[18] Pragmatists and ideologues rejected gender as an ascriptive and

ecologists'' (34 percent of the parliamentarians and party executive). The magnitude of this residual category and the vagueness of his other categories cast doubt on his claim that the "realist" wing of the party has declined and is displaced by "traditional socialists."

18. The Green strongholds of Hamburg, West Berlin, Hesse, and Bremen chose no woman to serve as a parliamentarian among the eleven initially elected and their alternates. The states of Bavaria, Rhineland Palatinate, and Schleswig Holstein, with marginal left-libertarian mobilization, selected three women for twelve positions (25 percent), whereas in the states of North Rhine–Westphalia, Lower Saxony, and Baden-Württemberg, with fairly strong movements but limited left-libertarian subcultures, 45 percent of the deputies and alternates were women.

particularist criterion of nomination, while lobbyists endorsed it as a key criterion of movementist recruitment. By the mid-1980s, however, when Green women had everywhere successfully pressed for a formal rule requiring the equal representation of sexes in all political offices, the Greens' radical and moderate wings began to use the gender issue for strategic purposes. Skillful politicians have tried to exploit the conflicting pressures many militants experience when they must choose between a male adherent of their own wing and a female candidate suspected of supporting another wing.

This game has been played by both pragmatists and ideologues, although the majority of outspoken feminists in the party leans in favor of radical positions. This is particularly the case where women have called for electoral lists excluding men because of the men's allegedly more instrumentalist, competitive political style. In Hamburg, after an intense debate between women and men, an electoral list of only female candidates was nominated for the 1986 state elections.[19] The most vocal opponents of this idea were ecosocialist women who argued that an exclusive women's list would endanger the party's commitment to universalist, egalitarian values and create the appearance that all major social problems derive from a conflict between men and women. In the end, however, the women's list was approved by a majority as a way of strengthening the radical wing and improving the party's electoral appeal.

The politicization of factions and the new criteria of recruitment have contributed to the emergence of a group of prominent women and men who are publicly recognized in the mass media as Green speakers. This has given rise to another criterion of political recruitment clearly inconsistent with the initial movementist selection of candidates. Party militants are slowly discovering and accepting rhetorically powerful politicians of both sexes as an indispensable resource for enhancing voter identification and guaranteeing the party's public credibility and continuity of policy. As a Hamburg militant put it, his state party is strongly influenced by a single "astounding political personality," who is crucial not only to outlining the party's strategy, but also to maintaining voter loyalty. A fundamentalist member of the Green federal parliamentary group remarked that the party cannot abandon the "political talents" it discovered in the first decade of its existence. In fact, eight of the most effective Green federal parliamentarians in the 1983–87 session were returned for the 1987–90 session.[20] Further, a number of militants who had

19. This debate is documented in the membership newsletter of the Hamburg Green Alternative List. Compare *GAL Rundbrief* (February 1984), 87–90, (March 1984), 13–23, (April 1984), 58–64, and (May 1984), 86–87. For a review of Green policy on women candidates, see Schöller (1985:78–97).

20. My assertion is based on subjective judgment, although a content analysis of the frequency with which the eight parliamentarians appeared in the mass media would support my assessment. They are: Marie-Louise Beck-Oberdorf, Petra Kelly, Hubert Kleinert, Christa Nickels, Otto Schily, Waltraud Schoppe, Eckhart Stratmann, and Antje Vollmer.

distinguished themselves in state parliaments joined the party's federal parliamentary group.

Thus, in moderate and radical wings alike, the principle that candidates should be political amateurs is being replaced by substantive political criteria such as effectiveness in representing a particular stand. Without question, this trend toward politicization of recruitment for elected office constitutes a shift away from the logic of constituency representation.

Professional Recruitment

In areas with low left-libertarian mobilization where parties are in a weak electoral position, movementist recruitment to elected office tends to be displaced by a third recruitment style, professional recruitment. Once party militants learn how unpredictable elected representatives chosen according to movementist criteria are, pragmatists in particular begin to value a candidate's reliability as a party activist, formal qualifications and competence, willingness to cooperate with others, popularity, and seniority in the party. While politicized recruitment emphasizes a candidate's programmatic and strategic position, professional recruitment is more concerned with demonstrated contributions to the party organization and effectiveness in communicating party views to a broader audience.

Several circumstances favor a professional recruitment style. The absence of factions and the dominance of pragmatists eliminate intense political disagreements as a source of intraparty competition. Further, a weak social movement sector in a party's environment makes it difficult to engage in movementist recruitment. Finally, pragmatists put more weight on organizational loyalty and party discipline, qualities the professional recruitment style values, than do radical supporters of the new logic of constituency representation with its open, fluid participatory politics. These three conditions favoring professional recruitment prevail in some of the less mobilized Green state parties (such as Bavaria or Rhineland Palatinate), in Agalev, and especially in Ecolo.

In Agalev and Ecolo pragmatists and moderate lobbyists dominate the parties operating in an environment with limited left-libertarian mobilization. Moreover, the decentralized nomination process in individual electoral districts helps to depoliticize the choice of parliamentary candidates. Belgian interviewees almost unanimously claim that proven militancy in the party organization is decisive for nomination. Since nominations take place in electoral districts and involve small numbers of participants, most activists know each other well and select the most popular and highly esteemed members. Interviewees mention as decisive such personal qualifications as integrity, sympathetic personality, trust, and friendship. In this context it is not surprising that long-term party membership, if not seniority, plays a greater role in Agalev and Ecolo than in the Greens. Whereas 71 percent of

Agalev's and Ecolo's elected officers in parliament and municipal councils who were interviewed for this study had joined their party or its precursor organization before 1980, the same is true of only 37 percent of the elected officers in the Greens.

The importance of proven organizational involvement is evidenced by the fact that many Agalev and Ecolo nominees for promising electoral positions have previously served on the parties' executive committees. In the Greens this career path has been common only in state party organizations located on the periphery of the left-libertarian cleavage.[21] In addition to being candidates themselves, Agalev's and Ecolo's holders of national party office often play a role in monitoring district recruitment choices. Ecolo's federal steering committee, guided by key personalities in the executive, decided to review all nominations for the 1985 parliamentary elections and indeed intervened in several districts.[22] Although the Agalev steering committee eventually backed off from similar supervision, the executive and secretariat were involved in district recruitment decisions behind the scenes.

Agalev and Ecolo interviewees are generally skeptical about recruiting nonmembers to electoral lists because they do not find them representative of the party. Ecolo has never fielded an "open list" of candidates. Agalev, however, with an environment of somewhat higher movement activism than Ecolo, has occasionally adopted elements of a movementist recruitment style. For instance, the party chose a feminist nonmember as nominee in the Antwerp district for the 1985 national election on a position likely to be elected to parliament. Nevertheless, professional criteria are more decisive in Agalev than movement activism. Efforts to place a prominent leader of the Flemish anti-nuclear movement on the 1985 electoral list failed when key militants objected to external recruitment.[23]

Ecolo feminists in particular encountered great difficulty in establishing gender as a criterion in the nomination process. Almost all male Ecolo militants and even many women interviewed for this study rejected parity between the sexes as a formal rule for candidate selection because political abilities should be ranked higher than constituency representation. In Ecolo, and even more so in Agalev and the Greens, more radical feminists reject professional criteria such as expertise, qualifications, or competence. In their view these arguments are thinly veiled efforts to bar women from political power and push the party toward a strategy of accommodation with existing

21. In the Green federal parliamentary party in the 1983–87 term, eighteen of fifty-six militants had served on state or national party executives. The highest percentage of former party executives came from Bavaria and Baden-Württemberg, i.e., areas closer to the periphery of the left-libertarian cleavage.

22. See the Ecolo steering committee's decision to enact a "procedure of concentration," *Ecolo Infos,* no. 57 (May 15, 1985), 22.

23. The intraparty debate on Agalev's open list policy is reflected in the minutes of the steering group session of April 20, 1985, 3–4 and 6.

political institutions.[24] Women who subscribe to professional criteria of competence, in contrast, fear that women are often elected only because of gender and feel uncomfortable as "tokens." Others are troubled by the political particularism the gender criterion inserts into ecology parties.

Since feminists have no strong voice in Ecolo, the party has made few efforts to recruit women to its electoral lists. At the national level women have been represented only in the less powerful house of the Belgian parliament, the Senate. Moreover, these come from an older generation of socially or ecologically active women uninterested in broader feminist and political programs. Feminists in Ecolo have criticized the party's recruitment practices but have failed to get their own candidates nominated to leading positions on the list.[25] As the Antwerp case shows, Agalev has made more serious efforts to recruit women. Yet even these militants emphasize the difficulty of nominating women, particularly since the party does not fully back feminist positions on abortion because of its Catholic heritage and voter preference.

Thus, while Agalev has made some efforts to incorporate a movementist nomination style, Ecolo is firmly wedded to a professional recruitment pattern. The difference between the Belgian parties reflects the greater strength of the movement sector in Flanders as compared to Wallonia. With the exception of local centers of left-libertarian mobilization such as the Brussels Ecolo section and Agalev's Ghent district party, there are few signs of competition among political factions in the recruitment process.

Conclusion

The three styles of recruitment for political office in ecology parties are summarized in Table 36. Each ideal typical style is associated with a complex set of criteria and a different principle of representation. The movementist style represents the attributes and concerns of specific protest groups, the politicized style represents the strategic and programmatic preferences of party activists, and the professional style represents interest in organizational cohesiveness, stability, and electoral effectiveness.

The significance of each style varies with the environment in which ecology parties operate. In addition to the three familiar contextual variables, which are left-libertarian cleavage mobilization, national political institutions, and competitive strength, I have added a fourth one, the *timing* of nomination procedures in the historical growth of the parties. Movementist recruitment

24. A female municipal councilor of the Alternative List in Berlin says: "And in the interest of women: Let us abandon the rule of experts and go toward the principle that really everyone can learn everything, with some time and solidary support. Women are always paralyzed by the notion of 'competence' and one has to find out on one's own that only experience and practice will remove this respect." *Stachlige Argumente*, no. 27 (July–August 1984), 20.

25. These complaints about opportunities for women in Ecolo were made in an open letter a feminist member of the party executive, Myriam Kenens, circulated in Liège: "A tous les membres de la Régionale Ecolo-Liège, en particulier aux hommes," June 28, 1985.

Table 36
Three types of recrutiment for elected office in ecology parties

	Movementist recruitment	*Politicized recruitment*	*Professional recruitment*
Selection criteria			
Movement activism	important	less important	unimportant
Ascriptive criteria (age, occupation, residence)	important	unimportant	unimportant
Gender	important	important	unimportant
Affiliation with political current	unimportant	important	medium important
Reputation in mass media	unimportant	important	important
History of party involvement	unimportant	medium important	important
Party loyalty	unimportant	unimportant	important
Previous party office	liability	unimportant	important
Opportunity structure			
Level of cleavage mobilization	(medium) high	high	low
National political context	more in West Germany	more in West Germany	more in Belgium
Party's competitive position	weak	strong	weak or strong
Maturation: first or subsequent nomination of candidates	first nomination	subsequent nomination	subsequent nomination
Calculus of ambition			
Type of party activists attracted	lobbyists	pragmatists and ideologues	pragmatists
Type of political ambition with greatest likelihood to run	amateurs: "discrete" ambition	political entrepreneurs: "progressive" ambition	functionaries: "stationary" ambition
Impact of the differential mobilization of party activists in the selection procedures	intermediate	important	unimportant

was particularly pronounced in West German centers of left-libertarian cleavage mobilization in the early development of the Greens when the party was still in a very weak competitive position. In these areas later on high cleavage mobilization and a strengthening competitive position led to a politicized recruitment style. In contrast, on the periphery of left-libertarian mobilization, particularly in Agalev and Ecolo, a professional style has evolved.

The movementist style best approximates the amateur logic of constituency representation in ecology parties, but they tend to abandon it because it has unintended, perverse effects. They discover that movementist policy was based on a fallacy: Constituencies and leaders who share a common sociopolitical background and history of activism in left-libertarian movements do not necessarily have identical interests when parties must make strategic choices in the parliamentary or electoral arenas.

Both styles that emerged as the parties matured rationalize selection procedures and move closer to a logic of party competition that puts a premium on the nominees' *reliability* and *predictability*. Politicized recruitment in particular simplifies the party activists' and the voters' choice because it clearly reveals the candidates' and the parties' political positions. Moreover, in both the professional and the politicized style, what counts is how effectively candidates can present the party in the news media and help voters to identify personalities with specific strategies and political demands. The nomination of charismatic political entrepreneurs in particular contributes to a *personalization of political programs* which facilitates voter mobilization.

Each of the recruitment styles also tends to coincide with a particular type of ambition activists hold when they seek office. Where party militants demand a movementist recruitment style, candidates with discrete ambitions and a background as lobbyists from social movements have the greatest chance of being nominated. Later on in the centers of left-libertarian mobilization politicized recruitment style favors political entrepreneurs with progressive ambitions. Lastly, the professional recruitment style on the periphery of left-libertarian mobilization tends to reward the aspirations of functionaries. It must be kept in mind, however, that these schematic simplifications represent only trends. Even where politicized and professional recruitment plays an increasing role, movementist criteria have not been entirely abandoned in ecology parties.

Differential mobilization of participants in nomination procedures affects the choice of nominees depending on the style of recruitment that prevails. The more ideologues, pragmatists, and lobbyists are polarized, and the more politicized the procedure, the more a broad involvement of party activists favors pragmatist candidates. Conversely, a lower turnout of participants in the nomination process helps ideologues. In areas with low mobilization, low intraparty factionalism, and therefore a prevalence of pragmatists, a professional recruitment style prevails, little influenced by the turnout. Movementist recruitment, finally, is an intermediate case in which higher turnouts may marginally advantage moderates.

The distribution of political preferences, recruitment styles, and results of nominations for electoral office in ecology parties cast doubt on the accuracy of McKenzie's sweeping "law of curvilinear disparity" according to which activists are more radical than party leaders elected to legislatures.[26] Studies of rank-and-file radicalism usually select national conference participants as their reference group of party activists, neglecting the more moderate localists who are often inclined to stay home. McKenzie's law would therefore at least have to be rephrased as a "law of middle-level radicalism" stating that cosmopolitan party activists are more radical than localists and legislative representatives.[27]

Particularly in ecology parties with their loose, stratarchal organization, most cosmopolitans belong to a middle stratum which is neither tied into firm local networks of communication nor into the party leadership connecting the parties to institutions of political representation and the electorate. Middle-level radicals discount the disadvantages of political participation and have a strong preference for getting involved in national politics. But their chances of being chosen for important electoral office are limited because recruitment for these offices is one of the few instances when the more pragmatic and localist rank and file becomes involved in national party politics. For this reason, radical middle-level ecologists at best manage to dominate the parties' steering committees and executives, which have little influence on parliamentary policy. Thus, middle-level activists are more out of step with broad sentiment among local party members and voters than either grassroots militants or party leaders in elected office.

Michels, McKenzie, and many others have explained the moderation of a party's parliamentarians predominantly with a socialization theory. Parliamentary institutions slowly change the behavior even of radical deputies. Moreover, the exigencies of electoral success force them to defend more moderate policies. The recruitment of electoral candidates in ecology parties, however, demonstrates that the differential mobilization of party activists in

26. The law was formulated in McKenzie's (1955) study of British parties, but became familiar to party scholars with Michels' work. Empirically, the law has been examined by Costantini (1963), May (1973), McClosky et al. (1960), Searing (1986), and Steel and Tsurutani (1986). Kavanagh (1985) and McKenzie (1982) explore the normative implications of these findings, arguing that party oligarchy is justified in order to give voters a say in party policies.

27. Evidence for this hypothesis abounds. Whiteley (1983:44) found that municipal councilors and parliamentarians in the British Labour party were about equally moderate, parliamentary candidates were more radical, and delegates to party conventions were the most radical group. In the Austrian parties Stiefbold (1974) encountered more extremism in the layer of party activists directly below the leadership than in the grassroots members. In the Danish Socialist People's party, rank-and-file activists support moderate social reform more strongly than party delegates calling for more radical change (Logue 1982:226). Also in voluntary associations, particularly labor unions, numerous studies have noted "middle-level radicalism" (cf. Sabel 1981:229–32).

personnel decisions is also important in explaining the moderation of a party's legislators. Ecology parties go through a learning process in which substantial groups of moderate rank-and-file activists come to embrace electoral considerations as a rationale for choosing parliamentary representatives.

Professional and politicized recruitment styles move ecology parties closer to the logic of party competition prevailing in conventional Belgian and West German parties and in the major parties of other parliamentary democracies. In all such parties a candidate's personal abilities, organizational loyalty, and political stance play an important role in recruitment for electoral office.[28] Yet there remain important differences between conventional and left-libertarian parties. In conventional parties the role of local and national party executives in screening and selecting candidates is extensive, particularly in systems with proportional representation and multi-member electoral districts. In ecology parties, however, this role is negligible, with the partial exception of Ecolo. Further, in traditional parties political functionaries and career politicians represent the most common pattern of political ambition. In ecology parties amateurs still play an important role. Moreover, even where they are displaced by political entrepreneurs, their lifestyle, aspirations, and political behavior differ dramatically from those of career politicians in conventional parties. Finally, while in conventional parties strong linkages to organized interest groups and proportional representation of special interests are a dominant concern, such rationales play next to no role in ecology parties. On the surface, movementist recruitment criteria seem to point into the direction of special interest representation. Yet, as I discuss in the next chapter, left-libertarian movements and ecology parties lack the patterns of linkage that could establish and enforce a quasi-corporatist system of movement representation in party politics.

On the whole, recruitment patterns are still evolving in ecology parties. But they exhibit a stronger pull toward a logic of party competition than we encountered when we examined the parties' commitment mechanisms, their dynamic of local party sections, or even their patterns of organizational communication and control. This pull articulates itself either in a personalization of politics around prominent postmaterialist political entrepreneurs and a politicized style of recruitment for electoral office, or a routinization of politics around functionaries and a professional recruitment style. Still, the modest involvement of the ecology party apparatus in recruitment procedures, the outlook and behavior of political entrepreneurs, and the absence of strong interest group control of the nomination process preserve essential differences between conventional Belgian and West German parties and their new left-libertarian competitors.

28. The nomination of Belgian party candidates for parliament has been studied by Ceulers (1977) and Obler (1974). Instructive German studies include Preusse (1981), Pumm (1977), and Zeuner (1970). See also Ranney's (1968; 1981) work on candidate selection in Britain and the Unites States and Wertman's (1977) study of Italian recruitment.

8 | Reaching Out

Divorced from other means of political participation, voting for a party or candidate expresses citizens' policy preferences without much precision or sophistication. It tells a party little about its constituency's perceptions, demands, and fears. For this reason, parties in competitive democracies rely on elaborate secondary linkage networks to sound out and direct their constituencies. Ecology as well as conventional parties view nonelectoral linkages to their constituencies as important channels of communication. But whereas conventional Belgian and West German parties have close organizational and political bonds to centralized economic and cultural interest groups, the ecologists prefer the ideal of fluid, open networks of interaction between their parties and social movements. Left-libertarian movements and parties are both ideologically committed to decentralized nonhierarchical forms of political action. Both reject the conventional corporatist model of linkage between parties and interest groups, as well as the Leninist model in which a revolutionary party exercises authority over mass organizations (see Rossanvallon 1982). Rather than imposing themselves on left-libertarian movements, ecology parties should serve as the movements' "mouthpieces" representing their demands in parliamentary institutions.

In practice, relations between movements and ecology parties have fallen short of such expectations in many areas. Party activists are now trying to revaluate their initial beliefs about movement-party linkages. Of the Hamburg Greens Rainer says that initially most militants subscribed to the "mouthpiece doctrine," but have begun to reassess their position. He argues that party activists had overrated the movements' capacity to insist on change. He emphasizes that the Hamburg Greens are more radical than the movements and the movements are no counterbalance to the party's increasing pragmatism. Faced with a decline of movements in the mid-1980s, the party must now create its own extraparliamentary protest rather than rely solely on naturally mobilized groups. According to Kurt, another Hamburg Green, movement groups often no longer mobilize on their own but expect the party to publicize and pursue their demands. Other militants from Hamburg observe that citizens' initiatives with limited, well-defined demands do not consider the Greens to be their main benefactors, but turn to whatever party promises to meet their needs. Rainer notes that among Hamburg's vast range of groups some are unwilling to communicate with the Greens, particularly social policy and self-help groups for women, young people, and the unemployed. Angelika, who participates in a women's group, comments that feminists are averse to dealing with any party, including the Greens. Most militants agree that contacts between Greens and movements depend on the initiative of individual activists, primarily elected parliamentarians. In general, the Hamburg section has too few militants to establish an ongoing dialogue with all relevant movements in its area.

Hessian Green activists have had more experience with movement groups, especially since their party began to support the Social Democratic state government. Dirk is puzzled by what he called a "schizophrenia" in the movements: On the one hand, movement groups are uncompromising in their own particular demands, but on the other they urge the Greens to make far-reaching concessions in negotiations with the Social Democrats as long as their own demands are met. Gertrud, another Hessian activist, fears the movement groups are beginning to treat the Greens as a "service organization" pressing for movement demands but having no say over movement strategy. Jürgen notices that since the Greens began to participate in the Hessian government, an increasing number of movement groups have turned to the Green parliamentary party and have acted like self-serving pressure group lobbies, while in a city like Frankfurt where the local Greens are part of the opposition in the city council, movement-party linkages remain weak.

In other Belgian and German party sections, movements take great care to remain nonpartisan and dislike direct contacts with the party. In Ecolo, Rudi recalls he had to see the leaders of an environmental protection group in secrecy because they did not want it to be known they had invited party representatives. Torsten, a Green parliamentarian from southern Germany, complains that "we have made the mistake of believing we are the representatives of the peace initiatives." Although some movements have overcome this arms-length relationship to the party, activists still find the breadth and continuity of movement-party linkages limited.

These are some of the recurring perceptions and experiences militants report about linkages with constituency groups, meaning direct interactions between party activists and more or less organized external constituencies.[1]

---

1. My definition is considerably narrower than Lawson's (1980:3) notion of linkages as the "substantive connection between rulers and ruled." Lawson also includes indirect linkages,

At the individual level activists establish linkage through overlapping involvement in ecology parties and social movements. At the collective level linkages are created by the interaction of party representatives (executives, parliamentarians) and movement spokespeople. In a study of Norwegian parties, Valen and Katz (1964:313) distinguished four types of organized linkages: (1) overlapping leadership, (2) party subgroups representing external interest organizations, (3) liaison committees between interest groups and parties, and (4) the collective affiliation of interest associations with parties.

In left-libertarian parties individual linkage is more likely to emerge than collective linkage: given the preference for fluid, nonhierarchical structure in left-libertarian ideology, collective linkages remain confined to occasional, selective interactions between movement and party representatives or a clientelism where movements retain their internal autonomy but regularly extract favors from the ecology party. To some extent, at least, the weakness of collective and organized linkages as a medium of party-constituency communication can be compensated for by what I call "cultural interpenetration," a continuous flow of symbols and ideas between parties and constituencies. Joint celebrations, cultural and protest events including both party and movement activists, and the left-libertarian mass media are examples of cultural interpenetration: the transmission of ideas and visions from sympathizers to parties and vice versa. In this sense, parties can thrive on the intellectual creativity of external supporters.

Particularly in centers of left-libertarian mobilization, an extensive infrastructure of pubs, cafés, health food stores, repair shops, theater groups, preschools organized by parents, women's clinics, local news media, and university groups facilitates the cultural interpenetration of ecology parties and their constituencies. Yet even here, given the pace and pressure of decision making in political parties, cultural interpenetration is often too slow and diffuse to affect party strategy directly. The parties' need for constituency input cannot be fully satisfied by cultural linkages alone. For this reason militants find direct discussion of policies and initiatives by individuals and organizational units in movements and parties important. While the left-libertarian vision of politics calls for a fluid cultural interpenetration between civil society and parties, parliamentary practice requires more immediate linkages directed toward specific purposes and policies. Up to now the left-libertarian vision of politics appears to have had more effect on linkage patterns than the institutional constraints and opportunities of parliamentary policy making. Direct linkages remain relatively weak in the eyes of most activists. Moreover, they bring about unintended effects which reinforce a stratarchal distribution of power.

---

such as the demographic and cultural representativeness of a party's leadership for its electoral constituencies or its influence on policies favorable to its constituencies.

Table 37
Party preferences of sympathizers and opponents of new social movements in Belgium and West Germany, 1982

	Christian Democrats	Social Democrats	Liberal democrats	Ecology parties
West Germany				
Ecology movement	−35.2	−1.3	−1.9	+29.2
Anti-nuclear movement	−35.0	+2.2	−2.5	+26.9
Peace movement	−26.5	+8.0	−2.7	+17.1
Belgium				
Ecology movement	−3.6	−4.2	−8.6	+18.6
Anti-nuclear movement	−10.3	−0.1	−8.2	+12.4
Peace movement	−2.4	−7.5	−9.2	+9.6

Note: percentage differences between supporters and opponents of each movement among supporters of a party
Source: Muller-Rommel (1984b: Table 1), based on Eurobarometer 17.

Linkages through Joint Activism

Surveys indicate that most Belgian and West German ecology party sympathizers support the ecology, anti-nuclear, and peace movements.[2] Yet the reverse is not necessarily true. In 1982 at the height of the European peace protests against NATO nuclear armament, not only the Greens but also the German Social Democrats were backed by more supporters than opponents of the anti-nuclear and the peace movements (Table 37). Even the West German liberals, Belgian Christian democrats, and Belgian socialists attracted almost as many movement supporters as opponents. Only the German Christian Democrats and the Belgian liberal parties clearly draw more opponents than supporters of new social movements. Thus, although ecology parties appeal to a considerable *segment* of movement supporters, they are not the movements' party representatives as such. The majority of movement sympathizers still backs one of the conventional parties. Because in Belgium the party spectrum is not as clearly polarized around left-libertarian issues as in West Germany, the linkage between movement support and Agalev or Ecolo affiliation is relatively tenuous. In both countries the peace movement appeals to the most heterogeneous group of voters, while ecology and anti-nuclear movement supporters are more concentrated in ecology parties.

The more deeply individuals are involved in protest events, organizations, and leadership of left-libertarian movements, however, the more likely they are to support ecology parties. In a West German survey 64 percent of those

2. In Belgium (Deschouwer and Stouthuysen 1984:16) as well as in West Germany (Schultze 1987:7; Veen 1984: 11) ecology party voters have different attitudes on defense, foreign policy, and environmental affairs than the average voter.

who claimed membership in the peace movement voiced their support of the Greens. Among voters who claimed to be ''strong supporters'' of the peace movement, but not ''members,'' however, Green support amounted to only 20 percent, while 64 percent endorsed the Social Democrats (Schmitt 1987a). In the absence of reliable data, the comparatively high involvement of ecology party activists in left-libertarian movements reported in Chapter 4 (Figure 3) may serve as additional indirect evidence that preference for ecology parties and the extent of involvement in left-libertarian movements are closely related to each other. Yet this association is not proof of a permanent and stable linkage. Recent joiners of ecology parties have less movement experience, and many movement activists have syndicalist or populist anti-party resentments even against ecology parties. Moreover, the parties often cannot maintain the loyalty of their new members.

These findings show that it is unlikely that ecology parties have simply absorbed most of the activists who used to be involved in left-libertarian movements. Agalev, Ecolo, and Green interviewees regret that their party work is leaving them little time for activism in protest movements. But the overall number of party activists—a total of at most 10,000 regulars in the Greens and about 800 in Agalev and Ecolo combined—pales in comparison to the number of participants in groups and events organized by anti-nuclear, peace, and feminist movements, thus disproving the contention that left-libertarian movements have been weakened because the parties drew away their activists.

Overall, joint activism in protest events and party organization is a significant but quite limited form of linkage between ecology parties and social movements. Only a small fraction of movement supporters get involved in ecology parties and, with the decline of activism among Belgian and West German movements in the mid-1980s, the parties' ties to these mobilized constituencies appear to have weakened.

How Movements Address Ecology Parties

Since ecology party militants do not see social movements as mere ''transmission belts'' executing tasks defined by the party, they have accorded them a role as creative and initiating agents in movement-party linkages. This self-restraint if not self-denial in limiting the party role in directing political mobilization in civil society is consistent with the widespread lack of organizational loyalty in ecology parties. Movements are considered as not only complementary but also superior avenues of left-libertarian politics; parties must follow the movements, not lead them. Organizational loyalty and the survival of the parties are less relevant than reaching the left-libertarian objectives. In the words of one militant, ''Green ideas must be realized, even at the expense of the party, as long as substantive progress toward our political objectives is accomplished.'' As a consequence party activists usually expect social movements to initiate linkages. Movements have developed at least four different patterns of linkage to ecology parties which I describe in order of increasing density of communication and coordination: (1) arms-length relations, (2) selective communication, (3) clientelism, and (4) organized ties.

Militants often report that movements shy away from direct contact with ecology parties out of the desire to allay suspicion that they are partisan. On the one hand, these attitudes are fuelled by a principled aversion to political parties grounded in the same populist or syndicalist reservations that limit party membership. On the other hand, movement activists avoid appealing to ecology parties because of the tactical consideration that it would risk undermining their ability to mobilize a strong political coalition around a particular issue among supporters of different parties. The wide distribution of party preferences among movement sympathizers evidenced in Table 37 illustrates that this rationale is warranted.

A further reason for limited linkages is the decline of many left-libertarian movements in the mid-1980s, especially the anti-nuclear and peace movements. Many other left-libertarian groups, particularly women's self-help organizations and the alternative economy sector of cooperatives, restaurants, repair shops, and social services, appear to have reached a saturation level and prefer to avoid political involvement. The attenuation of linkages is further exacerbated by the emergence of self-help efforts by the new poor, such as the young unemployed, to which left-libertarian ''middle-class'' parties have little access given their political agenda and support base. In all these instances an arms-length relationship develops between parties and movements in which contact is restricted to a minimum and regular mutual commitments generally do not exist.

A second level of cooperation is probably the most common in movement-party linkages. It involves *selective communication* and interaction between ecology party militants and the spokespeople of social movements. These contacts are almost exclusively oriented toward *elected* representatives of ecology parties in municipal councils or parliaments and address specific *individuals* in the parties, not the party or even parliamentary groups at large. Olivier from Ecolo's parliamentary party states that ''groups will work with you as an individual member of parliament, but they are afraid of being 'devoured' by the party.'' Familiar ideological reservations play a role in this strategy. Philippe from Liège observes that people contact Ecolo but do not want to be part of the ''politique politicienne [politicians' politics].''

Ecology party municipal councilors and deputies find selective interaction with representatives from movement groups a common and useful input. Most of the parliamentary initiatives and questions submitted by the Green deputies to the Lower Saxony state parliament, for instance, originate with action groups and local party units.[3] In addition, movement activists ask deputies to initiate investigations, review administrative decisions, draft bills, and submit legislative motions. Parliamentarians receive countless petitions, appeals, and letters from individual constituents pleading for help with everything from conflict with the public administration to personal problems. Interviewees mentioned the plight of released prison inmates, poor people struggling with welfare agencies, conscientious objectors resisting the draft, and foreign political refugees applying for asylum.

Selective interaction between elected deputies and movement constituencies remains idiosyncratic, diverse, and sporadic because the patterns of mobilization in most left-libertarian groups rule out more stable, routinized linkages. Movement activists do not turn to the party as party, but to elected representatives with opportunities and resources for placing an issue on the public agenda. This means that the strategic control of communication across organizational boundaries, a critical power resource, almost entirely rests with elected representatives.

Selective interaction between parties and movements reinforces tendencies I have identified in the intraorganizational analysis in Chapter 6: the irrelevance of the party organization and the focal position of its elected representatives in all strategic interactions. Party militants and elected representatives prefer an entrepreneurial political style that treats interactions with constituencies as personal rather than organizational. For instance, when asked about her relations to movement constituencies in her county, one Green councilor declares she never does things as or considers herself as a representative of the party, but only as "Dorothea," an individual who evaluates movement demands and initiatives in light of her personal values and political concerns. External ties increase the representatives' autonomy from others in the party and become a source of legitimation for political action (Zeuner 1983:111). When deputies disagree with other party militants they often invoke the policy or strategic preference of movement constituencies to justify their position.

Most interviewees do believe that selective communication is the form of linkage most closely corresponding to the parties' logic of constituency representation. It is stronger than an arms-length relation and allows for direct contact between party and movement. At the same time it preserves movement autonomy and avoids organizational ties that might undermine the nonhierarchical and fluid, decentralized character of the linkage.

The third level of cooperation, *clientelism,* reaches the threshold at which party militants feel uncomfortable about too much interdependence. In their view, movements seeking clientelistic linkage wish to shift the burden of

3. See Die Grünen im Landtag von Niedersachsen (1984), 5, 42, 59, and 63.

protest mobilization to the party and to have their interests represented through intraparliamentary initiatives and debates. From the movements' point of view this strategy is rational if it expends less energy than extraparliamentary protest but is at least equally effective. From the party militants' point of view, clientelistic representation undermines the belief that movements rather than parties should lead left-libertarian struggles. Militants resentfully call clientelistic linkage ''proxy politics'' (*Stellvertreterpolitik*) and complain that the representation of movement demands in legislatures is doomed to be insincere and ineffective unless it is backed up by credible extraparliamentary mobilization. In Hesse, for instance, a local citizens' initiative asked Green state parliamentarians to stop a highway project, but when Green deputies investigated the case they found that nobody at the local level had voiced protest against the project during the planning process.[4]

Instrumental, clientelistic linkages often create tensions between movements and ecology parties. Party militants chafe at the movements' free rider attitude, while movement constituencies grow impatient if the parties do not respond immediately to their demands. Movement activists, observing the slow machinery of parliamentary politics, underestimate the deputies' workload and the procedural and political difficulties of placing a new issue on parliamentary agendas.

Militants also find that movement organizations willing to enter a clientelistic relationship with the party typically advocate policies that would benefit only a narrow constituency. Broader political accountability is, for them, an extraneous concern, as is the compatibility of their demands with those of other party constituencies. Hessian Green interviewees, for instance, recall an environmental group that considered the cancellation of a new hazardous waste facility important enough to decide the fate of the party's alliance with the Social Democrats, but was willing to agree to policy compromises with the Social Democrats in most other policy areas.

Where movement organizations ask for public financing of their activities and projects, such as cooperative enterprises, young farmers committed to ecological farming techniques, or women's self-help groups, they often refuse to place their demands in a broader set of political priorities or to submit to financial and political oversight. A Green militant aptly summarizes the logic of clientelism with the motto ''Money yes, substantive cooperation with and accountability to the party, no.''[5] This particularism and instrumentalism

4. Die Grünen im Hessischen Landtag, *Landtags–Info*, no. 2 (1985).
5. In Hesse the Regional Association of Alternative Enterprises became an especially vocal pressure group, convincing the Greens and the state administration to subsidize cooperative firms. The *Grüne Hessenzeitung*, 4 (September 1984), 10 satirically describes the association's particularistic philosophy which evades a definition of what a cooperative enterprise worthy of public funding is: ''The principles of the circle are as follows: 1. We all want money. 2. If you don't ask me any questions, I will not ask you any questions. There is little discussion,

encounters resistance from most party militants. Dirk, a Hessian Green state parliamentarian, reports that ''we had to make clear to the association of cooperative enterprises that the party was not interested in them as such, but only as vehicles in a comprehensive strategy to lower youth unemployment.''

The dilemma of clientelistic linkage illustrates the difference between political parties and movements and the limitations of pursuing a logic of constituency representation. Whereas movements typically express a narrow range of often well-defined demands, parties find themselves forced to consider tradeoffs in a variety of policy demands and to create a minimum level of consistency in their plans of action. This imperative, of course, is more easily realized by pragmatists and ideologues than lobbyists, who are more inclined to follow a particularistic strategy: As long as this hazardous waste dump is not built in our neighborhood or our houses for battered women receive state financing, why should we care whether nuclear power plants keep running or welfare benefits are cut?

It must be kept in mind, however, that clientelistic linkages are sought by only a few movements and confined to particularly favorable circumstances, such as the participation of an ecology party in a government alliance. Ecology parties even less frequently engage in the fourth linkage mechanism, *organizational ties* to movements, which are established through internal suborganizations, coordinating committees between parties and constituencies, or written policy agreements and joint decision procedures. In Agalev and Ecolo even the movements from which the parties developed, Anders Gaan Leven and Amis de la Terre, insist on their autonomy over any formal organizational interdependence.[6]

Thus, organizational ties between ecology parties and movements rarely develop. Agalev, Ecolo, and the Greens formally participated in the national steering committees of the Belgian and West German peace movements. Yet interviewees in both countries found that even in this instance ecology parties were not represented according to their true strength but as only one among numerous supporting organizations and groups. An almost symbiotic party-movement linkage exists in only one West German case, that of a radical organization of retired people, the Grey Panthers. The Grey Panthers accepted the Greens as their parliamentary representatives in a formal agreement, probably because the group has virtually no access to any other party or labor union. In 1987 the organization's resolute chairwoman and undisputed leader was elected to the German parliament on the Green electoral ticket.

applications for money are not reviewed, and there is no debate about the criteria defining a collective self-managed enterprise. The only linking bond is the love of money.''

6. *Amis de la Terre*'s membership journal in fact published complaints about Ecolo's turn to institutional politics. See Marc Vanhellemont and Dominique Thibaut, ''Le futur n'est plus ce qu'il était,'' *Champs Libre,* no. 64 (September 1985), 34–36.

The distribution of the four patterns of party-movement linkage reveals the importance of constituency mobilization and left-libertarian ideology. The predominance of arms-length relations and selective communication between parties and movements, as opposed to clientelism or organizational linkage, stems from rejection of centralization, hierarchy, and formal organization. Variations of linkage patterns can be explained in terms of already familiar variables shaping the environment of left-libertarian party politics.

Different levels of left-libertarian mobilization affect the nature and strength of party-movement ties. On the periphery of mobilization with a relative paucity of social movements and a populist preference for remaining above parties while uniting the community against outside intruders (government, industry), the most typical linkages are arms-length relations and occasional selective communications. Thus, a "Green Front" of 300 local organizations to save the Black Forest from acid rain rejected requests by the Social Democrats and the Greens to participate officially in the protest coalition.[7] Similarly, the Belgian nature protection associations keep Agalev and Ecolo at a distance.

In centers of left-libertarian politics movement activists are more willing to ally themselves with ecology parties. Protest events joined by movement groups from centers and peripheries reveal different linkage strategies. In West German protests against nuclear power (Kitschelt 1980: chap. 5) and the extension of airports (Rucht 1984b:216–37), the movement groups located on the rural periphery of the left-libertarian cleavage remained nonpartisan and limited their demands to the operational objectives of the struggles, while groups from the centers went on to attack the existing parties and became openly partisan supporters of the Greens.

Most left-libertarian movements on the periphery are confined to the politics of space (environment, land use, transportation, military installations, and the like). They focus on specific, clear-cut decisions such as whether or not to build an industrial facility. They engage in single-issue radicalism but fall far short of a general critique of economic and political institutions. They tend to be defensive, pragmatic, and instrumental, and usually have only short-term objectives. For this reason they are less amenable to broad politicization of their activists and opt for arms-length relations to parties. At most they communicate with parties on a case by case basis or become free riders by shifting the burden of action to the parties.

Social identity movements, however such as feminist and self-help groups, cultural activities, and social services, involve complx, extensive, and prolonged efforts to change group identities, life-chances, attitudes, and institutions, rather than focus on decisions. Their social criticism is more com-

7. Cf. *Tageszeitung* (April 15, 1985).

prehensive and ideological than that of environmental movements. Organizational autonomy and grassroots participation have a strong expressive significance for these groups and make them more likely to subscribe to a syndicalist view hostile to parties. Yet because of the long-term nature of their objectives, they are inclined to engage in clientelistic relations with ecology parties to acquire funds for their activities. Thus, party militants observe two different, if not contradictory, views of party-movement linkages taken by movement activists such as feminist groups. On the one hand, these groups insist on their autonomy and reject party bonds but on the other, they expect the parties to fight for public funding of their projects. As a consequence of the Hessian Green/Social Democratic alliance, efforts to get public funding for left-libertarian projects met with some success. But feminists were often disillusioned by the administrative constraints of fiscal accountability that acceptance of subsidies carries.

The Hessian example demonstrates the importance of another factor in shaping movement-party linkages, the party's *competitive position*. Interviewees in Agalev, Ecolo, and the Greens are all familiar with the following scenario: Movement activists turn to the municipal councilors or parliamentarians of their parties if (1) they are part of a governing majority or (2) no other party is willing to publicize their demands. Representatives of movements in Hesse in 1984 and 1985 decisively threw in their weight to support pragmatic Greens who favored an alliance with the Social Democratic minority state government. The backing of environmental, feminist, and cooperative business movements lent legitimacy to the moderate strategy and undercut the credibility of the radical party faction. Thus, an alliance of pragmatists and lobbyists defeated the ideologues who had dominated the Hessian Greens up to 1983. In light of this experience, ideologues have second thoughts about whether ecology parties are a "mouthpiece" of social movements or, because of the movements' reformist myopia, must set an independent agenda.

At the local level many socialist green coalitions or informal alliances have facilitated similar intraparty configurations. In Freiburg, for instance, Green city councilors represent 16 percent of the voters and participate in shifting majorities in the city council. Because they have extracted a number of favors for their constituencies from the city government, they have comparatively strong, though informal and personal, relations with key figures in the Freiburg movement sector. Although many party militants are ideologues, these opportunities and linkages have facilitated a moderate Green strategy on the city council. Green municipal councilors, in cooperation with local movement organizations, support the incremental reforms backed by majorities in the council. Similarly, Ecolo formed a city government with the socialists in Liège, in 1982, and its contacts extend into the social movement community. Linkages in that case are limited by the relatively narrow range of left-libertarian movements in a declining industrial city embroiled in a fiscal crisis, restricting Ecolo's capacity to reshape municipal politics.

In places where the Social Democratic party is in power and ecologists remain in the opposition, movements are sometimes better off turning to the SPD. Movement activists show little sentimentality or loyalty in their dealings with parties, and in fact Green activists reinforce this behavior. Rainer, a well-placed Hamburg Green, argues he encourages movement activists to take their demands to the governing Social Democrats rather than to the Greens as a party of opposition. In some instances, however, the ecologists are the only parties who want to listen to social movement groups. Harry, a municipal councilor from Antwerp, sees social movement groups turn to Agalev as an opposition party because the governing Christian democratic and socialist majority on the council was unwilling to respond to their concerns.

Where both socialist and ecology parties are in opposition, they occasionally compete for movement support. The movements, however, have little incentive to commit themselves to a single party. In Frankfurt the Green municipal councilors in the 1980–84 electoral term belonged to the radical party wing, and many movement and party activists perceived their uncompromising strategy as impractical. Independent local women's groups, for instance, supported a Social Democratic proposal to create an office for the equalization of women, while the Green councilors argued the initiative did not go far enough and opposed it. Because of these and similar tensions between Green city councilors and local movements, linkages between the Frankfurt Greens and external constituencies remained tenuous.

In Belgium there are fewer linkages between movements and ecology parties than in West Germany. Limited left-libertarian mobilization and the weak competitive position of Agalev and Ecolo are two reasons. The structure of the party system and its less polarized political culture may also be responsible. Belgium's more fragmented party system makes it unlikely that movements will commit themselves to a particular party. Moreover, Belgian left-libertarian movements reject the pillarized, institutionalized relations prevailing among the Christian, liberal, and socialist parties and their occupational or religious interest groups. Movement activists, therefore, have little inclination to create an alternative pillar by associating too closely with ecology parties. West Germany's institutional and cultural polarization, however, makes it more difficult for movements to escape identification with a particular party. These national differences suggest why Belgian party militants perceive a greater distance from social movement groups than do their West German counterparts.

Up to this point the comparison of party-movement relations in different settings and opportunity structures has created a fairly static impression of linkages, yet on the contrary they are evolving, as party and movement activists learn to interact with each other. Where movement activists realize that municipal councilors and parliamentarians from ecology parties are committed to their demands, they are more willing to set aside their reservations about partisan identification. What may have worked against these improvements in party-movement linkages, however, is the broad downward trend of social protest in the mid-1980s which has limited the potential for contact between the parties and their mobilized constituencies. Even in a center of left-libertarian activism like Hamburg, Green militants worry about the decline of political protest that often leaves the party as the only standard bearer of left-libertarian causes.

In spite of these variations in party-movement linkages both in context and over time, it remains true that the form of mobilization in left-libertarian movements and the parties' logic of constituency representation discourage close interorganizational ties. Party militants have counted on spontaneous cultural interpenetration and dense informal networks of communication with left-libertarian movements, an expectation which has been realized to a lesser extent than militants had originally anticipated. In light of these experiences, militants have had to rethink earlier prescriptions for ecology parties as nothing more than advocates for social movements.

How Parties Address Movements

The initial view of party-movement linkages, as expressed in countless declarations and statements in the early years of the ecology parties, relied on four interdependent doctrines. First, party militants conceived of left-libertarian politics as a zero-sum game: because there is a fixed pool of activists, the more activists the parties attract the fewer will remain in social movements. Too much recruiting by the parties was thought to drain the movements. Only a small group of Green, Agalev, and Ecolo interviewees still support this view.[8] Predictably, lobbyists who have had direct involvement in movements are most inclined to see the rise of the parties as a cause of the movements' decline. Other activists, if they construct any causal tradeoff, more often argue the reverse: Parties have gained active supporters because the political effectiveness of movements is inherently limited.

A second doctrine maintained that movements are the true fountain of left-libertarian radicalism, while parties are prone to electoralism and co-optation. Again, practical experience has led many activists to revise this view. Both pragmatists and ideologues reject the often particularist, myopic, and instrumental behavior of movements and argue that parties need to develop broader political visions than movements. For ideologues many social movements are too moderate and limited in their demands, while pragmatists

8. A similar finding is reported in Zeuner (1985:10–11).

support incremental policy change but worry about the movements' special interest pressure group politics.

Ideologues and pragmatists now also call into question two other doctrines about party-movement linkages: extrainstitutional struggles led by social movements have priority over electoral politics and political parties are the movements' advocates in legislatures. What unites ideologues and pragmatists is the view that parties must actively stimulate and organize the mobilization of left-libertarian forces beyond issues raised by social movements. Ideologues believe that ecology parties must radicalize movements by leading extra-parliamentary struggles and by an educational strategy showing that the conventional parties are incapable of carrying out reform. Pragmatists, however, see the party as a corrective to movement particularism that develops coherent reform perspectives and brings about legislative policy change.

The interventionist approach supported by ideologues and pragmatists and the passive one advocated by lobbyists are linked to different operational theories about political mobilization. Lobbyists believe in a crisis/breakdown theory: As the social and environmental crises of industrial society intensify, radical social movements will mobilize and strengthen the party. Faced with a decline of the social movements, ecology parties must adopt wait-and-see strategies preserving their purity until the next wave of movements appears. Pragmatists and ideologues, however, insist that left-libertarian parties should mobilize critical resources to push forward social struggles, which will lead either to a dramatic transformation of social institutions, as the radicals hope, or an incremental reform policy, as the moderates prefer. The parties cannot wait for a breakdown of society, but must intensify political controversies with all means at their disposal.[9]

Table 38 summarizes the three different views of party-movement linkages expressed by the older movementist orthodoxy in ecology parties as well as the right and left revisionism of ideologues and pragmatists. It is not without irony that contemporary debates about external linkages and political strategy within ecology parties closely parallel those of socialist parties in the first half of this century. The German Social Democratic party, for instance, was divided between a fundamentalist center waiting for the breakdown of capitalism, and pressure from both left radicals and moderate reformers to go ahead with more activist party strategies (see Schorske 1955; Groh 1973). With lobbyists caught in the middle, ideologues called for a radical strategy of political mobilization, polarization, or at times even insurrection, while moderate pragmatists moved toward a logic of party competition and electoralism.

9. In terms of sociological theory, lobbyists adhere to a "relative deprivation" and "crisis" theory of political protest, pragmatists and ideologues to a "resource mobilization" theory. For the different approaches see Oberschall (1973), Piven and Cloward (1977: chap. 1), and Tilly (1978).

Table 38
Evaluations of party-movement linkages in ecology parties

Strategic choices	Older movementist orthodoxy: lobbyists	Leftist revisionism: ideologues	Rightist revisionism: pragmatists
1. Is there a zero-sum game between party growth and movement decline?	Yes, the rise of the party drains activists from the movements into the much less important party work.	No, the careers of movements and parties are causally independent from each other. Or the decline of the movements causes the rise of the parties.	No, essentially subscribes to the same views as the ideologues.
2. Are left-libertarian movements more radical and creative than the parties?	Yes, the movements "push" the reluctant parties that are in danger of being absorbed by the system into a more radical direction.	No, the movements are usually too selective and limited in defining political goals to develop a broad program and a consistently radical strategy.	No, the movements are reformist, but too particularistic and short-sighted in their strategic approach to achieve lasting social reforms.
3. Should party strategies follow the movements' political demands?	Yes, the parties express the movements' demands and should themselves behave like movements. This position denies fundamental differences between movements and parties.	No, a party is qualitatively different from movements. It has educational "vanguard" tasks to raise political consciousness and develop a broad program for social transformation.	No, a party is qualitatively different from movements. It develops coherent reform perspectives through detailed policy proposals and the mobilization of political support for them.
4. Are the parties' parliamentarians the movements' "mouthpiece"?	Yes, parliamentary representatives are useful only as representatives of social movements. The parties should abstain from representing unmobilized groups.	No, the complexity of social change and the limited horizon of movements require that parties go beyond the movements' demands. Parties also represent unmobilized constituencies.	No, agrees with the ideologues' assessment that parties have to go beyond movement demands but proposes to follow a different strategy: use parliaments to effect public policy reform.

In practice, however, the ideologues' and pragmatists' search for more active linkages to social movements has encountered many obstacles. The parties have limited personnel and financial resources and hence only modest organizational capabilities for mobilizing movements or providing incentives to seek closer contacts with the parties. Further, populist or syndicalist anti-party sensitivities common within left-libertarian movements are still working against stronger linkages. Finally, an activist approach to social movements frequently leads to intraparty conflict as the parties select issues, positions, movement groups, and forms of action necessary to party-movement linkages.

The parties' most visible activist linkage effort has therefore been confined primarily to staging regular protest events.[10] Party-organized protests are expected to enhance the cultural interpenetration of ecology parties and movements and underline party solidarity with movement demands. In some ways even campaign activities have taken on the character of almost festive protest rallies featuring avant-garde musicians, poets, and comedians sympathetic to left-libertarian causes. This style of campaigning, perfected especially by the Greens, clearly shows that ecology parties are more than vehicles for transmitting demands to political decision makers and are part of a cultural drive to change existing institutions and values.

Nevertheless, many militants realize that the parties have limited appeal to broad movement constituencies. In Hamburg, for instance, Greens interpreted it as a defeat when only 1,000 people responded to the party's call for the blockade of a chemical plant that had discharged large amounts of dioxin. Interviewees also regretted that the party did not publicly celebrate the facility's eventual shutdown. Similarly, Ecolo and Agalev militants felt they missed an opportunity to mobilize environmental protest and support for their parties when a ship loaded with nuclear waste materials sank off the Belgian cost in 1985.[11]

Ecology parties can gain visibility and media coverage for protest events quite easily if their leadership makes a point of being seen at them. A leader of the Hamburg Greens in parliament was arrested while participating in a squatters' occupation of an abandoned house. Green federal parliamentarians staged a peace demonstration in East Berlin and were arrested. Ecolo and Agalev parliamentarians trespassed onto the NATO base at Florennes to protest the planned stationing of new nuclear missiles and the arrest of

10. The national Green party regularly organizes or supports protest events about nuclear power, peace, feminism, the Third World, economic issues, and environmental pollution (cf. Die Grünen, Bundesvorstand, 1985:58–59). In Agalev a local group and the movement *De Groene Fietsers* organized demonstrations against a liquid natural gas harbor at Zeebrugge (*Het Volk,* September 9, 1983). And Ecolo is active in the coalition to fight French nuclear power plants near the Belgian border.

11. *Ecolo Infos,* no. 57 (May 15, 1985), 11.

previous demonstrators at the site. They spent two days in jail and faced trial when their parliamentary immunity expired. Other protest actions by prominent party activists have included hunger strikes and the occupation of embassies abroad. Agalev and Ecolo leaders took over the Belgian embassy in Paris to draw attention to the stationing of French nuclear power plants on the Belgian border. German Greens occupied their country's South African embassy to protest against West German trade with a racist regime. The visits of Belgian and West German ecology parliamentarians to governments and leftist groups in Central America and black Africa, the rebels of Afghanistan, and the PLO in Lebanon are messages to the constituencies of Third World support groups and international civil rights initiatives at home.

Ecology parties have also used parliaments as sites to stage symbolic protests that draw attention to special grievances and reinforce the identification of movement activists with the parties. In the view of one Ecolo militant, people rally around the party when it inserts "real life" into parliaments with protest events.[12] In all ecology parties, as a subtle protest, deputies have refused to comply with their parliaments' dress code and to employ the standard opening address to the assmbly when they speak in the legislature (see Berschien 1984). Green parliamentarians are more inclined to disrupt official procedure than are their more moderate Belgian colleagues. Green deputies once unrolled a banner during a speech by the chancellor. On another occasion Green deputies were excluded from the parliamentary session because of "improper conduct" in their attack on the government. In a spectacular and controversial gesture, the Hesse Greens had one of its members spill blood on a U.S. general at a Hessian state government reception, an action intended to draw attention to U.S. military intervention throughout the world.

As outreach to constituencies the parties symbolic actions and protest events have a limited impact. Events must be innovative, humorous, unusual, outrageous, and surprising, or else they go unnoticed by the mass media. As one Green deputy points out, arriving at the legislature on a bicycle matters to the public only once, thereafter its newsworthiness vanishes. Olivier from Ecolo argues that actions are successful only if the media cover them, but the media are highly selective and ignore other than truly spectacular, unprecedented actions.[13] As a consequence symbolic activities take place intermittently and have only a short-term effect on the consciousness of constituency groups. Many militants, therefore, warn that these activities have no real long-term payoff.[14]

12. Cf. Suzanne Van Rokeghem, "Les hirondelles du parlement," *Ecolo Infos,* no. 43 (June 1983), 20.

13. Agalev and Ecolo parliamentarians, for instance, complained that their occupation of the Belgian embassy in Paris did not get enough media attention. Cf. *Ecolo Infos,* no. 5 (March 1982).

14. Cf. the report of Ecolo parliamentary deputies Daras and Deleuze, in *Ecolo Infos,* no. 57 (May 15, 1985), 15–16. Compare also the view of radicals in Ecolo's Brussels district: "Ecolo

Creative actions featuring well-known party activists may also convey a message inconsistent with the parties' logic of constituency representation. As some interviewees explain, prominent leaders reinforce their privileged access to the mass media by staging special events and thus, in the long run, increase the parties' dependence on them. Moreover, such actions may trigger intraparty conflict, particularly in the Greens where protest is more militant and the party more divided along political lines. Prominent militants rarely consult their party before engaging in protest events or even feel they are politically accountable to the party. Although many members may disagree with either the content or the form of the protest event, the media attribute leaders' actions to the party as a whole. The ecosocialist wing of the Greens, for instance, harshly criticized the Green participants in the East Berlin peace demonstration. The blood spilling action in Hesse set off an intense intraparty clash between moderates and radicals (see Die Grünen im Hessischen Landtag 1983). In a third instance a Green federal parliamentarian and specialist on higher education refused to attend a large rally of liberal and progressive students protesting government efforts to streamline the universities because she identified with more radical students boycotting the protest event, a decision criticized by the majority of her colleagues in the Green parliamentary party.

Green strategy in the peace movement led to another intraparty conflict. Because the Greens support disarmament in both the East and the West, they wished to adopt the slogan of the repressed East German peace movement "Swords to Plowshares" for a national demonstration against President Reagan's vist to Bonn in 1982. But when communist groups in the organizing committee of the event opposed the slogan, the Green representative agreed to a compromise formula in hectic last minute negotiations, a concession opposed by members of the party executive and the steering committee.[15] A similar dispute between factions over protest activities arose in Ecolo when the party's national executive rejected participation in the Marche des Jeunes pour l'Emploi, organized by unions and leftist groups. While the executive declared the demonstration supported a "productionist" economic strategy and could not be backed by ecologists, the more left-wing Ecolo section in Brussels called for participation.

Beyond party-led protest events, ecologists have increasingly searched for intermediate party-movement linkages combining cultural interpenetration with more permanent organizational ties, yet have attained only limited re-

has become a master in the art of organizing actions as spectacular as they are punctual (for example the 'action automobile' at the station of the Leopold quarter in Brussels), which are certainly formidable propaganda coups but are not at all integrated into a campaign to raise people's consciousness [*sensibilisation*] and to mobilize them, for example, for the defense of public transportation." (Jean Fauchet, Jean Flinker, Denis Leduc, "Pourquoi nous ne voterons la charte," *Ecolo Infos*, supplement to no. 46 (October 15, 1984), 62.

15. See the protocol of the meeting of the Green national executive on May 8, 1982.

sults. In Chapter 7, I argued that open list candidacies of movement activists who are not party members are a linkage mechanism that generates considerable doubt about the candidates' representativeness and democratic legitimacy in speaking for the party or making decisions on its behalf. With their relative financial affluence, the German Greens have been able to try two other linkages. They funnel grants or loans through so-called "ecofunds" to constituencies such as protest groups or cooperative enterprises. The financing criteria and philosophy of these ecofunds vary from state to state.[16] Some militants, however, question whether these monies contribute to a broadening cultural linkage between movements and parties or finance groups with purely instrumental, financial interest in the party.[17] A second linkage strategy has been to finance educational foundations offering seminars and retreats on questions relating to left-libertarian politics. Because of West Germany's abundant state and federal funding of party foundations, the Greens have increasingly followed this route.[18]

Both Belgian and West German ecology parties lack mass media backed by or sympathetic to the party that could reach many of their voters. The Greens are in a better position than Agalev or Ecolo because the countercultural daily newspaper *Tageszeitung,* with a circulation of about 50,000, supports them. Moreover, numerous weekly and monthly independent local magazines sympathize with the Greens. While Agalev and Ecolo lack comparable outlets, in Flanders at least the established press is quite willing to report on ecology party activities and even opens its columns to contributions from party spokespeople.[19]

Ecology parties have shown little initiative in establishing formal linkages to movement organizations or interest groups, such as the umbrella organizations of national peace and environmental movements where the parties are far less represented than corresponds to their actual mass support in the movement. One major West German umbrella organization of environmental groups, the Bundesverband der Bürgerinitiativen Umweltschutz (BBU) has been skillfully dominated by Social Democrats for a number of years, although its individual member groups often lean toward the Greens.

16. In North Rhine-Westphalia most of the money goes to alternative enterprises. Hamburg finances initiatives concerned with international affairs. In West Berlin and Hesse women's projects and Third World groups have priority (*Frankfurter Rundschau,* September 3, 1983). Up to the summer of 1985, Green ecofunds disbursed over five million Marks, *Tageszeitung* (August 14, 1985).

17. See *Grünes NRW Info,* 3 (July 1983), 15.

18. Intraparty controversies over acceptance of state financing and the ensuing dependence on existing institutions as well as over the organizational form and policy of the Green ecological foundations have been intense. See my brief discussion in Chapter 4.

19. Most important is the socialist daily, *De Morgen,* which is widely read by Agalev militants, and the weekly magazine *Knaack. Le Soir* in Wallonia every now and then permits Ecolo to write a column.

Contacts to established professional and economic interest associations pose particular problems for ecology parties. While ideological reservations directed party activists away from such contacts in the past, the parties' exposure to parliaments and municipal councils dealing with a broad policy agenda began to change this attitude in the mid-1980s.[20] Yet relations to labor unions which are located in the political orbit of Christian democratic and socialist parties in Belgium and West Germany have remained uneasy and marked by profound disagreements about the future of industry, jobs, and economic growth. These tensions have also created conflict within the Greens about the party's policy toward labor unions.[21] In Wallonia a majority of Ecolo members appears to be opposed to unions, while in Flanders a rapprochement between Agalev and the unions may face fewer obstacles (see Vervliet 1983). Ecologists and unions are furthest apart in the old steel and coal regions of Wallonia in Belgium and North Rhine–Westphalia in West Germany but are somewhat more compatible in areas with large service sector employment and high-technology industries such as Flanders and parts of West Germany (Baden-Württemberg, Hesse). Unions in the service/high-technology sectors feel less threatened by ecologists' demands and their members are more inclined to left-libertarian political preferences.

As might be expected, all activist party linkages to external constituencies are most likely to occur in the core regions of left-libertarian movement mobilization. In these areas there is more likelihood of mass media with left-libertarian sympathies and contact with labor unions. Moreover, party members are more radical and inclined toward party-led protest activities than in areas with less left-libertarian mobilization. Finally, due to broad electoral support in the centers of cleavage mobilization, ecology parties are financially more resourceful and can employ these means to establish linkages. The German Green state parties have more resources for building linkages than Agalev or Ecolo. Overall, however, the parties' efforts to reach out to their external constituencies are still very tentative and are hampered by many intellectual, cultural, and institutional obstacles.

Conclusion

Patterns of party-movement linkage are strongly influenced by ideology, but they have yielded some unintended consequences. The militants have avoided imposing a hierarchical supremacy of the party on left-libertarian movements, but alternative linkages through overlapping activism, continuous communi-

---

20. Compare the account of a Green parliamentarian in Lower Saxony in Die Grünen im Landtag von Niedersachsen (1984:67).

21. As an example of these controversies, see the clash of opinions between members of the Green parliamentary party and the party executive. Die Grünen, Bundesvorstand (1985), 20–21.

cation, cultural interpenetration, and joint protest actions have not materialized to the extent most of those interviewed originally expected. The parties that entered the political arena to strengthen the bond between citizen and the decision-making process in fact often find themselves further removed from their constituencies than do conventional parties.

Cultural interpenetration of party and constituencies, the informal transfer of symbols and messages both ways, is probably the ecologists' primary linkage to movements and voters. But cultural linkages constitute inherently weak, diffuse ties which do not transmit specific preferences and information that could guide strategy and policy. Weak ties can nevertheless contribute to a network of strong bonds if they are sufficiently numerous (Granovetter 1978). With a small number of party activists, cultural ties may not reach a significant threshold of density even in left-libertarian strongholds, as activists from places like Frankfurt and Hamburg attest. Because strong or numerous ties fail to evolve spontaneously, some activists claim that ecology parties are rapidly changing from "movement parties" into "parties of conviction," representing the left-libertarian movements' conscience but having little interaction with them (Haupt 1984). Commenting on what this transformation means, an Ecolo city councilor from Liège argues that militants must stop worrying about the weakness of their external ties and start focusing on what should be the ecologists' message to the electorate: "Our message should be clear, bright, and pure—that the other parties are rotten."

The highly intermittent, selective communication between ecology parties and left-libertarian movements strengthens the importance of individual political entrepreneurs and parliamentarians in shaping the parties' external appeal. In a stratarchal, fragmented party structure elected representatives become go-betweens for the parties and their external constituencies wherever communication occurs. On the one hand, the external linkages reinforce a disjointed, stratarchal distribution of power inside the parties. On the other, the fluidity and malleability of internal and external lines of communication keep the parties and their political entrepreneurs receptive to new external demands that suddenly emerge and find no other political representative. While fluid organization may not preserve the continuous democratic participation of rank-and-file militants or external constituencies in the parties, it does enhance their political flexibility to respond innovatively to new conditions.

In this sense, Jose, an Ecolo activist from Liège, warns that strong external linkages that would reduce the parties to mere advocates of existing constituencies could immobilize the party and reduce its political appeal. In order to create innovative capacity, he claims, ecology parties must remain autonomous from outside pressure groups, consciously limit their communication with broad constituencies, and be willing to pay the political price that comes with weak external linkages: electoral volatility and limited electoral appeal. This recommendation closely matches the hypothesis of academic observers that social movements and open, flexible political parties may be a complement and corrective to the firmly institutionalized state parties existing throughout much of Western Europe.[22]

Within these broad generalizations, familiar forces can be identified. Movements are generally more inclined to communicate with ecology parties in areas where the left-libertarian cleavage is highly mobilized, traditional elites reject the new parties, and where ecology parties are in a strong competitive position. In these areas party militants are most willing to abandon an essentially passive view of linkages and call for more efforts by the parties themselves to initiate them.

Even though these forms of party-movement ties lead to unintended results, the actual linkages are still very different from those characteristic of conventional Belgian and German parties. Shefter (1977) has identified patronage and strong organizational ties to interest groups as two alternative forms of linkage between parties and civil society. Patronage becomes the prime linkage where parties have power to disburse selective benefits to their constituencies. Where parties are divorced from the state apparatus and oppose an incumbent political and economic elite, they develop a mass organization and tight organizational linkages to interest groups. "Pillars" and "camps" surrounding a party are a functional equivalent to patronage providing selective incentives for loyalty to the party. The socialist and Christian mass parties in Belgium and Germany, with a multitude of affiliated economic, social, and cultural associations, originally represented defensive reactions of homogeneous religious or class collectivities against a capitalist and secular society (Hellemans 1985).

Today, conventional Belgian and West German mass parties have experienced a decline of subcultural milieux and associations but combine organizational pillarization and patronage as linkage patterns between state and civil society. The strong ideological and hierarchical bonds between parties and interest associations have waned, yet conventional parties have supplemented them with a fine-tuned clientelism and patronage system that works through numerous state and party suborganizations (see Billiet 1984; Dyson 1977). The source of organizational linkage and mass membership is no longer a defensive ideological community, but the power over resources, positions, and policies that state parties exercise based on their symbiosis with the public administration.

For the time being, ecology parties have no control over the machinery of the state, thus barring them and their constituencies from patronage, nor are

---

22. Especially important contributions are Berger (1979), Olsen (1983), and Smith (1976b).

they able and willing to develop a mass organization. Hence, their linkages are built on cultural interpenetration and highly selective communication with left-libertarian movement activists, establishing only a weak bond between civil society and politics. Yet parties with fluid external relations and weak internal organization with active political entrepreneurs are more likely to call for innovation and represent new demands in the arena of party competition than conventional mass and state parties.

9 | The Temptations of Power

In the June 1982 Hamburg state elections, the Social Democrats lost their majority. That election also brought the Green Alternative List (GAL) into the Hamburg House of Deputies (Bürgerschaft) for the first time. Together the two parties had a majority of seats. Initially hesitant, the SPD soon agreed to negotiate with the GAL for its support of a Social Democratic minority government. In return the GAL asked the SPD to meet eight demands, among them withdrawing Hamburg's utilities from several nuclear power plants, halting further extension of the city's port facilities, and cancelling austerity measures in the social and educational state budget. Although several of these demands were part of the Social Democratic party program, the SPD now rejected them citing the city's deteriorating fiscal and industrial condition. In response the GAL did everything to portray the SPD as a traitor to its own constituency and engaged in political maneuvers designed to reveal dissension in the SPD. One such tactic was a GAL motion to declare Hamburg a nuclear free zone, a locally popular demand that would have forced Social Democrats to oppose the SPD federal government's policy of supporting new American nuclear missiles in West Germany. The Hamburg SPD had no intention of discussing substantive policies for forming a government with the GAL, avoided making any specific commitments, and attempted to force the GAL to support the SPD minority government's state budget unconditionally. The SPD wanted to demonstrate that the GAL could make the state "ungovernable" and would not cooperate in constructive policy making. Consequently, negotiations between the two parties collapsed. By the end of 1982 the SPD was riding on a wave of national support, following the resignation of its popular chancellor, Helmut Schmidt. New state elections in Hamburg returned a Social Democratic majority and forced the GAL onto the opposition bench.

Four years later an almost identical situation arose. In November 1986 the Hamburg SPD lost the state election but could have formed a majority coalition with the GAL, the big election winner. The climate between the two parties, however, was so poisoned that negotiations never got under way. Eventually the SPD called for new elections in which it improved its voter support enough to form a majority government with the liberals. The GAL, in contrast, gave up all gains made in the previous election and remained in the opposition.

In Hesse similar electoral results led to a very different outcome. State elections in September 1982 left both the Christian Democratic/Liberal camp and the Social Democrats in a minority position. The Greens, representing 8 percent of the voters, held the key to a coalition. The initial situation resembled that of Hamburg in many respects. Both sides were insincere in their negotiations. The SPD avoided committing itself to serious bargaining with the Greens and tried to force them into accepting the state budget as a precondition for futher talks. The Greens set out on a policy of confrontation with the SPD over its support of nuclear power and the controversial extension of the Frankfurt airport. Most Green deputies initially identified with the Greens' fundamentalist wing and were at most prepared to support the SPD minority government only on select issues. After the collapse of negotiations between GAL and SPD in Hamburg, most Hessian Green deputies thought the major goal of negotiations with the Social Democrats ought to be maximizing Green public support in new elections.[1]

Throughout the winter and spring of 1983 internal conflicts over Green party strategy intensified, particularly when the Green deputies approved a preliminary budget bill to demonstrate they were negotiating with the Social Democrats in good faith. But eventually, in Hesse as in Hamburg, these negotiations failed and new elections were scheduled for September 1983. Yet in contrast to Hamburg, these elections resulted in no clear parliamentary majority, although they strengthened the SPD while Green support declined precipitously from 8 to 5.9 percent. As a consequence of these changes, both Greens and Social Democrats changed their strategies and negotiated an agreement on a common program allowing the Greens to "tolerate" an SPD minority government without holding any executive positions. The new strategy sharply divided the Greens but finally won the support of a firm two thirds majority at a state party convention.

Not long after the toleration agreement went into effect, the alliance was disrupted as quarrels between SPD and Greens over licensing the expansion of nuclear fuel production plants broke out. The alliance was suspended for over six months but eventually resumed as a formal coalition between Social

1. Compare protocol of the meeting of the Hessian Green parliamentary party on October 12, 1982.

Democrats and Greens in November 1985. The Greens received the ministry for environmental affairs and the position of a deputy secretary for women's affairs. When in late 1986 the Greens and the SPD again found themselves at odds over the nuclear power issue, the Social Democratic prime minister outsted his Green cabinet colleague and the coalition collapsed. This decision came in the aftermath of Green electoral gains and SPD losses in the 1987 federal election and increasing conflicts within the SPD about the party's strategy toward the Greens. The Hesse SPD indicated it was willing to renew the socialist-green coalition, but lost heavily in the ensuing state elections, while the Greens, also affirming their willingness to enter another coalition, substantially increased their vote. Yet Christian Democrats and Liberals won a narrow majority and thus ended the experimental coalition.

Belgium provides another example of alliance strategy. After the 1985 national elections the Christian democrats and liberals together controlled exactly one half of the seats in the Walloon regional council. In this situation the Ecolo leadership decided to negotiate with these parties for an alliance on selected issues, such as environmental and energy policies.[2] Ecolo's strategy led to a sharp intraparty conflict with a bloc of radical militants, most of whom were from the Brussels district, opposed to any accommodation with the liberal/conservative Walloon regional government. In the end Ecolo's steering committee and a national convention endorsed the moderate strategy by solid majorities but censured the leadership for making crucial moves without prior consultation of the party rank and file. Since the liberals refused to agree to Ecolo's demands, however, the alliance never materialized. As a consequence of the conflict a number of radicals left Ecolo and founded their own leftist ecology party in Brussels. In the 1987 elections Ecolo maintained its electorate without making further advances, while the new radical party failed to win measurable support.

Aside from numerous local alliances, up to 1987 the three cases I have sketched are the only instances in which ecology parties were in a *strong competitive position* with a chance to influence the formation of government alliances directly. Like nothing else, competitive strength forces ecology parties to choose between the logics of constituency representation and party competition. A no-compromise strategy preserves ideological purity and appeals to ideologues and hard-line lobbyists. It reinforces a party's electoral support among its staunchest supporters. Willingness to engage in government alliances, in contrast, builds intraparty coalitions of pragmatists and lobbyists and may increase a party's attractiveness to marginal sympathizers, thus strengthening its electoral support, provided its core followers are not alienated by compromises.

2. The major provisions of a proposed agreement are documented in *La Cité,* (March 24, 1986), 1–2.

In this chapter I analyze factors influencing the ecologists' choice between electoralist strategies of alliance building and adversarial strategies of fundamental opposition to all established parties. Then I explore the consequences of the parties' organization and internal cohesiveness associated with each strategy.

The Politics of Alliance Formation

Formal theories of coalition building in competitive party systems have been primarily concerned with the size, composition, payoff structure, and durability of the coalitions.[3] They employ the size and ideological orientation of parties as key indpendent variables. The explanatory power of coalition theories is limited, however, because they cannot reconstruct how individual parties perceive the costs and benefits of government participation and select strategies.[4] Browne (1982:338), in fact, remarks that actors often perceive the gains and losses of coalitions very differently than the theories suggest. He also notes that coalition theories are unrealistic as long as they conceive of alliance formation as static and discrete, unconnected to events of the past or the actors' expectations about the future. Building on Browne, Pridham (1986) argues that the explanatory yield of coalition theories can be increased only if they examine the institutions, the history of party systems, the relations between parties, the parties' ideologies, their internal organization and decision-making processes, and their sociopolitical environment.

In my analysis of strategic choice in ecology parties, not all of these conditions are considered. I make some effort, however, to explain the parties' strategic posture with respect to (1) the structure of the party systems in which they operate, (2) their shifting electoral position vis-à-vis other parties and their own history of electoral support, and (3) organizational forces within parties influencing the formation of coalitions. Figure 8 summarizes the framework I elaborate in this section and apply to the three instances in

3. As surveys of the state of the art, see Browne (1982) and Browne and Franklin (1986). Compare also Dodd (1976) and the more recent contributions by Lijphart (1984: chap. 7), Luebbert (1984), and Strom (1984).

4. Luebbert (1984:230) claims that, compared to general patterns of coalition formation, the task of determining the likelihood of alliance in individual instances is trivial and can be answered by most informed observers, so does not need theoretical explanation. I disagree with this assessment. Individual parties often face great internal controversies in selecting strategies and it is well worth reconstructing their process of decision making. If anything, explaining general patterns of coalition formation is trivial compared to the process of strategic choice within political parties. As Laver (1986:33) argues, the problem of formal coalition theories is not that they are bad or wrong, but "[t]he problem is that they do not set out to do much that is interesting." Luebbert's own model of intraparty conditions for external bargaining strategies (section 3 of his article) is insufficient to provide an analysis of strategic choice at the level of the individual party because it builds on a misleading dichotomy of party "leaders" and "followers" too thin to reconstruct the behavior of party activists.

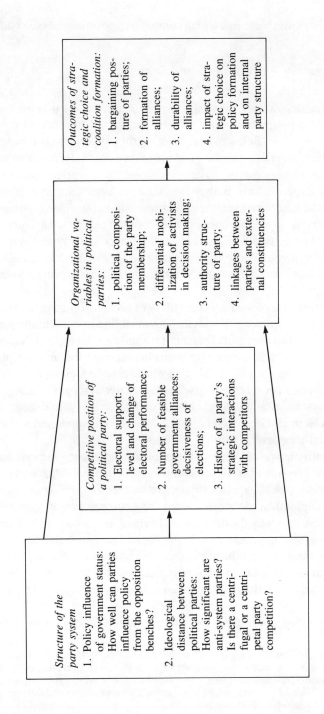

Figure 8. Determinants of strategic choice in political parties

Structure of the party system

1. Policy influence of government status: How well can parties influence policy from the opposition benches?

2. Ideological distance between political parties: How significant are anti-system parties? Is there a centrifugal or a centripetal party competition?

Competitive position of a political party:

1. Electoral support: level and change of electoral performance;

2. Number of feasible government alliances: decisiveness of elections;

3. History of a party's strategic interactions with competitors

Organizational variables in political parties:

1. political composition of the party membership;

2. differential mobilization of activists in decision making;

3. authority structure of party;

4. linkages between parties and external constituencies

Outcomes of strategic choice and coalition formation:

1. bargaining posture of parties;

2. formation of alliances;

3. durability of alliances;

4. impact of strategic choice on policy formation and on internal party structure

which ecology parties were in a strong competitive position and faced difficult strategic choices.

The Structure of Party Systems and Strategic Choice

Rational politicians seek government participation if (1) it helps them to influence public policy and voter support and (2) if they find compatible coalition partners.[5] In Belgium and West Germany government status is a decisive influence on policy making and thus creates a strong incentive to seek coalitions. Opposition parties have only limited and indirect control over policy making, particularly if they are not associated with strong interest groups, as is the case with the Greens, Agalev, and Ecolo. The importance of government status, however, does not help much to explain coalition politics in Hamburg, Hesse, and Wallonia. In each instance government status was relevant yet the parties chose diverse coalition strategies. The influence of government status may be a necessary but not sufficient inducement to engage in coalitions.

A second structural condition is the ability of parties to engage in alliances. Coalitions form only among ideologically compatible parties. In the past the Belgian and West German party systems have shown a centripetal dynamic in which all relevant parties compete for voters in the center and, in principle, are able to coalesce with each other. This may have changed with the rise of left-libertarian parties. Yet relatively few ecology party sympathizers support a radical anti-system strategy or challenge parliamentary democracy.[6] Even among West German Green voters, in 1987 80 percent supported a coalition with the Social Democrats (Schmitt 1987b:348).

Subnationally, however, voter sentiment may vary among regions according to high or low left-libertarian mobilization. Where mobilization is high and polarized we would expect a stricter commitment of ecology parties to a radical, uncompromising strategy toward their competitors. In general, this hypothesis is borne out by the three cases. In Hamburg, with very intense left-libertarian cleavage, negotiations with the Social Democrats failed. In Hesse, with high to medium mobilization, the Greens at first hesitated but later succumbed to the temptation of government status. In Wallonia, finally, Ecolo was willing not only to engage in an alliance but to support a right-wing government.

Even in Hamburg, however, the Greens' radical strategy was not elec-

---

5. In the specification of my argument, I am relying in part on Luebbert (1984) and Strom (1984). They have convincingly shown that many variables traditionally held responsible for the formation of minority, minimum winning, or oversized coalitions in fact explain very little.

6. Compare Table 12 showing that 74.4 percent of Green supporters and 80.6 percent of Agalev and Ecolo supporters see themselves as "moderately left" or "moderate."

torally rewarded. When the GAL refused to negotiate sincerely with the Social Democrats in 1986–87, it was abandoned by more than a third of its voters in the ensuing election. Thus, even in Hamburg a large portion of Green supporters wanted a moderate strategy. And in Hesse the Greens changed their strategic stance only after a torturous process that took close to three years. What structural coalition theories leave undiscussed, then, are the conditions under which parties learn to adopt new strategies and the internal process of collective decision making. These shifting circumstances and organizational deliberations are key to understanding the role of individual parties in the formation of government alliances.

The Parties' Competitive Position

The choice between cooperative and adversarial strategies becomes operative for ecology parties only if there are other parties which (1) show some ideological and strategic affinity to them and (2) have won or are expected to win enough votes to help form a government majority. If this situation materializes, ecologists are in a strong competitive position and internal strategic debate heats up. But there are further conditions which define how strong this competitive position is and how militants interpret the potential for alliances.

First, the level and change of a party's electoral support from one election to the next affect its bargaining power and perception of the strategic situation. The smaller its electoral support, the less likely the party will be able to wrest significant concessions from a potential coalition partner. In this respect, Hamburg, Hesse, and Wallonia offered equally dismal prospects for an alliance between the ecologists and other parties. In each case the potential partners received four to seven times as many votes as the ecologists.

Militants interpret changes in their party's electoral support as confirmation or repudiation of strategic stances. When ecologists gain parliamentary seats for the first time, they interpret this success as a vindication of radical strategies and are unlikely to negotiate with potential alliance partners immediately. Further electoral success reinforces noncooperative strategies. If, however, noncooperation is followed by an electoral performance below expectations, activists may reconsider past strategies.

In Hamburg the GAL saw little reason to ally itself with the Social Democrats after its initial success in the June 1982 elections. Militants also interpreted the party's strong performance in the December 1982 and 1986 state elections and in the March 1983 and January 1987 national elections as endorsement of a noncooperative strategy. Only the May 1987 elections, in which the party suffered serious losses, started to change that perception, but by then the party had again lost its strong competitive position. In Hesse and Wallonia the situation was different. In Hesse the Greens' initial success in the

1982 state elections (8 percent of the vote) led them to reject a cooperative stance. But when electoral support dropped to 5.9 percent in the 1983 elections, many activitists responded by advocating cooperation with the SPD. Similarly, many Green militants interpreted the weaker than expected performance of their party in the 1985 state elections in Saarland, Berlin, and North Rhine-Westphalia as signs that the voters opposed noncooperative strategies.

In Belgium Ecolo's electoral support in the 1985 national election barely exceeded that of 1981 and represented a dramatic decline compared to the 1982 local and the 1984 European elections. Subsequently, the party leadership abandoned its past strategy and initiated negotiations with the Christian/liberal alliance in Wallonia's regional assembly. Agalev in Flanders, in contrast, gained votes significantly in 1985 and was not pleased with Ecolo's efforts to reach an accommodation with Wallonia's conservative government.

A second influence on a party's bargaining power is the number of alternative coalitions it can threaten to join if its bargaining partners fail to respond to its demands (Laver 1986:41–42). In Hesse, Hamburg, and Wallonia ecology parties had only a single option to join a coalition and so in this respect were in a weak bargaining position. Yet the strength of their bargaining position also depended on the number of threats their negotiation partners could make. The Social Democrats in Hesse and Hamburg in the early 1980s could threaten the Greens only with new elections, not with alternative alliances. In 1987, however, the Hamburg Social Democrats increased their bargaining power by demonstrating that an alternative alliance with the liberals was possible. Similarly, Social Democratic politicians in other states such as Lower Saxony indicated that they might seek coalitions with the liberals, thus weakening the bargaining clout of the Greens. In Belgium the highly fragmented party system gives conventional parties many opportunities to withdraw from alliances with Agalev and Ecolo and would limit the ecologists' bargaining power in serious negotiations.[7]

On the one hand, the existence of few viable coalition alternatives is a blessing for ecology parties, increasing their bargaining strength. On the other, however, it is a curse because it makes elections highly decisive for government formation. Voters can calculate in advance which coalition they will support. When voters are able to link policy and strategic preferences, they tie the parties' hands in alliance negotiations. Parties lose their ability to withdraw from alliances if it is clear their voters support participation in a coalition government, weakening their bargaining position. Moreover, since governing parties are more likely to lose votes in subsequent elections than opposition parties, electoral decisiveness and government participation also lower a party's electoral chances (Strom 1984).

Applying this logic to ecology parties makes it clear why intraparty conflict

---

7. This situation is demonstrated at the local level by the breakup of the municipal coalitions in the villages of Schoten and Meise in which Agalev had participated.

over strategy is more intense in the Greens than in Agalev or Ecolo. Because West Germany has few parties and highly decisive elections, voters may easily hold parties responsible for strategic choices and government alliances. Voters put great pressure on the Greens to join coalitions with the Social Democrats. At the same time the party system increases the downside electoral risk of this strategy because the Greens are in a relatively weak bargaining position and therefore unable to influence the public policies of a coalition government profoundly. Agalev and Ecolo operate in a fragmented, centripetal party system in which elections have little decisiveness and parties have many options for forming coalitions. The Belgian ecologists preserve greater strategic maneuverability and are less likely to be rewarded or penalized by their voters for pursuing a particular strategy. This may explain why Ecolo's negotiations with the Christian/liberal Walloon regional government and their eventual failure did little to destabilize the party's electoral support in the 1987 elections that followed. As a consequence strategic disagreements in the Belgian ecology parties tend to be less fierce than in the Greens.

In addition to change in electoral support and the number of coalition alternatives, a third factor affecting strategy is the history of a party's interaction with opponents. When a party faces a chance to join an alliance for the first time, the interaction is probably perceived as a single-shot prisoner's dilemma game. Cooperation may be preferable to noncooperation for both sides, but if one party cheats while the other cooperates, the sucker will lose more than if it had refused cooperation. Mutual distrust and lack of experience with cooperation discourage alliances. For these reasons, neither in Hamburg nor in Hesse did the 1982 state elections lead to serious negotiations about alliances. The Greens treated the Social Democrats as adversaries, who in turn saw the Greens as a protest party that was bound to disappear quickly and did not deserve serious consideration. As Hamburg Green militants put it, the SPD did not test the GAL's willingness to compromise.

If the alliance game is played repeatedly and the parties continue to find themselves in a prisoner's dilemma situation, the chance of cooperation may improve (see Axelrod 1984; Hardin 1982). In Hamburg negotiations between the Greens and the Social Democrats in 1982 and in 1986–7 were confined to two distinct single-shot games separated by four years of Social Democratic one-party rule. Similarly, in Wallonia negotiations between Ecolo and the regional government were a single-shot game in which the liberals were unwilling to make concessions. But in Hesse the SPD and the Greens found themselves in a stalemate in two consecutive electoral terms. In this configuration, strategists in both parties began to realize each party would benefit from cooperation. But as the instability of the resulting alliance shows, more than two iterations are probably needed to yield stable cooperative results.[8]

8. For this reason it is quite unlikely that any national-level coalition of Greens and Social Democrats could emerge without much experience with such coalitions at the local and state

Party Structure and Decision Making

A structural and temporal analysis of party strategy still assumes that parties are homogeneous groups of decision makers rather than coalitions of activists with different preferences and ideas. Drawing on the variations in intraparty groups and patterns of decision making discussed in previous chapters, we can now drop this simplifying assumption. Examining the stances of intraparty groups helps us to answer an important question coalition theories have ignored up to now: How do political actors perceive and calculate the costs and benefits of coalition formation? More specifically, how do they assess tradeoffs between gaining government office and making policy concessions (Laver 1986:39–40)?

In ecology parties ideologues and pragmatists develop two very different cognitive and normative frameworks for evaluating the payoffs of coalitions, while lobbyists usually take an intermediate position.[9] For pragmatists, policy gains *and* electoral support are equally important goals. They treat parliamentarism as a set of institutions in which realistic gains can be accomplished, especially if they can democratize parliamentarism and increase the role of parliament vis-à-vis the executive branch (Verheyen 1985). Electoral returns and the voice of the voter pass an important verdict on parties' democratic legitimacy and performance.

For radical ideologues the parliament is at most an arena for publicizing ecological demands, gaining information about the functioning of the system, and demonstrating the inability of conventional parties to engage in reform. In the words of a Hamburg radical, "it is impossible to affect society's foundations through parliament." In this view electoral support and government office are much less important than the mobilization of social movements and indirect policy gains brought about by the disruption of existing institutions. Jan, a Hessian radical, argues that the Greens should adhere to a fundamentalist position even if this strategy reduced its electoral support below the 5 percent threshold of parliamentary representation.[10]

---

level. Also government changes in West Germany from a Christian Democratic/Liberal government to a SPD/FDP coalition in 1966–69 and return to the former configuration in 1982 were prepared by local and state level alliances of the parties that eventually formed the federal government.

9. The literature on party strategy in the Greens is by now too voluminous to review here. For the radical position see especially Arbeitsgemeinschaft Radikalökologisches Forum (1984), Bahro (1984a and b), Ebermann (1983), and Ebermann and Trampert (1984:263–79). For the moderate position see Fischer (1983), Hasenclever (1982b), Kostede (1983) and Wiesenthal (1985b). Both sides are represented in Bickerich (1985) and Kluge (1984). In Belgium, because of the weaker competitive position of Agalev and Ecolo no equivalent debate has taken place and most activists are comparatively moderate by West German standards.

10. On another occasion, fundamentalists declared that "the true Green project is too fundamental for electoral campaigns," and "presently no more than 4.6 percent of the voters [in the 1985 NRW state election] can be won for the Green project." Saral Sakar, "Wer ist denn nun wirklich schuld?" in *Kommune*, 3, 6 (June 1985), 48–49.

Table 39
Ecology party militants' perception of the payoffs from different coalition strategies in a single-shot game with one potential alliance partner

Moderates' perceived payoff matrix

		Strategic posture of potential alliance partner		
		Cooperative a	Uncommitted b	Uncooperative c
Strategic pos-	Cooperative A	3,3	3,2	3,0
ture of the	Uncommitted B	2,3	2,2	2,0
ecology party	Uncooperative C	0,2	0,2	1,1

Radicals' perceived payoff matrix

		Strategic posture of potential alliance partner		
		Cooperative a	Uncommitted b	Uncooperative c
Strategic pos-	Cooperative A	0,3	1,2	1,1
ture of the	Uncommitted B	1,1	2,1	3,1
ecology party	Uncooperative C	1,1	2,1	3,0

We can try to model the two extremes of strategic radicalism and pragmatism in terms of two hypothetical payoff matrices in Table 39 representing the ideologues' and pragmatists' expectations about the payoffs of different strategies. In each case the ecology party and its potential alliance partner(s) choose between three strategies revealed to the voters before elections: willingness to cooperate, an uncommitted position, and noncooperation. The payoffs represent a combination of electoral support and policy gains. The highest payoff value (3) indicates both substantial policy and electoral gains, the lowest value (0) neither policy nor electoral gains. It is also important to realize that party activists are not only interested in the *absolute payoffs* derived from a strategy but also in the payoffs *in relation to those of alliance partners or competitors.*[11]

For moderate ecologists cooperative strategies are dominant and yield the highest payoff both in terms of votes and policy gains, providing that the potential alliance partner takes a cooperative stance (strategies Aa, Ab and Ba in model I). The definitely worst results are incurred when ecology parties oppose cooperation with a potential partner in favor of it (strategies Ca and Cb). If potential allies choose a noncooperative strategy, noncooperative ecology parties are expected to get a somewhat greater share of votes (strategy

11. Of course, the game represented in Table 39 does not cover all the factors influencing the payoffs of ecology parties and potential alliance partners. In reality this game is nested into a broader game in which the strategic choices of party adversaries not potential alliance partners of the ecologists also play a decisive role. For the sake of reconstructing the actors' perspective on strategic choice in ecology parties, the reduced model is sufficient.

Cc). In this variable-sum game the total benefits for both parties depend on mutual choice of strategies. The moderates' perception of payoffs leads them to see equilibrium strategy as cooperation with potential alliance partners (strategy Aa).

For radical ecologists, model II represents a typical payoff matrix. Here, the absolutely and relatively best political outcome for ecology parties is both players' unwillingness to cooperate in the game, while the worst outcome for ecology parties is a cooperative stance by both parties (Cc versus Aa). Cooperative stances produce gains only as long as they are not honored by the potential alliance party (especially strategy Ac). Noncooperative strategies are expected to yield the highest electoral and policy payoffs in the long run, especially when other parties are noncooperative and not competing for the same voters.

The critical question now is to identify the conditions and processes that lead to the predominance of one or the other cognitive and normative framework in the evaluation of costs and benefits for ecology parties. Using the preceding chapters on intraparty dynamics, we can identify four processes that change the balance of power in ecology parties, when their competitive position changes.[12] These four mechanisms are (1) the recruitment of activists (Chapter 4), (2) the differential mobilization of militants in decision procedures (Chapters 6 and 7), (3) the evolution of the parties' authority structure (Chapters 5 and 6), and (4) the changing nature of linkages between parties and external constituencies (Chapter 8).

First, as ecology parties gain electoral support and become competitive, they attract more pragmatists. Particularly when in a strong competitive position, pragmatists feel they can tip a party's political balance toward moderate strategies. In Hesse recruitment of pragmatists in fact shifted the strategic balance in the Greens. In Hamburg radicals were too well entrenched and the periods during which the party held a strong competitive position too brief to bring about a similar effect. In Wallonia moderates always had a majority.

Second, localists who are mostly pragmatists get more involved in state and national party politics when the party is in a strong electoral position. Membership turnout at conventions deciding party strategy in Hamburg, Hesse, and Wallonia was always much higher than at other meetings. In Hamburg, however, the radicals' hold on the party was too strong to tip the balance of

12. The shift in the balance of power is the same everywhere *regardless* of the initial distribution of ideologues, lobbyists, and pragmatists in the parties, which is determined by levels of cleavage mobilization and the polarization between left-libertarian and conventional politics in a country. The initial distribution of intraparty activists decides, however, whether a shift of a certain magnitude will alter the balance of power between groups of activists sufficiently to yield a new dominant intraparty coalition as a consequence of the party's new competitive position.

intraparty power even though the moderates' turnout increased during strategic bargaining with the SPD.

Third, as parties move into a strong electoral position, their internal authority structure changes. Since conventions, on their own, usually deliver vague and undecisive resolutions, as we have seen in Hamburg and Hesse, a crucial role is played by emerging informal groups of charismatic political entrepreneurs and parliamentarians, who are in a strong position of power in negotiations with the potential alliance partner. In Hamburg militants found party conventions of little help in determining party strategy in negotiations with the SPD, and reported that instead an inner circle of about ten to twenty activists was crucial. In the Hessian Greens determined leadership was initially absent when the party moved into a strong competitive position and party conventions did little to clarify strategy.[13] The parliamentarians and a handful of informal pragmatic leaders eventually took the initiative and staked out the party's moderate course which was then ratified by the rank and file. In Wallonia there existed from the very beginning an inner circle that decided Ecolo's strategy.

Political leaders define the stakes involved in strategic choice in different ways, depending on whether they favor or oppose alliances with other parties. Because discussions about matters of principle always remain somewhat vague and easily disguise disagreements among the participants, they are less divisive in intraparty debates or in bargaining with alliance partners than in negotiations about precise modalities of policy (Luebbert 1984:237). Hence, in order to facilitate intraparty consensus and a coalition agreement with the SPD, Hessian Green moderate leaders invoked principles of policy rather than precise timing and operational policy implementation. Radical leaders, in contrast, emphasized operational steps in order to complicate the consensus building process both inside the Greens and between the Greens and the Social Democrats. These activists heightened the militants' awareness of the tradeoffs between winning government office and actual policy gains. Comparing Green strategies in Hesse and Hamburg, one Hamburg interviewee observes that the Hessian moderates emphasized the general atmosphere of cooperation in the bargaining process with the SPD, while the Hamburg radicals confronted the SPD with more clear-cut operational demands.

Fourth, social movements influence the parties' strategic choice through changing linkages. In Wallonia, where left-libertarian movements are weak, environmentalists and feminists outside the party had little input. In Hamburg there is a radical movement subculture with little sympathy for the Social Democrats and ties into the Greens through work groups and personal linkages. Angelika, a Green member of the Hamburg House of Deputies in the

---

13. Compare the report in *Tageszeitung,* November 2, 1982, on a convention of the Hessian state party.

1982–86 legislative period, states "the local alternative scene would have been appalled had we tolerated an SPD minority government." In Hesse, in contrast, the environmental movements in particular were more concerned with practical policy reforms and supported a socialist-green alliance. Hessian Green parliamentarians recall that a crucial turning point toward a moderate strategy occurred in the spring of 1983 when they voted against a resolution to fight acid rain in the state legislature because the Social Democrats had not accepted an amendment to shut down all nuclear power plants. The Green parliamentarians' intransigent position triggered an uproar among local militants and environmental organizations and forced them to reconsider the virtues of cooperation based on compromise. When the Greens remained in a strong competitive position after the September 1983 Hessian elections, social movement organizations in areas such as energy, ecology, women's affairs, agriculture, and cooperative enterprises strongly endorsed a moderate alliance strategy and actively participated in the Greens' preparations for negotiations with the SPD.

Comparison of internal decision making in the Hamburg and Hessian Greens shows that the extraordinary fluidity of internal and external alignments and political mobilization as well as the initial absence of strong leadership facilitated a rapid change in political strategy. In Hesse the party's openness permitted an influx of moderate newcomers to displace the fundamentalist core of militants who came mostly from Frankfurt and had dominated the party organization from 1980 to 1982. In Hamburg, however, both the internal party leadership and the social movement constituencies remained opposed to a strategic shift and gave less leeway to a mobilization of pragmatists from the rank-and-file party sections. Greater organizational rigidity and more centralized authority enabled the party to stay its radical course. In Wallonia, finally, Ecolo's leadership and activists were both committed to moderation. Its fairly centralized power structure enabled the leadership to engage in negotiations with other parties without consulting its own rank and file in advance.

Alliance Formation: Conditions and Payoffs

Structure, competitiveness, and internal organization affect the parties' strategic choice. Table 40 summarizes the conditions favorable or unfavorable to coalition formation for ecology parties in Hamburg, Hesse, and Wallonia. Given the small number of cases in which ecology parties have held a strong competitive position, we cannot weigh the relative importance of the various factors and at the same time make the model more parsimonious.

My reconstruction of alliance strategies contradicts Michels' (1911/ 1962:205–11) classic treatment of the subject. He explains the strategic moderation of working-class parties by the ambitions of party leaders to rise to

Table 40
Structural, conjunctural, and intraparty conditions conducive to moderate (+) or radical (−) alliance strategies

	Hamburg 1982 and 1986	Hesse 1982–1987	Wallonia 1985–1986
Structural conditions			
1. Policy impact of government participation	+	+	+
2. Ideological distance between ecology parties and alliance partners	−	+/−	+/−
Conjunctural conditions (parties' competitive position)			
3. Level of the ecology parties' electoral support	−	−	−
4. Change of electoral support compared to previous election	−	+	+/−
5. Number of feasible alliances among parties	+	+	−
6. Iteration of the bargaining game	−	+	−
Intraparty balance of power			
7. Recruitment of ideologues, lobbyists, and pragmatists	−	+	+
8. Differential mobilization of activists	−	+	+
9. The position of external movement constituencies	−	+	+/−
10. Authority structure of the party	−	+/−	+/−
Overall ratio of conditions favorable and adverse to moderate alliance strategy	2 : 8	8 : 2	5 : 5

positions of power and status. His purely psychological theory neglects the background conditions that influence strategic decisions as well as the party activists' cognitive frameworks and their rational calculation of the payoffs deriving from different strategies. Michels does note in passing that French parliamentarism, as opposed to German pre–World War I autocracy, enabled the socialists to join a government alliance while their German counterparts were compelled to stay in the opposition (ibid. 133). But he does not acknowledge the theoretical significance of his observation that objective conditions in the parties' environment and internal debates, political institutions, competitive position, and intraparty coalitions, not simply the motives of vain and self-serving party leaders, structure party strategy choices.

Within ecology parties radicals prefer Michels' psychological and motiva-

tional explanation of moderation because it places all the blame for moderation on organizational hierarchy, meaning corrupt party leaders, and disguises
the narrow support base for radical strategies even among the parties' rank-
and-file followers. Moderates predictably emphasize the role of institutional
environment, opportunity, and rank-and-file mobilization in deciding strategy. In this sense, voluntarist conspiracy models and structural and/or behavioral reconstructions of party politics are not purely academic reflections
on party dynamic, but are arguments in the political struggle itself.

Given the small number of instances in which the parties have been able to
choose from different strategies and the even smaller set of cases in which they
were actually in a strong competitive position, we cannot yet assess the
outcome of the choices in terms of the durability of coalitions and executive
office holding, long-term electoral support, and policy gains. Only electoral
support in West Germany provides a reasonable number of instances for
assessing the impact of strategic posture throughout a legislative term on
subsequent election results.

Table 41 reports the percentage changes in electoral support for the Greens
and the Social Democrats from the first election in which the Greens participated (1980–83) to subsequent state or national elections (1982–1987). I have
coded the parties' strategic stances based on their own declarations before
elections and the voters' perception of the situation, as revealed by preelection
surveys and mass media coverage.[14] Most controversial is the coding of cases
10 (West Berlin 1985) and 11 (Hamburg 1986) where I have coded Green
strategy as uncommitted rather than uncooperative. The West Berlin coding
overall appears more reasonable because the Alternative List was unable to
define a clear strategic course before the election. The Hamburg GAL fielded
a solely women's slate of candidates which blurred the radical strategic
position of the party for many voters during the campaign.

The payoff matrix shows that the Greens on average did best where they
pursued a cooperative strategy, but an uncommitted strategy comes in a close
second. They clearly performed worst where they subscribed to a radical
uncooperative strategy. The SPD, in contrast, contained their losses where
they pursued an uncommitted or uncooperative strategy. If both parties try to
maximize their expected yields the strategic combination Ab represents an
equilibrium. If both try to *maximize their minimum payoffs* they will end up
pursuing Bb. The actual payoff structure is not entirely consistent with either
the radical or the moderate cognitive framework presented in Table 39,
although it clearly lends more support to the moderate position. Overall,
cooperative strategies yield better electoral results than radical strategies.

---

14. Detailed analyses of each state election are provided by the *Zeitschrift für Parlamentsfragen* which was used to code the cases.

Table 41

Green and SPD electoral performance in state and national elections, 1983–87 (percent change of electoral support compared to previous elections)

		Strategic posture of the Social Democratic Party		
		a. Cooperative	*b. Uncommitted*	*c. Uncooperative*
Strategic posture of the Green party	A. Cooperative	1. +3.5/−6.0 (Hesse 1987)		
	B. Uncommitted		2. +0.6/+5.6 (Lower Saxony 1986) 3. +4.8/−0.8 (Bremen 1987) 4. +2.3/−0.1 (Baden-Württemberg 1984) 5. +3.7/−4.4 (Bavaria 1986) 6. +1.4/−0.8 (Rhineland Palatinate 1987) 7. −2.1/+3.4 (Hesse 1983) 8. +0.3/+1.5 (Schleswig-Holstein 1987)	
	C. Uncooperative			9. +2.7/−1.2 (Federal election 1987) 10. +3.4/−5.9 (West Berlin 1985) 11. +3.6/−9.6 (Hamburg 1986) 12. −0.9/+8.6 (Hamburg 12/1982) 13. −3.4/+3.3 (Hamburg 1987) 14. +1.6/+3.7 (North Rhine–Westphalia 1985) 15. −0.4/+3.2 (Saarland 1985)

Note: with the exception of case 9, all elections are state elections. In each case, the first percentage figure refers to Green electoral performance, the second to that of the SPD.

Table 42 pushes the strategic analysis one step further. The Greens win votes in all elections (+1.5%) no matter what strategy they choose, while the Social Democrats just about balance gains and losses. To calculate the impact of a strategy, we must set aside this underlying voter trend by subtracting the base change from the parties' actual electoral yield. I have done this in the payoff calculations for each party, based on their strategic choice, starting in row 1 of Table 42. It is clear that the Greens do best in absolute and relative terms when they cooperate with the SPD (row 1.1) and worst when they are uncooperative (row 1.3). The reverse applies to the Social Democrats (rows 2.1–2.3). The dilemma of West German party competition, then, is that the Greens have an incentive to cooperate while the Social Democrats do not. This configuration may explain why moderates in the Greens often encounter great difficulty convincing their party to choose a moderate strategy.

Rows 3 and 4 shed more light on the parties' uneven performance. When there is a reasonable expectation before an election that the Greens will gain a strong competitive position and may go on to form an alliance with the SPD, they do considerably worse than their baseline trend (row 3 and 3.2), a situation they can remedy only if they do not antagonize the SPD or openly declare their willingness to cooperate with the Social Democrats (row 3.1). The SPD, on the other hand, has little to gain from cooperative gestures toward the Greens. It does best when the party is uncooperative (row 3.4), especially when the Greens are also uncooperative (row 3.2). The Greens do best and the Social Democrats do worst when the parties have little chance of forming a coalition (row 4). Apparently, voters feel more inclined to vote for a Green party firmly locked into the role of parliamentary opposition than the Greens as power-brokers between Social Democrats and the conservative/liberal party bloc.

Whether the SPD is already in government or not has little independent effect on the electoral performance of either party (row 5). Yet again, the Greens' strategic stances account for wide variations in electoral performance (rows 5.1 and 5.2). Given that swings in Green voter support often amount to 30 percent or more of previous showings, and occasionally go even higher than that, it is likely that many Green supporters are strategic voters who are very sensitive to the party's political stance and competitive environment.[15]

15. In regard to voters' strategic behavior, there are also dramatic differences in Green support in state and federal elections which I can only touch upon. To take the most glaring example, in the 1983 national elections the Greens received 5.2 percent of the vote in the state of Schleswig Holstein but only 3.6 percent in the state election held one week later. In the same state the Greens received 8 percent in the January 1987 national elections, but only 3.9 percent in the state election of September 1987. That these swings are not simply due to the radicalism of the Schleswig Holstein Green state party but reflect genuine differences between state and national elections is evidenced by similar discrepancies between state and national performance elsewhere. In Bremen a moderate Green party received 14.5 percent in the January 1987 national election but only 10.2 percent in the September 1987 state election.

Table 42

Green and SPD electoral performance in state and national elections: further analysis of the influence of strategic choice on electoral outcomes

	Greens	SPD
Basic trend of electoral performance,	*+1.5%*	*+0.0%*
regardless of strategic choice (all 15 cases)	*Percent change minus basic trend*	
	Greens	SPD
1. Green strategy		
1.1 cooperative (cases 1–3)	+1.5%	−0.4%
1.2 uncommitted (cases 4–6 and 9–11)	+1.4	−3.7
1.3 uncooperative (cases 7–8 and 12–15)	−2.3	+4.0
2. SPD strategy		
2.1 cooperative (case 1)	+2.0	−6.0
2.2 uncommitted (cases 2–8)	−0.2	+0.3
2.3 uncooperative (cases 9–15)	−0.2	+0.3
3. Strong competitiveness of the Greens expected (cases 1–2, 7, 8, 12–15)	−1.6	+2.9
3.1 Greens cooperative or uncommitted (cases 1, 2)	+0.6	−0.2
3.2 Greens uncooperative (cases 7, 8, and 12–15)	−2.3	+4.0
3.3 SPD cooperative or uncommitted (cases 1, 2, 7, and 8)	−0.9	+1.1
3.4 SPD uncooperative (cases 12–15)	−2.3	+1.7
4. Weak competitiveness of the Greens expected (cases 3–6, 9–11, all with cooperative or uncommitted strategy)	+2.2	−3.8
5. SPD government incumbency (cases 1, 3, 7, 11–14)	−0.5	+0.4
5.1 Greens cooperative or uncommitted (cases 1, 3, 11)	+2.5	−5.5
5.2 Greens uncooperative (cases 7, 12, 13, 14)	−2.7	+4.8

Strategic voters sympathetic to the Greens most value the goal of preventing a conservative government alliance of Christian Democrats and the FDP. The safest bet for reaching this goal is to vote for the Social Democrats, particularly where a conservative alliance risks losing its majority. A vote for the Greens supports this strategic objective only if the Greens endorse an alliance with the SPD or are at least not openly hostile to the idea. In this respect, the argument of the Green pragmatists that radical strategic stances hurt the party at the polls is borne out.

Because of Ecolo's and Agalev's much less exposed strategic position and the small number of elections that can be compared, it is not possible to perform an analysis of the interaction between strategic stances and voter support equivalent to that of the Greens.[16] In the 1985 and 1987 elections, Agalev, Ecolo, and their potential alliance partners chose strategy Bb in table 41 and the results were roughly equivalent to the German ones. The ecology parties, particularly Agalev, strengthened their position, while the socialist parties held steady or slightly improved. Since Belgian election returns per se have a limited impact on government formation, it is unlikely, however, that strategic issues played an important role in the voters' choice.

The game theoretic analysis of Green and Social Democratic strategy in this section faces one obvious limitation. It reconstructs the choice of strategy as a single-shot game in fifteen independent cases, yet not as a sequence of strategic moves in which the parties affect each other's strategy while playing the game through a number of iterations. In fact, it is quite possible that in the course of the game the *payoffs,* or the voters' willingness to honor given strategies, themselves change. For this reason, the model presented here has only very modest predictive value and must be refined as more data on the link between the choice of strategy and electoral performance become available.

The Politics of Organizational Form:
Living with Dissent

Strategic debates in ecology parties influence which organizational reforms activists advocate, and affect the viability of internal political pluralism. How much disagreement should be permitted? How important is a cohesive policy and a more formalized party structure? As I argued in Chapter 4, these questions divide ecology parties into more than two groups. Moderate and radical strategic tendencies are often internally divided on the choice of a more instrumental or a more fluid, participatory party organization. These divisions are quite highly elaborated in the West German Greens, while they remain more muted in the less factionalized Belgian parties.

In the Greens strategic moderates fall into two groups, each pursuing a different path toward organizational reform. The realists believe in an instrumental organization with formal accountability of office holders, clear principles of representation, and more cohesiveness in order to make the party more attractive to marginal voters. As Roland, a strong supporter of realism says, "we no longer receive a reward from the voters for being incalculable and disruptive in parliament." In contrast, ecolibertarians call for a decentralized, fluid organization to maintain their libertarian and communitarian aspirations (see Ökolibertäre Grüne 1984:54). Ecolibertarians oppose discipline and formalization and demand a return to liberal principles of representation, a "free

16. The only data points in Belgium are the national elections of 1981, 1985, and 1987. The 1982 local election and the European elections of 1979 and 1984 are difficult to compare to national elections.

mandate'' for party members in elected office. Ecolibertarians expect that an open, fluid party will preclude dominance of small radical sects, which can entrench themselves only if the party makes access to its core decision-making arenas more difficult.

Strategic radicals also square off into two camps. The larger camp, the fundamentalists, share with the ecolibertarians a commitment to the party's fluid, participatory form, precisely because they fear the realists are correct in believing that a stronger organization will make the party more moderate and more predictable. They reject the professionalization of party offices since it would increase the pragmatists' incentives to run for these offices too. When asked why she opposed professionalized party executives, a Hessian fundamentalist spontaneously responded: ''Because then the realists would capture these positions too.'' The smaller radical camp, the ecosocialists, are more inclined to build on remanants of socialist party theory and favor a more structured, organized party in order to develop long-term radical strategies. In their view, it is precisely the organizational fluidity of ecology parties that undermines a consistent radical stance and promotes electoral reformism. Thus, they subscribe to the same theoretical reasoning about the organizational causes of party strategy as the ecolibertarians but take a diametrically opposed normative position. Because open, informal party organization weakens long-term radical commitment, the party should adopt stricter discipline and build a stronger apparatus.

The theoretical underpinnings of the positions taken by realists and fundamentalists on the one hand, and ecolibertarians and ecosocialists on the other, boil down to the following competing propositions:

P 1: Formal party organization reinforces moderate strategies. Therefore, realists welcome this form of organization while fundamentalists fear it.

P 2: Formal party organization reinforces radical strategies. Hence, ecosocialists call for formalization, while ecolibertarians reject it.

Evidence presented in this study lends mixed support to the two propositions. Comparison of the Belgian and West German ecology parties shows that more formal organization coincides with more moderate strategies in Belgium (proposition 1), yet the fluidity and informality of the Greens has enabled the moderates to occupy key positions (proposition 2). And in all three parties strong tendencies to personalize power counterbalance efforts to rationalize party structures through formalization. Finally, the motives behind their commitment mechanisms make it unlikely that ecology parties could support formalized, disciplined structures similar to those found in the conventional parties.

Although strategic factionalism and sharp controversy over organizational development are more widespread in the Greens than in the Belgian parties, the Greens are more tolerant of internal pluralism and disagreement. In the eyes of many of its supporters, internal pluralism is precisely what sets the Green party apart from the established political parties which frantically seek to maintain unity and suffocate internal debate. Internal dissension in the Greens is viewed as a productive force. In this vein, moderates often argue that radicals should not be completely pushed out of positions of influence but serve as the party's watchdog and conscience. One interviewee jokingly suggests a compromise with his fundamentalist opponents according to the principle "you get the party organization and we get the parliamentary party." The decentralization of the Greens makes it possible to convert factional conflicts into positive-sum games in which minorities receive "side payments" keeping it worthwhile for them to stay in the party.[17]

In contrast, many of the Agalev and Ecolo interviewees are more concerned with the unity and ideological homogeneity of their parties. Many fear that former New Left activists will overwhelm the ecology parties and commit the same mistakes of sectarianism and factionalism that marked the failure in the 1970s of the "small left," as the Flemish call radical Trotskyist and Maoist groups. Belgian militants, particularly in Ecolo, express little tolerance for leftist minority factions. When asked about factionalism in Ecolo Brussels, Philippe, a member of Ecolo's party executive, exclaims: "What would we lose if the Left leaves? The party executive wants them to leave." Michel, another member of the executive, categorically states that leftists have no place in the party. Others add that a permanent opposition should form its own party. In Agalev, where an organized left opposition is absent, many militants also opt against cooperation with New Left groups. When militants of the Ghent Agalev section considered a joint list with leftist groups in the 1982 local elections, the party executive threatened to exclude the initiators from Agalev.

In the Greens endorsement of organizational pluralism goes together with the rejection of efforts to create a new comprehensive political ideology. Many activists no longer believe that alternatives to modern society can be derived from a consistent set of first principles or that the existing society can be interpreted as the embodiment of a single principle of organization. In the words of an influential activist, "in a society that has so many contradictions the Greens cannot be without contradictions."[18] This ideological and practical pluralism, fallibilism, or agnosticism is closely intertwined with a rejection of centralized, bureaucratic political organization. Militants often associate a certain pride with being competent in a specific policy area rather than

17. For the logic of side-payments to opposition groups in political parties compare Barnes (1968).

18. Quotation from Antje Vollmer's interview in *Stern* (April 17, 1986) 172.

proselytizing for an all-encompassing ideology. Paul, a militant from Hamburg, notices with relief that individuals obsessed with "grand theory" and the exegesis of the "Marxist classics" have left the GAL's work group on economic policy and have been replaced by activists concerned with the down to earth economic problems of the Hamburg region.

Of the three ecology parties Ecolo is the most concerned with a general belief system and commitment to a shared ideology. In 1984 and 1985 Ecolo's core group of militants devoted three general assemblies to discussing a "declaration of principles." Ecolo interviewees in general prove more concerned with drawing a line between "true ecologists" and other militants than their colleagues in either Agalev or the Greens. There also appears to be an affinity between the search for ideological coherence and organizational loyalty on the one hand and a lack of tolerance for internal dissension on the other. In Ecolo organizational loyalty is more pronounced (Chapter 4) and the party is considered more important than social movements as a vehicle for left-libertarian change.

These observations should not suggest that decentralized, pluralist parties do not face internal crises or tensions and disappoint militants' expectations. Many examples of perverse effects throughout this study have shown otherwise. They also do not suggest that a pluralist, tolerant party reinforces social solidarity and the democratic legitimacy of its procedures. The lack of shared convictions about proper decision procedures is responsible for the ease with which activists jettison standards of courtesy and mutual respect whenever programmatic and strategic conflict appears. As a French ecologist aptly remarked about problems in his country's ecology party: "In other words, the ecologists reject the legitimate violence of a disciplinary order (the institutions, the state, the hierarchy, the boss), but in turn expose themselves to an internal violence that is often expressed in unjustifiable verbal attacks (which can explain the very small number of women in the party organs) or splits or exclusions which are always regrettable." (Cochet 1985:3)

When ecology parties are in a strong enough electoral position to consider alliances with other parties, social, substantive, and temporal techniques to mitigate intraparty conflict—compromise, side-payments, delaying tactics—fail to work. Decisions must be made under time pressure, involve discrete either/or choices, and leave little room for sufficiently attractive side-payments to intraparty minorities opposing the proposed strategy. While ecology parties, just as most other parties, generally avoid narrow majority decisions on important issues in order to prevent the exodus of defeated minorities, discrete strategic choices leave no democratic alternative to majority rule, unless blocking minorities are allowed to hold parties hostage to their demands. In this sense, a strong competitive position endangers the fluid, decentralized, pluralist structure so important in ecology parties to maintaining a coalition of diverse left-libertarian forces. At the same time, however, a decentralized organization and decision process undermines the parties' capacity to make lasting strategic commitments. Yet again we encounter a tension between ecology parties' logic of constituency representation and logic of party competition.

Nevertheless, the Greens have survived their first decade of existence without a major split, with the exception of the exit of conservative fringe groups in 1979 and 1980. Ecolo in Wallonia, with comparatively high internal homogeneity and integration and located on a periphery of the left-libertarian cleavage, however, suffered a serious split in 1986 when its leftist faction formed its own "Party for an Ecological Left." Thus we encounter the paradox that the party with the fewest ideological divisions proved to be the most vulnerable to factionalism. The greater capacity of the Greens to live with internal pluralism can be explained in terms of the higher left-libertarian cleavage mobilization in West Germany, promoting greater diversity among party activists. But the explanation also must include three interconnected institutional and historical particularities that differentiate Belgium and West Germany.

First, in West Germany electoral rules force the different Green factions to rely on each other. Since the threshold of parliamentary representation is 5 percent of the vote, a serious split could easily eliminate the Greens from the parliaments. The activists are very much aware of the fact "that we are all dependent on each other." One ecosocialist from Hamburg envisions a future split of the Greens into a left and a right party if the party's electorate continues to grow, but for the time being see a "compelling force to remain united." In Belgium, in contrast, thresholds of electoral representation vary across districts. In Brussels it is as low as 2 percent of the popular vote and thus encourages splinter factions to run on their own. In smaller districts the threshold is much higher and ecologists cannot afford to run on competing lists.

Second, the structure of party competition explains the greater tolerance of the Greens for internal pluralism. The West German party system is less fractionalized and yields a relatively greater ideological distance between ecologists and conventional parties. In Belgium the field of parties is more crowded and the ideological distance between them is less great, for instance between Agalev and the Flemish socialists, the Christian Democrats, or the Flemish nationalists.[19] As a consequence, the cost of exit and search for an

19. Swyngedouw and Billiet's (1988) analysis of voter movements in the 1987 Belgian elections shows that Agalev wins votes from a variety of parties, primarily from the Flemish nationalists, the small New Left parties, and also the Christian democrats. Gains from and losses to the Flemish socialists cancel each other out. In contrast, the West German Greens win most votes at the expense of the SPD. Thus, patterns of vote switching shed light on the different position of ecology parties in the Belgian and West German party systems.

alternative party catering to their preferred policy mix is probably higher for discontented West German Green militants than for Agalev or Ecolo activists in Belgium. For this reason West German militants are more likely to resort to voice rather than exit when they disagree with party policy.

Third, in response to the electoral and party system, and against the backdrop of different levels of polarization in the Belgian and West German political culture (Chapter 1), the New Left has developed quite different relationships to ecology parties. In Belgium the radical Left had always been tolerated and communists were represented in parliament until 1985. Similarly, the New Left parties could propagandize their ideas without official impediments, while their doctrinaire thinking attracted few followers. Thus, the Belgian New Left could never mobilize much support nor provoke a strong backlash by existing elites. The ecologists of the late 1970s and early 1980s, therefore, viewed the New Left as ineffective and outmoded.

In West Germany since the 1960s, however, an escalating conflict between elements of the orthodox New Left and the state took place which climaxed in the Radicalism Decree barring candidates from public service on the basis of political criteria and the terrorist acts committed by New Left fringe groups. The electoral success of the Greens liberated the German New Left from the political ghetto into which it had cornered itself or had been driven by the existing parties and elites.[20] Many Green interviewees wish to distance themselves from their own past involvement in New Left organizations and interpret the Greens as a new beginning in a more pluralist, open spirit. For example, Tom, a moderate Green from Frankfurt, recalls how he avoided becoming a terrorist in the 1970s "by a hair's breadth," and later on realized that it was imperative to break with the rigid politics of New Left sects and build the Greens as a broad political alliance. This "conversion" was experienced by many former New Left activists and explains why most New Left groups could not maintain a separate political identity once the Greens began to flourish. Even where New Left militants set out to form their own factions within the Greens, such as the Hamburg "Group Z," these groups soon disintegrated when they were confronted with topics unfamiliar to the traditional New Left agenda, such as ecology. Moreover, the opportunities Green parliamentary representation offers to exercise political influence led to strategic divisions among former New Left allies.

In light of the polarized German political culture in the aftermath of the 1960s student movement, the growing tolerance for political pluralism and

20. The annual reports of the *Bundesverfassungsschutz*, the agency charged with observing and prosecuting those engaged in anti-constitutional activities, have been a symbol of this politics of ghettoization. Based on arbitrary criteria subject to no judicial or parliamentary control, the agency has labeled political groups as "enemies of the constitution" and monitored their activities.

disagreements among leftist activists represents an innovation. The slowness and inconsistency of decision making in the Greens is, from this perspective, an important achievment which breaks with a long tradition in German political behavior: "This unwieldiness [of decision making in the Greens], however, also amounts to [the party's] real strength in a country that has never enjoyed democratic diversity, color, adventurousness, and the playful in politics."[21]

Conclusion

The account of strategic choice and factionalism within ecology parties in this chapter is consistent with the generalizations of comparative studies on factionalism in political parties.[22] Factionalism tends to increase the more a party emphasizes the democratization of society as one of its overriding goals. Factionalism further spreads when a party caters to heterogeneous electoral constituencies and interest groups while electoral thresholds force them into a coalition under the umbrella of a single party. Also, great ideological distance between parties encourages factionalism because dissatisfied militants will voice internal opposition rather than search for an alternative party. Finally, the weakness of party organization itself promotes factionalism. Among ecology parties, the Greens are the most tolerant of strategic diversity, Agalev comes second, and Ecolo is least receptive. National political institutions, the mobilization of left-libertarian cleavage, and the parties' competitive position explain these differences.

As I have shown in the first part of this chapter, many forces determine a party's strategic stance when it finds itself in a strong competitive position. Ironically, in left-libertarian strongholds where ecology parties tend to be most radical, heterogeneous, and decentralized, they are also most likely to receive sufficient voter support to assume a strong competitive position. This configuration, in turn, intensifies pressure to choose between a logic of party competition pursuing electoral success and a logic of constituency representation insisting on the party's core demands and renouncing government office to avoid compromising the party's ideals.

In the short run, lack of strong party organization hastens the adoption of a logic of party competition. Recruitment of pragmatists, differential mobilization of activists, changing linkages to external movement organizations, and emerging party leaders all contribute to this process. Again we encounter a perverse effect. Precisely because ecology parties develop a fluid and open

---

21. Quotation from Antje Vollmer's interview in *Stern* (April 17, 1986), 172.

22. I am primarily concerned with strategic and ideological factionalism, not with clientelistic and group factionalism. An important comparative study of this subject is Raschke (1977). Compare also Beller and Belloni (1978) and Hine (1982).

THE TEMPTATIONS OF POWER   275

structure setting them apart from their conventional competitors, they are easily swayed by the lures of government participation and so move to a moderate strategy of alliance building. In the long run, however, fluid party organization and commitment to a consistent electoral strategy aiming at executive responsibility inevitably clash. This dilemma illustrates once again why it is so difficult to build and maintain political parties representing left-libertarian constituencies.

10 | The Future of
Left-Libertarian Politics

Left-libertarian parties constitute one aspect of a two-pronged political transformation in Western Europe: electoral *realignment* and organizational *dealignment* between citizens and political parties. They attract an electorate remarkably uniform across national boundaries: young, educated professionals working in the urban public service sector and overproportionally female, at least among supporters under thirty-five. Organizationally, however, the ties between left-libertarian parties and their electorates are weak, and the parties have limited capacity and inclination to strengthen them. The parties in fact introduce new patterns of interest intermediation between citizen and political decision-making elites. Yet this new politics does not coincide exactly with what party founders initially endorsed or expected.

After a brief review of the main findings, in this final chapter I raise two broader issues addressing the significance of the left-libertarian political experience for contemporary democracy. The first issue focuses on the lasting impact left-libertarian parties may have on European competitive party systems. How persistent are the new left-libertarian demands and patterns of political mobilization? Will they affect the working of democracies even if particular left-libertarian parties were to collapse from their internal contradictions? The second issue deals with problems in the normative theory of associational life that are posed by the unique form of organization left-libertarian parties have tried to develop. What models of democratic politics *can* and *ought* to be pursued by left-libertarian parties in modern democracies?

Mass Parties versus Left-Libertarian
Framework Parties

Ecology parties have translated the left-libertarian rejection of conventional mass parties, centralized interest group intermediation, and bureaucratic state control of civil society as articulated by contemporary social movements into a new form of party organization. I have argued that (1) ecology parties realize essential tenets of a new logic of constituency representation but that (2) this logic creates unintended, perverse effects and that (3) the extent to which the new logic and its consequences occur depends on external contingencies and the interplay of coalitions within these parties.

Constituency Representation and the Constraints of Party Competition

In those European democracies where sizable left-libertarian parties such as Agalev, Ecolo, and the Greens have appeared, the dominant political forces are "mass apparatus parties" (Mintzel 1984) which have a large membership and hierarchical, partially professionalized organizations that are closely intertwined with the state executive and complex networks of corporatist interest intermediation. Left-libertarian parties, in contrast, develop loosely coupled, fluid organizations that lack cohesiveness, involve only a small number of activists, establish tenuous, intermittent linkages to social movements and interest groups, and build party leadership on postmaterialist political entrepreneurs. Quite appropriately, Raschke (1983; 1985:261–62) has labeled left-libertarian parties "postindustrial framework parties."

Ecology parties attract only small numbers of members because their constituencies lack organizational loyalty, reject formal party affiliation, and are primarily driven by varying purposive motivations that do not converge in a single, unified ideology. These orientations and motivations explain the volatile patterns of involvement in ecology parties. In contrast, the dominant conventional parties maintain a mass membership. Even the conservative parties have increased their organizational strength and encapsulation of voters considerably. Moreover, there are indications that conventional parties rely increasingly on material rather than purposive or social commitment mechanisms to attract activists (Chapter 4).

Local as well as regional and national ecology party organizations lack a firm, institutionalized power structure crystallized around executive leadership. This contributes to an open, contingent process of decision making in meetings of local party sections as well as in party conventions. Also neither municipal councilors nor elected parliamentarians constitute cohesive, disciplined centers of power and control over the parties (Chapters 5 and 6). In contrast, conventional mass apparatus parties develop a professional core of party secretaries and executives that maintains vertical and horizontal communication across the party organization. This core not only organizes campaign activities and membership recruitment drives but also maintains the web of political intermediation with interest groups and control over the public administration. Modern mass parties combine bureaucratic organization with a centralization of authority around highly visible leadership personalities holding both party and electoral office. Parliamentary groups in legislatures are usually disciplined, cohesive organizations clearly subordinated to the leadership.

Organizational patterns also influence the recruitment of leadership personnel. At least initially, ecology parties recruited party executives and nominees for electoral office using ascriptive criteria and the candidates' past involvement in social movements, rather than their political stance, organizational loyalty, and ability to articulate political ideas. Further, a new type of political entrepreneur who alternately lives "for" politics without being independently wealthy or "off" politics without seeking a continuous professional political career track has emerged in the parties. In contrast, conventional parties recruit political leaders according to quasi-professional career patterns in which candidates have to prove themselves in progressively more demanding and responsible positions and usually represent clearly identifiable group and political interests (Chapter 7).

With respect to external linkages, ecology parties seek to avoid "pillarized" interorganizational systems of tightly coupled linkages to interest groups and respect the autonomy of left-libertarian movements. The parties reject both the Leninist view of movements as the parties' "transmission belts" to civil society as well as the neocorporatist practice of interlocking elites and organized bonds between party and interest group functionaries commonly found in mass apparatus parties. Instead, left-libertarian parties rely on informal contacts between individual party militants and movement organizers, joint activism in protest events, and occasionally the symbolic redeployment of political institutions (parliaments, embassies) as sites of demonstrations and direct political intervention (Chapter 8).

Political mobilization and organizational form influence strategic choice. At least initially, ecology parties interpreted parliamentary involvement as a continuation of political protest by novel means. And the open, fluid internal party structure, combined with often sharp internal political disagreements among ideologues, lobbyists, and pragmatists, continues to contribute to volatility in the parties' external strategies. This in turn increases the uncertainty voters face when they try to determine whether left-libertarian parties will in fact adhere to the strategies they reveal before elections. Conventional parties, however, build strategic consistency on the inertia of the party apparatus and its complex machinery of internal decision making. Under most conditions the strategic and programmatic stances of conventional parties shift only marginally in the aftermath of elections, thus allowing voters to establish a comparatively tight connection between their expression of party preference and the parties' actual behavior (Chapter 9).[1]

---

1. As I argue in Chapter 9, the decisiveness of elections varies across countries and constitutes an intervening variable not captured in my brief recapitulation.

By pursuing a logic of constituency representation, however, ecology parties unleash a host of perverse effects. These unintended results derive from mistaken assumptions about commitment to left-libertarian politics and from resource constraints imposed on political participation. They lead to a number of dilemmas and tradeoffs, to which militants begin to respond as the parties evolve.

Contrary to the belief that political participation is a superior good which all people seek and enjoy for its own sake, militants rationally calculate the costs and benefits of political involvement in light of their limited resources and alternative preferences. Aside from populist or syndicalist anti-party bias, the militants' rational calculation of time investment in politics explains the narrow base of activism in ecology parties. Moreover, it helps us to understand why ecology parties develop loosely coupled, stratarchal systems of communication and decision making with horizontally and vertically semi-autonomous party sections and elites. Many militants shy away from assignments with low rates of return on investment, in terms of yielding little political influence, but demanding great time commitments. Militants do not invest enough resources in the political organization to maintain a continuous and highly interactive process of communication. Further, loosely coupled, stratarchal organization promotes the rise of political entrepreneurship because it enables actors with the most resources and most intense political preferences to dominate the decision-making process. The result is competition among cliques of political entrepreneurs, unrepresentativeness of party executives for the rank and file, and a disjointed process of decision making, all phenomena that appear to many activists as perverse effects.

Militants misperceive motivations and commitments because they are unaware that activists choose them according to the scarcity of resources, a second source of perverse effects. Individual party members are unequally endowed with resources and capabilities for engaging in political participation. Since loose left-libertarian party organizations provide no corrective to enhance the influence of resource-poor militants and constrain those of resourceful activists, the actual distribution of power in ecology parties violates the egalitarian and participatory ideals held by many activists. These experiences often discourage membership participation and fuel sharp intraparty conflicts (Chapter 4).

Resource scarcity slows down the process of collective decision making and constrains participation. Arrangements for national party conventions, for instance, may take months to prepare and are costly in terms of money and time. Consequently, informal groups of leaders and activists who can communicate with each other easily make decisions under time pressure and thus place resourceful political entrepreneurs in a focal position (Chapters 5 through 7). In a similar vein, external linkages to constituency groups are maintained by individual parliamentarians and entrepreneurs who are influential and can rapidly respond to outside demands. This in turn enhances the authority of competing party elites and also attenuates the scope and intensity of interaction between left-libertarian parties and social constituencies (Chapter 8).

There is little evidence, however, that left-libertarian entrepreneurs constitute a cohesive elite with interests and preferences that differ from those of the rank and file and pursue personal advantage. Rather than approximating Michels' "strong" syndicalist conception of oligarchy, ecology parties develop weak, fragmented oligarchies of competing leaders who represent segments of rank-and-file activists at different levels of the parties' stratarchal organizations. Party activists have been successful in preventing the emergence of a power center; but rather than shifting to the rank and file, power— the ability to bring about collective action—evaporates in a stratarchal organization riddled by group pluralism (see Edler 1987:36). This outcome has caused activists to react in two different ways: on the one hand, they have intensified efforts to realize party democracy and on the other have adopted a more sympathetic stance toward elements of a logic of party competition.

Intensified efforts to realize party democracy have been promoted by party ideologues and are intellectually driven by the syndicalist interpretation of Michels' theory of oligarchy. Although I have argued that this theory misrepresents the actual dynamic of left-libertarian parties, its effectiveness is based on the sociological "Thomas theorem," which holds that what individuals define as social reality has real, though not always intended, consequences. Because a syndicalist theory of party oligarchy gives a distorted picture of reality, its practical application, through efforts to reduce the positional power of party executives or the resources they control (short tenure periods, low incomes, and the like), reinforces rather than alleviates the observed perverse effects. Organizational reforms based on a syndicalist view of political parties misperceive the motive for running for office as material self-interest rather than a desire to be politically efficacious. This view also ignores the scarcity of resources rank-and-file militants have available for getting involved in politics and controlling the parties' decision-making process. These reforms unwittingly speed up the vicious circle of grassroots control in ecology parties (Chapter 6) that fosters trends to make political power unaccountable by causing it to migrate toward informal elites of entrepreneurs and parliamentarians with media access.

In other respects left-libertarian parties, especially their pragmatic activists, have responded to these perverse effects by modifying expectations and behavior and by adopting elements of a logic of party competition. These tendencies have developed most strongly in all those activities that link the parties to broader electoral and political audiences. Most importantly, many municipal councilors and parliamentarians have accepted the routines of institutional politics in parliaments or city councils. Because of their key role in defining strategy, party activists have made efforts to rationalize the process of nomination for elected office by abandoning the movementist style of recruitment and adopting a candidate's political stance and/or commitment to the party as leading recruitment criteria (Chapter 7). Moreover, where parties have found themselves in a strong competitive position for forming government alliances, they have felt the temptations of exercising executive power (Chapter 9). In contrast to Michels' argument, however, these processes were not driven by autonomous actions of party elites but by complex internal processes involving the influx of pragmatic rank-and-file activists, differential mobilization of militants in party conventions, changing external linkage patterns between left-libertarian movements and ecology parties, and new criteria for the nomination of the parties' electoral candidates.

To conclude, ecology parties develop a new *internal* form of organization that differs from that of conventional Belgian and West German mass parties and is characterized by a narrower base of voter encapsulation and participation, less centralization of power, and less organizational coherence. In their *external* behavior, however, particularly in the choice of electoral candidates, the emphasis on visible leadership, and strategies of alliance building, they show some signs of moving toward a logic of party competition. Ecology parties apparently try to overcome the tension between both logics by *segmenting different organizational and strategic relations*. On the one hand, the internal party organization caters to ideological sensibilities by preserving a fluid, informal, participatory dynamic. On the other, external strategies are increasingly geared toward the realities of political power and party competition in parliamentary democracies. In other words, internally the parties are charting a course to communicative skills that maintain participatory openness and flexibility in spite of the perverse effects identified by the activists themselves. Externally they are attempting to develop instrumental strategic capacity for coping successfully with political adversaries and exercising influence over public policy.[2] The parties lack the administrative means to organize and control a large social constituency, but they are receptive to new demands and left-libertarian forms of social mobilization. They create a stratarchal, informal organization but nevertheless participate in the arena of party competition where, at least in parliamentary democracies, parties with a centralized, professional apparatus and stable leadership have held an advantage.

The Environment of Left-Libertarian Parties

The cross-national and subnational comparison of Belgian and West German ecology party units showed that their structure and strategy vary in

2. Jürgen Habermas (1971:37–42) criticized the Leninist model of party organization and recommended that an emancipatory organization must function internally according to commu-

different political environments. The choice between a logic of constituency representation and a logic of party competition hinges on the relative strength of three groups of internal activists—ideologues, lobbyists, and pragmatists—and on the coalitions they enter within a party. Group strength and propensity toward internal coalition formation in turn are influenced by three conditions in the environment of the parties: the mobilization of the political cleaveage a party expresses, the openness and accessibility of existing elites and institutions to a party's demands, and a party's competitive position vis-à-vis its adversaries in the electoral arena. The link between external conditions and internal choices in parties is established through (1) patterns of recruiting activists (Chapter 4), (2) the differential mobilization of activists in decision making and competition for political office (Chapters 6, 7, and 9), and (3) external linkages to mobilized constituency organizations (Chapters 8 and 9).

Among left-libertarian parties, those (sub)organizations (1) located in areas with high cleavage mobilization, (2) facing hostile incumbent elites and relatively closed institutional settings, and (3) finding themselves in a weak competitive position have the greatest propensity of moving toward a radical logic of constituency representation. In these party units ideologues represent a large share of the militants, are likely to form coalitions with lobbyists, and conflict with pragmatists. Intraparty frictions are intensified further when parties receive contradictory cues from their environment (particularly where cleavage mobilization is high), the existing institutions and elites are openly hostile, and parties get sufficient electoral support to achieve a strong competitive position. They are then forced to choose between a radical strategy of opposition on principle and a moderate strategy of entering a government coalition and/or alliances to push through policy reforms. In this process ideologues and pragmatists mobilize against each other and vie for the support of the lobbyists.

Where left-libertarian parties operate in an environment of (1) low cleavage mobilization and (2) relatively porous, open institutional settings and also assume (3) a strong competitive position, it is likely that pragmatists will prevail and intraparty conflicts will remain relatively subdued. In this case the party will be most inclined to follow a logic of party competition and it is improbable that sizable and sharply differentiated groups of ideologues and lobbyists will emerge to confront the pragmatists. More generally, the closer any party moves toward a centrist position in a party system in terms of cleavage polarization, institutional access, and competitive position, the fewer sharp internal strategic conflicts will appear.

nicative standards and externally according to standards of instrumental and strategic rationality. Although ecology parties appear to be far removed from Habermas' vision of communicative interaction, they involve new capacities for articulating and including interests in the political debate that are currently excluded from established parties.

The comparison of the Belgian and West German ecology parties and of subunits within Agalev, Ecolo, and the Greens bears out these points. At the national level, in contrast to the Belgian Agalev and Ecolo, the West German Greens are located in an environment of higher cleavage mobilization and greater institutional rigidity. Consequently, the West German party has many more ideologues and lobbyists than its Belgian counterparts. Moreover, the Greens tend to be in a stronger competitive position than the Belgian parties. The tension between high cleavage mobilization and institutional rigidity on the one hand, and the lures of a strong competitive position on the other, explain why the Greens encounter more intraparty conflict than Agalev or Ecolo.

At the subnational level the same argument is confirmed. Among the Green state party organizations compared in this study, Hamburg constitutes the most mobilized left-libertarian environment but has put the party in a weak competitive position except for brief interludes. As a consequence it has the most radical Green party, pursuing an almost pure logic of constituency representation. The Baden-Württemberg Greens, at the other end of the spectrum, are located in a relatively less mobilized left-libertarian environment and have shown a greater propensity toward moderation and a logic of party competition, even though they are in a weak competitive position. Hesse is in the middle of the spectrum with medium left-libertarian mobilization which coincided with a strong competitive position from 1982 to 1987. The Hessian Greens, therefore, have gone through the most intense internal conflict among ideologues, lobbyists, and pragmatists, with a coalition of the latter two prevailing in the end. In Belgium both Agalev and Ecolo face similar institutional settings and weak competitive positions but the level of left-libertarian mobilization differs between the two regions. In Flanders the left-libertarian cleavage is distinctly more articulated than in economically depressed Wallonia. As a consequence Agalev has more party ideologues and lobbyists than Ecolo and is also more committed to a logic of constituency representation.

The applicability of the theoretical framework to explanation for structural developments and strategic choices in political parties is not confined to left-libertarian parties. Conventional parties in advanced democracies have moved toward a logic of party competition because they rely on cleavages undergoing a process of demobilization (class, religion), have been included in the existing institutions of interest intermediation, and are frequently in an electorally very competitive position. Yet even here variations between parties and over time, especially among socialist parties on the left and conservative parties on the right, should illuminate the varying role of intraparty groups and external conditions in the choice of organizational forms and external strategies.

Ecology Parties and the Future of West European Party Systems

Even though left-libertarian parties represent new social movements and their sympathizers vigorously, they still draw on comparatively limited voter support even in Belgium, Denmark, and West Germany, where they have made their greatest electoral inroads. It is an open question, then, whether the new parties constitute a fringe phenomenon in European democracies or will prove to be resilient enough to become permanent and increasingly powerful participants in the existing party systems. I will outline several arguments in favor of expecting, on balance, a growing importance of left-libertarian parties in Western Europe and then discuss a number of forces that may temper their success or even precipitate their collapse. In any case, however, the persistence of particular left-libertarian *parties* must be distinguished from the presence of left-libertarian *politics,* no matter which parties represent left-libertarian constituencies. It is quite possible that specialized left-libertarian parties are a fleeting phenomenon but that the specific style of left-libertarian political mobilization and its logic of constituency representation will survive. Conventional parties might successfully defeat left-libertarian parties, but at the price of being transformed by left-libertarian demands and patterns of political action.

The Persistence of Left-Libertarian Parties

In most West European parliamentary democracies, parties are more than vehicles for electoral competition. They are immersed in complex networks of interest intermediation between civil society and government. Parties are threads of a finely woven web of communication which includes interest groups, social movements, and state bureaucracies. Thus, they are also agents for recruiting political elites, articulating and representing interest groups, and designing as well as implementing public policy. The first argument, then, in favor of expecting left-libertarian parties to persist has to do with the highly differentiated and relatively stable institutional configurations linking capitalist markets, neocorporatist patterns of interest intermediation, and bureaucratic mass apparatus parties in almost all countries where sizable left-libertarian parties have appeared. As long as these institutions prevail, left-libertarian demands are likely to arise and find an outlet in new political parties. Left-libertarian movements and parties seek to build an alternative network of political communication that its creators expect to eventually displace established neocorporatist patterns. This alternative calls for open, flexible, and decentralized links between government and civil society. It emphasizes a maximum of responsiveness, innovation, and open conflict in the political process, while the established neocorporatist techniques of political regulation stress stability, continuity, and consensus.

Party and party system theories that emphasize voter maximization alone have produced fruitful insights into the nature of party competition but have not fully understood the interplay of party activism, organization, and strategy formation, because they have underemphasized the parties' immersion in the intricate institutional networks of politics of which party competition is only one arena. The persistence of left-libertarian parties may be due largely to their refusal to accept techniques of voter maximization and to their resistance to full participation in the established state/civil society networks. Here we touch upon a second reason to expect the longevity of left-libertarian parties. The established mass apparatus parties have become victims of their own success by overextending themselves in deploying techniques to maximize votes. In this process their political message has become so diffuse, oriented toward the political status quo, and incapable of responding to new demands that they can no longer reach well-defined, new left-libertarian constituencies with strong sentiments about particular policy issues and a goal of transforming modern politics (Offe 1980; Raschke 1982). Left-libertarian challenges to conventional parties are especially serious since they reject the focal position of parties in the process of policy formation altogether. Left-libertarian politics employs the form of party organization ultimately to reduce the role parties play in the intermediation between state and society and to limit the central state in the governance of society.

It is the irony of modern mass apparatus and state parties that their techniques of acquiring electoral hegemony and centrality in the process of policy formation have generated a new challenge to the basic institutional framework of party competition and the corporatist welfare state for the first time in Europe since World War II. Left-libertarian parties with their stratarchal, informal organization have introduced a new flexibility and innovative capacity in political systems that have solidified around highly organized cleavages and institutions of political bargaining. Their organizational dealignment from voters and mobilized social constituencies symbolizes a new style of democratic politics. Internally, the fluidity and openness of loosely coupled parties encourage new ideas, surprise strategies, and a high level of debate and conflict among party militants. Externally, the new form of organization questions the centrality of party itself for interest intermediation between state and society.

Left-libertarian electoral constituencies and new forms of party organization have arisen not only in West Germany and Belgium but also in other countries. A third argument for expecting the longevity of left-libertarian parties and of their unique form of mobilization, then, is the similarity of ideas, electorates, and organizational forms that characterize these parties in a considerable number of countries although they have developed independently of each other. Left-libertarian parties everywhere are primarily populated by intellectuals and employees in the public service sector.[3] Women play a relatively greater role in them than in their conventional competitors.[4] All studies of left-libertarian parties have also found their purposive, participatory, and social commitment mechanisms characterized by weaknesses and contradictions similar to those I observed in Agalev, Ecolo, and the Greens. Consequently, left-libertarian parties are largely unable to encapsulate their electorate in a mass organization and therefore have extraordinarily low member/voter ratios. Left-libertarian parties have also shunned tightly integrated formal structures. As Wilson (1962:232–39; 251–57) remarked about a precursor to left-libertarian politics, the U.S. Democratic Club Movement, its members had an aversion to formal organization and encountered great difficulty in coordinating their activities. Similarly, the Scandinavian left-libertarian parties have more the character of electoral alliances than of disciplined party organizations (Lorenz 1982:42; Lund 1982:74–75). The Socialist People's party (SPP) in Denmark reduced the role of the parliamentary leader during its libertarian transformation in the 1970s. In the same vein, the Dutch Pacifist Socialist party (PSP) is a conglomerate of largely independent partial groups such as local sections, party executive, and parliamentary deputies (Gerretsen and Van der Linden 1982:101).

In external relations to left-libertarian movement constituencies, remarkable similarities also exist among all left-libertarian parties. In the Netherlands the PSP has a loose, arms-length relationship to left-libertarian movements (Jacobs and Roebroek 1983:108). Relations to working-class organizations remain tenuous, even where left-libertarian parties originated in a socialist milieu. The Danish SPP, for instance, has not benefited from the unions' conflict with the social democrats (Logue 1982:261). This parallels similar difficulties of the Belgian and West German ecology parties in relating to the labor movement.

With respect to strategic alliances, most left-libertarian parties express ideological pluralism and steer a rather erratic course. Moreover, they are strategically factionalized and thus develop a limited capacity to act cohesively.[5] In countries where left-libertarian parties have existed since the 1960s, strategies have wavered between fundamental opposition and rapprochment to the established parties. Splits and factionalism such as in the Dutch PSP, the French PSU, or the Danish SPP were often motivated by

3. See Logue (1982: chaps. 7 and 8) on the Scandinavian left-libertarian parties. The same is true of early left-libertarian efforts such as the Democratic Club movement in the United States (Wilson 1962:258–88) and the French PSU (Hauss 1978: chap. 9).

4. See Gerretsen and Van der Linden (1982) on the Netherlands, Kergoat (1982) on the French PSU, and Lorenz (1982) on the Norwegian left socialists.

5. On ideological divisions compare Wilson (1962:348) on the Democratic Club Movement, Hauss (1978:182) on the French PSU, Lund (1982:74) on the Norwegian left socialists, and Gerretsen and Van der Linden (1982) on the Dutch PSP.

strategic disagreements. Dutch, Danish, Norwegian, and Swedish left-libertarians have occasionally cooperated with social democratic governments. Where they withdrew from the alliance when internal strategic conflicts erupted, they were badly beaten in ensuing elections.[6]

Skeptics who do not see a future for a unique left-libertarian political form, and conventional party theorists who emphasize the constraints of electoral competition, argue that new parties might start out with a radical idea but will soon adopt the electorally most efficient strategies (Robertson 1976:101–5). An example for this life cycle of party formation is the German Social Democratic party which took about thirty-five years, from 1875 to about 1910, to become a modern mass party (Schorske 1955). The German Christian Democrats needed thirty years (1946–1975) to create a mass organization (Mintzel 1975; Schönbohm 1985). A similar life cycle argument has been made most recently for the West German Greens (Offe 1986).

Three arguments against the life cycle model, however, must be taken seriously. First, the strategic wavering of left-libertarian parties in Western Europe shows they are not following a unilinear path of adaptation and accommodation to existing party systems. Second, in the case of Agalev, Ecolo, and the Greens, and also that of other, often older left-libertarian parties, only a limited number of indications confirm an internal learning process at the end of which the parties will follow a logic of party competition. Third, it must not be forgotten that in socialist, conservative, or Christian parties a collectivist ideology prevailed which facilitated a commitment to organizational discipline and the subordination of the individual to a formal leadership, features important for the working of conventional parties within a logic of party competition. Because of their militants' individualist, anti-organizational predispositions and ideas, left-libertarian parties, at least with respect to their internal organization, are much less conducive to transformation into established molds. In their external strategies, however, learning through experience may lead them to adopt some elements of a logic of party competition such as developing firmer constituency ties, recognizing the importance of visible party leaders, and engaging in moderate alliance strategies when opportunities arise.

On balance, left-libertarian parties constitute the vanguard of a certain Americanization of European politics. They foster a libertarian, individualist mode of political action. A fluid subculture, provocative issues, and charismatic personalities hold the parties together rather than comprehensive, con-

---

6. The Danish SPP fell from 10.9 percent to 6.1 percent in 1968 after withdrawing its support for a social democratic minority government. Another episode of cooperation between the two parties ended in 1973 after two years and led to a fall of the SPP's vote from 9.1 to 6 percent. The Dutch Democrats '66 experienced a similar defeat in the 1982 national elections after they had supported a Christian democratic government and then withdrew.

sistent programs, cohesive organization, or solidarity. The key personalities draw much of their influence from access to the mass media. Party supporters constitute loose coalitions that mobilize intermittently and are more inspired by a specific cause than a comprehensive world view or encompassing strategy of political action. Even where left-libertarian parties are willing to adopt moderate alliance strategies, their internal decision-making process and style of conflict resolution appears to preclude their becoming bureaucratic mass apparatus parties akin to the conventional European socialist, Christian, and conservative parties.

At times, the rhetoric of left-libertarian political entrepreneurs is reminiscent of the attack by progressive reform politicians on established urban party machines in the United States at the beginning of the century. Nevertheless, although the participatory, individualist tendencies in left-libertarian politics clearly show parallels to the American model, one should not take this comparison to U.S. party politics too far. The historical, institutional, and cultural circumstances of the left-libertarian challenge in Europe are too different from American politics to suggest unequivocally an Americanization of European democracies. In fact, it is precisely the ecology parties' tendency to Americanize European politics that clashes with institutional constraints likely to undermine their viability, unless they learn to live within the existing systems of party competition.

Destabilizing Tendencies in Left-Libertarian Parties

Unconventional organizational forms and programs help left-libertarian parties to attract a well-defined electorate, but lack of internal cohesion, integration, and consistency as well as limited strategic capability constrain their electoral appeal and undercut their influence on policy making, given the existing patterns of interest intermediation. The new parties seize upon demands not represented by existing groups and parties but cannot aggregate and coordinate interests to the extent necessary for successful policy influence in a liberal corporatist polity. This weakness is succinctly stated by Peter Glotz, the general secretary of the German Social Democrats in the mid-1980s, in criticizing the Greens for failing to accomplish two essential tasks: "Good parties stand out by their capacity to manage a double process of integration: on the political level, an integration of wings which are present in all living parties; on the societal level, an integration of diverse groups and strata which yields more than an aggregation of particular interests."[7]

In parliamentary systems with cohesive parties competing for the control of government, the left-libertarian form of constituency representation creates

7. Peter Glotz, "Grüne Politik. Diskrepanz zwischen Diagnose und Therapie," *Tageszeitung* (May 15, 1985).

exceptional vulnerabilities that can quickly trigger the demise of the new parties. First, the small, fluid, stratarchal left-libertarian parties have little democratic legitimacy as party organizations. For strategically calculating voters, they offer few assurances that they will pursue the policies revealed before an election. The absence of organizational loyalty and the often intense conflict among the small number of left-libertarian militants further erode the parties' electoral reputation. Second, in the competition for votes, the organizational dealignment of the parties from their electorate may turn into a liability. Left-libertarian voters have more loyalty to their ideas and issues than to specific parties. Their intellectual sophistication predisposes them to vote strategically rather than to identify with a party.

The organizational *dealignment* of parties and voters may thus endanger the electoral *realignment* upon which left-libertarian parties have been built. This becomes especially relevant when a third factor is taken into account, the parties' uncertain strategic stances and limited influence on public policy. Left-libertarian parties have no control over organized constituencies whose mobilization could be employed as a threat to extract policy concessions from their opponents. Left-libertarian parties generally lack the organizational, ideological, and strategic prerequisites for becoming governing parties in highly institutionalized, liberal corporatist polities. While they may occasionally support governments, their major impact on existing patterns of policy making is the *power of negation,* their ability to set limits to the maneuvering of conventional parties and thereby to influence public policy indirectly.

Sophisticated left-libertarian voters may realize the parties' limited policy-making capacities and ability to make strategic commitments, a perception that may explain the extraordinary volatility in the parties' electorate. Not only in the West German Greens, but also in other left-libertarian parties such as the Danish, Norwegian, or Dutch left-libertarian parties, electoral support has varied widely from one election to the next. And in some countries, such as France, Italy, and the Netherlands, the rise and demise of left-libertarian parties shows how uncertain is their ability to weather the storms of internal strategic conflict and electoral swings.

Left-libertarian parties are thus caught in a dilemma. If they rationalize their organization and strategy, they risk the support of their libertarian core constituencies and the legitimacy of their claim to change the democratic process. If they adhere to their meta-political goal of transforming the patterns of state/civil society linkages and base their party on organizational dealignment, they fail to win the support of a large reliable electorate and of marginal sympathizers.

The parties' combination of electoral realignment with an organizational dealignment of party and constituency groups encounters serious obstacles in corporatist welfare states. It is therefore quite possible that the left-libertarian cleavage defies political organization in the form of stable new parties. If the existing cohort of left-libertarian parties were to disappear, would this prove that the left-libertarian cleavage has no long-term impact on European party systems?

Left-Libertarianism in Established Parties

In order to assess the significance of left-libertarian politics in case left-libertarian parties fail, two easily conflated issues must be separated: the occurrence of electoral realignment on the one hand, and the rise of new parties or changes in the relative strength of existing parties on the other. Electoral (re)alignments have to do with the loyalty of identifiable social constituencies to parties or party blocs. This definition of (re)alignment focuses on the demand side of electoral politics. Whether electoral (re)alignment leads to changes in the composition and relative strength of parties, however, depends on the supply side of political alternatives.[8] Where left-libertarian parties fail, a left-libertarian realignment may nevertheless take place if (1) there is a bloc of left-libertarian voters with a common policy preference (demand side) and (2) a conventional party sets out to capture the left-libertarian vote by catering to its demands and expectations.

If left-libertarian voters support a conventional party because they have more confidence in its strategic competence and political effectiveness, they bring about electoral realignment without emergence of a new party. According to my arguments in Chapters 1 and 9, this situation is likely to arise under two conditions. First, traditional social democratic and socialist parties are in the opposition but in a sufficiently strong competitive position to raise expectations that the replacement of a rightist government is possible. As opposition parties, socialists can appeal to both left-libertarian and traditional working-class voters without revealing the practical tensions between the policies advocated by each of these constituencies. Second, left-libertarians will be more likely to vote for the socialist competitor if the genuinely left-libertarian parties cannot agree on a moderate strategy of cooperation with a socialist government and are beset by internal factionalism.

If conventional leftist parties defeat new left-libertarian competitors, however, they will experience similar challenges to their organizational form and

8. Dalton et al. (1984a:13) do not strictly separate these two dimensions and define realignments as "significant shifts in the group bases of party coalitions, and usually [?] in the distribution of popular support among the parties as a result." (My question mark.) Later in the book, however, they discuss the conditions that affect the supply side of new parties and realignments and make it possible that voter blocks shift across parties (Dalton et al. 1984b:463–72). Criticizing the American literature on partisan realignment, Brady (1985) pointed out its excessive concern with the electoral demand side and analyzed how institutions (such as electoral systems, districting, etc.) affect the capacity of parties to express an electoral realignment at the legislative level.

strategic capabilities as left-libertarian parties themselves. Socialist parties thus would internalize conflict over participatory politics and patterns of interest intermediation between state and civil society that characterize left-libertarian parties. That conventional left parties could face these internal challenges is not mere speculation. Since the late 1960s social democratic, socialist, and at times even communist parties have competed for left-libertarian electorates. But this strategy has created serious intraparty factionalism, in several instances decreasing the parties' electoral competitiveness and forcing them into the opposition. The Belgian, Danish, Dutch, West German, and most recently the Austrian social democrats are the most notable examples. In some ways even struggles within the British Labour party are affected by left-libertarian politics.[9] Only in countries where the left-libertarian cleavage is less mobilized, such as the Mediterranean democracies, have socialist parties not faced this problem (Hine 1986).

If socialist parties try to cater to left-libertarian electoral constituencies, they face a dilemma which is the mirror image of that encountered by left-libertarian parties. If they remain mass apparatus parties, sticking to the established ground rules of party competition and interest intermediation, they maintain their strategic viability and capacity to operate as state parties in the process of policy formation, but consciously give up competition for left-libertarian votes. If they compete for left-libertarian voters they face the risk that an influx of left-libertarian activists will weaken their capacity to govern and function as mass apparatus parties. Where socialist parties have tried to combine both strategies, they have experienced intense internal conflict over the substance of left-libertarian demands and the procedures of intraparty decision making. Hence, socialist parties find themselves in the awkward position of having to choose between the model of state party which may preserve their capacity to govern in the short run, and the model of postindustrial framework party which drives them into the opposition by weakening their strategic capability and alienating some of their working-class supporters.

To summarize, it would be a mistake to see the organizational dealignment of parties and constituencies as a trend confined to left-libertarian parties, for electoral realignments may precipitate organizational dealignment in existing mass parties, too (Smith 1984). The left-libertarian pressure to restructure the relations between state and civil society and the ensuing new differentiation and polarization of parties is more significant and pervasive than an exclusive focus on genuinely left-libertarian parties might suggest. The latter are, as it were, the laboratories in which new patterns of interest intermediation and

9. The case of Britain is ambiguous for two reasons. First, many left-libertarians have supported the social democratic/liberal Alliance. Second, within Labour a radical Old Left has teamed up with New Left libertarian forces against the moderate party factions.

policy innovation are explored. They signal far-reaching changes in the bases and patterns of political participation that make a restoration of the undisputed hegemony of the mass apparatus party unlikely.

This change in modern party systems compels us to reconsider a number of popular theorems about the transformation of parties in modern democracies. In the 1950s Duverger (1954) speculated that a "contagion from the left" would lead all parties to adopt the structural properties of socialist mass parties in order to remain electorally competitive.[10] In the 1960s Epstein (1967:234–60) proposed precisely the opposite, a "contagion from the right" or a dissolution of mass party organization under the impact of changed campaign styles, the growing role of the mass media, and new techniques of party financing. Both proposals contain an element of truth but are only partially valid in view of the experience of the 1970s and 1980s. Duverger's prediction that, with some time lag, conservative parties in Europe would indeed improve the scope, articulation, and cohesiveness of their organizations turned out to be correct, but he did not anticipate the counter-tendencies of organizational dissolution on the Left promoted by new left-libertarian forces. Nor did Epstein predict the growth and persistence of party organization on the right.

Both Epstein and Duverger implicitly accepted too much of Kirchheimer's catch-all party thesis and derived their predictions too exclusively from the structural constraints of electoral competition for them to consider the role of political parties in the entire network of interest intermediation in modern democracies and the influence of new ideas on the development of political parties. As a consequence they underrated the possible tendency, at least in corporatist welfare states, toward *structural differentiation, if not polarization* among political parties. On the one hand, conventional parties have been increasingly transformed from being representatives of electoral constituencies into agencies of policy making, or state parties. But on the other a left-libertarian backlash against hierarchical state/society relations leads to new parties or at least opposition voices inside the dominant state parties of the conventional Left.

The structural differentiation of modern party systems is also not fully captured by the popular "decline-of-parties" literature of the 1970s, which maintains that issue related political mobilization would undermine party cohesiveness.[11] In contrast to the debates of the 1950s and 1960s, the decline-of-parties literature broadened the theoretical horizon beyond the narrow focus of electoral competition to consider the role of parties in the entire

10. I accept the dominant reception and interpretation of Duverger's (1954) typology of political parties, although John May (1969) has shown that it does not fully reflect Duverger's theory.
11. For inventories of hypotheses on the "decline of parties," see Berger (1979), Harmel and Janda (1982: 123–24), Lehner and Schubert (1984, Mair (1984), and Offe (1980).

network of democratic interest intermediation. Yet its sweeping generalizations tend to miss the importance of the new polarization between state parties and left-libertarian framework parties. The expectation of party theorists from Weber and Michels to the present time that a single formula can capture the common development of all parties will in all likelihood remain unrealized. Left-libertarian parties and their relation to newly mobilized constituencies caution us that unique political beliefs and practices in the complex web of modern democracies do not permit us to treat all parties as entities obeying a single logic.

Normative Theory of Associational Life and the Left-Libertarian Experience

This book treats the structure and strategy of ecology parties as dependent variables shaped by rival groups of party activists, each with distinct preference schedules. Although a number of organizational and strategic characteristics separate left-libertarian from conventional politics, in many ways the actual practice of left-libertarian parties does not meet their activists' expectations of a radically different form of democratic participation. Obviously, left-libertarian experiences raise important normative questions of democratic theory not adequately addressed by a purely descriptive and analytical perspective. In conclusion I take the opportunity to offer some preliminary thoughts on the following three questions. (1) How desirable is it to abandon the conventional mass apparatus party model? (2) How desirable is it to adopt the present model of left-libertarian framework parties? (3) Are there other alternatives worth considering for the design of left-libertarian parties? I first outline three important objectives of relevant democratic choice procedures, and then turn to the methods parties can employ to realize these objectives.

Democracy is a system of governance that establishes as tight a link as possible between the preferences of individual citizens and the results of collective choice. On the procedural level, the minimum condition for democracy is that all citizens must have a chance to make their voice heard in the collective choice process and that decisions (such as choice of government or policy) are reversible when the population's preferences change. Under certain conditions, it is logically impossible to aggregate individual preferences democratically into consistent collective choices (Arrow 1963). Empirically more important constraints on democracy may be the resource scarcity and high transaction costs (time) in collective choice procedures (Buchanan and Tullock 1962), citizens' limited incentives for engaging in collective decision making (Dahl 1956), and the inertia of the institutions, interests, and values around which an existing political order is crystallized.

Political parties competing in elections are one vehicle linking citizens to the democratic decision-making process. They aggregate preferences in the process, yet they have obligations to at least three democratic principals. First, parties are responsible to voters who have endorsed their policies and candidates in elections. Electoral success thus determines the parties' democratic *effectiveness* and *legitimacy*. Votes and elections, however, do not reflect the nature and intensity of popular support for specific policies and courses of action advocated by a party. Hence, parties do well to heed a second and third group of principals. Voluntary associations and mobilized constituencies express demands and positions on individual issues and request the parties' support between elections. The parties' democratic qualifications thus also depend on their *responsiveness* to constituency groups, especially if they attract a large following and express intense preferences on a policy issue. Finally, party activists, through their continuous participation in party debates, generate a more complex, differentiated view of popular policy demands than is provided by the electorate's simple act of voting. Activists maintain a party's organizational viability as long as it caters to their objectives and aspirations. The importance of the parties' *accountability* as a mode of democratic legitimation increases with the member/voter ratio and the mobilization of members in intraparty debates.

Electoral effectiveness, constituency responsiveness, and accountability to party militants are three complementary criteria which improve the democratic legitimacy of party governance. Ideally, parties should make all three criteria compatible. In some respects this compatibility hinges upon the substantive preferences and policies supported by voters, constituencies, militants, and party leaders. In other respects, however, compatibility also depends on the structure of parties themselves. Two dimensions of organizational design are particularly important: (1) the formalization of intraparty decision-making processes and (2) the degree of centralization and personalization of political authority accorded to party leaders.

The formalization of intraparty procedures increases the accountability of party leaders to the rank and file because it reduces the leadership's range of discretionary authority. Since it lends continuity to a party's policy objectives, thus guaranteeing voters that a party will indeed support the policies it revealed before an election, it also tends to increase electoral effectiveness. Yet formalization circumscribes a party's ability to respond to new constituencies and policy demands because formalized decision procedures inevitably create barriers to change that are difficult to overcome. Highly fluid, informal rules of decision making in parties have the reverse effect. They increase the capacity to respond to new demands but decrease the accountability of internal decision making and also electoral effectiveness.

Like formalization, the centralization and personalization of political authority tend to increase a party's electoral effectiveness. Visible political

leaders simplify the choice of party for many voters and, as with formalization, guarantee the continuity of the party's stance beyond an electoral contest. Unlike formalization, centralization of authority reduces the accountability of party leadership to the rank and file. This increase in the leaders' range
of discretion, however, enables them to enhance their responsiveness to new
demands and challenges from external constituencies, precisely because the
personalization of their authority relaxes constraints on their decision making.

Cross-tabulation of each organizational strategy yields four ideal-typical
organizational forms of modern parties (Table 43). The "democratic payoffs" of each form can be calculated by adding up the positive effects ($+1$)
and the negative effects (-1) each structural property produces for electoral
effectiveness, constituency responsiveness, and membership accountability.
First of all, the Table shows *there is no organizational strategy simultaneously
maximizing all three criteria of democratic legitimacy*. In contrast to Arrow's
logical impossibility theorem of democratic choice, we could call this an
empirical impossibility theorem of democratic representation and legitimacy
by party governance. In selecting an organizational form party activists inevitably face tradeoffs among democratic objectives. The normative discourse
about party structures in competitive democracies thus revolves around arguments justifying specific tradeoffs between competing organizational forms.

Cell 4 corresponds to the choice left-libertarian parties have initially made
(decentralization/low formalization). As I have argued throughout this book,
militants in ecology parties approximating a logic of constituency representation are not content with its results. Normative criteria of democratic legitimacy tell us why: Stratarchal, disjointed framework parties are neither particularly responsive to their constituencies, because linkages are loose and
intermittent (Chapter 8), nor very accountable to their militants, because
power is diffuse and resides with informal cliques and political entrepreneurs
(Chapter 6). Where this form of organization does worst, however, is in terms
of its electoral effectiveness and legitimacy. Because the parties provide few
structural means for establishing a clear link between the voters' choices and
the actual strategies pursued by the parties after elections, these parties can
count only on limited, volatile electoral support.

Cell 1 represents the reverse situation of cell 4 both in structural respects as
well as democratic payoffs. Centralization of authority and formalized decision-making procedures are attributes of conventional European mass apparatus parties. Both features bolster their electoral effectiveness and have led
party theorists to reject more decentralized, informal, and fluid internal decision-making procedures. From Michels and Weber to the present, the meta-
phor of the party as an army fighting against competing armies has been
invoked to defend a centralist, disciplined organization as a norm of democratic competition. As Wilson (1962:347–51) noted in one of the first studies

Table 43
Four patterns of party organization and their consequences for democratic rule and legitimacy

Formalization of the intraparty decision-making procedures	*Centralization/personalization of authority*	
	High electoral effectiveness: +1 constituency responsiveness: +1 membership accountability: −1	**Low** electoral effectiveness: −1 constituency responsiveness: −1 membership accountability: +1
High electoral effectiveness: +1 constituency responsiveness: −1 membership accountability: +1	Conventional European mass apparatus party effectiveness: +2 responsiveness: +/−0 accountability: +/−0	Formal party democracy accountability: +2 effectiveness: +/−0 responsiveness: −2
Low electoral effectiveness: −1 constituency responsiveness: +1 membership accountability: −1	Entrepreneurial framework party responsiveness: +2 effectiveness: +/−0 accountability: −2	Stratarchal postindustrial framework party responsiveness: +/−0 accountability: +/−0 effectiveness: −2

of left-libertarian politics, it is contradictory to combine a participatory, decentralized, leaderless party organization with the external imperatives of electoral competition: "The party is an agent of conflict, an instrument of political warfare, for which internal democracy is about as useful as it would be for an army. . . . Program implies discipline, but discipline, as the history of West European socialist parties abundantly suggests, is the enemy of party democracy." (Wilson 1962:347–49)

Here Wilson expresses the consensus of modern "realist" theories of party politics maintaining that internal party democracy and electoral effectiveness are technically incompatible. Giving this argument a normative turn, McKenzie (1955; 1982) and others have suggested that societal democracy and party competition can function only as long as intraparty democracy is firmly suppressed by the party leadership. Empirically, this argument rests on the assumption that militants systematically distort the general population's preferences and are always more radical than party leaders, a proposition I challenged in Chapter 2 and 7. For a purely normative analysis, however, it is more important to note that McKenzie and his followers claim that the demands and wishes of party militants—and, implicitly, also those of mobilized constituency organizations such as labor unions or left-libertarian social movements—are irrelevant to the democratic legitimacy of political parties. In other words, the "realist" theory of democracy asserts that the contest for votes is a satisfactory democratic mode of linking citizens and state. Hence, it rejects responsiveness to constituency groups and accountability to activists as criteria of a democratic order.

The rise of left-libertarian parties shows, however, that sizable groups in modern society have developed a contrary view of democracy and party legitimacy. These groups call for a different balance of electoral effectiveness, democratic accountability, and constituency responsiveness. Wilson's and McKenzie's model may work well in democracies where either (1) cleavages are not highly polarized or (2) parties are able to cater to very large, homogeneous groups of voters firmly tied to the political orbit of a party. As party identification weakens and more sizable electorates vote on issues cutting across the established lines of political interest aggregation represented by mass parties, it is arguable whether the principle of electoral effectiveness maintains its supremacy vis-à-vis the principles of constituency responsiveness and membership accountability. As the state intervenes in more and more spheres of civil society, voting for parties or individual candidates becomes too indirect a mode of democratic communication to satisfy citizens. Mass apparatus parties face the problem that they cannot serve groups with highly specific and intense political concerns. At the same time, greater popular demand for participatory involvement in policy making calls into question the ability of conventional parties to continue to rank electoral effectiveness higher than constituency responsiveness or accountability.

For this reason the common wisdom of mainstream empirical and normative democratic theory maintaining that political parties are structurally compelled and normatively obliged to adopt a logic of party competition with
centralized, personalized authority and formal control of the party apparatus,
becomes questionable. Yet we have seen that the stratarchal, disjointed dynamic of left-libertarian parties hardly represents an improvement on the
structural problems of democratic politics to which these parties initially
respond (cell 4 in Table 43). For this reason it is worthwhile to explore two
other options we have not yet considered but which have played a role in the
learning process left-libertarian party activists themselves have initiated when
faced with the perverse effects and structural constraints to which a fluid,
stratarchal framework party is subjected.

Ecology party pragmatists in particular, but also some of the more instrumental ideologues (ecosocialists), favor a greater formalization of decision
making while simultaneously avoiding centralization of political authority
(cell 2). The key idea behind a more formalized party is to strengthen the
accountability of party leaders to rank-and-file militants through more rigorous principles of *representation* and *delegation* of authority. Formal representation would enhance the influence of resource-poor activists in relation to the
informal elites of permanently mobilized militants. It would combine formal
office and actual power and accountability. Furthermore, professionalization
of office and greater emphasis on intraorganizational criteria of advancement
would create incentives for militants to run for less popular party offices.

A formalized democratic party, however, runs into strong resistance on
several counts. Formalization undermines the vision of community and openness many militants in the parties still hold. What may be more significant in
the long run—a fear shared even by pragmatists—is that a stronger formal
organization will undermine the parties' *responsiveness* to its external constituencies. Ecology parties operate in complex, changing environments. They
try to represent new and dynamic social demands crystallized around unstable
social milieus and ideologies. The more turbulent an organization's environment, the less bureaucratic organizations with formal rules, clear chains of
command, and routine programs are able to respond to and cope with external
demands.[12] Formalization would foster a rigidity that would remove the most
important potential advantage left-libertarian parties have over their conventional competitors: their ability to place new issues on the political agenda and
catch their adversaries off-guard. Moreover, advocates of more intraparty
democracy must confront the question of *how relevant* it is as a way of

12. I am relying here on the findings of structural contingency theories of organization, such
as Emery and Trist (1965), Perrow (1972) and Thompson (1967). Similarly, Sharkansky
(1970:126) notes that political parties lack the routine tasks and communications with their
environment that would facilitate formal bureaucratization.

legitimizing left-libertarian parties, since they have by far the lowest member/voter ratio among electorally significant northwest European parties. How much democratic legitimacy can a party gain from becoming accountable to 0.2 percent of its electorate rather than 0.1 percent?

For this reason left-libertarian parties may consider a third option of reform located in cell 3 of Table 43: maintain an informal, fluid party structure but enhance the authority of political entrepreneurs over crucial decisions and increase their political visibility and responsibility. In practice, the fluid, decentralized ecology parties have already accommodated to a certain personalization of political power. Yet this study has shown that for many militants politcal entrepreneurs are also the villains, the shadowy figures who bring about the perverse effects that undermine intraparty democracy. What would be needed to implement reform option three, then, is less a structural and strategic transformation than a conscious recognition of the importance of political entrepreneurs. The militants would have to subscribe to a new democratic theory to legitimize the factual rather than the idealized difference of ecology parties from their conventional competitors. An entrepreneurial framework organization increases the capacity of left-libertarian parties to seize on new topics and develop new political ideas far beyond what is possible in conventional parties (democratic responsiveness). At the same time, left-libertarian parties would remove some of the roadblocks limiting their electoral effectiveness.

The cost of an entrepreneurial framework would have to be borne primarily by the party activists because no other form of organization promises an equally limited accountability of the leadership to them. At first sight, therefore, this model appears to face insurmountable obstacles to its implementation. Yet five conditions may increase its feasibility. First, the recognition of entrepreneurial authority represents less of a departure from de facto power distribution than formalization of party structure. Second, political entrepreneurs do not form a cohesive leadership with separate interests but a set of competing cliques, offering alternative political visions on which members are requested to vote periodically. Intraparty democracy will therefore be preserved as competition among rival cliques. Third, entrepreneurial leadership can be constrained by plebiscitary procedures (intraparty primaries, referendums) to which leaders have to submit themselves at certain intervals.

Fourth, since a postindustrial framework party lacks a mass organization, the ability of political entrepreneurs to dominate it will always be limited because they lack the resources, the patronage, and the personnel to implement their ideas against resistance from the rank and file or from external constituencies. Postindustrial political entrepreneurs rely on the *power of persuasion* rather than on that of bureaucratic control. To accept greater personalization of authority, party militants would have to subscribe to a model of democracy which lies somewhere between the "anarchy" of grassroots control and the oligarchy of party leaders. Lewin (1980:16–19) has called this new model *interactive democracy.*[13] Interactive democracy relies on the debate and active participation of the rank and file in critical strategic choices but allows leaders to make responsible decisions on behalf of the entire collectivity even when they are not directly approved by the rank and file. On the part of party militants interactive democracy presupposes some willingness to accept leadership but also a certain "civic spirit" (Lewin) and loyalty to the party.

Fifth, the power of the leadership in left-libertarian framework parties without bureaucracy is limited by the relatively weak role the parties could play in the policy-making process. The parties lack extensive patronage networks and centralized external constituency organizations that could serve as "transmission belts" for strategies chosen by party leaders. These limitations of party power are not pious hopes without corresponding evidence in reality but represent traits of left-libertarian politics that can already be observed in practice.

Left-libertarian parties signal a devolution of the role of parties in the policy process and require other vehicles of political interest intermediation linking state and civil society to fill the void. A comparable devolution of political parties had already been called for and expected by early party theorists. Ostrogorski, the first student of party organization, claimed that industrial society is divided into too many groups and issue cleavages to afford a generalization and simplification of political alternatives around the package deals a few parties can offer (Ostrogorski 1902/64:327–29). Instead, he envisioned special interest groups with single issue objectives as the prime agents of policy making (ibid. 356–57). He believed these groups should be embedded in a decentralized social and political structure that would facilitate participatory self-government.

Criticizing Ostrogorski's vision, Lipset argues that the lower classes especially can gain power only through centralized political machines and democratic party competition: "The failure to recognize that organized parties, party machines, even party oligarchies, contribute to the operation of democracy at every level of government, is the great defect of Ostrogorski's analysis." (Lipset 1964:lxiii)

Lipset is probably correct in his observation that the organization of class cleavage intrinsically depends on large party machines. But with the transformation of cleavage structures in modern capitalist democracies and the left-libertarian movements' and parties' challenge to the established networks of interest intermediation, Ostrogorski's analysis is gaining new importance.

13. A similar suggestion has been made by Günther (1979:11–17) who contrasts consultative-representative democracy to receptive-representative democracy.

Mass and state parties may have exhausted their capacity to mobilize and incorporate new political demands into the existing patterns of linkage between state and civil society. At least on the left side of the political spectrum where groups demand a more participatory society, the cohesion of mass parties is being undermined, bringing about a pluralization of forms of conflict resolution through new parties, interest groups, and social movements (see Olsen 1983). If nothing else, the Belgian and West German ecology parties are one sign of the momentum left-libertarian calls for a democratization of society have gained in the 1980s.

Appendix | Research Design and Methodology

Research Design

Kenneth Janda (1983:319) found that all empirical comparative studies of party organization across nations would fit into a single briefcase. In his view comparative research is hampered by the fact that party organization is hard to define and is a fluid empirical phenomenon. Moreover, practical requirements (such as language competence) and political accessibility have kept the number of comparative studies low. The few in-depth comparative analyses of political parties rely primarily on secondary materials (see Lawson 1976).

Over the past fifteen years Janda and his associates have made an effort to develop a "most different systems" comparison of parties in a wide variety of political settings to explore common factors shaping their structure and behavior. They have collected a large inventory of data on 147 parties in 53 countries.[1] Based on secondary analysis of case studies, Janda identifies a host of variables for which values can be determined across a wide range of parties. Janda's studies have yielded a number of plausible and significant results. They demonstrate that institutional properties of political regimes influence the structure of parties (Harmel and Janda 1982). They also confirm Duverger's theory of mass and cadre parties, which identifies leftism as the major determinant of high structural articulation in political parties (Janda and King 1985).

Nevertheless, a survey-type most different systems comparison of parties has several drawbacks. First, the reliability and validity of the data about a large set of political parties is often poor and/or the coding of variables is open to debate. Moreover, only those indicators can be included in the survey for which data on a sufficient number of cases can be identified. As a consequence

1. Compare Harmel and Janda (1982), Janda (1980; 1983), and Janda and King (1985).

the most different systems approach relies predominantly on the *formal structure* of political parties, as laid down in party statutes. Most analysts of complex organizations would argue that in practice, however, the formal structure is of limited use for understanding behavioral patterns and power relations in parties. Particularly in voluntary organizations, the informal, personalized networks of communication may be more important (Horch 1982). Ecology parties, in their zeal to minimize the role of formal structures, are an extreme case in which the formal statutes of the parties say relatively little about the actual process of communication and control in the organization. Using Janda's (1980) operational variables, the parties would appear not very different from their Belgian and West German competitors.

For these reasons I have chosen a "most similar systems" design for comparing a very limited number of parties. In this design all parties operate in a similar basic institutional setting (advanced industrial democracies with parliamentary government) and only select environmental features vary from case to case. This design enabled me to collect in-depth data on each case which broadens the range, reliability, and validity of the information used in the analysis.

Of course, there are always more variables than cases in most similar systems analyses. The capacity to generalize research findings based on this research design is thus limited (Lijphart 1971). I have been able, however, to increase the number of cases beyond the three ecology parties in Belgium and West Germany (1) by breaking down the ecology parties into smaller subnational units and (2) by comparing them to traditional Belgian and West German party organizations which have been examined in numerous other empirical studies. This disaggregation makes it possible to test some of my hypotheses about the link between the environment of political parties and their internal process against a broader set of cases.

Two critical environmental determinants of party organization vary across smaller subnational party units: the mobilization of left-libertarian social movements and the competitive position of the parties. In my interviews I gathered data on thirty-three Green district party organizations and eighteen Ecolo and Agalev local organizations. Using information on each district's population size and degree of urbanization, its occupational profile, its electoral support of ecology parties and, most importantly, the breadth and intensity of its left-libertarian social movements, I have classified each district according to its level of left-libertarian cleavage mobilization. Because I lack precise measures of mobilization and a method of aggregating values on each of the other variables, there is an ineradicable element of judgment in this procedure. Table 44 provides the list of all party districts or (in Belgium) local sections that I have classified as having high, medium, or low left-libertarian mobilization. In the actual analysis I have usually dropped the distinction

Table 44
Local party organizations covered in interviews

		West Germany	Belgium
Level of left-libertarian mobilization	High	Bielefeld, Bochum, Bremen, Frankfurt, Freiburg, Heidelberg, Hamburg, Karlsruhe, Konstanz, Marburg, Nürnberg, Tübingen	Brussels (Ecolo), Brussels (Agalev), Ghent, Leuven (city), Ottignies/Louvain-la-Neuve
	Medium	Gross-Gerau, Hochtaunus, Kaiserslautern, Offenbach, Pforzheim, Pinneberg, Regensburg, Rems-Murr, Stuttgart, Wiesbaden	Antwerp, Mechelen, Liège, Namur
	Low	Bergstrasse, Böblingen, Celle, Emmendingen, Erdingen, Ettlingen, Geilenkirchen, Hersfeld, Hof, Offenburg, Schwäbisch-Gemünd, Vogelsberg	Furnaux, Grand-Hallet, Leuven (county), Ghent (county), Lontzen, Scheldewindeke, St. Antonius-Zoersel

between low and medium levels of mobilization. Only the difference between the centers of left-libertarian politics and both periphery and "semi-periphery" appears to account for differences of party organization.

The relative number of districts in the centers of left-libertarian conflict is smaller in Belgium than in West Germany. This is not a bias in my sampling process but attributable to the relative absence of highly mobilized party districts in Belgium even if we correct for the different size of the two countries. Moreover, the Belgian districts with high left-libertarian mobilization are, in general, still less mobilized than their West German counterparts. When we aggregate the level of cleavage mobilization in individual districts to create a summary index of the national environment of party organization, the Greens operate in an environment of higher left-libertarian mobilization than either Agalev or Ecolo.

The competitive position of ecology parties has been measured in terms of their actual or expected ability to form coalition governments with other parties so inclined. As I have shown in Chapter 9, only in Hesse (1982–1987), in Hamburg (1982 and 1987), and marginally in Wallonia, ecology parties found themselves in a strong position at the state or national level. In a number of German state elections, however, the competition between the conservative/liberal coalition government and the Social Democrats and Greens was close enough to expect the possibility of a socialist-green alliance. The *prospect* of this situation alone may fuel changes within parties, e.g., the influx of pragmatic militants and increasing strategic factionalism, which enable us to infer what happens if parties *actually* gain a strong electoral position. In numerous local governments such as Bielefeld, Freiburg, Liège, Nuremberg, Tübingen, and Wiesbaden, ecology parties have occupied a strong electoral position. Yet the stakes of local politics are too low to count these cases as serious tests of party dynamics under conditions of strong electoral competitiveness.

Data Collection

In the literature on political party organizations at least two different approaches have been employed to gather and analyze data. On the one hand, most American and a few European studies rely on interview surveys among party militants.[2] On the other hand, most European research builds on direct observation of party meetings, in-depth open interviews with party functionaries, or documentary analysis.[3] The choice of empirical research techniques is influenced by the object of analysis itself. Surveys are useful instruments for exploring the individual party members' motivations, perceptions, and behaviors, but they are less well adapted to the analysis of organizational structures and processes. Political organizations in particular must be studied with other than survey techniques to shed light on the distribution of power and decision-making authority.[4]

A second reason why survey techniques are of limited help in the analysis of highly structured parties concerns the sensitivity of the data researchers are trying to gather. Political parties refuse to unveil their power structures to the outside observer and usually prohibit surveys on delicate political issues. Information about their internal organization, or even their militants' attitudes, may become weapons in the hands of the adversary. In the case of ecology parties, particularly in areas with high mobilization, there is another reason why it is difficult to use survey techniques. Many militants reject "hard" social science based on survey research because they perceive this approach as a "tool of political domination" and part of the same technocratic logic they fight politically. In West Germany this sensitivity about surveys has been further increased by a prolonged national controversy over a new census

2. Some of the best research in this tradition is Eldersveld (1964) and Kornberg et al. (1979). For studies on European parties compare Barnes (1967), Falke (1982), Hauss (1978), Logue (1982), Valen and Katz (1964), and most recently the very interesting study by Greven (1987) which includes a small number of Green activists from one single party district. An effort to test some of the hypotheses underlying this book through a survey taken among Belgian Agalev and Ecolo activists is in preparation. See Kitschelt and Hellemans (forthcoming).

3. Significant studies using this approach are Günther (1979), Jenson and Ross (1984), Lammert (1976), Lohmar (1963), Mayntz (1959), McKenzie (1955), Minkin (1978), Mintzel (1975), and Raschke (1974).

4. This point has been forcefully made by Warwick (1975) in his research on the power structure of the U.S. Department of State.

Table 45
Selection of interviewees—region

	West Germany	Belgium	
Areas with a high mobilization of left-libertarian movements	47	19	N = 66
Areas with a medium mobilization of left-libertarian movements	26	21	N = 47 ⎫
Areas with a low mobilization of left-libertarian movements	13	8	N = 21 ⎭ N = 68

questionnaire. Its first draft was successfully blocked by the Greens and other organizations in the early 1980s through demonstrations and lawsuits in which the West German constitutional court found the questionnaire to constitute a serious infringement of civil liberties. For these reasons the German Greens are not amenable to survey research.[5] In Agalev and Ecolo the situation is more favorable. With the aid of the party secretariats, a colleague and I were able to carry out a survey among 260 party militants who attended national party conferences in October 1985. Because comparable data for the West German Greens are lacking, findings of this study will be reported elsewhere (Kitschelt and Hellemans forthcoming).

As an alternative to the survey I interviewed key party militants at local, state, and national levels of the party organization. Over a period of nine months, I conducted 134 interviews, eighty-six in West Germany and forty-eight in Belgium, at various research sites. Four criteria governed my selection of interviewees. First, all had to be active participants in the ecology parties for at least one, but preferably several, years. Second, I chose interviewees from a wide variety of regional party organizations. In the West German Greens, for instance, I selected national politicians from strongholds and weak party districts. I then interviewed activists in three state party headquarters and in the seats of the state party parliamentary groups in Hamburg, Hesse, and Baden-Württemberg. In order to increase the scope of data on different elements of ecology party organizations further, I visited strongholds and areas of weak support within each state. A similar procedure was followed in Belgium. Table 45 disaggregates the interviewed party militants by area of left-libertarian cleavage mobilization. While the total number of interviews in the centers and peripheries of the cleavage is about the same, it varies by country. In Belgium more activists from the semi-periphery were

5. A social scientist in the Green national executive confided to me that his efforts to carry out a survey among party militants had failed repeatedly because of political objections. These political obstacles are exacerbated by practical ones. The Greens lack a national membership file, thus ruling out a randomized sampling technique.

Table 46
Selection of interviewees—office

	West Germany	Belgium	
Members of state and national parliaments	42	7	N = 49
Municipal councilors	20	14	N = 34
Members of state and national party executives	16	18	N = 34
Administrative employees/other activists	8	9	N = 17

interviewed than in West Germany because there are relatively few areas of high mobilization in Belgium.

In order to include activists with different experiences and perspectives on ecology parties, I employed office holding as the third criterion for selecting interviewees. I interviewed (1) elected representatives in state and national parliaments, (2) municipal councilors, (3) members of the parties' regional or national executive boards, and (4) salaried party employees and a very few volunteer workers in the parties' administrative organization (editors of membership newsletters, etc.). In the few instances where activists had held several offices, they were classified according to the most influential office they had held. Table 46 provides a breakdown of the 134 interviewees according to office.

The emphasis on office holders and cadre activists in ecology parties might suggest a one-sided image of the parties' actual operation which excludes the perspective of the marginally involved rank-and-file militants. But in fact most of the interviewed militants had extensive experience with diverse aspects of party life. Moreover, municipal councilors at least work very close to the grassroots level of party organization. Based on observations in my occasional participation in local party meetings, I believe that the interviews do not distort the experiences of rank-and-file militants.

Strategy toward other parties and the degree of radicalism of party programs are subjects of many intense debates within ecology parties. For this reason it was imperative to include all relevant strategic tendencies in the interviews. Affiliation with factions and tendencies provided the fourth criterion for selecting militants for this study. A careful matching of political tendencies in the pool of interviewees also ensures detection of differences in perception of party politics linked to an interviewee's affiliation. In practice, different views of the party by faction were caused more by the evaluation of party processes than disagreements about the actual functioning of the parties. Table 47 divides the entire pool of interviewees into three groups. Party members could identify themselves as "radical," "uncommitted," or "moderate." The imbalance of radicals and moderates in Agalev and Ecolo is not a sampling

Table 47
Selection of interviewees—political tendencies: strategic commitment

	West Germany	Belgium	
Moderates	27	37	N = 64
Uncommitted	25	8	N = 33
Radicals	34	3	N = 37

error but due to the difficulty of encountering radicals among the core party militants.

The interviews were built on a semistructured schedule of questions that invited the miltants to interpret their political experience in the party. They were first asked to give a brief account of their own political biography, which included information on their initial political activities, and their affiliation with parties, interest groups, and social movements before joining the ecology party. This introduction was followed by a battery of questions concerning motivations and aspirations, and included the political significance of membership, the (co)existence of different political generations in the party, and the turnover of activists.

The next set of questions turned to the local party organization. The level and distribution of participation, topics of debate in meetings, links between the local level and the central party organs, and ties among elected representatives of the local party organizations were discussed. If the interviewee was a municipal councilor, a number of questions concerned his or her activities in the council.

The questionnaire went on to query the activists' choice of career paths inside the parties and explored motivations and opportunities for seeking political office. This topic served as a transition to discussing the role and performance of various decision-making bodies in the parties at large, such as parliamentary party groups, party executives, and national conventions. The interviewees were asked to report their own experiences, and to address questions such as the cohesiveness, centralization of authority, and process of consensus building within the parties.

The next section of the interview concerned the contacts interviewees maintained with external constituency groups or other nonparty political actors. Municipal councilors and members of parliament in particular were asked to list their regular conversation partners and describe their cooperation with social movement activists. The final topic of the interviews concerned evaluation of imminent internal and external party strategy and of the broader national role the parties (should) play. I asked interviewees to explain their parties' factional divisions and to assess the relative strength and style of political argument typical of each faction. I also asked them to compare their own party to other ecology parties. In Belgium most interviewees had sufficient knowledge to compare their own ecology party to its counterpart across the linguistic border in Belgium and to the West German Greens. Yet very few German Greens had ever read or heard of the Belgian ecology parties and often were unable to recognize their names.

Two factors determined the precise range and intensity with which certain topics were covered in the interviews. First, the ability of an interviewee to answer the questions often depended on his or her experience in a certain arena of party politics. As a rule most time was devoted to those aspects the interviewee was most familiar with. Second, the time constraints of the interviewee were a deciding factor. The less time an interviewee could afford for the conversation, the more my questions focused on the core areas of an activist's political involvement. Questions concerning the political biography and membership were asked in all cases.

Although the questions were not always asked in the same sequence and wording, but brought up in the flow of the conversation, each item was transcribed from interview notes with a uniform code number in a standard sequence for all questions. Answers to individual questions could thus be easily retrieved from each interview. In the data analysis, all statements belonging to one code number were systematically drawn together from the interviews and then examined to detect general patterns and variations of experiences. Given that the number of interviews is quite small by normal survey research standards, the data are usually not reported in quantitative form. An exception are strictly individual-level data, for instance information about the socioeconomic status and political biography. I have also refrained from giving lengthy quotations or paraphrases of interview responses in order to pare the text to a manageable length.

As is evidenced by the paucity of references to other materials and studies about ecology parties, virtually all information reported in Chapters 4 through 9 is taken from the interviews and the large amount of other primary materials such as party documents, membership newsletters, and news media coverage analyzed in the preparation of this study. At the time of this writing, no single major analysis of ecology parties in the social sciences has yet been published.

Bibliography

Abrahamson, Paul R., and Ronald Inglehart. 1986. "Generational Replacement and Value Change in Six West European Societies." *American Journal of Political Science*, 30, no. 1: 1–25.

Agalev. 1981. *Echt nieuw & echt anders*. Borgerhout: Uitgeverij Stil-Leven.

———. 1982. *Statuten*. Brussels: Agalev.

———. 1983. "Beginselverklaring." In: *Blad Groen*, 2, special issue.

——— 1985a *Krachtlijnenprogramma AGALEV '85*. Brussels: Agalev.

——— 1985b *Vier jaar groénen in het parlament. 1981–1985*. Brussels: Agalev.

Agalev, Werkgroep Economie. 1984. *Op Mensenmaat. Een Groene Kijk op Economie*. Brussels: Dirk Vansitjan, Uitgever.

Alber, Jens. 1985. "Modernisierung, neue Spannungslinien und die politischen Chancen der Grünen." *Politische Vierteljahresschriften*, 26, no. 3: 211–26.

Aldrich, John H. 1983. "A Downsian Spatial Model with Party Activism." *American Political Science Review*, 77, no. 4: 974–90.

Alemann, Ulrich v. and Rolf Heinze eds. 1979. *Verbände und Staat. Vom Pluralismus zum Korporatismus. Analysen, Positionen, Dokumente*. Opladen: Westdeutscher Verlag.

Alternative Liste Fraktion. 1984. *Rechenschaftsbericht der Fraktion der AL Berlin, 1983/84*. Berlin: AL Fraktion.

Andersen, Jorgen Goul. 1984. "Decline of Class Voting or Change in Class Voting? Social Classes and Party Choice in Denmark in the 1970s." *European Journal of Political Research*, 12, no. 3: 243–59.

Arbeitsgemeinschaft Radikalökologische Foren. 1984. *Radikalökologische Politik. Dokumentation radikalökologischer Diskussionsbeiträge in den Grünen Hessen*. Frankfurt: Eigendruck.

Arrow, Kenneth. 1963. *Social Choice and Individual Values*, 2d ed. New Haven, Conn.: Yale University Press.

Ash, Roberta. 1972. *Social Movements in America*. Chicago: Markham.

Axelrod, Robert. 1984. *The Evolution of Cooperation*. New York: Basic Books.

Badura, Bernhard and Jürgen Reese. 1976. *Jungparlamentarier in Bonn. Ihre Sozialisation im Deutschen Bundestag*. Stuttgart: fromann-holzboog.

Bahro, Rudolf. 1984a. "Fundamentalistisches zur Krise der Grünen." In: *Kommune*, 2, no. 6: 47–50.

——. 1984b. *Pfeiler am anderen Ufer: Beiträge zur Politik der Grünen von Hagen bis Karlsruhe*. Berlin: Befreiung.

Baker, Kendall L., Russel Dalton, and Kai Hildebrandt. 1981. *Germany Transformed: Political Culture and the New Politics*. Cambridge, Mass.: Harvard University Press.

Barnes, Samuel H. 1967. *Party Democracy: Politics in an Italian Socialist Federation*. New Haven and London: Yale University Press.

——. 1968. "Party Democracy and the Logic of Collective Action," 105–38. In William J. Crotty, ed., *Approaches to the Study of Party Organization*. Boston: Allyn and Bacon.

Barnes, Samuel H., and Max Kaase, eds. 1979. *Political Action. Mass Participation in Five Western Democracies*. Beverly Hills: Sage.

Bartolini, Stefano. 1983. "The Membership of Mass Parties: The Social Democratic Experience, 1889–1978," 177–220. In: Hans Daalder and Peter Mair, eds., *Western European Party Systems. Stability and Change*. Beverly Hills, Calif. Sage.

Baumgarten, Jürgen, ed. 1982. *Linkssozialisten in Europa. Alternative zu Sozialdemokratie und kommunistischen Parteien*. Hamburg: Junius.

Beaufays, Jean, Michel Hermans, and Pierre Verjans. 1983. "Les élections communales a Liège: cartels, polarisation et les écologistes au pouvoir." In: *Res Publica*, 25, no. 2/3: 391–415.

Beck, Ulrich. 1983. "Jenseits von Stand und Klasse? Soziale Ungleichheiten, gesellschaftliche Individualisierungsprozesse und die Entstehung neuer sozialer Formationen und Identitäten." *Soziale Welt*, 34, no. 1: 35–74.

Beckenbach, Frank, Jo Müller, Reinhard Pfriem, and Eckhard Stratmann, eds. 1985. *Grüne Wirtschaftspolitik. Machbare Utopien*. Cologne: Kiepenheuer und Witsch.

Becker, Horst, and Bodo Hombach. 1983. *Die SPD von Innen. Bestandaufnahme an der Basis der Partei*. Bonn: Verlag Neue Gesellschaft.

Beddermann, Carl. 1978. "Die 'Grüne Liste Umweltschutz' in Niedersachsen," 105–16. In: Rudolf Brun, ed., *Der Grüne Protest*. Frankfurt/Main: Fischer.

Bell, Daniel. 1973. *The Coming of Post-industrial Society: A Venture in Social Forecasting*. New York: Basic Books.

——. 1976. *The Cultural Contradictions of Capitalism*. New York: Basic Books.

Beller, Dennis C., and Frank P. Belloni. 1978. *Faction Politics. Political Parties and Factionalism in Comparative Perspective*. Santa Barbara, Calif.: ABC/Clio.

Berger, Johannes, Joachim Müller and Reinhard Pfriem, eds. 1982. *Kongress "Zukunft der Arbeit." Materialienband*. Hannover SOAK.

Berger, Johannes, and Norbert Kostede. 1983. "Fundamentalopposition und Reformpolitik", 13–27. In: Wolfgang Kraushaar, ed. *Was sollen die Grünen im Parlament?* Berlin: Verlag Neue Kritik.

Berger, Manfred, Wolfgang G. Gibowski, Dieter Roth, and Wolfgang Schulte. 1983. "Regierungswechsel und politische Einstellungen: Eine Analyse der Bundestagswahl 1983." *Zeitschrift für Parlamentsfragen*, 14, no. 4: 556–82.

——. 1987. "Die Konsolidierung der Wende. Eine Analyse der Bundestagswahl 1987." *Zeitschrift für Parlamentsfragen*, 18, no. 2: 253–84.

Berger, Suzanne. 1979. "Politics and Anti-politics in Western Europe in the Seventies." *Daedalus*, 108, no. 2: 27–50.

——. 1981. ed. *Organizing Interest Groups in Western Europe*. New York: Cambridge University Press.

Bergmann, Eckhard, and Dietmar Krischausky. 1985. "Wirtschaftsreform. Die verlorene Utopie?" *Kommune*, 3, no. 5: 47–59.

Bergmann, Joachim, Gerhard Brandt, Klaus Körber, Otto Mohl, and Claus Offe. 1969. "Herrschaft, Klassenverhältnis und Schichtung," 67–87. In: Theodor W. Adorno, ed., *Spätkapitalismus oder Industriegesellschaft?* Stuttgart: Enke.

Berschien, Helmut. 1984. "Liebe Freundinnen und Freunde! Über die Sprache der Grünen im Bundestag," 73–84. In Klaus Gotto and Hans Joachim Veen eds., *Die Grünen. Partei wider Willen.* Mainz: v. Hase & Koehler.

Beywl, Wolfgang, and Hartmut Brombach 1984. "Neue Selbstorganisation. Zwischen kultureller Autonomie und politischer Vereinnahmung," *Aus Politik und Zeitgeschichte,* 34, no. 11 (March 17, 1984): 15–29.

Bickerich, Wolfram, ed. 1985. *SPD und Grüne. Das neue Bündnis?* Reinbek: Rowohlt.

Billiet, J. 1984. "On Belgian Pillarization. Changing Perspectives." *Acta Politica,* 19, no. 1: 117–28.

Billiet, J., and Luc Huyse. 1984. "Verzorgingsstaat en verzuiling: een dubbelzinnige relatie." *Tijdschrift voor Sociologie,* 5, no. 1/2: 129–51.

Boch, Rudolf, Rainer Schiller-Dickhut, and Michael Winter. 1981. "Die alternative Wahlbewegung und die Kommunalpolitik. Das Beispiel Bielefeld," 9–43. In: *Alternative Stadtpolitik.* Hamburg: Verlag für das Studium der Arbeiterbewegung.

Bolaffi, Angelo, and Otto Kallscheuer. 1983. "Die Grünen: Farbenlehre eines politischen Paradoxes. Zwischen neuen Bewegungen und Veränderung der Politik." *Prokla,* 13, no. 2: 62–105.

Boudon, Raymond. 1977. *Effets pervers et ordre social.* Paris: Presses Universitaires de France.

———. 1984. *La logique du désordre.* Paris: Presses Universitaires de France.

Boy, Daniel. 1981. "Le vote écologiste en 1978." *Revue française de science politique,* 31, no. 2: 394–416.

Brady, David B. 1985. "A Reevaluation of Realignments in American Politics: Evidence from the House of Representatives." *American Political Science Review,* 79, no. 1: 28–49.

Brand, Jack. 1973. "Party Organization and the Recruitment of Councillors," *British Journal of Political Science,* 3, no. 4: 473–86.

Brand, Karl-Werner, Detlef Büsser, and Dieter Rucht. 1983. *Aufbruch in eine andere Gesellschaft. Neue soziale Bewegungen in der Bundesrepublik.* Frankfurt/Main: Campus.

Braunthal, Gerard. 1983. *The West German Social Democrats, 1969–1982: Profile of a Party in Power.* Boulder: Westview Press.

Briem, Jürgen. 1976. *Der SDS. Die Geschichte des bedeutendsten Studentenverbandes der Bundesrepublik seit 1945.* Frankfurt: Paedex Verlag.

Browne, Eric C. 1982. "Conclusion: Considerations on the Construction of a Theory of Cabinet Coalition Behavior," 335–57. In Eric C. Browne and John Dreijmanis, eds., *Government Coalitions in Western Democracies.* New York: Longman.

Browne, Eric C., and Mark N. Franklin. 1986. "Editors' Introduction: New Directions in Coalition Research." *Legislative Studies Quarterly* 11, no. 4: 469–83.

Brun, Rudolf ed. 1978. *Der grüne Protest.* Frankfurt/Main: Fischer.

Buchanan, James M., and Gordon Tullock. 1962. *The Calculus of Consent. Logical Foundations of Constitutional Democracy.* Ann Arbor: University of Michigan Press.

Bühnemann, Michael, Michael Wendt, and Jürgen Wituschek, eds. 1984. *AL. Die Alternative Liste Berlin.* Berlin: LitPol.

Bundervoet, Jan. 1983. "Vakbond en politiek in crisistijd," *Res Publica,* 25, no.2–3: 220–36.

Bürklin, Wilhelm P. 1984a. *Grüne Politik. Ideologische Zyklen, Wähler und Parteiensystem.* Opladen: Westdeutscher Verlag.

———. 1984b. "Value Change and Partisan Realignment in West Germany, 1970–1983. Recent Findings and Some Political Interpretations." Paper presented at the 1984 APSA Convention. Washington, August 30–September 2.

——. 1985a. "The Greens: Ecology and the New Left," 187–218. In: H. G. Wallach and George K. Romoser, eds., *West German Politics in the Mid-Eighties. Crisis and Continuity*. New York: Praeger.

——. 1985b. "The German Greens: The Post-Industrial Non-Established and the Party System," *International Political Science Review*, 6, no. 4: 463–81.

——. 1987. "Governing left parties frustrating the radical non-established Left: the rise and inevitable decline of the Greens," *European Sociological Review*, 3, no. 2: 109–26.

Buyle, Daniel 1985. "Van pechstrook naar paradigma. De groenen in Vlaanderen." *De nieuwe Mand*, 28, no. 1: 16–27.

Cameron, David. 1984. "Social Democracy, Corporatism, Labour Quiescence, and the Representation of Economic Interest in Advanced Capitalist Society," 143–78. In: John H. Goldthorpe, *Order and Conflict in Contemporary Capitalism*. Oxford: Oxford University Press.

Case, John, and Rosemary C. R. Taylor, eds. 1979. *Coops, Communes and Collectives. Experiments in Social Change in the 1960s and 1970s*. New York: Pantheon Books.

Castles, Francis G. 1982. "The Impact of Parties on Public Expenditure," 21–96. In: Castles, ed., *The Impact of Parties*. Beverly Hills, Calif.: Sage.

Ceulers, Jan. 1977. "De lijstensamenstelling in de Belgische Socialistische Partij," *Res Publica*, 19, no. 3: 411–21.

——. 1981. (directing debate) "Evaluatie van de Partiecratie," *Res Publica*, 23, no. 2/3: 155–77.

Claeys, Paul H., and Nicole Loeb-Mayer. 1984. "Le 'para-fédéralisme' Belge. Une tentative de conciliation par la cloisonnement." In: *International Political Science Review*, 5, no. 4:473–90.

Clark, Peter B., and James Q. Wilson. 1961. "Incentive Systems: A Theory of Organizations." *Administrative Science Quarterly*, 6, no. 1:129–66.

Cochet, Yves. 1985. Analyse de l'électorat écologiste. France, 1984–85. Paris, unpublished manuscript.

Cohen, Michael D., James G. March, and Johan P. Olsen. 1972. "A Garbage Can Model of Organizational Choice." *Administrative Science Quarterly*, 17, no. 1: 1–25.

Conway, M. Margret, and Frank B. Feigert. 1968. "Motivation, Incentive Systems, and the Political Party Organization." *American Political Science Review*, 62, no. 4: 1159–73.

Cook, Philip J. 1971. "Robert Michels's Political Parties in Perspective." *Journal of Politics*, 33, no. 3: 773–96.

Costantini, Edmond 1963. "Intraparty Attitude Conflict: Democratic Party Leadership in California." *Western Political Quarterly* 16 (1963): 956–72.

Crotty, William J. 1970. "A Perspective for the Comparative Analysis of Political Parties." *Comparative Politics*, 3, no. 3: 267–96.

Crozier, Michel. 1964. *The Bureaucratic Phenomenon*. Chicago: Chicago University Press.

Curtis, Russell C., and Louis A. Zurcher. 1974. "Social Movements: An Analytical Exploration of Organizational Forms." *Social Problems*, 21, no. 3: 356–70.

Daalder, Hans, and Peter Mair, eds. 1983. *Western European Party Systems. Continuity and Change*. Beverly Hills, Calif: Sage.

Dahl, Robert A. 1956. *A Preface to Democratic Theory*. Chicago: Chicago University Press.

Dalton, Russell J. 1984a. "The West German Party System between Two Ages," 104–33. In: Russell J. Dalton, Scott C. Flanagan, and Paul Allen Beck eds., *Electoral Change in Advanced Industrial Democracies*. Princeton, New Jersey: Princeton University Press.

——. 1984b. Environmentalism and Value Change in Western Democracies. Paper prepared for delivery at the 1984 annual meeting of the American Political Science Association. Washington, August 30–September 2.

Dalton, Russell J., Scott C. Flanagan, and Paul Allen Beck. 1984a. "Electoral Change in Advanced Industrial Democracies," 3–22. In Dalton, Flanagan, and Beck, eds., *Electoral Change in Advanced Industrial Democracies*. Princeton, New Jersey: Princeton University Press.

——. 1984b. "Political Forces and Partisan Change", 451–76 in idem, eds., *Electoral Change in Advanced Industrial Democracies*. Princeton, New Jersey: Princeton University Press.

Defeyt, Philippe. 1985. Radioscopie de l'électorat écologiste. Unpublished paper, Namur 1985.

De Graeve-Lismont, Edith, 1975. "Het oppositioneel gedrag van de belgische staatsburger," *Res Publica*, 17, no. 4: 517–43.

DeNardo, James. 1985. *Power in Numbers. The Political Strategy of Protest and Rebellion*. Princeton, New Jersey: Princeton University Press.

Denver, D. T., and J. M. Bochel. 1973. "The Political Socialization of Activists in the British Communist Party." *The British Journal of Political Science*, 3, no. 1: 53–71.

De Roose, Frank. 1984. "De Groene Golf. Over de nationale diversiteit van een internationaal fenomeen." *De Groene Schriften*, 7: 33–61.

Deschouwer, Kris, and Patrick-Edward Stouthuysen. 1984. "L'Electorat d'Agalev." *CRISP. Courrier Hébdomadaire*, no. 1061 (December 7).

Dewachter, Wilfried and Edi Clijsters. 1982. "Belgium. Political Stability despite Coalition Crises," 187–216. In: Eric C. Browne and John Dreijmanis, eds., *Government Coalitions in Western Democracies*. New York: Longman.

De Winter, Lieven. 1981. "De parteipolitisering als instrument van particratie. Een overzicht van de ontwikkeling sinds de Tweede Wereldoorlog." *Res Publica*, 23, no. 1: 53–107.

Dierickx, Luido. 1979. *Denkwegen naar en globale visie. Meer dan een milieubeweging*. Enlarged edition March 1982. Ursel: De Groene Schriften.

Dittberner, Jürgen. 1970. "Die Rolle der Parteitage im Prozess der innerparteilichen Willensbildung," *Politische Vierteljahresschriften*, 11, no. 2/3: 236–68.

Dodd, Lawrence C. 1976. *Coalitions in Parliamentary Government*. Princeton, N.J.: Princeton University Press.

Dolive, Linda. 1976. *Electoral Politics at the Local Level in the German Federal Republic*. Gainesville: The University Presses of Florida.

Donati, Paolo R. 1984. "Organization Between Movement and Institution." *Social Science Information*, 23, no. 4/5: 837–59.

Downs, Anthony. 1957. *An Economic Theory of Democracy*. New York: Harper and Row.

——. 1967. *Inside Bureaucracy*. Boston: Little, Brown.

Drewitz, Ingeborg, ed. 1983. *The German Women's Movement*. Bonn: Hohwacht.

Duverger, Maurice. 1954. *Political Parties*. London: Methuen.

Dyson, Kenneth H. F. 1977. *Party, State, and Bureaucracy in Western Germany*. Beverly Hills: Sage.

——. 1982. "West Germany. The Search for a Rationalist Consensus," 16–46. In: Jeremy Richardson, ed., *Policy Styles in Western Europe*. Boston: Allen and Unwin.

Ebermann, Thomas. 1983. "Wer verbreitet hier eigentlich parlamentarische Illusionen?" 140–47. In: Wolfgang Kraushaar, ed., *Was sollen die Grünen im Parlament?* Berlin: Verlag Neue Kritik.

Ebermann, Thomas, and Rainer Trampert. 1984. *Die Zukunft der Grünen. Ein realistisches Konzept fur eine radikale Partei.* Hamburg: Konkret Verlag.

Ecolo. 1981. *Propositions des écologistes. Une autre manière de faire de la politique.* Namur: Ecolo.

———. 1982. *Une autre manière de vivre sa commune. Propositions des écologistes.* Namur: Ecolo.

———. 1985a. *Déclaration de Peruwelz-Louvain-La-Neuve. Exprimant les principes fondamentaux du Movement Ecolo.* Namur: Ecolo.

———. 1985b. "Textes préparatoires à l'assemblée générale socio-économique." *Ecolo Infos,* no. 56, May 12, 1985.

———. 1985c. *Quatre ans d'action politique.* Namur: Centre d'études et de formation en écologie. Namur: Ecolo.

———. 1985d. "Les Statuts du Mouvement Ecolo." *Ecolo Infos,* numéro spécial, February 1985.

Edler, Kurt. 1987. "Die GAL im eigenen Ghetto. Struktureller und ideologischer Hintergrund einer Wahlniederlage," *Kommune,* 5, no. 9: 35–39.

Eisinger, Peter K. 1973. "The Conditions of Protest Behavior in American Cities." *American Political Science Review,* 67, no. 1: 11–28.

Elder, Neil, and Rolf Gooderham. 1978. "The Centre Parties of Norway and Sweden," *Government and Opposition,* 13, no. 2: 218–35.

Eldersveld, Samuel J. 1964. *Political Parties: A Behavioral Analysis.* Chicago: Rand McNally.

———. 1982. *Political Parties in American Society.* New York: Basic Books.

———. 1983. "Motivations for Party Activism. Multi-National Uniformities and Differences." *International Political Science Review,* 4, no. 1: 57–70.

Ellemers, J. E. 1984. "Pillarization or a Process of Modernization." *Acta Politica,* 19, no. 1: 129–44.

Elster, Jon. 1979. *Ulysses and the Sirens.* Cambridge: Cambridge University Press.

———. 1985. *Making Sense of Marx.* Cambridge: Cambridge University Press.

———. 1986. "Introduction," 1–33. In Jon Elster, ed., *Rational Choice.* New York: New York University Press.

Emery, Fred E., and Eric L. Trist. 1965. "The Casual Texture of Organizational Environments." In: *Human Relations,* 18, no. 1: 21–32.

Epstein, Leon D. 1967. *Political Parties in Western Democracies.* New York: Praeger.

Etzioni, Amitai. 1960. "Two Approaches to Organizational Analysis: A Critique and a Suggestion." *Administrative Science Quarterly,* 5, no. 2: 257–78.

Falke, Wolfgang. 1982. *Die Mitglieder der CDU.* Berlin: Duncker & Humblot.

Feist, Ursula, Dieter Fröhlich, and Hubert Krieger. 1984. "Die politischen Einstellungen von Arbeitslosen." *Aus Politik und Zeitgeschichte,* 34 (November 10, 1984), no. 45: 3–17.

Fischer, Joschka. 1983. "Für einen grünen Radikalreformismus," 35–46. In: Wolfgang Kraushaar, ed., *Was sollen die Grünen im Parlament?* Berlin: Verlag Neue Kritik.

Fitzmaurice, John. 1983. *The Politics of Belgium. Crises and Compromise in a Plural Society.* New York: St. Martin's Press.

Flora, Peter, and Arnold Heidenheimer, eds. 1981. *The Development of Welfare States in Europe and America.* New Brunswick: Transaction Books.

Florizoone, Patrick. 1985. *De Gronen. Ideen, bewegingen en partijen.* Deurne: Kluver.

Fogt, Helmut. 1982. *Politische Generationen.* Opladen: Westdeutscher Verlag.

———. 1983. "Die Grünen in den Parlamenten der Bundesrepublik. Ein Soziogramm." *Zeitschrift für Parlamentsfragen,* 14, no. 4: 500–17.

——. 1984. "Basisdemokratie oder Herrschaft der Aktivisten? Zum Politikverständnis der Grünen," *Politische Vierteljahresschriften*, 25, no. 1: 97–114.

——. 1986. "Die Mandatsträger der Grünen. Zur sozialen und politischen Herkunft der alternativen Parteielite." *Aus Politik und Zeitgeschichte*, 36, no. 11: 16–33.

Fogt, Helmut and Pavel Uttitz. 1984. "Die Wähler der Grünen 1980–1983: Systemkritischer neuer Mittelstand," *Zeitschrift für Parlamentsfragen*, 15, no. 2: 210–26.

Foucault, Michel. 1983. "Afterword: The Subject of Power," 208–26. In Hubert L. Dreyfus and Paul Rabinow, *Michel Foucault. Beyond Structuralism and Hermeneutics.* 2d. ed. Chicago: Chicago University Press.

Freeman, Jo. 1975. *The Politics of Women's Liberation.* New York: Longman.

Frognier, André-Paul. 1975. "Vote, classe sociale et réligion/pratique réligieuse." *Res Publica*, 17, no. 4: 479–90.

Gamson, William. 1975. *The Strategy of Social Protest.* Homewood, Ill: Dorsey.

Garraud, Philippe. 1979. "Politique électro-nucléaire et mobilisation. La tentative de constitution d'un enjeu." *Revue française de science politique*, 29, no. 3: 448–74.

Garwin, Tom. 1976. "Local Party Activists in Dublin. Socialization, Recruitment, and Incentives," *British Journal of Political Science*, 6, no. 3: 369–80.

Gerlach, Luther P., and Virginia H. Hine. 1970. *People, Power, and Change. Movements of Social Transformation.* Indianapolis, Ind.: Bobbs-Merrill.

Gerretsen, Rob, and Marcel Van der Linden. 1982. "Die Pazifistisch-Sozialistische Partei der Niederlande (PSP)," 85–106. In Jürgen Baumgarten, ed., *Linkssozialisten in Europa.* Hamburg: Junius.

Gitlin, Todd. 1980. *The Whole World Is Watching. Mass Media in the Making and Unmaking of the New Left.* Berkeley, Calif: University of California Press.

Gotto, Klaus, and Hans Joachim Veen eds. 1984, *Die Grünen. Partei wider Willen.* Mainz: Hase & Köhler.

Granovetter, Mark S. 1978. "The Strength of Weak Ties." *American Journal of Sociology*, 78, no. 6: 1360–80.

Greven, Michael Thomas. 1987. *Parteimitglieder. Ein politischer Essay.* Opladen: Leske und Buderich.

Groh, Dieter. 1973. *Negative Integration und revolutionarer Attentismus. Die deutsche Socialdemokratie am Vorabend des Ersten Weltkriegs.* Berlin: Propylaen.

Grün Alternative Liste Hamburg. 1982. *Programm für Hamburg.* Hamburg: GAL.

Die Grünen. 1980. *Das Bundesprogramm.* Bonn: Die Grünen.

——. 1983. *Bundeswirtschaftsprogramm.* Bonn: Die Grünen.

Die Grünen, Bundesvorstand. 1985. *Rechenschaftsbericht des Bundesvorstandes.* Bonn: Die Grünen.

Die Grünen im Bundestag. 1984. *Bericht zur Lage der Fraktion.* March 1984. Bonn: Die Grünen.

——. 1985. *Rechenschaftsbericht.* December 1985. Bonn: Die Grünen.

Die Grünen im Hessischen Landtag. 1983 *Die Würde einer Uniform ist antastbar. Die Aktion der Landtagsgruppe beim Empfang der U.S. Kommandeure im Wiesbadener Schloss am 3. August 1983.* Wiesbaden: Die Grünen.

Die Grünen im Landtag von Niedersachsen. 1984. *Zwei Jahre im Parlament.* Hanover: Landtagsfraktion.

Die Grünen in Baden-Württemberg. 1984. *Programm zur Landtagswahl 1984.* Stuttgart: Die Grünen.

Die Grünen in Hessen. 1982. *Landesprogramm.* Frankfurt: Die Grünen.

Die Grünen Nordrhein Westfalen. 1985. *Landesprogramm. Unser dickstes Ei.* April 1985. Düsseldorf: Die Grünen.

Gundelach, Peter. 1984. "Social Transformation and New Forms of Voluntary Associations." *Social Science Information,* 23, no. 6: 1049–81.

Günther, Klaus. 1979. *Sozialdemokratie und Demokratie 1946–1966. Die SPD und das Problem der Verschränkung innerparteilicher und bundesrepublikanischer Demokratie.* Bonn: Verlag Neue Gesellschaft.

Gurr, Ted Robert. 1970. *Why Men Rebel.* Princeton, N.J.: Princeton University Press.

Gusfield, Joseph R. 1981. "Social Movements and Social Change: Perspectives of Linearity and Change," 317–339. In: Louis Kriesberg, ed., *Research in Social Movements, Conflict and Change,* vol. 4.

Gyorgy, Anna and Friends. 1979. *No Nukes. Everyone's Guide to Nuclear Power.* Boston: Southend Press.

Habermas, Jürgen. 1971. *Theorie und Praxis.* Rev. edition. Frankfurt, Main: Suhrkamp.

———. 1975. *Legitimationsprobleme im Spätkapitalismus.* Frankfurt, Main: Suhrkamp.

———. 1981. *Theorie des kommunikativen Handelns,* 2. Frankfurt, Main: Suhrkamp.

———. 1985. *Die neue Unübersichtlichkeit.* Frankfurt, Main: Suhrkamp.

Hallensleben, Anna. 1984. *Von der Grünen Liste zur Grünen Partei?* Göttingen: Musterschmidt.

Hands, Gordon. 1971. "Roberto Michels and the Study of Political Parties." *British Journal of Political Science,* 1, no. 2: 155–72.

Hansen, Jan Bo. 1982. "Die Grünen (und die Roten) in Danemark." *Links,* 17, no. 186: 27–28.

Hansen, John Mark. 1985. "The Political Economy of Group Membership." *American Political Science Review* 79, no. 1: 79–96.

Hardin, Russell. 1982. *Collective Action.* Baltimore: Johns Hopkins University Press.

Harmel, Robert and John D. Robertson. 1985. "Formation and Success of New Parties. A Cross-National Analysis." *International Political Science Review,* 6, no. 4: 501–23.

Hasenclever, Connie, and Wolf-Dieter Hasenclever. 1982. *Grüne Zeiten. Politik fur eine lebenswerte Zukunft.* Munich: Kösel Verlag.

Hasenclever, Wolf-Dieter. 1982a, "Die Grünen und die Parlamente," *Zeitschrift für Parlamentsfragen,* 13, no. 3: 417–22.

———. 1982b. "Die Grünen im Landtag von Baden-Württemberg. Bilanz nach zwei Jahren Parlamentspraxis," 101–19. In: Jörg Mettke ed., *Die Grünen. Regierungspartner von morgen?* Reinbek: Rowohlt.

Haungs, Peter. 1973. "Die Bundesrepublik—ein Parteienstaat? Kritische Anmerkungen zu einem wissenschaftlichen Mythos." *Zeitschrift für Parlamentsfragen,* 4, no. 4: 502–24.

zu einem wissenschaftlichen Mythos." *Zeitschrift für Parlamentsfragen,* 4, no. 4: 502–24.

Haupt, Volker. 1984. "Zum Dilemma der Alternativen Liste. Die Niederlagen der sozialen Bewegungen und das Fehlen einer linken Oppositionspartei," 175–83. In: Michael Bühnemann, Michael Wendt, and Jürgen Wituschek eds., *AL. Die Alternative Liste Berlin.* Berlin: LitPol.

Hauss, Charles. 1978. *The New Left in France. The Unified Socialist Party.* Westport, Conn: Greenwood.

Hauss, Charles and David Rayside. 1978. "The Development of New Parties," 31–57. In: Louis Maisel and Joseph Cooper eds., *Political Parties. Development and Decay.* Beverly Hills: Sage.

Heidar, Knut. 1984. "Party Power. Approaches to a Field of Unfilled Classics," *Scandinavian Political Studies,* 7, no. 1: 1–16.

Heisler, Martin O. 1974. "Institutionalizing Societal Cleavages in a Cooptive Polity. The Growing Importance of the Output Side in Belgium", 178–220. In: Martin O. Heisler, ed., *Politics in Europe. Structures and Processes in Some Postindustrial Democracies.* New York: McKay.

Hellemans, Staf. 1985. "Elementen voor een algemene theorie van verzuiling." *Tijdschrift voor Sociologie,* 6, no. 3: 235–58.

Hermans, Rita. 1984. "Die Hälfte des Himmels? Über alternative Frauen, Frauen und die AL, Frauen in der AL," 99–115. In: Michael Bühnemann, Michael Wendt, and Jürgen Wituschek eds. *AL. Die Alternative Liste Berlin.* Berlin: LitPol.

Hickson, D. J., C. R. Hinings, C. A. Lee, R. E. Schneck, and J. M. Pennings. 1971. "A Strategic Contingencies Theory of Intraorganizational Power." *Administrative Science Quarterly,* 16, no. 2: 216–29.

Hill, Keith. 1974. "Belgium. Political Change in a Segmented Society," 29–107. In: Richard Rose ed., *Electoral Behavior. A Comparative Handbook.* New York: Free Press.

Hine, David. 1982. "Factionalism in West European Parties. A Framework for Analysis." *West European Politics,* 5, no. 1: 36–53.

——. 1986. "Leaders and Followers. Democracy and Manageability in the Social Democratic Parties of Western Europe," 261–90 in William E. Paterson and Alastair H. Thomas eds., *The Future of Social Democracy.* Oxford: Clarendon Press.

Hirschman, Albert. 1970. *Exit, Voice and Loyalty.* Cambridge, Mass.: Harvard University Press.

——. 1981. *Shifting Involvements.* Princeton, N.J.: Princeton University Press.

Hofstetter, C. Richard. 1971. "The Amateur Politician. A Problem in Construct Validation." *Midwest Journal of Political Science,* 15, no. 1: 31–56.

Holvoet, Luk. 1980. "Jaren 70: Integratie en versplintering," *De nieuwe Mand,* 22, no. 10: 679–700.

Hoplitschek, Ernst. 1981. "Die Alternativen und die 'Macht' ", 144–55. In: *Alternative Stadtpolitik,* Hamburg: Verlag für das Studium der Arbeiterbewegung.

——. 1983. "Kontrolle ist schlecht. Uber die alternative Angst vor der Mündigkeit des einzelnen." *Freibeuter,* no. 15: 69–77.

Horacek, Milan. 1982. "Zwischen den Etablierten und uns liegen Welten," 120–34. In: Jörg Mettke ed., *Die Grünen. Regierungspartner von morgen?* Reinbek: Rowohlt.

Horch, Heinz-Dieter. 1982. *Strukturbesonderheiten freiwilliger Vereinigungen.* Frankfurt, Main: Campus.

Huber, Joseph. 1980. *Wer soll das alles ändern? Die Alternativen der Alternativbewegung.* Berlin: Rotbuch.

Huyse, Luc. 1980. *De gewapende vrede. Politiek in Belgie na 1945.* Leuven: Kritak.

——. 1983. "Breuklijnen in de Belgische samenleving." *Tijdschrift voor Sociologie,* 4. no. 1–2: 9–25.

——. 1984. "Pillarization Reconsidered." *Acta Politica,* 19, no. 1: 145–58.

Inglehart, Ronald. 1977. *The Silent Revolution.* Princeton, N.J.: Princeton University Press.

——. 1984a. "Changing Paradigms in Comparative Political Behavior," 429–69. In: Ada W. Finifter ed., *Political Science. The State of the Discipline.* Washington, D.C.: APSA.

——. 1984b. "The Changing Structure of Political Cleavages in Western Societies," 25–69. In: Russell J. Dalton, Scott C. Flanagan, and Paul Allen Beck, eds., *Electoral Change in Advanced Western Democracies.* Princeton, N.J.: Princeton University Press.

——. 1985. "Aggregate Stability and Individual-Level Flux in Mass Belief Systems: The Level of Analysis Paradox." *American Political Science Review,* 79, no. 1: 97–116.

Institut National de Statistique. 1985. *Annuaire Statistique de la Belgique,* 105. Brussels: Institut National de Statistique.

International Labor Office. 1985. *The Cost of Social Security: Eleventh International Inquiry 1978-1980.* Geneva: ILO.

Irwin, Galen, and Karl Dittrich. 1984. "And the Walls Came Tumbling Down. Party Dealignment in the Netherlands," 267-97. In: Russel J. Dalton, Scott C. Flanagan, and Paul Allen Beck, eds., *Electoral Change in Advanced Western Democracies.* Princeton, N.J.: Princeton University Press.

Ismayr, Wolfgang. 1985. "Die Grünen im Bundestag: Parlamentarisierung und Basisanbindung." *Zeitschrift für Parlamentsfragen,* 16, no. 3: 299-321.

Jacobs, Danny, and Joop Roebroek. 1983. *Nieuwe sociale Bewegingen in Vlaanderen en Nederland.* Antwerpen: Uitgeverij Leon Lesoil.

Jäger, Brigitte, and Claudia Pinl. 1985. *Zwischen Rotation und Routine. Die Grünen im Bundestag.* Cologne: Kiepenheuer und Witsch.

James, C. C. 1978. "Social Credit and the Values Party," 149-167. In: Howard R. Penniman, ed., *New Zealand at the Polls. The General Election of 1978.* Washington, D.C.: American Enterprise Institute.

Janda, Kenneth, 1980. *Political Parties. A Cross-National Survey.* New York: Macmillan.

———. 1983. "Cross-National Measures of Party Organization and Organization Theory." *European Journal of Political Research,* 11, no. 3: 319-32.

Janda, Kenneth, and Desmond S. King. 1985. "Formalizing and Testing Duverger's Theories on Political Parties," *Comparative Political Studies,* 18, no. 2: 139-69.

Jenson, Jane, and George Ross. 1984. *The View from Inside. A French Communist Cell in Crisis.* Berkeley, Calif.: University of California Press.

Kaack, Heino. 1971. *Geschichte und Struktur des deutschen Parteiensystems.* Opladen: Westdeutscher Verlag.

Kanter, Rosabeth Moss. 1972. *Commitment and Community: Communes and Utopia in Sociological Perspective.* Cambridge, Mass.: Harvard University Press.

Katzenstein, Peter J. 1982. "West Germany as Number Two: Reflections on the German Model," 199-215. In: Andrei S. Markovits, ed., *The Political Economy of West Germany. Modell Deutschland.* New York: Praeger.

———. 1985. *Small States in World Markets.* Ithaca, N.Y.: Cornell University Press.

———. 1987. *Policy and Politics in West Germany: A Semi-Sovereign State.* Philadelphia: Temple University Press.

Katznelson, Ira, and Aristide R. Zolberg, eds. 1986. *Working Class Formation: Nineteenth Century Patterns in Western Europe and the United States.* Princeton, N.J.: Princeton University Press.

Kavanagh, Dennis. 1985. "Power in British Political Parties. Iron Law or Special Pleading?" *West European Politics,* 8, no. 3: 5-22.

Kelly, Petra. 1982. "SPIEGEL-Gespräch mit Petra Kelly," 26-35. In: Jörg Mettke, ed., *Die Grünen. Regierungspartner von morgen?* Reinbek: Rowohlt.

Kergoat, Jacques. 1982. "Die Parti Socialiste Unifie in Frankreich," 107-29. In: Jürgen Baumgarten, ed., *Linkssozialisten in Europa.* Hamburg: Junius.

King, Anthony. 1969. "Political Parties in Western Democracies." *Polity,* 2, no. 2: 111-41.

———. 1976. "Modes of Executive-Legislative Relations: Great Britain, France and West Germany. *Legislative Studies Quarterly,* 1, no. 1: 11-36.

Kirchheimer, Otto. 1966. "The Transformation of the Western European Party Systems," 177-200. In: Joseph La Palombara and Myron Weiner, eds., *Political Parties and Political Development.* Princeton, N.J.: Princeton University Press.

Kirkpatrick, Jeanne, 1976. *The New Presidential Elite: Men and Women in National Politics.* New York: Russell Sage Foundation.

Kitschelt, Herbert. 1980. *Kernenergiepolitik. Arena eines gesellschaftlichen Konflikts.* Frankfurt, Main: Campus.

———. 1983. *Politik und Energie.* Frankfurt, Main: Campus.

———. 1984. *Der ökologische Diskurs.* Frankfurt, Main: Campus.

———. 1985a. "New Social Movements in West Germany and the United States," 273–324. In: Maurice Zeitlin, ed., *Political Power and Social Theory,* 5. Greenwich, Conn.: JAI-Press.

———. 1985b. "Zur Dynamik neuer sozialer Bewegungen in den USA. Strategien gesellschaftlichen Wandels und 'American Exceptionalism'," 248–305. In: Karl-Werner Brand, ed., *Neue soziale Bewegungen in Westeuropa und den USA.* Frankfurt, Main: Campus.

———. 1986. "Political Opportunity Structures and Political Protest: Anti-Nuclear Movements in Four Countries." *British Journal of Political Science,* 16. no. 1: 57–85.

———. 1988a. "Left-libertarian Parties: Explaining Innovation in Competitive Party Systems." *World Politics,* 40, no. 2: 194–234.

———. 1988b. "The Life Expectancy of Left-libertarian Parties. Do Structural Transformation or Economic Decline Explain Party Innovation?" *European Sociological Review,* 4.

———. 1989. "New Social Movements and the Decline of Party Organization." To appear in: Russell J. Dalton and Manfred Küchler, eds., *Challenging the Political Order.* New York: Oxford University Press.

Kitschelt, Herbert, in collaboration with Staf Hellemans. (forthcoming) Political Action in Left-libertarian Parties: Amateur Politics in the Belgian Ecology Parties. Duke University, July 1988.

Kitschelt, Herbert, and Helmut Wiesenthal. 1979. "Organization and Mass Action in the Political Works of Rosa Luxemburg." *Politics and Society,* 9, no. 2: 152–202.

Kleinert, Hubert and Jan Kuhnert. 1982. "Aufstieg und Fall des Marburger 'Ampelbündnisses'," 133–54. In: Jürgen Reents, ed., *Es grünt so rot.* Hamburg: Konkret Verlag.

Klingemann, Hans D. 1979. "Measuring Ideological Conceptualizations," 215–54. In: Samuel J. Barnes and Max Kaase eds., *Political Action.* Beverly Hills, Calif: Sage.

Klotzbach, Kurt. 1982. *Der Weg zur Staatspartei. Programmatik, praktische Politik und Organisation der deutschen Sozialdemokratie, 1945–1965.* Berlin und Bonn: J. H. W. Dietz, Nachfahren.

Klotzsch, Lilian, and Richard Stöss. 1984. "Die Grünen," 1509–98. In: Richard Stöss, ed., *Parteien-Handbuch.* Opladen: Westdeutscher Verlag.

Kluge, Thomas, ed. 1984. *Grüne Politik. Der Stand der Auseinandersetzung.* Frankfurt, Main: Fischer.

Knoke, David, and James R. Wood. 1981. *Organized for Action. Commitment in Voluntary Organizations.* New Brunswick, N.J.: Rutgers University Press.

Kornberg, Allan, Joel Smith, and Harold D. Clark. 1979. *Citizen Politicians—Canada: Party Officials in a Democratic Society.* Durham N.C.: North Carolina Academic Press.

Kostede, Norbert. 1983. "Mixtum Compositum. Der Preis für die Regierbarkeit." *Freibeuter,* no. 15: 59–68.

Kuhnle, Stein, Kaare Strom, and Lars Svasand. 1986. "The Norwegian Conservative Party. Setback in an Era of Strength." *West European Politics,* 9, no. 3: 448–71.

Kvistad, Greg O. 1987. "Between State and Society: Green Political Ideology in the Mid-1980s." *West European Politics,* 10, no. 2: 210–27.

Lagroye, Jacques, and Guy Lord. 1974. "Trois Fédérations de Partis Politiques. Esquisse de Typologie." *Revue Française de Science Politique*, 24, no. 3: 559–95.

Lambert, Gerard, Jean-Marie Pierlot, and Jean-Luc Roland. 1982. "Les Ecolos voient l'avenir autrement," *La revue nouvelle*, 38, no. 5–6: 543–47.

Lammert, Norbert. 1976. *Lokale Organisationsstrukturen innerparteilicher Willensbildung*. Mainz: Eichholz Verlag.

Lange, Peter. 1975. "The PCI at the Local Level: A Study of Strategic Performance," 259–304. In: Donald L. M. Blackmer and Sidney Tarrow, eds., *Communism in Italy and France*. Princeton, N.J.: Princeton University Press.

——. 1984. *Union Democracy and Liberal Corporatism: Exit, Voice, and Wage Regulation in Postwar Europe*. Center for International Studies, Cornell University: Western Societies Program, Occasional Paper No. 16.

Langer, Alexander. 1983. "Politik als Ware. Warum es in Italien keine Grüne, wohl aber eine Radikale Partei gibt." *Freibeuter*, 15: 82–92.

——. 1985. "Gewonnen! Wie Weiter?" *Kommune*, 3, no. 10: 42.

Langer, Thomas, and Rainer Link. 1981. "Ein Ausgangspunkt für zwei Wege. Über den Umgang mit Defiziten linker Politik in Hamburg," 128–43. In: *Alternative Stadtpolitik*. Hamburg: Verlag fur das Studium der Arbeiterbewegung.

Langguth, Gerd. 1983. *Protestbewegung. Entwicklung—Niedergang—Renaissance. Die Neue Linke seit 1968*. Cologne: Verlag Wissenschaft und Politik.

——. 1984. *Der Grüne Faktor. Von der Bewegung zur Partei?* Osnabrück: Fromm.

Lannoye, Paul. 1985. "Réflexions sur l'état du mouvement Ecolo," *Ecolo Infos*, no. 51 (February 1, 1985): 48–54.

Laver, Michael. 1986. "Between Theoretical Elegance and Political Reality: Deductive Models and Cabinet Coalitions in Europe," 32–44. In: Geoffrey Pridham, ed., *Coalition Behavior in Theory and Practice*. Cambridge: Cambridge University Press.

Lawson, Kay. 1976. *The Comparative Study of Political Parties*. New York: St. Martin's Press.

——. 1980. "Political Parties and Linkage," 3–24. In: Kay Lawson, ed., *Political Parties and Linkage. A Comparative Perspective*. New Haven, Conn.: Yale University Press.

Layton-Henry, Zig. 1976. "Constituency Autonomy in the Conservative Party." *Parliamentary Affairs*, 29, no. 4: 396–403.

——. 1983. ed., *Conservative Parties in Western Europe*. London: Macmillan.

Leggewie, Claus, and Roland de Miller, eds. 1977. *Der Wahlfisch. Ökologie-Bewegungen in Frankreich*. Berlin: Merve.

Lehmbruch, Gerhard. 1978. "Party and Federation in Germany: A Developmental Dilemma." *Government and Opposition*, 13, no. 2: 151–77.

——. 1979. "Liberal Corporatism and Party Government," 147–84. In Philippe C. Schmitter and Gerhard Lehmbruch, eds., *Trends Toward Corporatist Intermediation*. Beverly Hills, Calif.: Sage.

——. 1984. "Concertation and the Structure of Corporatist Networks," 60–80. In: John H. Goldthorpe, ed., *Order and Conflict in Contemporary Capitalism*. New York: Oxford University Press.

Lehner, Franz, and Klaus Schubert. 1984. "Party Government and the Political Control of Public Policy." *European Journal of Political Research*, 12, no. 2: 131–46.

Lehnert, Detlef. 1979. "Zur politischen Transformation der Deutschen Sozialdemokratie. Ein Interpretationsversuch für die Zeit des Übergangs zum organisierten Kapitalismus," 279–314. In: Jürgen Bergmann, Klaus Megerle, and Peter Steinbach, eds., *Geschichte und politische Wissenschaft*. Stuttgart: Klett-Cotta.

Lenin, Vladimir I. 1902/69. *What Is to Be Done?* New York: International Publishers.

Leonard, Dick. 1983. "BENELUX," 149–66. In: Vernon Bogdanor and David Butler, eds., *Democracy and Elections. Electoral Systems and their Political Consequences.* Cambridge: Cambridge University Press.

Leonardi, Robert. 1981. "The Victors. The Smaller Parties in the 1979 Italian Elections," 172–92. In: Howard R. Penniman, ed., *Italy at the Polls.* Washington, D.C.: American Enterprise Institute.

Leroy, Pierre. 1980. "Voor Outer en Heerd." *De nieuwe mand,* 23, no. 10: 701–11.

——. 1982. "Alternatief en autonoom bewegend Vlaanderen." *De nieuwe mand,* 25, no. 5: 351–64.

——. 1984. "Waar staan 'de groenen' in Vlaanderen voor?" *Ons Erfdeel,* 27, no. 4: 481–94.

Lewin, Leif. 1980. *Governing Trade Unions in Sweden.* Cambridge, Mass.: Harvard University Press.

Lijphart, Arend. 1971. "Comparative Politics and the Comparative Method." *American Political Science Review,* 65, no. 3: 682–93.

——. 1977a. "Political Theories and the Explanation of Ethnic Conflict in the Western World: Falsified Predictions and Plausible Postdictions," 46–64. In: Milton J. Esman ed., *Ethnic Conflict in the Western World.* Ithaca: Cornell University Press.

——. 1977b. *Democracy in Plural Societies. A Comparative Exploration.* New Haven, Conn.: Yale University Press.

——. 1981. ed., *Conflict and Coexistence in Belgium. The Dynamics of a Culturally Divided Society.* University of California at Berkeley: Institute of International Studies.

——. 1984. *Democracies. Patterns of Majoritarian and Consensus Government in Twenty-One Countries.* New Haven, Conn.: Yale University Press.

Lipset, Seymour Martin. 1962. "Introduction," 15–39. In: Robert Michels, *Political Parties.* New York: Free Press.

——. 1964. "Ostrogorski and the Analytical Approach to the Comparative Study of Political Parties," ix–lxv. In Mosei Ostrogorski, *Democracy and the Organization of Political Parties.* Edited and abridged by S. M. Lipset, 2 Vols., Garden City, N.Y.: Doubleday.

——. 1983. "Radicalism or Reformism: The Sources of Working-class Politics." *American Political Science Review,* 77, no. 1: 1–18.

Lipset, Seymour Martin, Martin A. Trow, and James S. Coleman. 1956. *Union Democracy.* New York: Free Press.

Lipset, Seymour Martin, and Stein Rokkan. 1967. "Cleavage Structures, Party Systems, and Voter Alignments. An Introduction," 1–64. In: Seymour Martin Lipset and Stein Rokkan, eds., *Party Systems and Voter Alignments. Cross-National Perspectives.* New York: Free Press.

Logue, John. 1982. *Socialism and Abundance. Radical Socialism in the Danish Welfare State.* Minneapolis: University of Minnesota Press.

Lohmar, Ulrich. 1963. *Innerparteiliche Demokratie.* Stuttgart: Enke.

Lorenz, Einhart. 1982. "Linkssozialismus in Norwegen," 33–57. In: Jürgen Baumgarten, ed., *Linkssozialisten in Europa.* Hamburg: Junius.

Lorwin, Val P. 1966. "Belgium. Religion, Class, and Language in National Politics," 147–87. In: Robert A. Dahl ed., *Political Opposition in Western Western Democracies.* New Haven, Conn.: Yale University Press.

——. 1971. "Segmented Pluralism: Ideological Cleavages and Political Cohesion in the Smaller European Democracies." *Comparative Politics,* 3, no. 3: 141–75.

Luebbert, Gregory M. 1984. "A Theory of Government Formation." *Comparative Political Studies,* 17, no. 2: 229–64.

Lüdke, Hans-Werner, and Olaf Dinne eds. 1980. *Die Grünen. Personen, Projekte, Pro-gramme*. Stuttgart: Seewald.

Lund, Baastrup. 1982. "Sozialistische Volkspartei (SF) und Linkssozialisten (VS). Dänische Parteien zwischen Sozialpartnerschaft und Klassenkampf," 58–84. In: Jürgen Baumgarten, ed., *Linkssozialisten in Europa*. Hamburg: Junius.

Luxemburg, Rosa. 1971. *Selected Political Writings*, ed. Dick Howard. New York: Monthly Review Press.

Mabille, Xavier, and Val R. Lorwin. 1977. "The Belgian Socialist Party." In William E. Patterson and Alastair M. Thomas, eds. *Social Democratic Parties in Western Europe*. New York: St. Martin's Press.

Maguire, Maria. 1983. "Is There Still Persistence? Electoral Change in Western Europe, 1948–1979," 67–94. In: Hans Daalder and Peter Mair, eds., *Western European Party Systems. Continuity and Change*. Beverly Hills, Calif.: Sage.

Mahaux, Philippe, and Jacques Moden. 1984. "Le movement Ecolo," *Centre de Recherche et Information Socio-Politique. Courrier Hébdomadaire*, No. 1045–1046.

Mair, Peter. 1984. "Party Politics in Contemporary Europe: A Challenge to Party?" *West European Politics*, 7, no. 4: 170–84.

Mansbridge, Jane J. 1980. *Beyond Adversary Democracy*. New York: Basic Books.

May, John D. 1965. "Democracy, Organization, Michels." *American Political Science Review*, 59, no. 2: 417–29.

——. 1969. "Democracy, Party 'Evolution,' Duverger." *Comparative Political Studies*, 2, no. 2: 216–48.

——. 1973. "Opinion Structure of Political Parties: The Special Law of Curvinlinear Disparity." *Political Studies*, 21, no. 2: 135–51.

Mayer-Tasch, Peter Cornelius. 1977. *Die Bürgerinitiativbewegung*. Reinbek: Rowohlt.

Mayntz, Renate. 1959. *Parteiengruppen in der Grosstadt*. Cologne and Opladen: Westdeutscher Verlag.

McAdam, Doug. 1982. *Political Process and the Development of Black Insurgency, 1930–1970*. Chicago: Chicago University Press.

McCarthy, John D., and Mayer N. Zald. 1977. "Resource Mobilization and Social Movements: A Partial Theory." *American Journal of Sociology*, 82, no. 6: 1212–41.

McCarthy, Patrick. 1981. "The Parliamentary and Nonparliamentary Parties of the Far Left," 193–211. In: Howard R. Penniman, ed., *Italy at the Polls, 1979*. Washington, D.C.: American Enterprise Institute.

McClosky, Hubert, Paul J. Hoffmann, and Rosemary O'Hara. 1960. "Issue Conflict and Consensus among Party Leaders and Followers." *American Political Science Review*, 54, no. 2: 406–27.

McKenzie, Robert T. 1955. *British Political Parties*. London: Heinemann. 1982. "Power in the Labour Party. The Issue of Intraparty Democracy," 191–202. In: Dennis Kavanagh, ed., *The Politics of the Labor Party*. London: George Allen & Unwin.

McRae, Kenneth D. 1986. *Conflict and Compromise in Multilingual Societies: Belgium*. Waterloo, Ontario: Wilfried Laurier University Press.

Melucci, Alberto. 1985. "The Symbolic Challenge of Contemporary Movements." *Social Research*, 52, no. 4: 789–816.

Merton, Robert K. 1968. *Social Theory and Social Structure*. Enlarged edition. New York: Free Press.

Mettke, Jörg, ed. 1982. *Die Grünen. Regierungspartner von morgen?* Reinbek: Rowohlt.

Meyer, John W., and Brian Rowan. 1977. "Institutionalized Organizations: Formal Structure as Myth and Ceremony." *American Journal of Sociology*, 83, no. 2: 230–363.

Mez, Lutz, ed. 1979. *Der Atomkonflikt. Atomindustrie, Atompolitik und Anti-Atombewegung im internationalen Vergleich*. Berlin: Olle & Wolter.

Michels, Robert. 1911/1962. *Political Parties: A Sociological Study of the Oligarchical Tendencies of Modern Democracy*. English edition. London: Collier-Macmillan.

Minkin, Lewis. 1978. *The Labour Party Conference. A Study in the Politics of Intra-Party Democracy*. London: Allen Lane.

Mintzel, Alf. 1975. *Die CSU. Anatomie einer konservativen Partei, 1945–1972*. Opladen: Westdeutscher Verlag.

———. 1984. *Die Volkspartei. Typus und Wirklichkeit*. Opladen: Westdeutscher Verlag.

Modeley, John. 1986. "Norway's 1985 Election: A Pro-Welfare Backlash." *West European Politics*, 9, no. 2: 289–92.

Moe, Terry M. 1980. *The Organization of Interests*. Chicago: University of Chicago Press.

Molitor, André. 1981. "The Reform of the Belgian Constitution," 139–53. In: Arend Lijphart, ed., *Conflict and Coexistence in Belgium*. University of California at Berkeley: Institute of International Studies.

Molitor, Michel. 1978. "Social Conflicts in Belgium," 21–51. In: Colin Crouch and Alessandro Pizzorno, eds., *The Resurgence of Class Conflict in Western Europe Since 1968*. New Hork: Holmes & Meyer.

Mombaur, Martin. 1982. " 'Im Parlament und auf der Strasse.' Die Doppelstrategie der Grünen Niedersachsen," 135–45. In: Jörg R. Mettke, ed., *Die Grünen. Regierungspartner von morgen?* Reinbek: Rowohlt.

Müller-Rommel, Ferdinand. 1982. " 'Parteien neuen Typs' in Westeuropa. Eine vergleichende Analyse." *Zeitschrift für Parlamentsfragen*, 13, no. 3: 369–90.

———. 1983. "Die Wahl zur Hamburger Bürgerschaft vom 19. 12. 1982. Die neue alte Mehrheit." *Zeitschrift für Parlamentsfragen*, 14, no. 1: 96–109.

———. 1984a. " 'Neue' soziale Bewegungen und 'neue' Parteien in Dänemark und den Niederlanden. Eine empirische Analyse." *Zeitschrift für Parlamentsfragen*, 15, no. 4.

———. 1984b. "Zum Verhältnis von neuen sozialen Bewegungen und neuen Konfliktdimensionen in den politischen Systemen Westeuropas. Eine empirische Analyse." *Sozialforschung*, 311–14 (August 24, 1984), and 411–17 (August 27, 1984).

———. 1985a. "New Social Movements and Smaller Parties: A Comparative Perspective." *West European Politics*, 8, no. 1: 41–54.

———. 1985b. "Social Movements and the Greens. New Internal Politics in Germany." *European Journal of Political Research*, 13, no. 1: 53–67.

———. 1985c. "The Greens in Western Europe. Similar But Different." *International Political Science Review*, 6, no. 4: 483–99.

———. 1987. "New Social Movements and New Political Parties: Preliminary Statements and Empirical Findings." In Russell J. Dalton and Manfred Küchler, *Challenging the Political Order*, forthcoming.

Mughan, Anthony. 1979. "Modernization and Ethnic Conflict in Belgium." *Political Studies*, 27, no. 1: 21–37.

Mushaben, Joyce Marie. 1985. "Cycles of Peace Protest in West Germany: Experiences From Three Decades." *West European Politics*, 8, no. 1: 24–40.

Narr, Wolf-Dieter, ed. 1977. *Auf dem Weg zum Einparteienstaat*. Opladen: Westdeutscher Verlag.

Nelkin, Dorothy, and Michael Pollak. 1980. "The Political Parties and the Nuclear Energy Debate in France and Germany." *Comparative Politcs*, 12, no. 2: 127–41.

Nelles, Wilfried. 1984. "Kollektive Identität und politisches Handeln in neuen sozialen Bewegungen." *Politische Vierteljahresschriften*, 25, no. 4: 425–40.

Neumann, Sigmund. 1932. *Die deutschen Parteien. Wesen und Wandel nach dem Krieg*. Berlin: Junker & Dünnhaupt. New ed. *Die Parteien der Weimarer Republik*. Stuttgart: Kohlhammer.

———. 1954. "Toward a Theory of Political Parties." *World Politics*, 6, no. 4: 549–63.

——. 1956. "Toward a Comparative Study of Political Parties," 395–421. In: Sigmund Neumann, ed., *Modern Political Parties. Approaches to Comparative Politics*. Chicago: Chicago University Press.

Nicolon, Alexandre, and Marie-Josephe Carrieu. 1979. "Les partis face au nucléaire et la contestation," 79–159. In: Francis Fagnani and Alexandre Nicolon, eds., *Nucléopolis. Materiaux pour l'analyse d'une société nucléaire*. Grenoble: Presses Universitaires de Grenoble.

Nugent, Neil. 1982. "The Strategies of the French Left: From the 1978 Defeat to the 1981 Victories," In: David S. Bell, ed., *Contemporary French Political Parties*. New York: St. Martin's Press.

Nullmeier, Frank, Harald Schulz, and Frauke Rubart. 1983. *Umweltbewegungen und Parteiensystem*. Hamburg: Quorum.

Oberschall, Anthony. 1973. *Social Conflict and Social Movements*. Englewood Cliffs, N.J.: Prentice Hall.

——. 1980. "Loosely Structured Collective Conflict: A Theory and Applications." *Research in Social Movements, Conflict and Change*, 3: 45–68.

Obler, Jeffrey. 1974. "Intraparty Democracy and the Selection of Parliamentary Candidates. The Belgian Case." *British Journal of Political Science*, 4, no. 2: 163–85.

Ökolibertäre Grüne. 1984. *Systemopposition oder Volkspartei? Gedanken zu Demokratie, Privatheit und Wirtschaft*. Berlin: Eigendruck.

Offe, Claus. 1969. "Politische Autorität und Klassenstrukturen," 135–64. In: Gisela Kress and Dieter Senghaas, eds., *Politikwissenschaft*. Frankfurt, Main: Fischer.

——. 1980. "Konkurrenzpartei und politische Identität," 26–42. In: Roland Roth, ed., *Parlamentarisches Ritual und politische Alternativen*. Frankfurt, Main: Campus.

——. 1981. "The Attribution of Public Status to Interest Groups. Observations on the West German Case," 123–58. In: Suzanne Berger, ed., *Organizing Interests in Western Europe*. New York: Cambridge University Press.

——. 1983. *Contradictions of the Welfare State*. Cambridge, Mass.: MIT Press.

——. 1985. *Disorganized Capitalism*. Cambridge, Mass.: MIT Press.

——. 1986. "Zwischen Bewegung und Partei. Die Grünen in der politischen 'Adoleszenzkrise'?" 40–60. In: Otto Kallscheuer, ed., *Die Grünen—Letzte Wahl?* West Berlin: Rotbuch.

——. 1987. "Democracy against the Welfare State? Structural Foundations of Neoconservative Political Opportunities." *Political Theory*, 15, no. 4: 501–37.

Offe, Claus, and Helmut Wiesenthal. 1980. "Two Logics of Collective Action." In: Maurice Zeitlin, ed., *Political Power and Social Theory*, 1: 67–115, Greenwich, Conn.: JAI Press.

——. 1985. "Die grüne Angst vorm 'Reformismus.' Durch Formfehler ins Formtief," 196–203. In Gabriel Falkenberg and Heiner Kesting, eds., *Eingriffe ins Diesseits. Beiträge zu einer radikalen Grünen Realpolitik*. Essen: Klartext Verlag.

Olsen, Johan P. 1983. *Organized Democracy. Political Institutions in a Welfare State. The Case of Norway*. Bergen: Universitetsforlaget.

Olson, Mancur. 1965. *The Logic of Collective Action*. Cambridge, Mass.: Harvard University Press.

Opielka, Michael. 1985. "Vom Sozialstaat zum ökologischen Gemeinwesen—Für eine neue Sozialpolitik," 206–25. In: Frank Beckenbach, Jo Müller, Reinhard Pfriem, and Eckhard Stratmann, eds., *Grüne Wirtschaftspolitik. Machbare Utopien*. Cologne: Kiepenheuer & Witsch.

Opielka, Michael, Martin Schmollinger, and Angelika Fohmann-Ritter, eds. 1984. *Die Zukunft des Sozialstaates*. Stuttgart: Die Grünen.

Organization of Economic Cooperation and Development. 1982. *Historical Statistics: 1960–1980*. Paris: OECD.

Ostrogorski, Mosei. 1902/1964. *Democracy and the Organization of Political Parties*. Edited and abridged by Seymour Martin Lipset, 2. Garden City, N.Y.: Doubleday Anchor.

Otto, Karl A., 1977, *Vom Ostermarsch zur APO*. Frankfurt Main: Campus.

Ozbudun, Ergun. 1970. "Party Cohesion in Western Democracies. A Causal Analysis." *Sage Professional Papers*, Series Number 001–006, 1: 303–88.

Pappi, Franz Urban. 1977. "Bewegungstendenzen des politisch-sozialen Systems in der Bundesrepublik Deutschland." *Politische Vierteljahresschriften*, 18, no. 2–3: 195–229.

———. 1984. "The West German Party System." *West European Politics*, 7, no. 4: 7–26.

Parodi, Jean-Luc, 1979. "Essai de problematique du mouvement écologiste. Les écologistes et la tentative politique," *Revue politique et parlementaire*, 80, no. 878: 25–43.

Peeters, Andre, and Ivo Vermeiren. 1980. *De Jaren Zeventig: Van Groen Naar Groenen*. Borgerhout: Uitgeverij Stil Leven.

Perrow, Charles. 1961. "The Analysis of Goals in Complex Organizations." *American Sociological Review*, 26, no. 6: 854–65.

———. 1972. *Complex Organizations. A Critical Essay*. Glenview, Ill.: Scott, Foresman.

Pfriem, Reinhard. 1985. "Marktwirtschaft, Planwirtschaft oder was?" 44–69. In: Frank Beckenbach, Jo Müller, Reinhard Pfriem and Eckhard Stratmann, eds., *Grüne Wirtschaftspolitik*. Cologne: Kiepenheuer & Witsch.

Pinard, Maurice. 1975. *The Rise of a Third Party. A Study in Crisis Politics*. Enlarged edition. Montreal: McGill-Queen's University Press.

Piven, Francis Fox, and Richard A. Cloward. 1977. *Poor People's Movements. Why They Succeed. How They Fail*. New York: Random House.

Potter, Tim. 1982. "Il Manifesto und Il Partito di Unita Proletaria (PdUP). Linke Kritik an der KPI," 1–32. In: Jürgen Baumgarten, ed., *Linkssozialisten in Europa*. Hamburg: Junius.

Powell, G. Bingham Jr. 1986. "American Voter Turnout in Comparative Perspective." *American Political Science Review*, 80, no. 1: 18–43.

Preusse, Detlev. 1981. *Gruppenbildungen und innerparteiliche Demokratie*. Königstein, Taunus: Hain.

Pridham, Geoffrey. 1986. "An Inductive Theoretical Framework of Coalition Behavior: Political Parties in Multi-Dimensional Perspective in Western Europe," 1–31. In: Geoffrey Pridham, ed., *Coalition Behavior in Theory and Practice. An Inductive Model for Western Europe*. Cambridge: Cambridge University Press.

Projektgruppe Grüner Morgentau, ed. 1986. *Ökologische Wirtschaftspolitik*. Frankfurt/Main: Campus.

Pütz, Helmut. 1974. *Innerparteiliche Willensbildung*. Mainz: v. Hase & Köhler.

Pumm, Günther. 1977. *Kandidatenauswahl und innerparteiliche Demokratie in der Hamburger SPD*. Frankfurt/Main: Lang.

Putnam, Robert D. 1973. *The Beliefs of Politicians. Ideology, Conflict, and Democracy in Britain and Italy*. New Haven, Conn.: Yale University Press.

Ragin, Charles. 1987. *The Comparative Method*. Berkeley: University of California Press.

Rammstedt, Otthein, ed. 1980. *Bürgerinitiativen in der Gesellschaft*. Villingen: Neckar Verlag.

Ranney, Austin. 1968. "Candidate Selection and Party Cohesion in Britain and the United States," 139–57. In: William J. Crotty, ed., *Approaches to the Study of Party Organization*. Boston: Allyn and Bacon.

——. 1981. "Candidate Selection," 75–106. In: David Butler, Howard R. Penniman, and Austin Ranney, eds., *Democracy at the Polls*. Washington, D.C.: American Enterprise Institute.

Raschke, Joachim. 1974. *Innerparteiliche Opposition. Die Linke in der Berliner SPD.* Hamburg: Hoffman & Campe.

——. 1977. *Organisierter Konflikt in westeuropäischen Parteien.* Opladen: Westdeutscher Verlag.

——. 1982. "Einleitung," 9–31. In: Joachim Raschke, ed., *Bürger und Parteien. Ansichten und Analysen einer schwierigen Beziehung.* Opladen: Westdeutscher Verlag.

——. 1983. "Jenseits der Volkspartei." *Das Argument,* 25, no. 1: 54–65.

——. 1985. *Soziale Bewegungen. Ein historisch-systematischer Grundriss.* Frankfurt/Main: Campus.

Reents, Jürgen, ed. 1982. *Es grünt so rot. Alternativen zwischen Mode und Modell.* Hamburg: Konkret Verlag.

Reif, Karlheinz. 1984. "Konsolidierungszeitpunkt, Polarisierung, Bipolarität. Einige Anmerkungen zu Rokkan, Sartori und dem Wandel europäischer Parteiensysteme," 142–52. In: Jürgen W. Falter, Christian Fenner, and Michael Th. Greven, eds., *Politische Willensbildung und Interessenvermittlung.* Opladen: Westdeutscher Verlag.

——. 1985. "Ten Second Order National Elections," 1–36. In: Karlheinz Reif, *The European Election.* Aldershot: Gower.

Riggs, Fred W. 1968. "Comparative Politics and the Study of Political Parties: A Structural Approach," 45–103. In: William J. Crotty, ed., *Approaches to the Study of Party Organization.* Boston: Allyn and Bacon.

——. 1975. "Organizational Structures and Contexts." *Administration and Society,* 7, no. 2: 150–90.

Robertson, David. 1976. *A Theory of Party Competition.* London: Wiley.

Rochon, Thomas. 1988. *Mobilizing for Peace in Western Europe.* Princeton, N.J.: Princeton University Press.

Rönsch, Horst Dieter. 1980. "Grüne Listen. Vorläufer oder Katalysatoren einer neuen Protestbewegung?" 375–434. In: Otthein Rammstedt, ed., *Bürgerinitiativen in der Gesellschaft.* Villingen: Neckar Verlag.

Rokkan, Stein. 1966. "Norway: Numerical Democracy and Corporate Pluralism," 70–115. In: Robert A. Dahl, ed., *Political Opposition in Western Democracies.* New Haven: Yale University Press.

Ronneberger, Franz, and Jürgen Walchshofer. 1975. "Parteien als Kommunikationssysteme," 115–60. In: Oscar W. Gabriel, ed., *Strukturprobleme des lokalen Parteiensystems.* Bonn: Eichholz Verlag.

Rosanvallon, Pierre. 1982. "La société politique," 174–78. In: Alain Touraine, ed., *Movements sociaux d'aujourd'hui. Acteurs et analystes.* Paris: Les Editions Ouvriers.

Rose, Richard. 1974. *The Problem of Party Government.* London: MacMillan.

——. 1984. *Politics in Britain.* 4th edition. Boston: Little, Brown.

Rose, Richard, and Derek W. Urwin. 1970. "Persistence and Change in Western Party Systems since 1945." *Political Studies,* 18, no. 3: 287–319.

Roth, Roland. 1985. "Neue soziale Bewegungen in der politischen Kultur der Bundesrepublik. Eine vorläufige Skizze," 20–82. In: Karl-Werner Brand, ed., *Neue soziale Bewegungen in Westeuropa und den USA.* Frankfurt/Main: Campus.

Rothschild-Whitt, Joyce. 1979. "The Collectivist Organization: An Alternative to Rational Bureaucratic Models." *American Sociological Review,* 44, no. 4: 509–27.

Rowies, Luc. 1975. *Les Partis Politiques en Belgique.* Brussels: Centre de Recherche et Information Socio-Politique.

Rubart, Frauke. 1983. "Schweden. Die Grüne Zentrumspartei und die neue(n) Umwelt-partei(en)," 79–127. In: Frank Nullmeier, Frauke Rubart, and Harald Schulz, *Um-weltbewegungen und Parteiensystem.* Hamburg: Quorum.

Rucht, Dieter. 1980. *Von Wyhl nach Gorleben.* Munich: Beck.

——. 1984a. "Zur Organisation der neuen sozialen Bewegungen," 609–20. In: Jürgen W. Falter, Christian Fenner, and Michael Th. Greven, eds., *Politische Willensbildung und Interessenvermittlung.* Opladen: Westdeutscher Verlag.

——. 1984b. *Flughafenprojekte als Politikum: Die Konflikte in Stuttgart, München, und Frankfurt.* Frankfurt/Main: Campus.

——. 1985. Parteien und Bewegungen als Modi kollektiven Handelns. March 1985, unpublished manuscript.

——. 1986. Themes, Logics and Arenas of Social Movements. Paper prepared for the Internation Workshop on Participation in Social Movements, "Transformation of Struc-ture into Action." Free University of Amsterdam, June 12–14.

Rüdig, Wolfgang. 1985a. "The Greens in Europe. Ecological Parties and the European Elections of 1984." *Parliamentary Affairs,* 38, no. 1: 56–72.

——. 1985b. "Die grüne Welle. Zur Entwicklung ökologischer Parteien in Europa," *Aus Politik und Zeitgeschichte,* 35, no. 45: 3–18.

Rüdig, Wolfgang, and Philip D. Lowe. 1986. "The Withered 'Greening' of British Politics. A Study of the Ecology Party." *Political Studies,* 34, no. 2: 262–84.

Sabel, Charles. 1981. "The Internal Politics of Trade Unions," 209–44. In: Suzanne Berger, ed., *Organizing Interests in Western Europe.* New York: Cambridge University Press.

Sack, Fritz, 1984. "Die Reaktion von Gesellschaft, Politik und Staat auf die Studenten-bewegung," 107–226. In: Fritz Sack and Heinz Steinert, eds., *Protest und Reaktion. Analysen zum Terrorismus,* 4/II. Opladen: Westdeutscher Verlag.

Sartori, Giovanni. 1966. "European Political Parties. The Case of Polarized Pluralism," 137–76. In: Joseph LaPalombara and Myron Weiner, eds., *Political Parties and Politi-cal Development.* Princeton, N.J.: Princeton University Press.

——. 1976. *Parties and Party Systems. A Framework for Analysis.* Cambridge: Cam-bridge University Press.

Savage, James. 1985. "Postmaterialism of the Left and Right: Political Conflict in Post-industrial Society." *Comparative Political Studies,* 17, no. 4: 431–51.

Schaper, Burkhard. 1984. "Die Entstehungsgeschichte der AL. Zu den Bedingungsfak-toren für die Entwicklung grüner/bunt/alternativer Wahllisten," 57–68. In: Michael Bühnemann, Michael Wendt, and Jürgen Wituschek, eds., *Die Alternative Liste Berlin.* Berlin: LitPol.

Scharpf, Fritz, Bernd Reissert, and Fritz Schnabel. 1976. *Politikverflechtung. Theorie und Empirie des kooperativen Föderalismus in der Bundesrepublik.* Kronberg/Taunus: Scriptor.

Schattschneider, E. E. 1960. *The Semi-Sovereign People: A Realist View of Democracy in America.* New York: Rinehart and Winston.

Schenk, Herrad. 1981. *Die feministische Herausforderung.* Munich: Beck.

Schlesinger, Joseph A. 1965. *Ambition and Politics. Political Careers in the United States.* Chicago: Rand McNally.

——. 1984. "On the Theory of Party Organization." *Journal of Politics,* 46, no. 2: 369–400.

Schmid, Thomas, 1983. "Über die Schwierigkeiten der Grünen, in Gesellschaft zu leben und zu denken." *Freibeuter,* no. 15: 44–58.

——. 1984. ed., *Befreiung von falscher Arbeit.* Berlin: Wagenbach.

Schmidt, Manfred. 1982. *Wohlfahrtsstaatliche Politik unter bürgerlichen und sozialdemokratischen Regierungen.* Frankfurt/Main: Campus.

——. 1984. "Demokratie, Wohlfahrtsstaat und neue soziale Bewegungen." *Aus Politik und Zeitgeschichte,* 34, no. 11 (February 17): 3–14.

——. 1985. *Der Schweizerische Weg zur Vollbeschaftigung.* Frankfurt/Main: Campus.

Schmitt, Rüdiger. 1987a. "Was bewegt die Friedensbewegung? Zum sicherheitspolitischen Protest der achtziger Jahre." *Zeitschrift für Parlamentsfragen,* 18, no. 1: 110–136.

——. 1987b. "Die hessische Landtagswahl vom 5. April 1987: SPD in der Modernisierungskrise," *Zeitschrift für Parlamentsfragen,* 18, no. 3: 343–61.

Schmitter, Philippe C. 1981. "Interest Intermediation and Regime Governability in Contemporary Western Europe and North America," pp. 287–330 in Suzanne Berger, ed. *Organizing Interests in Western Europe.* New York: Cambridge University Press.

Schmollinger, Horst W. 1983. "Die Wahl zum Berliner Abgeordnetenhaus vom 10 Mai 1981. Einbruch der Sozialliberalen." *Zeitschrift für Parlamentsfragen,* 14, no. 1: 38–57.

Schöller, Gertrud. 1985. *Feminismus und linke Politik.* Berlin: Quorum.

Schönbohm, Wulf. 1985. *Die CDU wird moderne Volkspartei. Selbstverständnis, Mitglieder, Organisation und Apparat 1950–1980.* Stuttgart: Klett-Cotta.

Schönhoven, Klaus. 1980. *Expansion und Konzentration. Studien zur Entwicklung der Freien Gewerkschaften im wilhelminischen Deutschland, 1890—1914.* Stuttgart: Klett-Cotta.

Schonfeld, William R. 1983. "Political Parties. The Functional Approach and the Structural Alternative." *Comparative Politics,* 15, no. 4: 477–99.

Schorske, Carl. 1955. *German Social Democracy, 1905–1917. The Development of the Great Schism.* Cambridge, Mass.: Harvard University Press.

Schultze, Rainer-Olaf. 1987. "Die Bundestagswahl 1987. Eine Bestätigung des Wandels." *Aus Politik und Zeitgeschichte,* 37, no. 12: 3–17.

Scott, Richard. 1981. *Organizations. Rational, Natural, and Open Systems.* Englewood Cliffs, N.J.: Prentice Hall.

Searing, Donald D. 1986. "A Theory of Political Socialization. Institutional Support and Deradicalization in Britain." *British Journal of Political Science,* 16, no. 3: 341–76.

Selle, Per, and Lars Svasand. 1983. "The Local Party Organization and Its Members. Between Randomness and Rationality." *Scandinavian Political Studies,* 6, no. 3: 211–29.

Sellin, Peter. 1984. "Die AL Berlin und die Bundesgrünen," 121–34. In: Michael Bühnemann, Michael Wendt, and Jürgen Wituschek, eds., *AL. Die Alternative Liste Berlin.* Berlin: LitPol.

Shamir, Michal. 1984. "Are Western Party Systems 'Frozen?' A Comparative Dynamic Analysis." *Comparative Political Studies,* 12, no. 1: 35–79.

Sharkansky, Ira. 1970. *The Routines of Politics.* New York: Van Nostrand.

Shefter, Martin. 1977. "Party and Patronage. Germany, England, and Italy." *Politics and Society,* 7, no. 4: 403–51.

Sik, Ota. 1985. "Dritter Weg und grüne Wirtschaftspolitik," 350–62. In: Franz Beckenbach, Jo Müller, Reinhard Pfriem, and Eckhard Stratmann, eds., *Grüne Wirtschaftspolitik.* Cologne: Kiepenheuer und Witsch.

Smelser, Neil. 1963. *The Theory of Collective Behavior.* New York: Free Press.

Smith, Gordon. 1976a. "West Germany and the Politics of Centrality." *Government and Opposition,* 11, no. 4: 387–407.

——. 1976b. "Social Movements and Party Systems in Western Europe," 331–54. In: M. Kolinsky and W. Patterson, eds., *Social and Political Movements in Western Europe*. New York: St. Martin's Press.

——. 1984. "Europäische Parteiensysteme. Stationen einer Entwicklung?", 14–22. In: Jürgen W. Falter, Christian Fenner, and Michael Th. Greven, eds., *Politische Willensbildung und Interessenvermittlung*. Opladen: Westdeutscher Verlag.

Smits, Jozef. 1984. *Demokratie op straat. Een analyze van de Betogingen in Belgie*. Leuven: Uitgeverij Acco.

Soule, John W., and James W. Clarke. 1970. "Amateurs and Professionals: A Study of Delegates to the 1968 Democratic National Convention." *American Political Science Review*, 64, no. 1: 888–98.

Spiss, Rainer, 1985. "Die Grünen in Italien. Das ungewisse 'Andere'," *Links*, 17, no. 5: 22–23.

Statistisches Bundesamt. 1984. *Statistisches Jahrbuch der Bundesrepublik Deutschland 1983*. Stuttgart: Kohlhammer.

Steel, Brent, and Takatsugu Tsurutani. 1986. "From Consensus to Dissensus. A Note on Postindustrial Political Parties." *Comparative Politics*, 18, no. 2: 235–48.

Steiner, Wolf. 1970. *SPD Parteitage 1964 und 1966. Analyse und Vergleich*. Meisenheim am Glan: Hain.

Steinert, Heinz. 1984. "Sozialstrukturelle Bedingungen des "linken Terrorismus" der 70er Jahre. Aufgrund eines Vergleichs der Entwicklungen in der Bundesrepublik Deutschland, in Italien, Frankreich und den Niederlanden," 388–601. In: Fritz Sack and Heinz Steinert, eds., *Protest und Reaktion. Analysen zum Terrorismus*. 4/II. Opladen: Westdeutscher Verlag.

Steininger Rudolf. 1984. *Soziologische Theorie der politischen Parteien*. Frankfurt/Main: Campus.

Stiefbold, Rodney. 1974. "Segmented Pluralism and Consociational Democracy in Austria: Problems of Political Stability and Change," 117–77. In: Martin O. Heisler, ed., *Politics in Europe*. New York: McKay.

Stöss, Richard. 1980. *Vom Nationalismus zum Umweltschutz. Die Deutsche Gemeinschaft/AUD im Parteiensystem der Bundesrepublik*. Opladen: Westdeutscher Verlag.

Stouthuysen, Patrick-Edward. 1981. De politieke identiteit von de ecologische beweging. Ongepubliceerde eindverhandeling. Frije Universiteit Brussel.

——. 1983. "De politieke identiteit van de Vlaamse groene partij Agalev." *Res Publica*, 25, no. 2/3: 349–75.

Strom, Kaare. 1984. "Minority Governments in Parliamentary Democracies. The Rationality of Nonwinning Cabinet Solutions." *Comparative Political Studies*, 17, no. 2: 199–227.

——. 1985. "Party Goals and Government Performance in Parliamentary Democracies." *American Political Science Review*, 79, no. 3: 738–54.

——. 1988. Institutions, Organizations, and Competitive Party Behavior. Paper prepared for presentation at the Annual Meeting of the Midwest Political Science Association, Chicago, April 14–16.

Swyngedouw, Marc. 1986. De Veranderingen van het Kiesgedrag in Vlaanderen Bij de Parlementsverkiezingen von 1981 en 1985. Een statistische Analyse. Bulletin no. 10 from the workgroup "Methods of Sociological Research." Catholic University of Leuven.

Swyngedouw, Marc, and Jaak Billiet. 1988. Van 13 tot 13. Een Analyse van de Veranderingen in het Kiesgedrag in Vlaanderen 1985–1987. Bulletin No. 19 of the Center for Data Collection and Analysis. Catholic University of Leuven.

Thomas, Alastair H. 1986. "Social Democracy in Scandinavia: Can Dominance Be Regained?" 172–222. In: William E. Paterson and Alastair H. Thomas, eds., *The Future of Social Democracy*. Oxford: Oxford University Press.

Thompson, James D. 1967. *Organizations in Action*. New York: McGraw Hill.

Tilly, Charles. 1978. *From Mobilization to Revolution*. Reading, Mass.: Addison Wesley.

Touraine, Alain. 1973. *La production de la société*. Paris: Seuil.

——. 1978. *La voix et le regard*. Paris: Seuil.

Touraine, Alain, François Dubet, Zsusza Hegedus, and Michel Wieviorka. 1980. *L'utopie anti-nucléaire*. Paris: Seuil.

Troitzsch, Klaus G. 1980. "Die Herausforderung der 'etablierten' Parteien durch die 'Grünen'," 260–82. In: Heino Kaack and Reinhold Roth, eds., *Handbuch des deutschen Parteiensystems*. Opladen: Leske & Buderich.

UNESCO. 1984. *Statistical Digest 1984*. Paris: UNESCO.

Unger, Roberto Mangabeira. 1975. *Knowledge and Politics*. New York: Free Press.

Urwin, Derek W. 1970. "Social Cleavages and Political Parties in Belgium: Problems of Institutionalization." *Political Studies*, 18, no. 3: 320–40.

——. 1983. "Harbinger, Fossil or Fleabite? Regionalism and the West European Party Mosaic," 221–52. In: Hans Daalder and Peter Mair, eds., *Western European Party Systems: Continuity and Change*. Beverly Hills, Calif.: Sage.

Uusitalo, Hannu. 1984. "Comparative Research on the Determinants of the Welfare State. The State of the Art." *European Journal of Political Research*, 12, no. 4: 403–22.

Vadrot, Claude-Marie. 1978. *L'écologie. Histoire d'une subversion*. Paris: Syros.

Valen, Henry, and Daniel Katz. 1964. *Political Parties in Norway*. Oslo: Universitetsforlaget.

Van den Brande, A. 1987. "Neo-corporatism and functional-integral power in Belgium," 95–119. In: Ilja Scholten, ed., *Political Stability and Neo-Corporatism*. Beverly Hills, Calif: Sage.

Van Haegendorn, Mieke. 1981. "Veranderingen in het Belgische partijenstelsel van 1945 tot 1980." *Res Publica*, 23, no. 1: 29–45.

Van Parijs, Philippe. 1982. "Functionalist Marxism Rehabilitated. A Comment on Elster." *Theory and Society*, 11, no. 4: 497–511.

Veen, Hans-Joachim. 1984. "Wer wählt grün? Zum Profil der Neuen Linken in der Wohlstandsgesellschaft." *Aus Politik und Zeitgeschichte*, 34, no. 35/36: 2–17.

Verba, Sidney, and Norman H. Nie. 1975. "Political Participation," 1–74. In: Fred I. Greenstein and Nelson W. Polsby, *Handbook of Political Science*, 4. Reading, Mass.: Addison Wesley.

Verheyen, Hans. 1985. "Ohne Basisdemokratie stirbt das Parlament," *Aus Politik und Zeitgeschichte*, 35, no. 6: 31–39.

Versteylen, Luc. 1981. *Wat nu met Agalev?* Borgerhout: Uitgeverij Stil Leven.

Vervliet, Miel. 1983. *Milieubeweging en Vakbeweging*. Ursel: De Groene Schriften 6.

Vollmer, Antje. 1984. *. . . und wehret Euch täglich*. Gütersloh: Siebenstern.

Von Beyme, Klaus. 1982. *Parteien in westlichen Demokratien*. Munich: Piper.

——. 1983. "Governments, Parliaments, and the Structure of Power in Political Parties," 341–67. In: Hans Daalder and Peter Mair, eds., *Western European Party Systems: Continuity and Change*. Beverly Hills, Calif.: Sage.

Warwick, D. P. (in collaboration with M. Meade and T. Reed). 1975, *A Theory of Public Bureaucracy*. Cambridge: Cambridge University Press.

Weber, Max. 1919/1958. "Politics as a Vocation," 77–128. In: Hans H. Gerth and C. Wright Mills, eds., *From Max Weber: Essays in Sociology*. New York: Oxford University Press.

——. 1958. *Gesammelte Politische Schriften*. Tübingen: Mohr.

——. 1968. *Economy and Society*. 2 vols. New York: Bedminster.

Wellhofer, E. Spencer. 1979. "Strategies for Party Organization and Voter Mobilization: Britain, Norway and Argentina. *Comparative Political Studies*, 12, no. 2: 169–204.

——. 1985. "The Electoral Effectiveness of Party Organization: Norway, 1945–1977." *Scandinavian Political Studies*, 8, no. 3: 171–85.

Wellhofer, E. Spencer, and Timothy M. Hennessey. 1974. "Models of Political Party Organization and Strategy: Some Analytic Approaches to Oligarchy," 279–316. In: Ivor Crewe, ed., *Elites in Western Democracy. British Political Sociology Yearbook*. London: Croom Helm.

Wertman, Douglas. 1977. "The Italian Electoral Process: The Elections of June 1976," 41–80. In: Howard R. Penniman, ed., *Italy at the Polls. The Parliamentary Elections of 1976*. Washington, D.C.: American Enterprise Institute.

——. 1981. "The Christian Democrats: Masters of Survival," 64–103. In: Howard R. Penniman, ed., *Italy at the Polls, 1979*. Washington, D.C.: American Enterprise Institute.

Whiteley, Paul. 1983. *The Labor Party in Crisis*. London: Methuen.

Wiesendahl, Elmar. 1980. *Parteien und Demokratie: Eine soziologische Analyse paradigmatischer Ansätze in der Parteienforschung*. Opladen: Leske.

——. 1984. "Wie politisch sind politische Parteien? Zu einigen vernachlässigten Aspekten der Organisationswirklichkeit politischer Parteien," 78–88. In: Jürgen W. Falter, Christian Fenner, and Michael Th. Greven, eds., *Politische Willensbildung und Interessenvermittlung*. Opladen: Westdeutscher Verlag.

Wiesenthal, Helmut. 1985a. "Die Grünen in Nordrhein Westfalen. Geschichte, Bedeutung, Programm und Willensbildung." In Ulrich v. Alemann, ed., *Parteien und Landtagswahlen in Nordrhein Westfalen*. Cologne: Kohlhammer.

——. 1985b. "Grün-Rational. Hintergrundüberlegungen zu einer zeitgemässen Strategie," 1–41. In: Gabriel Falkenberg and Heiner Kersting, eds., *Eingriffe ins Diesseits. Beiträge zu einer radikalen Grünen Realpolitik*. Essen: Klartext Verlag.

Willers, Peter. 1982. "Den Tiefschlag der Altparteien stören. Vom Auf und Ab der 'Grünen Liste' in Bremen," 159–78. In: Jörg R. Mettke, ed., *Die Grünen. Regierungspartner von morgen?* Reinbek: Rowohlt.

Wilson, Frank L. 1979. "The Revitalization of French Parties." *Comparative Political Studies*, 12, no. 1: 82–103.

——. 1980. "Sources of Party Transformation. The Case of France," 526–51. In: Peter Merkl, ed., *Western European Party Systems*. New York: Free Press.

Wilson, James Q. 1962. *The Amateur Democrat*. Chicago: The University of Chicago Press.

——. 1973. *Political Organizations*. New York: Basic Books.

Wippler, Reinhard. 1984. "Het oligarchieprobleem: Michels' ijzeren wet en latere probleem-oplossingen," *Mens en Maatschappij*, 59, no. 2:115–41.

Wright, Erik Olin. 1985. *Classes*. London: Verso.

Wright, William E. 1971. "Comparative Party Models. Rational-efficient and Party Democracy," 17–54. In: William E. Wright, ed., *A Comparative Study of Party Organization*. Columbus, Ohio: Merrill.

Zetterberg, Hans. 1980. *The Swedish Public and Nuclear Energy. The Referendum 1980*. Tokyo: UN University.

Zeuner, Bodo. 1970. *Kandidatenaufstellung zur Bundestagswahl 1965*. The Hague: Nijhoff.

——. 1983. "Aktuelle Anmerkungen zum Postulat der 'Basisdemokratie' bei den Grünen/Alternativen." *Prokla,* 13, no. 2: 106–17.

——. 1984. "Die Bedeutung der Grün/Alternativen Parteien fur Parteientheorien und -typologien," 119–30. In: Jürgen W. Falter, Christian Fenner, and Michael Th. Greven, eds., *Politische Willensbildung und Interessenvermittlung.* Opladen: Westdeutscher Verlag.

——. 1985 "Parlamentarisierung der Grünen." *Prokla,* 15, no. 4: 5–23.

Zeuner, Bodo, Lilian Klotzsch, Klaus Könemann, and Jörg Wischermann. 1982. Alternative im Parlament. Neue soziale Bewegungen und parlamentarische Repräsentation. Vorlage fur den Kongress der Deutschen Vereinigung für Politische Wissenschaft, Berlin, October 1982.

Zolberg, Aristide. 1977. "Splitting the Difference: Federalization without Federalism in Belgium," 103–42. In: Milton J. Esman, ed., *Ethnic Conflict in the Western World.* Ithaca: Cornell University Press.

——. 1978. "Belgium," 99–138. In: Raymond Grew, ed., *Crises of Political Development in Europe and the United States.* Princeton, N.J.: Princeton University Press.

Zoll, Ralf. 1974. *Wertheim III.* Munich: Beck.

Index

Library of Congress Cataloging-in-Publication Data
Kitschelt, Herbert.
    The logics of party formation: ecological politics in Belgium and West
Germany / Herbert Kitschelt.
    p.   cm.
    Bibliography: p.
    Includes index.
    ISBN 0–8014–2252–3 (alk. paper)
    1. Grünen (Political party)   2. Ecolo (Organization)   3. Agalev
(Organization)   4. Environmentalists—Germany (West)—Political
activity.   5. Environmentalists—Belgium—Political activity.
6. Political parties.   I. Title.
JN3971.A98G723443   1989
324.24—dc19   88–31871